THE INSIDERS'® GUIDE TO

South Carolina's Myrtle Beach & the GRAND STRAND

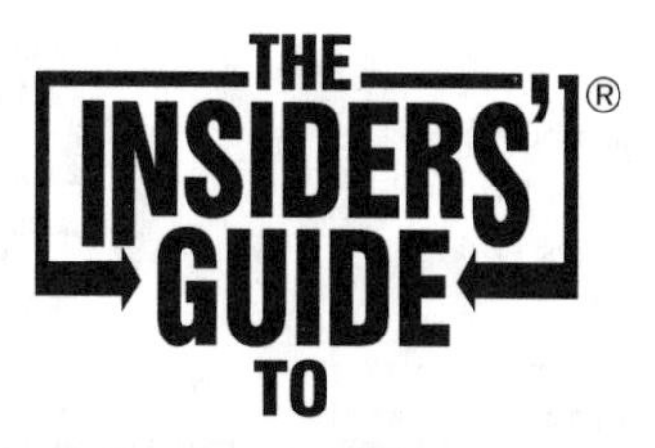

South Carolina's

Myrtle Beach & the GRAND STRAND

Including the communities of:

North Myrtle Beach • Surfside Beach
Garden City Beach • Murrells Inlet
Litchfield Beach • Pawley's Island
Georgetown • Conway
Brunswick County, NC

by
Kimberly Duncan Altman
and
Denise Mullen

The Insiders' Guides Inc.

Co-published and marketed by:
The Sun News
P.O. Box 406
Myrtle Beach, SC 29578
(803) 626-8555

Co-published and distributed by:
The Insiders' Guides Inc.
The Waterfront • Suites 12 &13
P.O. 2057
Manteo, NC 27954
(919) 473-6100

•

SECOND EDITION
1st printing

•

•

Printed in the United States
of America

•

ISBN 0-912367-71-7

The Sun News
Specialty Publications

Specialty Publications Manager
Jody Hazzard

Marketing Services Manager
Milton Miles

Advertising Specialty
Publications Manager
John Cioni

Account Representatives
John Plitt, Bill Jones, Melanie Boyer, Faith Campbell, Meg Daniel, Debbie Flinchum, Diane Hamilton-Forbes, Kim Hawkins, Chris Lee, Marian Lynam, Monica Parnell, Edie Shroup

Advertising Director
Phil LaPorte

The Insiders' Guides® Inc.

Publisher/Managing Editor
Beth P. Storie

President/General Manager
Michael McOwen

Vice President/Advertising
Murray Kasmenn

Creative Services Director
Mike Lay

Partnership Services Director
Giles Bissonnette

Project Editor
Dan DeGregory

On Line Services Director
David Haynes

Fulfillment Director
Gina Twiford

Sales and Marketing Director
Julie Ross

Controller
Claudette Forney

On the cover:
Photos by (clockwise from top left) Lafayette, Bill Scroggins and *The Sun News*

About the Authors

Kimberly Duncan Altman has lived in the Myrtle Beach area for more than 15 years and is active in a variety of community organizations including the President's Roundtable and Coastal Advertising and Marketing Professionals. Kimberly graduated from Myrtle Beach High School, Coastal Carolina University and the Myrtle Beach Chamber's Leadership Grand Strand Program, and takes pride in calling herself "nearly a native." As such, she is uniquely qualified to offer the *inside* scoop on the Grand Strand.

Kimberly's happiest times have been spent along this beach where she grew up, fell in love and made her life among the big-city excitement, small-town charm and rich history.

In October of 1993, Kimberly founded The Altman Group, a marketing firm in Pawleys Island that addresses a wide variety of marketing needs for small- to medium-size businesses, and she enjoys juggling the diverse commercial writing assignments that come her way. Prior to her current career, she worked in real estate and resort marketing. She also worked in development and marketing at Brookgreen Gardens, a much-loved local landmark.

Kimberly and Briley, her husband, have one daughter, Madison. In their free time they enjoy long walks, bike rides, reading and all kinds of music including gospel, classical and jazz.

Denise Mullen moved to Myrtle Beach from Canada in 1984. After recovering from initial culture shock, she fell in love with the coastal area and eased into the comfortable Lowcountry lifestyle.

After graduating from university, Denise lived and worked as a journalist for a chain of Toronto newspapers, wrote and produced a weekly cable news program and freelanced for a variety of publications. Just before relocating to Myrtle Beach, Denise put down the pen for a couple of years, drawn to the bright lights of the theater. A true stage gypsy, she traveled the theater circuit, working as an actress, set designer and producer.

Denise is the public information specialist for The Waccamaw Center for Mental Health in Horry County. She earned an M.A. in Business in 1993 as an adult student, has written freelance articles for *The Sun News* and has created promotional copy for numerous local marketing efforts.

A great believer in community service, Denise became the first woman president of the Myrtle Beach Jaycees in 1989 and was the recipient of *The Sun News'* Volunteer of the Year award that same year. She continues to advocate for citizens in her community through involvement on various boards and committees.

Still a newlywed, Denise married James Mulvanerton, a ceramic engineer turned restaurant owner, in October 1994. The couple live in the heart of Myrtle Beach. Denise avidly participates in step aerobics and has cultivated the largest array of houseplants and cats known to her friends.

Acknowledgments

Kimberly Altman

First, thanks to Daddy for bestowing upon me a love of words. My life is much richer than it could have been without that gift. And thanks to Mother for the genetic dose of creativity that helps me weave those words together in ways that delight me — if no one else.

Much gratitude is extended to those who worried with me, overlooked my acid moods and made me laugh when I didn't feel like laughing: Kelly — the dearest friend of all; Hugh — a constant ally; Linda, Susan and Ashlyn — who encourage me in ways they do not know; and, Lisa — whose friendship is a treasured constant in my life.

Last of all, and most importantly, I'd like to acknowledge Briley, my forbearing and marvelous husband, for being merciful with me and my eccentricities — though I am always undeserving. And thanks to Madison who is indisputably the most remarkable little girl in the world. Without the inspiration of her smiles, escapades and precocious love, nothing else would matter at all.

Denise Mullen

When working on a book like this on rather short deadlines, a writer truly needs to acknowledge and sincerely thank everyone who had the overwhelming urge to pummel her, but didn't. Thank you to everyone for being so understanding, and thanks to all who willingly gave information and assistance to this book.

On a very personal note, I want to extend a great big hug to my mother, who was with me throughout most of this process, making sure my clothes got laundered and that I got something to eat every day, and for being my "No. 1 one-woman fan club." I would also like to pay tribute to the late stray cat, Boo-Boo, who came into my life when I started this book and lost her life as the last chapter was being written. Boo-Boo spent many an hour as my mewing muse, purring adoringly and watching the computer screen cursor. Boo-Boo helped tremendously with the pet boarding and veterinary care section — she had very strong opinions on the subject. And a big thanks to my recently acquired husband who did his very best to stay out of my hair and let me work.

To my editors, Dan and Theresa, and to all who played a small part or large role in the development of this Insiders' Guide, my deepest gratitude.

Table of Contents

Directory of Maps

Photo: The Sun News

The Rice Museum in Georgetown.

How To Use This Book

This incredible 60-mile stretch of beach from Little River to Georgetown, appropriately dubbed The Grand Strand, is a vacationer's mecca. There's so much going on in any given area that, oftentimes, people need not wander beyond a 2-mile radius from their hotel to keep busy all day and night. We hope that this guide to South Carolina's favorite coastal resort will help you effectively plan your next visit here, your relocation or your retirement. One thing is sure, this guide will give you a true "Insider's" view of the Grand Strand from those of us who live, work and play here. This coastal stretch is one of the nation's top-10 fastest growing areas. The Grand Strand is a boomtown right now, with new construction going on nearly everywhere you look and new entertainment being announced on practically a weekly basis.

In producing the *Insiders' Guide to Myrtle Beach and The Grand Strand*, we have tried to lead you through the dizzying options of things to see and do. The chapters on Shopping, Restaurants, Nightlife, Annual Events, The Entertainment Explosion, Attractions and Arts and Culture should be good starting points for planning your activities. If you still have time and energy, the chapter on Daytrips can direct you to nearby cities of interest. The last thing we want is for you to get lost around here, so we've provided maps of the overall area, including main arteries and roadways. We also have used the regional headings of the North Strand, Myrtle Beach and the South Strand in certain chapters to orient you and save you travel time: Basically, the North Strand is anywhere to the north of Myrtle Beach proper, including Restaurant Row, and the South Strand is anywhere to the south. Continuing southward, once you've hit the Murrells Inlet area, you're in Georgetown County. This guide contains several listings from this sister region.

Whether you're staying for a weekend, week or permanently, this guide will help you find suitable accommodations or a roof over your head — check out the chapters on Accommodations and Real Estate. To make financial planning easier, we've coordinated a dollar sign key to give you a price range for places to eat and stay. However, prices quoted in this guide are subject to change, and each establishment reserves the right to make those changes. And, we do apologize here and now if you should contact any place mentioned in this guide only to find it out of business. As is typical of a resort area, there is so much new market competition here that its not unusual for a certain percentage of businesses to close their doors each year.

Other chapters provide vital information on child care, education, local laws, retirement and medical care. The Services and Utilities chapter provides a list of numbers for emergency help and assistant organizations. Please note that the area code for South Carolina (803) is the same throughout the state, so we didn't list it with the telephone number.

We hope the *Insiders' Guide to Myrtle Beach and The Grand Strand* will give you a real feel for this area and the opportunity to experience it to the fullest. With this information in hand, you'll fit right in as if you've been beachcombing all your life.

Myrtle Beach

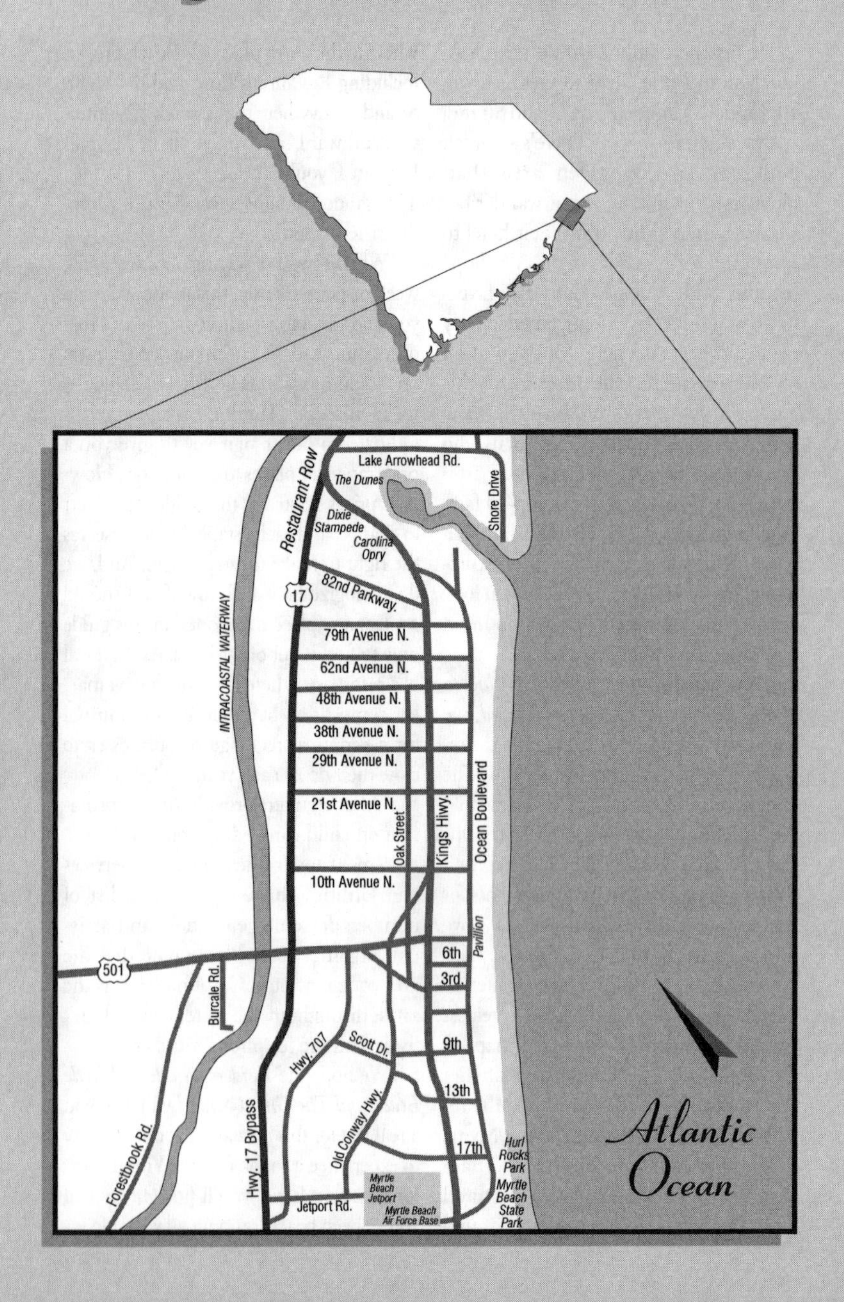

Inside The Grand Strand

The extraordinary natural beauty of this coastline, as well as its wealth of activities, makes the Grand Strand truly deserving of its name. Stretching for more than 60 miles along South Carolina's northern shore, this string of contiguous cities and smaller communities begins at the North Carolina line with the spirited fishing village of Little River. It extends all the way to the historic, oak-lined avenues of Georgetown where no fewer than four rivers spill into Winyah Bay.

There's more to do than you ever imagined . . . thousands of restaurants, dazzling nightlife, incomparable shopping and amusements galore. Wander off the beaten path and discover unexpected delights . . . unchanging salt marshes, silver Spanish moss, hammocks and ghost stories and petulant crabs tiptoeing 'cross tidal flats. Visit the Pavilion and ride every ride. Eat corn dogs and cotton candy. Memorize the feel of sand between your toes. Take a cruise. Enjoy a comedy show. Windsurf. Sleep in the sun. Go fishing. Swim and sail and dine and dance. Acquaint yourself with our winning combination of Lowcountry charm and uptown flair. It's like nothing you've known before.

North to south, stem to stern, the Grand Strand is a place of color . . . popsicle blue skies, rainbow-hued sailboats, sun-bleached sand and golden sunshine. The Grand Strand is a place of variety . . . curling breakers, shells beneath bare feet, soft breezes, and gulls pleading for the crumbled remains of a sandwich. The Grand Strand is a place of activity . . . wave and raft riding, board and body surfing, parasailing, jet skiing, novel reading, amusement parks, water parks, state parks and theaters galore. The Grand Strand is a place you'll come back to — again and again.

Little River

Where the Carolinas meet, the sun smiles on the charming fishing village of Little River. Here, nestled beneath the twisted arms of old weathered oaks, you'll discover an unhurried and uncommon side of the Grand Strand. From clutches of cheerful shops, an unexpected array of merchandise spills forth; shopping is bound to reveal surprises. You can also schedule a deep sea fishing excursion, take a cruise down the Intracoastal Waterway or hang around and chat with well-tanned fishermen while they haul in a day's catch. Restaurants, marinas and fresh seafood abound. Water is the undisputed King, and everyone is subject to its rule. Like the rest of the Grand Strand, Little River is growing rapidly, but it's still possible to discover marvelous pockets of solitude in this historic fishing village.

Each spring, thousands of people make a pilgrimage to Little River on the weekend following Mother's Day when the horseshoe area of the beloved waterfront hosts the **Blue Crab Festival** (see our Annual Events chapter). This special day-long event showcases live entertainment, oodles of arts and crafts displays and an abundance of scrumptious seafood.

North Strand

Folks who call the North Strand "home" boast that they have the world's widest beach. Though the claim is disputable, no one will deny that their beach is remarkably wide — especially when the tide is at low ebb. Unlike too many South Carolina beaches, there's still plenty of room to bask in the sun, take long walks, mastermind sandcastles and play volleyball and paddleball — even when the tide is high.

The North Strand is a firm beach, too — so firm that a favorite pastime of North Stranders has long been taking a drive on the shore. However, as the popularity of the North Strand beaches has soared, officials have been forced to severely restrict beach driving. Now, vehicles are allowed on the beach in North Myrtle only from December 1 through February 28 from 8 AM to 5 PM.

The North Strand is one of the few beaches where visitors are allowed to bike. Bicycles and a tricycle of sorts are popular forms of entertainment. (Both vehicles can be rented along the North Strand, so don't bother to bring your own.) On the three-wheelers, a goofy-looking but interesting (and attention-getting) way to see the beach, you sit in a semi-reclined position and peddle with your feet out front. It's a bit awkward at first, but you'll get the knack quickly. Although the big trikes have hand rests, you steer using your feet and the sway of your body. There are also attachments that allow you to bring the kids along.

As with the rest of the Grand Strand, the wide blue Atlantic stills merits top billing on the North Strand, but rapid development is quickly filling the area with luxury condos and modern hotels, shopping complexes, restaurants, golf courses and a country music theater or two.

North Myrtle Beach is the anchor of the North Strand area. The city was formed 25 years ago when Cherry Grove, Ocean Drive, Crescent Beach and Windy Hill merged into a single municipality. A veritable mecca for college students, North Myrtle is proud home to the state's shimmy-in-your-well-worn-Weejuns dance — the Carolina Shag. Despite the fact that North Myrtle Beach is "growing up" and changing in the process, it still isn't as densely developed as Myrtle Beach. Oceanfront accommodations are typically condominiums and small motels. And, you can still find front-row cottages. Their suitability for house parties, coupled with North Myrtle Beach's longstanding party reputation, make it a mainstay for collegiate men and women. From mid-May, when exams are over, until mid-June, you'll find it overflowing with celebrating students from all over the country. The area is probably second only to Daytona Beach in the number of college students it attracts. City officials estimate that 75,000 to 90,000 kids flock to the beach for dancing and romancing every Easter. Over the years, police have become especially strict about public drinking. Consequently, many have found themselves singing the jailhouse blues instead of dancing on the strand.

Traveling south from Little River, the **Cherry Grove** section will be your first North Myrtle stop. (Sea Mountain Highway is the only way into Cherry Grove.) Cherry Grove has its share of oceanfront condominiums and motels, but away

The Naming of the Strand

In magazines and newspapers, on billboards, in storefronts and phone books, wafting on the airwaves of radio and television, and rolling off the tongues of residents and tourists alike, you're bound to notice the much-loved moniker "The Grand Strand." The terminology is perfect, and most folks are so accustomed to the phrase, no one seems to give much thought to where it originated and exactly what it means. So, for the record, here's the story.

In 1949, a local reporter named Claude Dunnagan needed a title for a gossip and publicity column he was writing for the weekly *The Myrtle Beach Sun*. The information in his column covered a stretch of communities from Little River to the south end of Windy Hill Beach. He wanted something short and punchy but pertinent to the various areas on "his beat." So, like every good writer, he scoured his dictionary and thesaurus, arranged and rearranged different words, and came up with the very apt term "The Grand Strand." The original column appeared on December 3, 1949, and was filled with a brand of chatty news found in today's society columns. Very quickly, the term was picked up by other media, as well as the Chamber of Commerce, and it came to include a whole string of communities from the fishing village of Little River to the history-steeped streets of Georgetown.

Accolades to Mr. Dunnagan for coining the perfect phrase for one of the most beautiful stretches of coastline in the whole world!

from the ocean you'll find rows of stilted houses lining serpentine channels and inlets. Many Cherry Grove residents and tourists have handpicked their destination because they like catching, cleaning and cooking their own seafood.

Just about any time of day, **Hog Inlet** will be bustling with people fishing and shrimping, crabbing with chicken necks and dutifully checking their fish pots. Most fishermen troll up and down, seeking out the day's best fishing spot. At night, they gig for flounder. Hog Inlet has a public boat landing so you don't have to be lucky enough to own a home on the creek to partake of its bounty.

On the other side of Hog Inlet is **Waties Island**, a pristine piece of land donated to Coastal Carolina University's internationally renowned marine biology department. In recent years, archaeologists have found mysterious mounds of shells on Waties Island that were apparently built by Native Americans who followed schools of mullet and spot down the coast. Although they still aren't sure why the mounds were created, they have discovered enough pottery and well-worn arrowheads to ascertain that Indians once inhabited the island.

Along U.S. 17, **Ocean Drive**, **Crescent Beach**, **Atlantic Beach** and **Windy Hill** are pretty similar. In fact, if you're not a local, it's nigh to impossible to know when you've passed from one community into the next. On the ocean, you'll find more motels and condominiums in Ocean Drive and Crescent Beach. Windy Hill remains in a more natural state. Ocean Drive is best known as the place where the shag originated. There are several clubs in downtown Ocean Drive where Beach Music will never go out of style. Here, en masse, people do the dance that Lewis Grizzard described as "the jitterbug on Valium." You might be inspired to buy a pair of Bass Weejuns and become a shagger yourself. Locals know (but won't tell you 'til it's too late): Shagging is a highly contagious ailment.

Between the Windy Hill and Crescent Beach communities — though not a part of North Myrtle Beach — sits Atlantic Beach. Historically speaking, Atlantic Beach played an important role in the lives of blacks in the Carolinas, Georgia and Florida, as it was the only beach open to African Americans on the southern portion of the Atlantic Seaboard. Atlantic Beach has a few small motels and night spots and lots of cottages. Its one landmark, the open-air pavilion where the movie *Shag* was filmed, was irreparably damaged in Hurricane Hugo in 1989. Despite this loss, the treacherous storm effectively served as a downtown renovation project.

Briarcliffe Acres comes next. It is a very quiet, very upscale and almost solely residential little town that you'll probably miss if someone doesn't point it out. The residents incorporated some years ago to avoid outside influence. Just south beyond Briarcliffe, you'll run smack through the center of **Restaurant Row**. A line of restaurants, like a string of fine pearls, is situated on either side of U.S. 17 and offers up some of the best food in the world. Seafood, of course, is a specialty, but steaks, ribs and even down-home country cooking are available on this renowned strip. No matter how many restaurants open along this stretch, they all have waiting lines every night — believe us, it's worth the wait. The traffic is especially heavy during the dinner rush, which starts as early as 5 PM and continues until around 8 PM. (See our sidebar on Restaurant Row in the Restaurants chapter.)

Closest to Myrtle Beach is the unincorporated **Shore Drive** area. Highly developed and densely populated, this area sports huge high-rise condominiums, lots of retiree homes, a nearly constant flow of renters and timeshare purchasers and a couple of fine residential communities.

As for shopping, North Strand is paradise. **Barefoot Landing**, one of the state's top tourist attractions, is located on U.S. 17, just south of North Myrtle Beach. Built around a 20-acre freshwater lake, with more than 1,000 feet of floating dock on the Waterway and miles of boardwalks, Barefoot Landing features more than 100 specialty and retail shops, factory direct stores, and somewhere in the neighborhood of 12 waterfront restaurants. Attractions include the **Barefoot Carousel**, **Barefoot Princess Riverboat** and **The Alabama Theatre**. (See our Attractions and Shopping chapters.) More than seven million visitors streamed through this beautiful complex last year. Even the locals love it. You should also check out Briarcliffe Mall, the Galleria and Hidden Village.

In 1937, the North Strand had one log-cabin-style motel, one self-proclaimed "honky-tonk," one "filling station" and only a handful of homes. The area started booming after World War II. In 1954, Hugo's big sister, Hurricane Hazel, left most of the oceanfront houses sitting in the middle of Ocean Boulevard. But the residents' indefatigable spirit prevailed, and development continued stronger and faster than before. For good or for ill, there doesn't appear to be an end in sight.

Greater Myrtle Beach

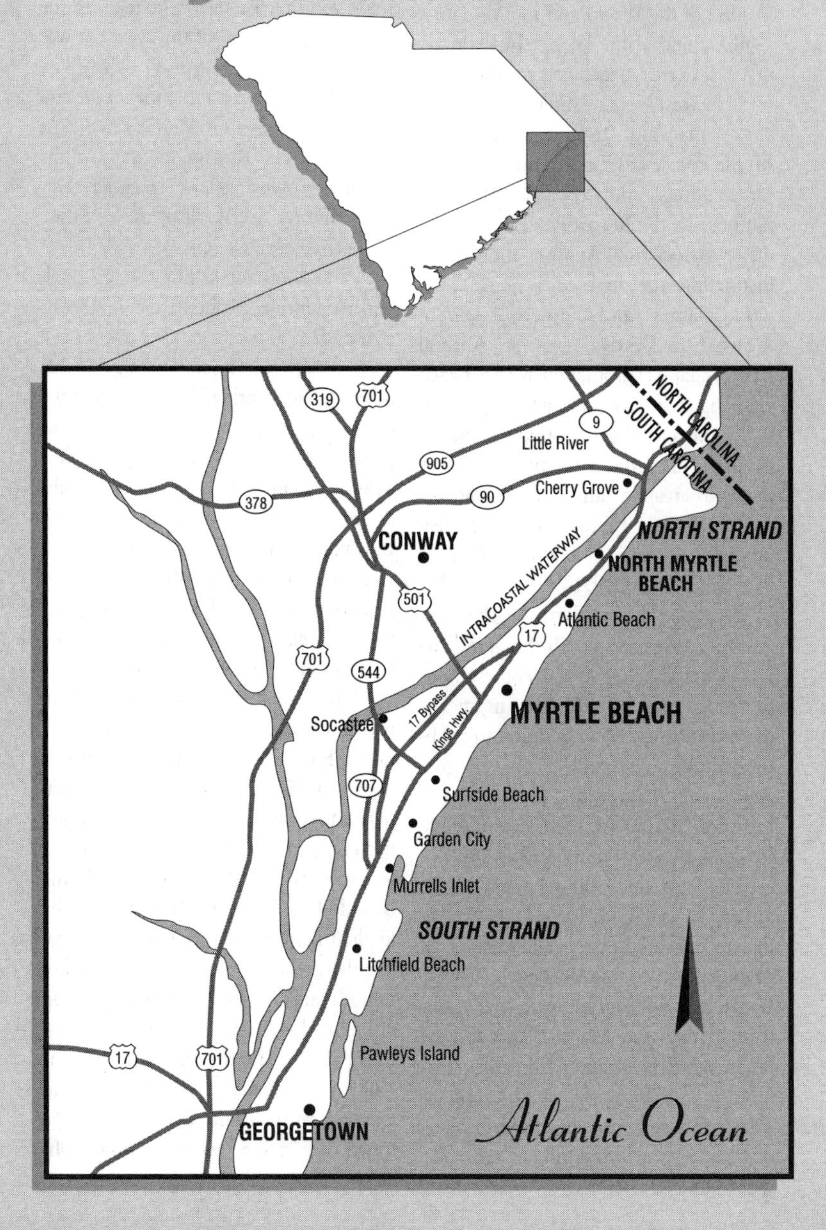

Myrtle Beach

Myrtle Beach is the largest of the Grand Strand beaches, the most developed and probably the most popular. The area has been billed the Seaside Golf Capital of the World, the Campground Capital of the World and the Miniature Golf Capital of the World. In February of 1994, Myrtle Beach was rated the second "Hottest New Destination" in *Destinations* magazine. In September of 1994, Myrtle Beach was listed as one of the "10 Outstanding Family RV Vacation Destinations" by the Recreational Vehicle Industry Association. Another of the many distinctions the city holds is home to the world's largest sand sculpture. As part of a **Sun Fun Festival** (see our Annual Events chapter) promotion, Myrtle Beach challenged the city of Long Beach, Washington, to a sand castle building competition. Hundreds of volunteers united forces to create a sand sculpture 86,536 feet (more than 16 miles) long. The feat landed the city in the Guinness Book of World Records in 1991.

Everyone knows, Myrtle Beach's most enviable attraction is still the grand Atlantic. But there are so many other things to do that the shoreline is by no means the only attraction. In addition to shopping, amusement parks, miniature golf, water parks, waterway cruises, golf and historical attractions, there's an absolute frenzy of theaters climbing skyward.

Even for the folks who have been around to watch, it's sometimes difficult to comprehend the explosion of development known as Myrtle Beach. Cherry Grove and Windy Hill were well established long before Myrtle Beach. On the other end of the Strand, Georgetown featured a flourishing rice empire resplendent with plantations when Myrtle Beach was nothing save mounds of sand and scrubby pine trees. People who passed through the area en route to more popular destinations noted Myrtle Beach's pristine beauty, but until the 1900s, no one seemed interested in staying.

F.G. Burroughs, a Conway businessman, was the visionary who realized the staggering potential of the area that was once known as Long Bay. In the late 1800s, he purchased a majority of the real estate now known as Myrtle Beach. (At one point, the Burroughs and Collins Company owned 80,000 splendid acres — including nearly all of the coastline between Little River and Murrells Inlet.) He earned a living selling the tar, pitch and turpentine gleaned from the area's rich timber.

Myrtle Beach was not easily accessible to the outside world until 1900, when the Conway & Seashore Railroad was completed. People began calling the area New Town. Late in 1900, New Town was officially renamed Myrtle Beach. (F.G. Burroughs' wife won a contest to name the area, choosing as a theme the myrtle bushes that grew so prolifically.) Then, in December of 1900, a telephone line connected Conway and Myrtle Beach for the first time.

The area's first motel, **Seaside Inn**, was constructed in 1901 under the direction of F.G.'s son, F.A. Burroughs. Room rates were $2 a day. Here's how a local newspaper described the inn: "Through the kindness of Mrs. Frank Burroughs, we were carried all over the handsome Seaside Inn. From the front steps to the kitchen perfect order and beauty reigns. On the broad piazzas are stands of hot house plants, giving the first impression of a refined and homelike welcome. Beautiful palms and ferns grace the spacious hallways, parlors and dining rooms, and all through the house is seen the magic touch of a refined woman's fingers. In

C.B. Berry, North Myrtle Beach Historian

When local folks have a question about the history of North Myrtle Beach, they don't necessarily go to the library or even the courthouse. They head straight for C.B. Berry, a Crescent Beach surveyor who carefully stores in his head everything from the area's most important incidents to amusing minutiae. Berry moved to the area in 1937 and has witnessed most of the North Strand's development. He has bountiful stories to tell — here's just one:

"The Indians lived here," Berry said, adding that they must have been Lumbee Indians from up around the Lumberton/Fayetteville, North Carolina, area. He believes they migrated to the area at certain times of year when the fishing was good. "We find evidence of that all the time on Waties Island." (Waties Island is an undeveloped island across Hog Inlet from Cherry Grove. It was recently donated to Coastal Carolina University for use by its marine science department.)

"I found an old Indian burial mound and I knew it was a burial mound because it had shells on it. The Indian custom was to place a rock on the mound when they walked by it, if there were rocks there. There were no rocks here so they used shells. They even put sticks on it if there were no rocks or other objects. It was just a custom of the Indians to put something on the burial mound when they were walking the paths that went by the mound. I found that mound on Waties Island and I carried two or three different groups from different colleges, one group from Alabama, students in archaeology, and they confirmed that it was a burial mound.

"Although Jim Michie, he had some questions about it. He's the former state archaeologist. He tried to dig into it with a shovel without making a real archaeological exploration of it. He questioned whether it was a burial mound, but you can go under the straw up on that mound and there's no other explanation as to why those shells are there and then I found another mound about 300 feet from the first one. It's got pine straw over it. It rises up about 15 to 20 feet high. It's higher than the other sand dunes around. It predates white civilization in America possibly a thousand years, it's hard to say."

"It's a pure forest now. I've tried to find it since then . . . I think the Indians probably didn't live permanently over there on the island. I think they came down here during fishing season because the fish were so prevalent, and of course for oysters and clams, too. Some of them lived there possibly during the summer time. I find Indian pottery most all places inland. If the land is high and close to water, you'll find Indian pottery — sometimes on top of the ground. In a plowed field when it rains, it will wash it and show it sometimes in the plowed field."

the well-furnished bedrooms a delightful sense of coziness and comfort pervades the atmosphere, and it is determined that no one who visits there this summer shall contract malaria for there are screens to all the windows and doors, and as extra precaution, canopies over all the beds. From the north side of the piazza a board walk led to a round dance pavilion. Big bones of a whale that rested in front of the hotel provided sport for the children as they stepped in and out of his jaw and jumped over his backbone."

People soon began building cottages. In 1910, lots sold for $25. Anyone who promised to build a $500 house on his or her lot received a second lot free of charge. Early residents enjoyed the area only as a secluded summer hideaway. The Burroughs family, for example, moved belongings to Myrtle Beach from Conway each summer on the railroad. F.G.'s granddaughter, Virginia Burroughs Marshall, remembers how the train pulled up to their home every spring. After making their way eastward with possessions that included cows and goats, the train stopped at their beach cottage and allowed them to unload for a peaceful summer. (Back then, semi-wild hogs sometimes ran sunbathers off the beach.)

Myrtle Beach took a giant step forward in 1925 when **John T. Woodside**, a wealthy textile magnate from Greenville, devised a plan to turn the promising resort into a playground for the rich and famous. Woodside purchased a vast tract of land from the Burroughs and quickly set to work building the luxurious **Ocean Forest Hotel**. Featuring chandeliers and an enormous ballroom, this classic high-rise was indisputably the most elegant building most Horryites had ever seen. (Ocean Forest was demolished in 1974.) Unfortunately, Woodside's most ambitious plan, Arcady, a recreational showplace for the wealthy, never became a reality, as the stock market crash of 1929 ushered in the Great Depression. Even so, the area continued to grow — albeit slowly.

By 1954 Myrtle Beach had grown into a modest but pleasant resort. Then Hurricane Hazel ripped ashore. Ironically, the wicked lady served as somewhat of an urban renewal project. When people began to rebuild storm ravaged properties, they built back bigger, stronger and more lavishly than before. The hammers have not been silent since.

You won't find many cottages in Myrtle Beach proper any more. But nestled among elegant new motels, you can find smaller facilities that have built their businesses on a reputation of personal service and reasonable rates. Most of these "mom and pop" motels cater to loyal families who return year after year.

Myrtle Beach is unofficially divided into four areas. The south end of the Boulevard is a solid line of accommodations — some big, some small. The mid-portion of town features entertainment and activities — from **The Myrtle Beach Pavilion** to the **Ripley's Believe It or Not! Museum**. Beginning around 32nd Avenue North, there is an exclusive residential district where permanent and summer residents coexist in beautiful, expensive homes. From 52nd Avenue northward, luxury motels and condominiums dominate the landscape.

Thankfully, Myrtle Beach officials have had the vision to keep the beach open to the public. Public beach accesses, many with parking, are provided every few blocks throughout the city. The city erected blue and yellow signs along the Boulevard several years ago to help folks recognize these access sites. Handicapped access to the beach is also provided. And,

Lowcountry Ghost Stories

Ghost stories are part and parcel of Lowcountry tradition. It's hard to imagine a coastal native unfamiliar with the oft-repeated stories of Gray Man and Alice of the Hermitage. For decades, hundreds have made pilgrimages to what is purported to be Alice's grave at the All Saints Cemetery in Pawleys Island. Legend has it Alice will appear to anyone holding a ring who walks backward around her grave 13 times, and a well-worn path encircles the simple gravestone. As for the Gray Man, he is widely known as a kind and benevolent ghost who warns unsuspecting folks of impending hurricanes. Along the Grand Strand, there hasn't been a hurricane yet without a Gray Man sighting. The best part of the story is that the property and possessions of those individuals lucky enough to encounter the famous phantom are spared the damage of raging winds and furious tides.

If the stories you read here whet your appetite for more other-worldly tales, just head for a local bookstore. Books on Southern ghosts abound.

"**Alice of the Hermitage**"

(We should preface this story by admitting that there has been confusion about the chronicle of Alice. Truth is, three Alice Flaggs called the Lowcountry home, and it's been difficult to determine exactly to which of the Alices this story pertains.)

In Murrells Inlet, in an era when the rice empire was at its zenith, one of the most beautiful plantations was The Hermitage, overlooking a breathtaking expanse of saltmarsh. The Flaggs, who owned the property, had a teenage daughter named Alice. Alice's brother, a respected doctor, traveled frequently. On one of his return visits he brought a friend who was quite successful in the mercantile business.

Although Dr. Flagg and the young fellow were friends, the "mere merchant" was not considered worthy to move in the Flagg's social circles. Given those circumstances, it was unfortunate that the young man and Alice struck up an immediate rapport, one that quickly transformed into love. Because of the difference in their social standings, Alice knew her brother would never ever allow her to marry his friend. Still, in private, they determined to marry without the family's consent as soon as she was old enough.

In the fall, Alice was sent to finishing school in Charleston. Dreading their long separation, the two lovers planned to be married as soon as her schooling was completed. To seal their promise, the mercantile man gave her a ring. Since she could not wear the ring openly, she wore it on a chain around her neck — well hidden from her family.

When summer ended, Alice and her boyfriend exchanged sad farewells. In Charleston, she went to many balls and met scads of eligible young men, but she never betrayed her promise. Without fail, she kept her ring close to her heart. At night, alone with her memories and her dreams, she would take out the beloved token, look at it longingly, and remember.

Without warning, Alice became very ill. Doctors were called but were unable to help. In desperation, school officials sent Alice back to her beloved Hermitage so her brother could care for her. She was only barely alive.

Often, as her fever climbed unmercifully and delirium took control, she talked about her betrothed. Initially, her unsuspecting brother didn't understand the gibberish. Then, one fateful night, he found her clutching the ring and mumbling about his friend. Suddenly, he understood their secret pact. In a rage, he snatched the ring from her neck and tossed it out the window into the swaying spartina grass. Alice — sick, desperate, disheartened — pleaded for understanding, but her brother remained impassive. A short time later, she died; whether from her mysterious illness or a broken heart, no one will ever know.

For burial, Alice was dressed in a beautiful white ball gown. Shortly thereafter, people began talking of encounters with a ghost about the grounds. When the Flaggs entertained friends from another part of the state, a little boy was put to bed in Alice's former room. Later, when the mother overheard her child talking, she opened the door and looked inside. The boy said he was talking to the lady in the window. She assured the child he had been asleep and dreaming, but he insisted a beautiful lady had given him a flower. He held up an unexplained magnolia blossom for his mother to see.

Years later, another family visited The Hermitage. Most guests had gone to the inlet to play in the water. One young woman, engaged to be married, choose to stay behind and read. Lying on a chaise lounge in Alice's room, with windows open to catch the salty breeze, she sensed she was not alone. The room's temperature dropped. Suddenly, her left hand lifted itself inexplicably, and her betrothal ring was literally removed from her finger. Suspended in midair for only a moment, it dropped to the floor.

Immediately, the feeling passed away. Terribly frightened, the young girl called her hosts who explained the story of the lonely Alice still searching for her ring.

"**The Gray Man of Pawleys Island**"

Two centuries ago, a young man came to Pawleys Island to visit his fiancée. More than a little anxious to see his beloved, he was galloping along a sandy coast at breakneck speed. Regrettably, his tired horse stumbled and the young man fell, broke his neck and drowned in the waves.

A century or so later, a young woman was staying at Pawleys Island in autumn, what used to be a desolate time of year. One morning, as she walked the beach, she became conscious of a young man, or someone she presumed to be a man, walking a distance behind but keeping pace with her.

Initially, she was unconcerned. But, for some distance, the man continued to maintain her pace. From afar, she could only distinguish the blurred, gray outline of a man. Concerned, she began to run. Still, the figure kept pace with her. Finally, home at last, she locked her doors and sat nervously, wondering if the stranger might come to her door. He did not.

Later that day, the weather changed. Vicious winds whipped wickedly, heavy clouds rolled in and rain poured. Though nervous about the weather, she wasn't sure what she should do. Eventually, there came a pounding at the door. An unknown voice called to her, a man's voice, telling her to leave quickly for high ground. Frantically, she answered "Yes, yes, I'll leave immediately." With only a few possessions in tow, she left Pawleys Island and headed inland.

After the hurricane passed, she returned to the island to find unmitigated devastation. Thankful to the faceless man who had warned her of the impending disaster, she repeatedly inquired about his identity. The old-timers looked askance, knowing she had been alone on the island.

Unrelenting, she continued to talk about the figure she had seen, and people soon understood. "Don't worry," they assured her, "it was only the Gray Man."

There are reports that the Gray Man was seen on Pawleys Island before Hugo roared ashore in 1989. A retired couple living on Pawleys was strolling the beach early in the day. Walking hand in hand, alone, the couple noticed a young man approaching, shrouded in an odd gray mist.

At the time, they didn't give the incident much thought and kept walking. But at a point when they should have passed the figure, they realized he was gone. Although they looked around frantically, they saw no one else.

Returning home, they listened to reports indicating Hugo was predicted to hit Pawleys Island directly. The couple left their home, returning after the storm. Devastation reigned. Entire houses had vanished. But returning to their own home, they found nothing damaged save the walkway to the beach. Nothing more.

If you're visiting Pawleys — any of the coastal areas in fact — and you glimpse a shadowy, unsubstantial gray figure, head inland without hesitation. No doubt, a hurricane is coming fast.

thanks to the efforts of several area civic clubs, beach services now offer specially designed wheelchairs that are easy to maneuver on the sand.

Myrtle Beach hosts many annual festivals. Two of the most popular are the Sun Fun Festival (usually held the first full weekend in June), and the Canadian American Days Festival (held in March to coincide with spring break for Canadian kids).

The **Sun Fun Festival**, more than 40 years old, originally served as an official kickoff for the long-anticipated summer season. Now that Myrtle Beach is a year-round tourist destination, the traditional Sun Fun Festival continues to offer four days of nonstop fun in early June. The now-famous festival frequently attracts national media attention. NBC's "Today Show" and ABC's "Good Morning America" have reported live from the festival, which features beauty and bikini contests, human checkers, sand castle building, a huge parade, children's games, musical and theatrical performances, cookouts, sailing regattas and much more.

Canadian-American Days, a much

newer festival, offers a jam-packed agenda, too. Can-Am, as locals call it, was developed in a visionary effort to extend the beach season by encouraging our neighbors from the Great White North to visit. During this 10-day festival, banks willingly exchange currency. Radio, television and newspapers headline Canadian news. And there are activities of every type imaginable — historical tours, parades, concerts and more. (See the Annual Events chapter for details.)

South Strand

Unofficially, the South Strand includes Surfside Beach, Garden City, Murrells Inlet, Litchfield Beach and Pawleys Island. In comparison to the rest of the Grand Strand, the South Strand subscribes to a more leisurely pace and lifestyle. Many praise this stretch of land — rich with marshland, uninhabited beaches, bountiful inlets and maritime forest — as the Carolina coast's finest treasure. For those same reasons, South Strand residents cherish their privacy and vigilantly protect the area's resources.

Surfside Beach was incorporated on March 14, 1964, with 881 residents. Today, the town's year-round population is more than 4,000. Immediately adjacent to Myrtle Beach and most like it in nature, Surfside Beach is growing by leaps and bounds, and traffic is more than a little frustrating during peak season.

In recent years, Surfside's roads and its water and sewer system have been completely modified. The town is preparing to construct a new police station and public works building and improve the Town Complex Administration Building. In addition, a new branch of the Horry County Library may be built at Fuller Park. U.S. 17 in Surfside is lined with restaurants, beachwear shops, attractions and retail areas. Accommodations along Surfside's oceanfront differ somewhat from Myrtle Beach. Fewer high-rises tower above the sun-scrubbed beaches, and cottages and condominiums treasure comfort more than fancy fittings.

Neighbor to Surfside Beach is **Garden City Beach**, a family-oriented retreat sporting hundreds of residential homes, summer cottages and condominiums. Surf fishing reels in many participants along the beach, also a favorite beachcomber retreat. The point where Atlantic Avenue punctuates Ocean Boulevard is the only area in Garden City that resembles the neon-splattered expanses of Myrtle Beach. Here, you'll find arcades and carnival-style food vendors. As for quieter pursuits, walking the Garden City pier is a popular pastime — particularly when a silvery Carolina moon is riding high.

The North Jetty of Garden City was built in 1979 with rocks weighing up to 200 pounds each. It extends 3,445 feet from the shore and stabilizes the inlet across the ocean so commercial and recreational boats never bog down. This ensures ideal boating conditions, regardless of tidal action, which is especially important for commercial fishermen who rely on the sea's bounty for their living.

South of Garden City is **Murrells Inlet**, the oldest fishing village in the state. Murrells Inlet was named for John Morrall who bought 610 acres on the inlet in 1731. This area's history, much like a Southern romantic novel, recounts stories of pirates patrolling the seaside and aristocratic plantation owners accumulating immense wealth. Fishing in the creeks and waterways of Murrells Inlet has been a way of life for generations, and the quiet community trumpets the fishing village as the Seafood Capital of South Carolina. Best known to tourists for many fine

Grover Cleveland Was Here

In his book *Pirates, Planters & Patriots*, local author Rod Gragg writes about a very famous visitor to the Grand Strand. In 1894, President Grover Cleveland came to the Lowcountry to hunt ducks. Cleveland's friend, Edward Alexander, a former Confederate General, owned property near Winyah Bay and overwhelmed the President with descriptions of rich hunting grounds near his home. So, in December 1894, the President sailed into Georgetown Harbor and spent five glorious days trudging through abandoned rice fields south of Myrtle Beach. The press provided elaborate daily reports of Cleveland's hunting successes, and the entire nation became fascinated with South Carolina's Lowcountry. Soon, letters requesting information about duck hunting and accommodations started pouring in — as did the hunters. Wealthy northern sportsmen fell in love with the area and began buying old rice plantations along the river. Natives referred to the phenomena as the "second Yankee invasion." The new plantation proprietors have had a dramatic impact on the Lowcountry's burgeoning education, arts and businesses — all because Grover Cleveland enjoyed hunting ducks.

seafood restaurants, Murrells Inlet also sports numerous antique shops.

The journey on U.S. 17 from Murrells Inlet to Litchfield is a quick but pretty trip. Densely wooded areas line the highway and give a sense of traveling back in time. Carefully manicured landscapes adorn the median along the main highway. Once known as Magnolia Beach, the popular resort of **Litchfield Beach** takes its name from Litchfield Plantation, a rice plantation on the Waccamaw River. The manor house is one of the few still-standing plantation homes surrounded by majestic oaks.

Litchfield's quaint shops, outstanding restaurants and various accommodations are reasonably new compared to the historic resort of Pawleys Island, just south of Litchfield. The beaches of Litchfield and Pawleys are among the widest, cleanest and best preserved on the South Carolina coast; however, much of the property is private and there are only a few public beach accesses. Though the accesses are clearly marked, parking is limited, which can be inconvenient.

Pawleys Island is one of the oldest resorts along the coastal Carolinas. In the 1800s, the tiny barrier island was a summer retreat for wealthy plantation owners and their families. Despite storms and the ravages of time, many of their cottages, weather-worn and rustic looking, still remain. Hence, for many years, the term "arrogantly shabby" has been used to describe Pawleys Island.

Today, Pawleys is known for its low-key lifestyle, handmade hammocks, and the Gray Man, a friendly spirit who warns of impending hurricanes (see our sidebar in this chapter). The cherished lifestyle is carefully protected by Islanders; the 2-mile island was incorporated into a township about a decade ago. Strict limitations exist on building codes, and the construction of high-rise condominiums and hotels is prohibited. A few bed and breakfast inns flourish, however, and offer a taste of beach living as it used to be . . . simple, unassuming and perfectly tranquil.

Photo: The Sun News

Beach volleyball tournaments are held regularly during the summer at Downwind Sails in Myrtle Beach.

Inside Getting Around

A vacation in Myrtle Beach is wonderful. It can calm even the most tense soul. So while you're sitting in traffic with the kids squabbling in the back seat, just remind yourself how nice your vacation is going to be.

Close your eyes and think about those gorgeous beaches with the sun shimmering on the water, feel that cool salt air wafting across your face and imagine yourself floating over those crisp clear waves. Now say to yourself every 5 or 10 minutes, "It really is worth it." Because it is.

The only distasteful part of your trip will be getting here and possibly getting around a little bit once you're here.

Getting Here

By Automobile

The popularity of the Grand Strand has soared in recent years with as many as 8.5 million to 9.5 million visitors pouring in every year. The problem is Horry County's roads just haven't kept up with the Grand Strand's popularity. But take it from those of us who have lived here for years: It's easy to avoid traffic snarls if you travel at the right times of day and night. Plan your trip so that you will be driving U.S. 501 into Myrtle Beach by 7 AM or after 7 PM, Monday through Thursday. Another rule of thumb is to stay off beach exit roads right after hotel checkout time on Sundays. You will be much better off to check out of your room, put the bags in the car and hang around town until late afternoon. That way, you can also get in one extra afternoon on the beach, which is far more pleasant than bumper-to-bumper driving.

If you're coming to the Grand Strand from eastern North Carolina, you might want to try I-40 E. or U.S. 17 S. to Wilmington, North Carolina. At Wilmington, you'll continue down U.S. 17 S. You should expect traffic to be moving pretty slowly along that stretch, unless you heed our previous advice and travel it early morning or late evening.

From Charleston, you'll want to take U.S. 17 N. It could be crowded at peak traffic times.

If you're traveling north on I-95, you'll take Exit 170 (clearly marked Myrtle Beach) just this side of Florence. You'll take U.S. 76 to U.S. 501 and follow it the rest of the way. Vacationers heading to North Strand beaches — Little River, Crescent Beach, Ocean Drive, Atlantic Beach and Windy Hill — will veer to the left at Marion, cross two lanes of U.S. 501 and continue on U.S. 76. At Nichols, take a right onto S.C. 9.

If you're traveling I-20, follow the signs toward Florence. The road will merge into I-95 North and bypass Florence. Then you'll take Exit 170, same as if you'd come the whole way on I-95.

If you're traveling south on I-95, you'll take Exit 193 at Dillon. Head toward Latta and then take U.S. 501. If you're going to North Myrtle Beach, you can take S.C. 9 all the way from Dillon.

If you're going to the South Strand, you might want to take S.C. 544. You'll turn to the right about 4 or 5 miles out of Conway off U.S. 501. S.C. 544 is a two-lane road. It's curvy and dangerous and frequently slowed by campers headed to the South Strand. The good news is that the new stationary bridge over the waterway is complete, so there's no more waiting for boats to pass through. It is now a straight overpass drive. You have the option of taking S.C. 544 or continuing on U.S. 501 and then connecting with U.S. 17 Bypass at the overpass about 10 miles out of Conway, just after the bridge at the Waccamaw Pottery complex. U.S. 501 and the U.S. 17 Bypass are much nicer roads than S.C. 544, but they'll add a few miles to your trip, and traffic is usually bad 7 AM to 7 PM or when it's raining. It's a toss up. Which one you pick will probably depend on what kind of road you prefer.

From Conway, most people will take U.S. 501. You'll find it most frustrating on Saturdays between about 11 AM and 3 PM.

State and local officials realize that motorists have problems getting to the Grand Strand, and they have several projects in the works that should help the situation. Plans are under way for a northern bypass around Conway beginning between Conway and Aynor and connecting to U.S. 17 at Briarcliffe Acres. The first step will be building a bridge over the Intracoastal Waterway. Although motorists will be able to see construction from the highway, other than having additional trucks on the road, the construction should not impede traffic.

The most optimistic estimates for completion of the northern bypass are late 1999 or early 2000, so there's still a lot of bad traffic days ahead.

Getting around in Myrtle Beach should be a little easier this year thanks to the widening of 21st Avenue N. between U.S. 17 and U.S. 17 Bypass. A project to widen a portion of Oak Street was finished ahead of schedule about mid-October in 1993. The project widened Oak Street to five lanes — four travel lanes and a turn lane — from 21st Avenue N. at the Myrtle Beach Convention Center to 29th Avenue N. From 29th Avenue N. to 38th Avenue N., the road was widened to three lanes — two travel lanes and a turn lane. The project also included curbs, guttering and sidewalks.

By Plane

An $18-million renovation project has put the **Myrtle Beach Jetport**, 448-1589, into the big-city league. The terminal has grown from 50,000 square feet to 120,000, and an upper level concourse has been added.

Rainy days no longer bring a polite attendant with an umbrella out to the planes to walk passengers into the terminal. Two jetways now connect the planes to the terminal and passengers need never get wet or cold.

Six airlines offer service to Myrtle Beach:

USAir, (800) 428-4322; Atlantic Southeast, (800) 282-3424, and Comair, (800) 282-3424, both Delta; Air South, (800) 247-7688; Continental Connection, (800) 525-0280, a commuter carrier for Continental Airlines; and Myrtle Beach Jet Express, (800) FUN 2 SUN.

Before February 16, 1995, direct flights

Navigating the Strand

Trying to navigate the Grand Strand can be a frustrating venture at first, because there seem to be so many names for the same routes. You'll hear "17 Bypass," "Kings Highway," "the Boulevard" and a host of others. We're going to try and make sense of all this for you.

The first thing to remember is that all main arteries along the Grand Strand run parallel with the Atlantic Ocean. Closest to the beach is Ocean Boulevard (a.k.a. The Boulevard or The 'Vard). Ocean Boulevard officially runs from Surfside Beach northward, breaks for 5 to 7 miles of private land and state park, and ends at 9000 Ocean Boulevard at Dunes Golf and Beach Club. Then it picks up again at 48th Avenue S. at Windy Hill beach and continues northward to Cherry Grove beach. Westward from Ocean Boulevard, the next main roadway is Kings Highway — commonly referred to as U.S. 17 or Business 17. Kings Highway is the proper name for this road in Myrtle Beach. To make a mental note, just remember that Kings Highway is also called "Business 17" because shops, restaurants and attractions galore line both sides of this main street. Kings Highway (U.S. 17) stretches from Georgetown all the way through South Carolina. Still moving west now, you'll come across the racing traffic of U.S. 17 Bypass or Alternate 17. True to its name, this highway's purpose is to bypass traffic on Kings Highway. The Bypass begins in Murrells Inlet and continues northward until it merges with Kings Highway at Dixie Stampede in the Restaurant Row district. Once you've merged here, the road remains Kings Highway northward to the Cherry Grove area; it then becomes U.S. 17 N.

If you really want to skip through town like a true native — anywhere from the Myrtle Beach Jetport to 48th Avenue N. in Myrtle Beach — here's how: Leaving the Jetport, take the first right turn onto South Broadway (road signs read S.C. 15). As you proceed, South Broadway will turn into West Broadway at the stoplights; the Bob Bible Honda dealership will be to your left. Keep in the center lanes that allow you to travel straight through this original downtown section of Myrtle Beach until you reach the third set of stoplights; then get in the left-turn lane. Turning left will put you on Oak Street; you'll wind through town to 38th Avenue N. Go straight through the 38th Avenue stoplights onto Pine Lakes Drive and pass through a lovely old residential section of Myrtle Beach all the way to 48th Avenue N.

to Myrtle Beach were a rarity. Now, the Myrtle Beach Jet Express can get you to the Strand in a jiffy from Newark (N.J.) International, Philadelphia International, Chicago's Midway and New York's J.F.K. airports. One flight departs daily (except Tuesday) from each location for the Myrtle Beach Jetport. One-way fares range from $69 to $119 from Chicago and from $59 to $119 from Newark, Philadelphia and New York. Reservations, based on availability, are accepted on a first-come, first-serve basis. And, guess what? . . . The Express may soon link Boston and Pittsburgh with Myrtle Beach as well.

You should be able to get to Myrtle Beach by air from just about anywhere in the United States. Unless you can book an express flight, you'll have to take a smaller commuter flight, probably from a major air terminal in Charlotte, North Carolina or Atlanta, Georgia.

Before March of 1993, the Jetport operated in connection with the Myrtle Beach Air Force Base. The Air Force closed its base in 1993, but service at the Jetport has not been affected. The Myrtle Beach Jetport is at the southern most part of Myrtle Beach, between U.S. 17 and U.S. 17 Bypass.

Horry County also operates the **Grand Strand Airport**, 448-1589, in North Myrtle Beach where private aircraft and corporate jets can land. It's open 24 hours a day. You don't have to notify anyone that you're coming, but be aware that all services close for business at 10 PM.

You can leave your craft for several days while you enjoy the beach. The airport is at 33rd Avenue S. and Terminal Avenue, just about one block from U.S. 17, pretty much in the heart of North Myrtle Beach.

Fixed-base operators at Grand Strand Airport are Air East and Ramp 66. Both services offer overnight tie down. Cost is $5 per night. Fuel is also available.

An Air East representative said some motels will pick up passengers. If Air East staffers have time and your accommodations aren't too far away, they will take you to your motel. Air East has also added Enterprise Rent-A-Car services, 361-0418 or 272-6161.

Ramp 66 has its own car rental service, featuring all new cars. Customers can use a car for an hour for free. After that, it's $8 per hour. They also have weekly rates. If you're coming into the airport at odd hours, you need to take care of your car rental ahead of time. Call (800) 433-8918.

There is also an airport for private planes and corporate jets outside Conway off U.S. 378. This airport is home for the North American Institute of Aviation, an international pilot training school. Overnight tie down is $2. (See our Day Care and Education chapter for more information.)

Rental Cars

Five companies — Avis, 448-1751; Hertz, (800) 654-3131 or 448-3191; Budget, 448-5630; National, (800) 227-7368 or 626-3687; and Payless, 448-3737 or (800) 729-5377 — rent cars and vans at the Jetport. Other rental car offices in the Myrtle Beach area include Alamo, (800) 327-9633, Thrifty, 626-6527, and U-Save, 626-3937. Coastal Cabs can take you to your lodging. They'll also provide a van if you go to the Executive Coach Service booth and request it.

By Bus

You should be able to get to Myrtle Beach on a Greyhound bus from just about any point in the United States. You'll find it easier during the summer when more buses are scheduled. The station, at Ninth Avenue N. in Myrtle Beach, is open from 8 AM to 1 PM and 3 PM to 7 PM. Call 448-2471 or (800) 231-2222 for details.

Coastal cabs will be on hand to get you to your accommodations.

By Train

Don't count on riding the train to your Grand Strand vacation. Florence and Dillon are the two closest places Amtrak

Photo: The Sun News

Don't forget your Frisbee before you head to the beach.

serves. The problem is you can't get to the Grand Strand from either of those cities unless you have friends who'll pick you up.

Some people used to ride Amtrak to Florence and catch the Greyhound bus on to Myrtle Beach. However, that bus was discontinued because there weren't enough people riding it.

Greyhound officials say it is possible the Florence to Myrtle Beach bus will be put back into action during the tourist season, but don't count on it. They recommend calling ahead before you buy your train ticket.

By Boat

The most scenic and perhaps most peaceful way to get to the Grand Strand is by boat. The Intracoastal Waterway runs 1,200 miles from Boston, Massachusetts, to Key West, Florida, parallel to the Atlantic Ocean. In 1932, the Army Corps of Engineers dug a 20-mile canal, connecting Little River to the Waccamaw River. This portion goes right through the Grand Strand.

Boaters can tie up at Barefoot Landing for a day of shopping and dining and an evening of country music at the new Alabama Theatre. There are numerous marinas along the waterway and Waccamaw River where boaters can spend the night, eat in a nice restaurant, buy groceries or have their motors tuned up.

Many of the marinas have signs along the waterway telling you what CB band to tune into to contact them.

Marinas along the Grand Strand area include Little River, Vereen's Marina, 280-6354, Bella Marina and Palmetto Shores, 249-4131, at the northern edge of Horry. On down, there's Hague Marina, 293-2141, just before Socastee; Bucksport, 397-5566, a very popular docking spot;

Coming South Via I-77?

Coming to the Grand Strand via I-77 from Western North Carolina, West Virginia, Ohio, Western Pennsylvania, Michigan and possibly Canada can be a trying time. We've consulted a couple of AAA offices for their best directions, but when we tried those routes we wound up spending a lot of time sitting in traffic. So, here's a favored route of some transplanted Northerners who call Myrtle Beach home: Travel I-77 S. through Charlotte, North Carolina, to Rock Hill, South Carolina. Just past Rock Hill, take Exit 77 onto U.S. 21 S. Stay on U.S. 21 for about 5 miles and exit east onto S.C. 5. Stay on S.C. 5 for about 5 miles until you reach U.S. 521. Head south on U.S. 521 to Lancaster. Outside of Lancaster, take S.C. 9 for about 3 miles to S.C. 903. Take S.C. 903 east for about 20 miles to S.C. 151 and turn right. Stay on S.C. 151 for about 40 miles to Darlington. Just outside of Darlington, take U.S. 52 toward Florence until it junctions with I-95. Take I-95 N. and follow the instructions included in this chapter from that point.

It sounds confusing, we know, but pull out your map and highlight the route in advance. Even though the roads look like two-laners on most maps, you actually will be on four-laners for most of the way, with the exception of the 60-mile or so stretch between Lancaster and McBee, South Carolina. Following these directions, it should take about 3½ hours to get from Charlotte to Myrtle Beach. If you don't want to bother with the back roads, we understand. If you prefer interstates, stay on I-77 to Columbia, South Carolina, then take I-20 to Florence and follow the directions included in this chapter from that point. The advantage is traveling all interstates, but it may take you a little longer.

There is a possibility that some relief is in sight. There's talk of an Interstate 73 that would begin in Michigan and run all the way down to Charleston, South Carolina. This proposal is in the very early planning stages, so don't expect this option anytime soon.

Wacca Wache at Wachesaw Landing, 651-2994 or 651-7171; Inlet Port Marina and Cedar Hills, 651-5805, in the Murrells Inlet area. (See our Watersports chapter for details about marinas.)

There is a city-owned marina in Conway, 248-1711, on the Waccamaw River. If you're traveling south on the waterway, you'll turn right at Enterprise Landing at Channel Marker 25. Then you'll head north for about 9 miles. Some boaters choose this course because of the beauty of the river. It's winding and has some sharp turns, so if your boat is longer than about 40 feet, you might not want to try it.

To navigate the waterway, it's a good idea to have a nautical map. The maps point out dangerous spots, marinas and buoys and describe available services at the marinas.

You won't find the waterway as crowded as U.S. 501, but it is a popular artery for travelers, recreational boaters and water skiers. You'll find the water crowded on weekends, especially the Waccamaw River.

Traffic in Myrtle Beach can be very heavy, especially on rainy days.

The stretch between Conway and Bucksport is especially charming, a wonderful place to get back in touch with nature. Egrets build their nests on the channel markers, and beautiful old trees overhang the water. If you're fortunate enough to travel at night, the moon glistens on the water and you can spot campfires back in the woods. At times, the campers will come to the bank and shout hearty hellos to the boaters.

Once You're Here . . .

Taxis

For easy, accessible travel it's always best to have an automobile when exploring the Grand Strand. Let's face it, to cover 60 miles of territory, any other mode of transportation will take considerable time. But there's nothing more expedient than a cab to simply get from point A to point B in good time. We will warn you that taxi fares are not cheap around here. To give you an idea of the usual cost, a run from the Myrtle Beach Jetport to a Myrtle Beach destination around 21st Avenue N. will be approximately $10 to $15. Try any of the following companies for service:

Carolina Cab	*626-2050*
City Cab	*448-5555*
Coastal Cab	*448-4444*
Coker's Cab	*448-4170*
Grand Strand Taxi, Inc.	*249-6705*
Hillside Taxi	*448-6652*
North Myrtle Beach Taxi	*272-0009*
Surfside Yellow Cab	*293-5515*
Yellow Cab	*448-3181*

Buses and Trolleys

Once you're in Myrtle Beach, you might want to walk or ride the **Coastal Rapid Public Transit Authority** bus whenever you can.

CRPTA runs buses and a San Francisco-looking trolley along Kings Highway (U.S. 17 Business) daily from Barefoot Landing to the north to Inlet Square Mall toward the south end. The trolley runs from 7:10 AM to 6:45 PM, depending upon the time of year. It comes along about every 40 minutes in the off-season. During tourist season, it comes by a little more frequently. Most motels and hotels have the schedules. Otherwise you can call 626-9138 to get the routes and times.

If you stand out near the road and wave, the trolley driver will stop and pick you up. A ride anywhere up and down the highway is $1. The driver cannot give you change.

Buses also go from Myrtle Square Mall to Inlet Square, Waccamaw Pottery, Conway, Briarcliffe and Barefoot Landing. A ticket to Conway is $1.25. The most expensive ride the service offers is from Loris to Myrtle Beach — a mere $2.

Inside Restaurants

To be a dieter on the Grand Strand is a lot like being a pagan in a village of missionaries. If dropping pounds is one of your vacation objectives, you'd better pack your Samsonite and head for the hills. And don't waste time. On the other hand, if you're up for a no-holds-barred gastronomic adventure, you are situated smack-dab in the middle of paradise. Sprinkled along the Carolina's 60-mile ribbon of sea and surf are more restaurants than your sun-baked brain can fathom . . . more than 1,400 in all. There's scarcely a bend in the road that doesn't offer up a panoply of tongue-teasing taste sensations! Unless you have several months of three-meal days to while away, there's no way you can sample them all.

If the thought of freshly caught seafood's got your mouth waterin', you'll find a slew of delectable choices to appease your rumbling tummy. Poised on the brink of the beautiful blue Atlantic, we take full advantage of our location to bring you some of the world's very best seafood. Calabash, a quaint little fishing village just a smidgen north of the South Carolina line, is filled with restaurants that specialize in seafood fare. Then again, an easy scoot down U.S. 17 South will land you in Murrells Inlet, another charming fishing village that teems with restaurants catering to seafood connoisseurs. Restaurant Row, on U.S. 17 North, sits midway along the Strand and boasts a bevy of options you just can't miss.

Although seafood enjoys premier popularity along the Strand, lots of other options deserve equal time. You can sample Japanese, French, Italian, Mexican and Chinese specialities. There's an intimate Australian pub, authentic German hangouts and charming round-table bistros. We're famous the whole world over for our lavish buffets, but we've mastered the art of intimate sit-down dinners too. We've got full-tilt elegant, and we've got shorts-and-swimsuits casual. And, when the Great Outdoors beckons, dozens of enterprises feature decks for dining and views galore. Take care not to skip the indigenous edibles — like grits, alligator stew, crawfish and "chicken bog" (a soupy mixture of rice, seasoned sausage, tender chicken and plenty of black pepper). Once you've sampled Lowcountry cooking — simmered slow and steeped in spices — you won't want to leave.

With more than 1,400 choices, it stands to reason that this chapter can't begin to do justice to the area's restaurants. We've opted to highlight a handful of favorites — mostly individually owned restaurants unique to this area. Of course, there are lots of good places for which we don't have room. And, there are plenty of regionally and nationally known names whose quality you can always count on:

Cracker Barrel, Shoney's, Quincy's, Red Lobster, Wendy's, The Olive Garden, Perkins', Pizza Hut, Fuddrucker's, TGI Fridays . . . the list is nearly endless.

Reservations are not necessary at the majority of restaurants, and — in deference to our laid-back lifestyle — some establishments don't accept them at all. However, lines are commonplace in this fair city of ours, so — whenever possible — it's a good idea to call ahead. If you just can't bring yourself to plan in advance, take heart in knowing we've learned a lot about feeding folks fast; lines usually move quickly. While you're waiting, people-watching will help you pass the time. And, lots of restaurants have bar areas where you can settle in for a drink or two until you can be seated.

The following key indicates the price range for an average dinner for two, including cocktails and a main course. Lunch fares usually run one-third to one-half less than the dinner prices.

Less than $20	*$*
$21 - $35	*$$*
$36 - $50	*$$$*
$51 and up	*$$$$*

North Strand

The Parson's Table

U.S. 17 N.
Little River *249-3702*
$$$ *All major credit cards*

The building in which The Parson's Table is located is filled with history. It was constructed in 1885 as the Little River Methodist Church. Today, the building has been converted into one of the finest restaurants we've ever enjoyed. The Academy Awards of the restaurant industry ranked it one of the Top 50 Best Overall restaurants in the United States. The Gourmet Diners Club of America bestowed its Silver Spoon Recipient Award on The Parson's Table. And, most recently, the Executive Chef was selected as one of the Best Chefs in America — joining the illustrious company of Wolfgang Puck and Louis Osteen.

Serving prime rib and filet mignon, roast duckling with raspberry demi-glaze, veal, pasta, seafood and oodles of calorie-laden desserts, this beautiful, history-steeped old church is among the Strand's very, very best. Don't leave without a cup of their Hawaiian Kona Coffee. The Parson's Table serves dinner only.

The Pier at Little River

4495 Mineola Ave.
Little River *249-2601*
$$$ *All major credit cards*

What do you have when you combine a European chef who worked in Marseille, France, an incredible view of the Intracoastal Waterway, indoor and outdoor dining and a splash of live entertainment (on Friday and Saturday evenings)? . . . You have an unbeatable recipe for casual fine dining.

The Pier at Little River is located in the historic fishing village of (you guessed it!) Little River. The menu is peppered with marvelous indulgences that, not unexpectedly, feature a French flair that's sadly uncommon in these parts. From tender veal and roast lamb to strip steaks, chicken, duck and seafood extraordinaire, this menu demands a herculean exercise in willpower. The grouper papillotte, baked in parchment paper with wine, capers, shallots and mushrooms, is a personal favorite. And the house special, the chowder-like Bouillabaisse Little River, is the absolute ultimate for seafood lovers.

The Pier at Little River is open for dinner every day except Sunday. Reservations are not required but are strongly recommended, particularly on weekend evenings.

The Brentwood Restaurant

4269 Luck St.
Little River — *249-2601*
$$ — *All major credit cards*

The Brentwood is a feast for all your senses. The first floor of this remodeled Victorian-styled restaurant, built in 1910, is reserved for dining. Upstairs, there is a European "salon" where guests can retire after dinner for dessert and drinks including espresso and capuccino. It's also the perfect place to relax and enjoy a leisurely bottle of wine with cheese. Toss in a game of backgammon, and you've got the makings for a splendid interlude.

The food is, quite simply, excellent. Prior to opening The Brentwood, chef and owner Bill Stublick worked for two of the North Strand's best-loved restaurants: The Parson's Table and Oak Harbour Inn. Those in the know will realize the value of those credentials. In addition to homemade desserts, the gourmet menu includes fresh veal, rack of lamb, fresh local seafood (the softshell crabs are extraordinary!), beef, pork and duck. Entrees include freshly baked bread, a crisp salad, your choice of rice pilaf or chantilly potatoes and a guaranteed-tasty vegetable of the day. A delicious vegetarian menu is also available.

The Brentwood is open for dinner Monday through Saturday. Seatings begin at 5 PM, and reservations are suggested but not required.

Maggie's Cafe

1535 U.S. 17
Little River — *249-4024*
$$ — *All major credit cards*

If you're a discriminating diner, this is one of the first places you should try on the Grand Strand. Located at the crest of the hill in Little River, Maggie's offers lunch seven days a week and dinner Tuesday through Saturday. Family groups with small children are welcome before 6:30 PM, but Maggie and Chef Alan Bell thank you for understanding that the dinner atmosphere is not appropriate for children after that time. This restaurant is the talk of the Strand for moderately priced "come as you are" dining. The food qualifies as gourmet, but don't be intimidated; it's not pretentious at all. At lunchtime, the seafood crêpes are a "can't miss" option, and, at dinner, Wisconsin veal with whiskey-pecan sauce is divinely different. Of course, Maggie's offers lots of fresh seafood choices, like lemon linguine with shrimp, scallops and smoked salmon, as well as chicken, beef, pork and salads, soups and appetizers.

Don't leave without taking Maggie's packaged seasoning and spice blends, dried fruit chutney and fresh homemade salad dressing to go. Maggie's is a smoke-free restaurant, so, if you must, fire one up before you come inside.

Sante Fe Station

1101 U.S. 17 N.
North Myrtle Beach *249-3463*
$$ *All major credit cards*

The single most distinctive thing about Sante Fe Station is the menu; it's bound to remind you of a metropolitan area phone book. It's enormous! And, it's wonderful. Sante Fe Station is fun — very youthful in atmosphere, but not at all trendy. Recently remodeled, they have a great bar and can whip up fabulous specialty drinks. There are 18 items on the appetizer menu alone! (Skip the reading: Order stuffed jalapeños or blackened lobster bites.) Entrees run the gamut from healthy salads and fresh seafood to fat sandwiches, steaks, burgers, chicken, and ribs. There's a kid's menu too. For dessert, the Key lime pie will soothe your sunburn. Better still, order a pitcher of Long Island iced tea and forget your worries. Sante Fe Station is open seven days a week for dinner only.

Apple Annie's

4711 U.S. 17 S.
North Myrtle Beach *272-2000*
$$ *All major credit cards*

Every year, Myrtle Beach's St. Andrew's Catholic School sponsors a fund-raiser called Taste of the Town. Every year, Apple Annie's lands on everyone's list of favorites. Everything is homemade — from salad dressings to sauces. The menu serves up scads of choices from raw bar specialities like Cajun spiced shrimp to salads, sandwiches, Italian selections, prime rib, chicken and pork chops. Perhaps best of all, Apple Annie's is genuinely enjoyable. The mood is light, and laughter is plentiful. Live bands play on Friday and Saturday nights, and there are more than 65 imported beers to sample. This locals' favorite, particularly with the younger set, serves lunch and dinner.

Cagney's Old Place

9911 U.S. 17 N., Restaurant Row
Myrtle Beach *449-3824*
$$$ *All major credit cards*

For nearly two decades, Cagney's Old Place has been a favorite local dining and dancing spot — and tourists have discovered our secret. There's ambiance aplenty and great food too. Many of the antiques that enliven Cagney's decor came from the Ocean Forest Hotel, a fabulous oceanfront hotel that was demolished in 1974. Cagney's specialty has always been prime rib, but everything is perfectly delicious. A children's menu is also available. *Southern Living* recommends this classic, and you know how high their standards are! Only dinner is served.

Chestnut Hill

9922 U.S. 17, Restaurant Row
Myrtle Beach *449-3984*
$$$ *All major credit cards*

When you walk into Chestnut Hill, the elegant decor may make you feel as though you've wandered onto Nob Hill instead. The menu does offer a number of gourmet dishes, but the stuffy air that is often part and parcel of elegant dining establishments is no where to be found. Service is friendly and accommodating,

Photo: Jody Hazzard, The Sun News

Restaurant Row is home to some of the best restaurants in the area.

Restaurant Row

Locals have referred to a strip of the U.S. Highway 17 Bypass as "Restaurant Row" for so long, we often forget visitors don't have the vaguest notion of what we mean. So, for the uninitiated, here's the explantation:

Restaurant Row represents a 2-mile portion of U.S 17 Bypass on the northernmost end of Myrtle Beach that is best known as the home to roughly 17 fabulous restaurants. Beginning at Lake Arrowhead Road near the Galleria, and extending to Briarcliffe Mall, Restaurant Row is notorious for some of the Strand's most frustrating traffic pileups. However, if you avoid the area during the height of the dinner rush — between 6 PM and 8 PM — the inconvenience is minimal. At any time, if you're looking for the best "eats" this area has to offer, getting in and out of Restaurant Row is a small price to pay.

"A Taste of the World" — that's Restaurant Row. Here are just a few of the names representing the quality and variety you'll find:

Bennett's Calabash features one of the beach's biggest and best buffets — with so many to choose from, that's a mouthful! With more than 80 items on the all-you-can-eat bar and a full menu to boot, Bennett's is the place to go to please everyone in your family. Don't show up unless you're really hungry!

For tenderness and flavor, **Shenanigan's** ages its steaks for at least 28 days. They hand pick fresh seafood and create a magnificent alfredo sauce from scratch. Every single day, professional butchers grind fresh chuck for outstanding burgers. They grind their own gourmet coffee beans, pour only premium liquors and hand squeeze oranges and grapefruits for your tropical drinks. It's pretty obvious, we think: Quality is the order of the day at Shenanigan's. *Golf* magazine called **The Gullyfield** "the best predominantly seafood restaurant around." Enjoy traditional, robust Lowcountry cuisine as it was meant to be enjoyed: always fresh and always graciously served. They offer hearty steaks, chicken and chops too. Gullyfield's overlooks a pretty lake, so come while the sun's still shining and enjoy the view.

At **Nakato**, a Japanese steakhouse, watching your meal being concocted is as much fun as eating it! Lobster, shrimp, chicken and steak fall under the chef's flashing knife as he prepares your meal — hibachi style — right at your table. For the adventurous, there's a sushi bar. Kids love the show. Make room for a glass of Japanese plum wine!

and the food is excellent. (Try anything grilled.) Guests always enjoy the picturesque view of the backyard lake — so, come before the sun sets if you can. The owner of Chestnut Hill, which opens daily at 5 PM, has several restaurants along the Strand, and he knows more than a thing or two about feeding hungry people. Don't miss this one.

Dick's Last Resort

4700 U.S. 17 S., Barefoot Landing
North Myrtle Beach *272-7794*
$$ *All major credit cards*

This place is billed as "the shame of Barefoot Landing," and we feel obligated to point out that you might want to think twice about ushering your kids into this barn-sized restaurant. A wisecracking staff serves up sloppy barbecue ribs, messy roasted chicken, boiled shrimp, crab legs, catfish and other hands-required delicacies in buckets. The attitude of the wait staff is anything but accommodating, and there's butcher paper instead of table cloths. The atmosphere teems with sexual innuendo — from the menu featuring drinks with lusty, carnal names to the anatomically correct paper hats the staff has been known to force customers to don. On the flip side, Dick's really does promise a unique dining experience — for adults and the savviest of youngsters at least. There's a staggering inventory of beer, and the messy food is plentiful and finger-lickin' good. (Forgive me, Colonel.) Seven nights a week, live entertainment ranging from jazz and rhythm and blues to beach music complements the staff's antics. Dick's also has a great deck where you can watch the alligators cavort in the freshwater lake. Lunch and dinner are served daily. If you're looking for something different and fun, this is the place to be.

Rosa Linda's Cafe

4635 U.S.17 S.
North Myrtle Beach *272-6823*
1803 N. Kings Hwy.
Myrtle Beach *626-3611*
5141 U.S. 17 S.
Murrells Inlet *651-2400*
$$ *All major credit cards*

The tastiest Mexican dishes this side of the border can be found at any one of Rosa Linda's three locations. Serving lunch and dinner, this locals' favorite caters to the spice of life — fun, good food and marvelous Margaritas. As soon as you've settled into your seat, you'll get a bowlful of complimentary tortilla chips with hot or mild salsa. (They're homemade!) Combine à la carte items like tostados, burritos, enchiladas and tacos made from beef, chicken or seafood for a hearty meal. Dinner specials, usually served with black beans and rice, include fajitas, chimichangas and grilled fish tampico. The fried ice cream is, of course, extraordinary. And, for you weight watchers, the pasta dishes and fresh salads are as good as the Mexican specialities. The menu boasts more than 140 items. All three locations serve lunch and dinner and showcase bars that are perfect for socializing. Plus, if you're staying within a 5-mile radius of any of the three locations, they'll deliver for free.

T Bonz Gill & Grill at Barefoot Landing

4732 U.S. 17 S.
North Myrtle Beach *272-7111*
$$ *All major credit cards*

T Bonz' big ole menu and spacious, if noisy, interior is fun, fun, fun. They serve up hearty portions of beef, grilled chicken, vegetarian entrees, seafood and more. Being Southern born-n-bred, we're particularly fond of the shrimp and grits specialty — a creamier dish of the snowy stuff has never been created. A vast selection of imported and domestic wines and beers is offered. We sometimes choose T Bonz just because they are so environmentally conscious. They recycle all their glass and cardboard and avoid the use of styrofoam. The atmosphere is casual, the price is affordable and kids are welcome. Open 11 AM until late night, T Bonz also offers light lunches and an after-hours social scene.

Thoroughbreds

U.S. 17 N.,Restaurant Row
Myrtle Beach *497-2636*
$$$$ *All major credit cards*

A favorite among locals and tourists, Thoroughbreds' popularity has grown by leaps and bounds since it opened in 1990. When the restaurant became unable to accommodate nightly reservations and the community's requests for public and private functions, Scott Harrelson, owner and operator, made the decision to overhaul. Not someone to do anything in a small way, Harrelson spent in excess of $500,000. And, it shows. The new Thoroughbreds — featuring four beautifully appointed dining rooms, an elegant piano bar and a captivating garden terrace — offers an unparalleled celebration of food, spirits, music and art.

Arguably, this is the single most elegant restaurant on the Strand. The wait staff is meticulously trained and very professional. Harp music is often highlighted. And candlelight abounds. The menu, which combines gourmet seafood and continental cuisine, is nothing shy of memorable. Caesar salads are prepared tableside. Beef is best, but there's chicken, veal, pork and even duck.

Lest you be fooled into thinking Thoroughbreds is too ritzy for your average vacation meal, think again. Yes, it's elegant, and you do need to dress up a bit, but the atmosphere is cozy, the staff is friendly and accommodating, and children are welcome. We think you'll be glad you donned your finery. This is a personal favorite.

Only dinner is served, and reservations are suggested.

Rossi's

9600 U.S.17 N., in the Galleria
Myrtle Beach *449-0481*
$$$ *All major credit cards*

Rossi's bills itself as "everything a restaurant ought to be," and we have to agree. A bevy of delights awaits your arrival: overly-generous servings of veal and homemade pasta, fresh seafood, and Black Angus beef; fine wines; a cozy dining room featuring weathered brick, stained glass and chandeliers; a piano bar; live entertainment; and desserts that'll make you do the two-step. Open for dinner only.

Damon's, The Place for Ribs

Barefoot Landing *272-5107*
2908 S. Ocean Blvd. *626-8000*
$$ *No Discover Cards*

Damon's is known locally for its mastery of red meat and exceptional value with every meal. Of course, it specializes in ribs and offers a signature appetizer, the onion loaf. Both Damon's are family-oriented restaurants located on a body of water. Its newest location on S. Ocean Boulevard replaces the former Downwind Trading Company restaurant. Right on the beach, facing the Atlantic, Damon's is open seven days a week for lunch and dinner.

Knickerbockers On the Water

Barefoot Landing *272-5900*
$$ *All major credit cards*

Knickerbockers offers more than 80 menu items including steaks, seafood, prime rib, barbecue, ribs, chicken, pasta and more. Serving lunch and dinner seven days a week, you can enjoy the spirited piano bar with live entertainment on the weekends. Very few patrons ask for doggy bags because alligators and sea turtles saunter right up to the watery end of the restaurant looking for leftovers! If you want to keep the kids entertained for hours with the purchase of a plate of french fries, this is the place to come.

Myrtle Beach

Collector's Cafe

7726 N. Kings Hwy.
Myrtle Beach *449-4815*
$$$ *All major credit cards*

Everyone has his or her own concept of a great restaurant. Some enjoy the casual, comfortable and unpretentious. Some like the blue-blood feeling they derive from the attentive service in an elegant restaurant. Still others prefer the intimacy of a neighborhood bar or coffee house. Amazingly, Collector's Cafe has managed to marry all three environments, and we can't imagine anyone who wouldn't be satisfied spending an evening here.

In the bar area, original paintings are artfully displayed along with a curious assortment of hand-painted bistro tables beneath soft lights. The dining room also features art, but its columns and high ceilings exude elegance. (There is also a dimly lit Gallery Room for the most intimate dining experience.) And, there's a grill room, too, with oversized wall hangings and hand-tiled table tops. Surrounded by art, you'll quickly see that Collector's Cafe serves up a feast for the senses, as well as for sustenance.

The restaurant bills itself as serving Mediterranean cuisine, which only seems a little daunting. Appetizers include the zucchini pancake with lobster and tomato basil cream and a grilled polenta triangle topped with mushroom ragout. A favored entree is beef medallions topped with grilled shrimp, roasted sweet peppers and Parmesan and rosemary oil. Of course, there are also pasta and salad selections, as well as veal, lots of fresh seafood and grilled breast of duck.

After dinner, take time to enjoy a steamed drink from the "Godiva Collection." And, don't forfeit dessert; you can walk an extra mile or two on the beach tomorrow. This is the latest, greatest place-to-be-seen on the Strand. Make a place for it on your itinerary. Collector's Cafe is open Monday through Saturday for dinner only.

Akel's House of Pancakes

6409 N. Kings Hwy.
Myrtle Beach *449-4815*
$ *All major credit cards*

For local color, don't miss Akel's; it's a Myrtle Beach landmark. In an area known for its stellar lineup of pancake houses, Akel's rates right up top. Whether for the food, the service or the all-night hours, we're not sure. The atmosphere is friendly and surprisingly familiar. Gossip, laughter and local news travels from one table to another; a meal here is as good as reading the local paper! Open 10 PM to 2 PM, Akel's is everybody's favorite way to wrap up a night on the town. Needless to say, it's a great way to start your morning, too. Come watch the locals in their element! While breakfast fare is the house speciality, they offer lots of sandwiches, salads and burgers, too.

The Bistro

208 N. 73rd Ave. N. (on Ocean Blvd.)
Myrtle Beach *449-0465*
$$$ *All major credit cards*

The Bistro is a very quaint restaurant

Serving Fresh Local Seafood, Handcut Steaks & Pasta Dishes.

"Winner Of Taste Of The Town 1993"

Serving Lunch & Dinner
Open 7 Days
Weekend Entertainment
Rock, Reggae & Blues

272-2000

Across From Barefoot Landing

The Pier at Little River

Casual Fine Dining On The Intracoastal Waterway In Historic Little River.

Veal, Beef, Chicken, Lamb, Steaks, Seafood,

House Special

Bouillabaisse "Little River"

4495-Mineola Ave., Little River

249-1220

The Brentwood
RESTAURANT

Gourmet Menu • Full Wine List

Chef Bill Stublick Of Brentwood, N.Y. Invites You To Dine In Our Turn Of The Century Victorian Great House

Reservations Suggested
Major Credit Cards

Turn At The Flashing Light in Little River

4269 Luck Ave., Little River
(803) 249-2601

THE TALK OF THE GRAND STRAND FOR MODERATELY PRICED COME AS YOU ARE FINE DINING

1535 Highway 17,
Little River, South Carolina
(803) 249-4024

Photo: Bill Scroggins, The Sun News

From seafood to salad, buffets offer something for everyone.

that serves sumptuous continental cuisine and extraordinary desserts. Indoors, about 40 people can enjoy the friendly atmosphere. If the weather cooperates, about 40 additional guests can dine on the patio. Specialties include veal, steaks, chicken and pasta dishes. The Bistro is open for lunch and dinner, and it's the perfect choice for a romantic interlude. Dinner is served from 6 PM at this longtime locals' favorite.

Corbin's Bar & Grill

6401 N. Kings Hwy.
Myrtle Beach — *497-0416*
$$ — *All major credit cards*

Corbin's may be best known for its big and busy bar area. It is very much a place for meeting people and is known as a hangout for the baby boomer crowd. In the dining room, the menu features variety that's bound to please. From California-style salads with avocados and bean sprouts to blue plate specials that showcase meatloaf, mashed potatoes and vegetables, the choices are eclectic — and good. The Sante Fe-style interior is decidedly "cool," and the live musical entertainment is hot.

Dagwoods

400 11th Ave. N.
Myrtle Beach — *448-0100*
$ — *No credit cards*

It takes two man-sized hands to handle the monstrous subs at Dagwoods. There's not a lot of ambiance — Dagwood's is working-class at its best — but with sandwiches and prices like these, who cares? Baskets of homemade bread (baked fresh every day!) and an authentic deli case greet you at the door — reminiscent of a Chicago deli. Choose from a variety of hot and cold sandwiches that showcase a mile-high stack of deli meats and cheeses. You can feast on burgers and Philly cheesesteaks, too. At lunchtime, local business folk frequent the place, so it's gotta be good. Dagwoods is open for lunch and dinner. Suggestion? Come for lunch and eat the other half of your sub for dinner!

Dirty Don's Oyster Bar & Grill

408 21st Ave. N.
Myrtle Beach *448-4881*
$$ *All major credit cards*

Dirty Don's is small in size but big on character. Serving lunch and dinner, Don's Bar & Grill features oyster shooters, clams on the half-shell, a variety of sandwiches and tasty "ragtime" fish stew. The catfish fingers are awesome, particularly with a salty Margarita. Bigger appetites are fond of the juicy steaks and man-size shrimp dinners. Dirty Don's is the perfect place to spend an afternoon out of the sun . . . noshing on appetizers and drinking tall cool ones.

The Library

1212 N. Kings Hwy.
Myrtle Beach *448-9242*
$$$$ *All major credit cards*

The Library is one of the most elegant restaurants in the entire South — recipient of guests' kudos as well as prestigious professional accolades. Offering consummate European cuisine and superior service, this restaurant has been quietly collecting fans since 1974. In a recent *Sun News* survey, locals voted The Library the "most romantic" dining spot on the Strand — with more than 1,400 restaurants, that's a real coup! The menu includes seafood, veal, duck, beef and chicken . . . first class all the way. The Library is open for dinner only.

Flamingo Seafood Grill

71st Ave. N.
Myrtle Beach *449-5388*
$$$ *All major credit cards*

Flamingo Grill's art deco decor, black lacquer accented with pink and blue neon, sets the pace for a trendy evening of dining. Owned by the same folks of Cagney's fame, this restaurant has become a favorite. The menu includes lots of fresh seafood prepared in a variety of ways. The grilled fish with Cajun spices is especially popular. Other entrees include pasta (the Pasta Flamingo is "delish"), chicken, prime rib and steaks. As an appetizer, the filet mignon chunks are outstanding. Save room for dessert; the Outrageous Derby Pie is . . . well . . . outrageous. A children's menu is also available. Flamingo Grill serves dinner only.

Latif's Bakery & Cafe

503 61st Ave. N.
Myrtle Beach *449-1716*
$$ *All major credit cards*

Latif's began as a modest French bakery more than a decade ago. Today, it has expanded to offer a truly delightful experience for brunch, lunch or dinner. The enclosed terrace is especially charming and will make you feel as though you've ambled in for a cup of espresso — somewhere on Paris' Left Bank. In addition to salads of fruit melange, rice noodles blended with chicken and homemade pasta, Latif's serves a variety of sandwiches on classic French croissants. Luncheon specials range from crabmeat quiche to seasonal soups served with warm French bread. The Chinese chicken salad is divine. Dinner often includes larger portions of daily lunch specials, as well as gourmet entrees like baked salmon, South Indian chicken curry and stuffed shrimp.

Latif's crowning glory is its treasure trove of desserts. Even *Bon Appetit* said so. We've traveled the world over and never found any to rate higher. The triple chocolate mocha mousse torte is beyond description. It's light as air going down, but once it hits your hips — watch out! There are scads of cheesecakes, all kinds of speciality cakes (yes, they sell by the slice), brownies, cookies, pecan tassies, chocolate eclairs, baklava and so much more. This is a heavenly place to brunch alone; you can drink espresso, read the paper and eat as much as you want while no one's watching. Brunch, lunch and dinner hours vary throughout the year, so please call ahead to determine business hours.

Mark's Delivery

2501 N. Kings Hwy.
Myrtle Beach *448-9999*
$$ *All major credit cards*

Good food doesn't get any easier than this. Myrtle Beach local Mark McBride brings delicious dining right to your door. The menu is surprisingly comprehensive and affordable . . . a mouthwatering lineup of sizzling steaks, hearty salads, rotisserie chicken, sandwiches, kebobs and yummy desserts. Delivery is free with a small minimum order, or you can call ahead to carry out. There's a dining room too. And, if you eat in, you can order beer and wine. All entrees are served with a big baked potato, fresh salad and a dinner roll. If there's a good movie on HBO, and the kid's are driving you crazy, Mark's is the way to go.

The Mayor's House

2606 N. Kings Hwy.
Myrtle Beach *448-9058*
$$$ *All major credit cards*

This is an exceptional dining experience in a charming Victorian restaurant that exudes romance. Just pronouncing some of the specialties, prepared by gourmet chefs, creates a sensual mood: coquille St. Jacques, soft shell crabs almondine, Châteaubriand for two and steak au poivre. Desserts like cherries jubilee, chocolate truffle mousse cake and praline pecan ice cream pie are — dare it be said — the crème de la crème! And the wine list is a veritable who's who of vintners. The Mayor's House offers private rooms, catering service for small parties and a lunch menu that's legendary among local business people.

River City Cafe

404 21st Ave. N.
Myrtle Beach *448-1990*
$ *No credit cards*

River City Cafe is the best hamburger joint on the beach for reasons only a bona fide hamburger connoisseur would appreciate. First, it's the perfect setting, a wooden-framed building that resembles an old beach house. Inside, the floors, benches and chairs are made of worn wood. Car tags, bumper stickers and party paraphernalia adorn the ceiling and walls. Customers serve themselves from the big bin of dry roasted peanuts and throw the empty shells on the floor — just oozes class, huh! But this all leads to the best part: huge, 100 percent pure beef burgers topped with a variety of fixins' like thick slabs of cheese, jalapeños, grilled onions, bacon, etc.

These burgers require two hands to manage, and, although it can be a little messy, it's worth several napkins. Don't forget the jumbo homemade onion rings. River City also serves a variety of other sandwiches and hot dogs. It's been said that only an ice-cold longneck bottle of beer truly complements River City Cafe's burgers. We think Jimmy Buffett's cheeseburger in paradise was inspired by this savory spot.

Sea Captain's House

3002 N. Ocean Blvd.
Myrtle Beach *448-8082*
$$$ *All major credit cards*

Back around 1930, the Sea Captain's House was a traditional family beach cottage. Converted to an oceanfront restaurant in 1962, it has remained a family-

Fine Dining At

Sea What Makes Us Famous.

World Famous Garlic Crabs
Live Maine Lobster
• All-U-Can-Eat
Salad & Raw Bar

Barefoot Landing 272-1062
Opening June,
Broadway at the Beach 444-2717

"Why Nibble On The Waste, When You Can Attack The Rack?"

Ribs • Prime Rib • Chicken
Famous Onion Loaf
Sunday Cocktails

Lunch 11AM-3PM
Dinner 3PM-Until
7 Days A Week
272-5107

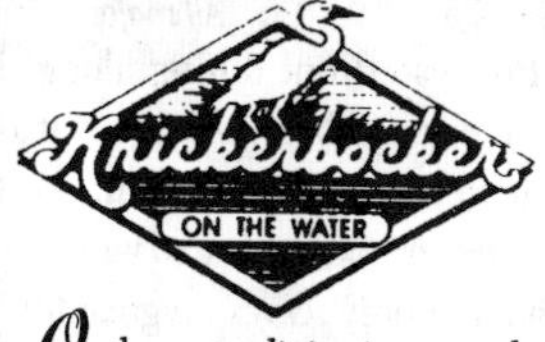

On the water dining in a casual atmosphere. Our fabulous 80 item menu is moderately priced, our portions extravagant.

Join us for tasty cuisine and entertainment. Some restaurants have the name, we have the food.

272-5900

COME HAVE FUN

COME GET EL BOW-DEEP IN BIG BUCKETS O' BEEF RIBS, ROAST CHICKY & CRAB LEGS- SURLY HELP & LOUD FREE MUSIC!

• 803-272-7794 •
4700 HWY 17-SOUTH
NORTH MYRTLE BEACH, SC

From Steaks To The Freshest Seafood You've Ever Tasted...Enjoy Barefoot Landing.

The East Coast's Most Exciting Waterfront Shopping, Dining and Entertainment Destination Center

Highway 17, North Myrtle Beach, SC • (803) 272-8349

owned and operated business to this day. Breakfast, lunch and dinner are served. If you enjoy understated elegance, delicious food and a panoramic view of the ocean, Sea Captain's House is sure to please. Specials range from grilled salmon fillets with roasted garlic sauce to baked breast of chicken topped with Cajun spiced shrimp. The kitchen staff is known for its culinary talents, particularly with seafood and Southern recipes.

Your vacation won't be complete until you visit this lovely Myrtle Beach landmark, another personal favorite.

Southside Freddie's

2300 S. Kings Hwy.
Myrtle Beach *626-9871*
$$ *All major credit cards*

The owner of the wildly successful Thoroughbreds restaurant created Southside Freddie's as his "alter ego" venture. While Thoroughbreds is elegant beyond compare, Southside Freddie's is relaxed and upbeat and features an eclectic menu you're bound to love. Start off with Freddie's onion loaf or Cajun fried oysters. (If you thought plain ole oysters were an aphrodisiac, wait 'til you try these!) Then, sink your teeth into slow-roasted chicken or mouthwatering smoked pork chops. You can even build your own all-you-can-eat pasta dinner or gourmet burger. They have yummy seafood specialities, too. Best of all, the prices are quite reasonable. Southside Freddie's is open for dinner only.

Villa Mare

7819 N. Kings Hwy. (behind NationsBank)
Myrtle Beach *449-8654*
$$ *No American Express*

This affordably priced Italian restaurant is an indisputable local favorite. Its simple, unassuming location in a strip mall around the corner from a grocery store is deceiving; this place has class. But, for all its class, it's not a bit pretentious. Clothing is casual; "come as you are, just come hungry," says Fred, the owner, in lilting Italian.

You'll find everything you'd expect on an Italian menu, from pastas to calzones, but the prices will pleasantly surprise you. You can order veal, chicken parmigiana, shrimp piccata and fettuccine alfredo and various pasta dishes, all made to order; absolutely everything is good. Plus, everyone is friendly and the atmosphere is light.

We think Villa Mare is a must for anyone who appreciates the best the Strand has to offer. Seating is limiting, so call ahead for reservations. Villa Mare is closed on Sundays.

South Strand

Anchor Inn

U.S. 17 Bus., (on the Waterfront)
Murrells Inlet *651-2295*
$$$ *All major credit cards*

For waterfront dining along the silvery creeks of Murrells Inlet, it doesn't get better than Anchor Inn. This two-story restaurant, decorated with rich, dark wood, not only serves up great food, they serve up a spectacular view of the Inlet. Full window walls bring the outdoors tableside. The menu is varied and includes a little of everything, from fresh local seafood to aged beef and tender prime rib.

Bovine's

U.S. 17 Bus. (On the Waterfront)
Murrells Inlet *651-2888*
$$$ *No American Express*

If ever a restaurant was fun, this is the one: expansive windows overlooking Lowcountry marsh; cozy lighting spilling shadows in every corner; exquisite

Hushpuppies!

If you aren't from the South, you may not be familiar with one of our best-loved culinary treats: hushpuppies. Hushpuppies are to seafood what french fries are to hamburgers. As a matter of fact, no self-respecting seafood restaurant would neglect serving you a heaping basket of these golden brown goodies.

Be sure to scare up a sample of this yummy Southern delicacy before you return home. The culinary roots of these tasty bits of deep-fried cornmeal batter have been traced back to the years following the War Between the States. During the Reconstruction, food was shockingly scarce, and one diet staple was corn meal. According to legend, many a mother fried up bits of corn batter to quiet the cries of hungry children — and dogs — with the words "Hush, child; hush, puppy!"

smells drifting from a wood-burning oven; and the low hum of happy patrons. Bovine's is the latest, greatest place-to-be-seen on the South Strand.

Bovine's decor is a tribute to the wonders of the west. Cowhide covered seats, rich, dark wood and the mounted head of a gargantuan bull reinforce the theme. The bar scene, separate from the main dining area, spotlights an awesome horseshoe-shaped bar, as well as electronic darts, a couple of mounted TVs and bistro tables scattered about. Comfy booths offer a ringside view of swaying spartina grass and the faraway, blooming lights of Garden City. Feels a little like the summertime hangouts of lost youth — only the patrons are seasoned and a bit more mellow. A great place for beer . . . and an individual-sized gourmet honey-crust pizza from the wood burning oven. A see-and-be-seen crowd always gathers after work.

As for the food, Bovine's recipe for success features a few ingredients unique to the area. First and foremost, you won't find anything swimming in grease. No all-you-can-eat buffets. Absolutely no "standard" fare. Nearly every selection on the titillating menu boasts a Southwestern slant. A great many choices come from the red hot, marvelously aromatic, igloo-shaped oven. The variety is quite impressive . . . from tender chargrilled chicken to melt-in-your-mouth steaks, seafood and pasta dishes, there's something for everyone.

Desserts are sinful and worth the mischief. The frozen vanilla honey mousse served with blackberry sauce is a sophisticated, grown-up version of an ice cream sundae. The homemade apple ligonberry cake will make you weak in the knees. There a showcase full of other decadent specialities too: Italian tortes, cheesecake and lots of chocolate. Bovine's serves dinner only, and reservations are accepted. This is a must.

The Captain's Restaurant

3655 U.S. 17 Bus.
Murrells Inlet *651-2416*
$$ *All major credit cards*

If you've got a hankerin' for that blue-blood feeling, head straight for The Captain's Restaurant. This beautiful old dining establishment has been in business for 25 years. On the Grand Strand, no restaurant lasts that long unless it's extraordinary, so you can be sure you'll enjoy your meal here.

Good ole Southern cooks, Mattie and Ernestine, have been laboring in the kitchen since The Captain's Restaurant first opened its doors, and they prepare seafood simply, classically and complemented by "from scratch" accompaniments. Everything is a treat for the palate, but if you love crabmeat, don't pass up the jumbo lump crabmeat dish. Big tender chunks of fresh, never frozen, crabmeat straight from the docks of McClellanville are pan broiled with a little butter, then served with drawn butter for dipping. It simple and simply unbeatable. Our second choice is scallops. The Captain serves none of the tiny bay scallops you find so many other places; here, you get a hearty plate of the oversized deep-sea kind everyone loves but can never seem to find. In addition to seafood, the dinner menu includes country ham, beef and chicken. And nearly everything on the "regular menu" is on the "senior menu" too. Featuring smaller portions and prices, this menu has been a real hit. The desserts are to-die-for.

The Captain serves lunch too. His salads are known far and wide. The shrimp salad, featuring capers and a tarragon-laced rémoulade sauce, is light and unusual. The Neptune salad, a longtime favorite, features shrimp, crabmeat and lobster. The avocado salad showcases crab meat and the sweetest shrimp we connoisseurs have ever discovered.

Not only is the food top-rate, The Captain's Restaurant — a quaint Cape-Cod structure overhung with centuries-old oaks — is steeped in history and beauty. All the bricks, columns, beams, mahogany wainscoting, pine floors and the tabby fireplace are original and authentic. Many of the architectural elements were salvaged from the ruins of Charleston's historic buildings.

In June, July and August, The Captain's Restaurant is open seven days a week for lunch and dinner. The rest of the year, the Captain takes Monday off. Reservations are not necessary.

The Charleston Cafe

815 Surfside Dr.
Surfside Beach — *238-2200*
$$$ — *All major credit cards*

Surfside Beach welcomed The Charleston Cafe with appropriate if inauspicious fanfare: Six hours after opening, Hurricane Hugo swept ashore and left the restaurant without power or water for 10 days. In years since, The Charleston Cafe has developed a fine reputation for romantic meals in an intimate setting, attentive and personable service and creative, attractively presented food. Specializing in certified Angus beef, local seafood, and veal and chicken dishes, The Charleston Cafe also offers a "light eaters" menu with smaller portions of well-liked items. The dessert menu is daunting, and servers parade the choices in front of you! Who can resist?! Also, The Charleston Cafe features a large list of wine by the glass. Lunch and dinner are served, and reservations are strongly suggested.

Beverage Station Cafe

U.S. 17 Bus.
Garden City — *651-3113*
$$ — *All major credit cards*

This spacious dining room is accented with brass fixtures, ceiling fans and lovely etched-glass partitions between booths. Beverage Station Cafe has been enjoyed for years by locals for the quality food, upbeat bar atmosphere and frequent musical entertainment.

The menu offers an abundant selection of appetizers, soups, salads, quiches, pita pockets, deli sandwiches, burgers, croissants, chicken, seafood and freshly baked desserts. Beverage Station is also home to the "Schnapping Center;" they stock a dozen different flavors of smooth, sweet Schnapps. Beverage Station Cafe serves lunch and dinner.

Conch Cafe

1482 N. Waccamaw Dr.
Garden City *651-6556*
$$$ *All major credit cards*

Dining at the Conch Cafe is like inviting 100 or so good friends to your beach house for grilled tuna, baked scallops, conch fritters, tenderloin, teriyaki chicken and shrimp, mussels in garlic butter and a mess of backfin crab cakes. Throw in a Happy Hour from 4 PM to 6 PM. Not a shabby way to host a party, huh? Did we mention the covered outdoor deck overlooking the ocean? It's great for star gazing and drinking tropical-sounding concoctions. Lunch and dinner are served.

Drunken Jack's Restaurant & Lounge

U.S. 17 Bus., (on the Waterfront)
Murrells Inlet *651-2044*
$$$ *All major credit cards*

As legend has it, Drunken Jack was a black-hearted pirate who patrolled Murrells Inlet, incessantly seeking treasure, until his alcohol abuse led him to a watery grave. His namesake, this time-tested restaurant and lounge is a preferred waterfront dining establishment in the Murrells Inlet area. Take time to have cocktails in the lounge and watch the fishing boats come in. Live musical entertainment is another treat. Seafood and steaks are the house specialties, including filet mignon; Lobster Theodore (chunks of lobster and cheese in a succulent cream sauce — beware your arteries!); frog legs, a true Southern delicacy; or Robinson Crusoe Special Seafood Coquille. Lowcountry specialties abound. A children's menu is offered. Drunken Jack's serves dinner only.

Flo's Place Restaurant & Raw Bar

U.S. 17 Bus.
Murrells Inlet *651-7222*
$$ *All major credit cards*

Hats go off to owner Flo Triska — literally! For years, she and husband Ralph have been running this upbeat Cajun-style restaurant, and people show their gratitude by donating their hats, all shapes and sizes, to the area's largest hat display — right in the restaurant. This wood-framed restaurant is set on the creek in Murrells Inlet and features Cajun and creole food that'll make you think you're in steamy New Orleans. In the spirit of Mardi Gras, the clientele has been known to form a Conga line through the indoor/outdoor dining room and to "eat, drink and be merry."

An all-time favorite menu item is the Dunkin' Pot, a large cast-iron kettle filled with jumbo spiced shrimp, clams, mussels, oysters, corn on the cob, red potatoes and crawfish. (If you don't know how to eat crawfish, Flo will come by and demonstrate. It's really elementary: Snap off the tail and suck the head first; then, peel the tail shell away, revealing the plump meat, and pop it in your mouth.) Another time-tested favorite is the Henry the Eighth rib eye, a 20-ounce, aptly-named wonder. Authentic PoBoy sandwiches, served on grilled French bread, are marvelous. There are several sensational appetizers, two of which incorporate alligator meat. The smoked alligator ribs are prepared in a honey-mustard dressing and cooked on the grill. The alligator stew

Photo: Bill Scroggins, The Sun News

Waterfront dining is an option at many Grand Strand restaurants.

contains more than 25 ingredients! Everything is made from scratch, and you can taste the difference. Quench your thirst with a pitcher of watermelons — a fruity punch with a kick of rum and vodka. "Good food, great time" says it all. Flo's Place is open for lunch and dinner, Monday through Saturday.

Gulfstream Cafe

1536 S. Waccamaw Dr.
Garden City *651-8808*
$$$ *All major credit cards*

Dining doesn't get better than an evening at Gulfstream — one of our personal favorites. This two-story restaurant sits high above the marsh and overlooks Murrells Inlet. Sunsets are spectacular and romantic. (Try to talk your host into giving you a table with a view.) Although dress is casual, the menu is upscale, and reservations are recommended. Appetizers range from crab-stuffed mushrooms to oysters on the half-shell. A popular appetizer is the Gulfstream sampler: stuffed shrimp, bacon-wrapped scallops, oysters Rockefeller, linguine with a delicate clam sauce and blackened fish. (Hope you're hungry.)

Our No. 1 entree choice is Gulfstream's tenderloin medallions: beef medallions topped with a Gulfstream crab cake and Béarnaise sauce, served with a baked potato and vegetables. We've eaten at Gulfstream many times, and have never had a bad night. Sounds impossible, but it's true. A children's menu is also available. Call now for tonight's reservation. Gulfstream Cafe is an absolute must.

Kyoto Japanese Steak House

U.S. 17 S.
Murrells Inlet *651-4616*
$$ *All major credit cards*

Kyoto's brings the beloved Japanese tradition of hibachi cooking right to your table. The chef, usually an authentic personality from the Orient, wows diners with tricks of his trade — knife juggling and flipping tiny shrimp tails from spatula to a small bowl high atop his chef's hat. All entrees are served with salad (the Gin-

What's a Calabash?

For those of you who are visiting the Myrtle Beach area for the first time, there might be some confusion about the meaning of a word that seems to appear everywhere, especially when the talk turns to great seafood: Calabash. No, it doesn't describe an Irish drinking festival or the latest pro wrestling move — it's the name of a tiny fishing village located just over the North Carolina border, and it's also the name of a legendary style of cooking developed there.

"Calabash-style" usually means deep-fried seafood that has been dipped in a light, seasoned batter, cooked golden brown and served very hot. "Calabash-style" also implies massive quantities and varieties of seafood: All-U-Can-Eat, in other words.

It all started in the 1930s when a budding restaurateur named Clinton Morse began serving up tubs full of steaming oysters near his boat dock. It caught on with locals, and the rest, as they say, is seafood history.

Today, that same sleepy fishing village contains more than two dozen seafood restaurants, and many of these original establishments have additional locations along the Grand Strand. Calabash in now known as the "Seafood Capital of the World"— the proof is in the pudding.

ger Root house dressing is the way to go) and a delicate onion soup.

The main course of chicken, beef or seafood and a variety of vegetables is then diced and cooked right before your eyes. It's so satisfying, you'll literally have to push yourself away from the table. A trip to Kyoto's is best enjoyed with a group and is a great way to celebrate a birthday, anniversary or other special occasion. Try the sushi bar, if you dare. And spring for a glass of sweet plum wine. Kyoto's serves dinner only, and reservations are strongly suggested.

Tyler's Cove

U.S. 17 S., at The Hammock Shops
Pawleys Island 237-1581
$$ *All major credit cards*

There used to be a theory: Restaurants shall be either luxurious and elegant or casual and not-so-elegant, and that is that, so you might as well get used to it. Well, Tyler's Cove flies in the face of all that.

Tyler's Cove. Very elegant and very relaxed. The veritable hub of the Pawleys Island locals' scene. Surrounded by oaks weeping moss and a couple dozen of the famous Hammock Shops, Tyler's Cove continues to garner rave reviews from natives and tourists. Not small, but decidedly cozy, this restaurant really does offer something for everyone. Somehow, the place is simultaneously perfect for starry-eyed lovers, families with children, business meetings and informal gatherings of friends.

The all-new menu runs the gamut from a lunchtime favorite, Cajun-fried chicken salad with honey-jalapeño dressing, to elegant evening indulgences like teriyaki marinated tuna with angel hair pancakes, or crab encrusted salmon with rice timbale and lobster sauce. And, consider this list of appetizers for a lesson in restraint: deep-fried alligator bites featuring Cajun sauce and peach chutney; triple cheese French onion soup; baked brie turnovers topped

with amaretto butter and toasted almonds; and melt-in-your-mouth bourbon-simmered shrimp. Entrees — all accompanied by a fresh salad, seasonal vegetables, a starch and a basket of truly exceptional, forever-hot rolls — include every hungry soul's desire . . . from tender Black Angus prime rib and roasted duckling to pork tenderloin served with Granny Smith apple sauce and a very wicked plate of fettuccine carbonara. (There's a special "Little Friends" menu too!) For the uninitiated, the menu suggests appropriate wines for each selection. Tyler's Cove is open for lunch and dinner.

Frank's Restaurant & Bar and Out Back At Frank's

U.S. 17 S.
Pawleys Island *237-1581*
$$$ *All major credit cards*

Frank's Restaurant & Bar, or just plain Frank's as locals call it, opened in 1988 and has been growing ever since. Today, locals often refer to Frank's as the best restaurant on the entire length of the Grand Strand. It's no wonder. Chef Pierce Culliton was educated at Johnson & Wells and has worked both east and west of the Mississippi, and he's an absolute master at combining different flavors. His creations feature an array of different influences — from Southwestern to French, Oriental and Thai. Frank's menu changes every night, and the selections are guaranteed to tempt the strongest dieter's resolve. Frank's solution for diners who can't choose is "small plates": portions larger than an appetizer but smaller than a full meal. Immensely popular, this option allows guests to sample several items in one sitting . . . and still have room for vintage wines and desserts.

Naturally, fresh seafood is a specialty, with options like sauteed cornmeal and black pepper-encrusted snapper. But, seafood is only a beginning. Free-range chicken and veal are often featured, along with crispy duck, roasted lamb and glazed fillets. Ummm. . . . Take note: Frank's serves dinner only, and they're closed on Sundays.

Out Back at Frank's is literally, as the name suggests, "out back" of the original restaurant. This second culinary venture grew out of the owner's desire for a casual lunchtime eatery and gourmet grocery, and Out Back combines the two concepts beautifully. The restaurant showcases all the soups, salads and sandwiches you might expect, but every selection boasts a special touch from chef Rosalyn Wyndam. For example, a typical BLT is transformed with marinated shrimp and grilled sourdough bread. A plain ole turkey sandwich becomes a culinary delight with roasted red pepper mayonnaise. After lunch, patrons enjoy browsing through an almost daunting collection of wines, cheeses, unusual spices and fresh deli items. There's even a butcher shop!

Like the original venture, Out Back at Frank's has been phenomenally successful. In fact, it has just begun serving dinner in season, as well as lunch. Dine inside or on the lovely outside deck with a Petanque court (similar to Bocce) and huge old oaks. Out Back at Frank's serves lunch and dinner every day except Sunday.

Inside **Accommodations**

Considering the Grand Strand offers literally thousands of accommodations for visitors, we have tried to narrow the scope to those establishments that consistently get positive reviews from the public. That's not to say that all others are dank tenements, but the numbers are far too vast to bring all the players into this arena. Lodging is in such demand along the Grand Strand that new facilities are being built as fast as you turn these pages, and smaller "mom and pop" hotels are abundant here. It would be safe to say that 95 percent of the hotels, motels and condominiums on the Grand Strand line both sides of Ocean Boulevard, the road that parallels the Atlantic Ocean from North Myrtle Beach to Surfside Beach and becomes Waccamaw Drive in Garden City. Don't be confused if you're riding along, in awe of the hundreds of lodging marquees, and the road detours west to U.S. 17 Business. A couple of miles of private property separate North Myrtle Beach from Myrtle Beach, and several campgrounds are located between Myrtle Beach and the end of the South Strand. Properties closest to the beach are considered "oceanfront." Properties with an "oceanview" refer to rooms that may have a view of the ocean but do not directly face it (on the side of the building) or, in some cases, rooms not located on the east of Ocean Boulevard. Rooms with a balcony or walkway are referred to as rooms with a "sideview." You may also run across terms like "poolside" or "streetside" that denote location within the property. Be sure to ask specific questions about the location of your room when confirming your reservation.

Those of you who travel with your pets may find it difficult to rent a room. The City of Myrtle Beach passed an ordinance that prohibits animals of any kind in the downtown area from March 1 through September 30. It seems there was a problem with pet owners bringing their pets and other exotic animals (boa constrictors, ferrets, iguanas) down to the heavily populated Pavilion area, causing quite a stir with other pedestrians. The law was passed to regulate any accidents or incidents caused by the animals. It just so happens the majority of hotels that did allow pets are located in this area. But, rest assured, neither Fluffy nor Fido need to spend the vacation alone because a few properties still accept small pets.

Like most resort areas, be prepared to make a deposit when calling in your reservation — it is required by the majority of properties and should be credited to your bill. Generally, a deposit equals a day's rent. To avoid hassles, use credit cards, cash or travelers checks to pay for everything because most local banks will not cash out of town personal checks unless you have an account with them or enough picture identification to satisfy the

FBI on a manhunt. Vital reservation information includes the time you plan to arrive, the number in your party, the length of your stay and the date you plan to depart. Although rooms are plentiful, the population of the area swells to almost four times its year-round size in the heat of summer, and all of these people need a place to lay their weary heads. Think twice if you want to drive to the beach and "find" a room, especially in the middle of the night. The tourism season blooms like the flowers each spring and peaks like the hot noonday sun each summer. As the autumn leaves fall, so do lodging rates; and in wintertime, snowbirds flock to the beach for cheap, cheap rates. In the '60s and '70s, most businesses rolled up the sidewalk from Labor Day until Easter. Today, that is a thing of the past; as the Grand Strand is quickly becoming a year-round resort, the majority of properties remain open throughout the year.

Hotels and Motels

These accommodations are listed according to location, ranging from the North Strand to Myrtle Beach to the South Strand. In accordance with the Americans With Disabilities Act, all of these properties should be handicapped accessible; establishments must comply to stay in business. Keep in mind when making reservations that most accommodations offer at least a 10 percent discount if you're staying a week or longer. Most also offer senior citizen, AAA and group discounts as well. Always ask about any special rates or entitlements. The following dollar sign key should provide you a good idea of lodging costs; it's based on the lowest room rate for two people (at least two double beds) per night in the middle of July, when hotel and motel rates are at their peak.

$50 to $75	$
$76 to $101	$$
$102 to $127	$$$
$128 to $153	$$$$
$154 and up	$$$$$

North Strand

Beach Cove Resort

4800 S. Ocean Blvd. — *272-4044*
North Myrtle Beach — *(800) 331-6533*
$$$$ — *All major credit cards*

Here's a getaway resort guaranteed to make your vacation a memorable one. Each of the 260 lavish suites are complete with two queen-size beds, kitchenettes and a private balcony overlooking the ocean. Meeting and banquet facilities are available. This resort features a unique oceanfront poolscape of smaller pools and walkovers amidst towering Palmetto trees and flowering shrubs. Other amenities include regular swimming pools, saunas and racquetball courts. For the children, activities are provided from Easter through the summer months. If you feel like dining on the property, take a table at the Tradewinds Cafe or catch the night life at Chases Lounge. Golf packages are offered at more than 70 championship golf courses in the area.

Blockade Runner Motor Inn

1910 N. Ocean Blvd
North Myrtle Beach — *249-3561*
$$ — *All major credit cards*

Located on the oceanfront in the popular Ocean Drive section of North Myrtle Beach, the Blockade Runner offers 72 two-bed units, including efficiencies, all of which overlook the ocean. In addition to an oceanfront pool and kiddie pool, guests can also enjoy the Jacuzzi and a delicious meal in the on-premises

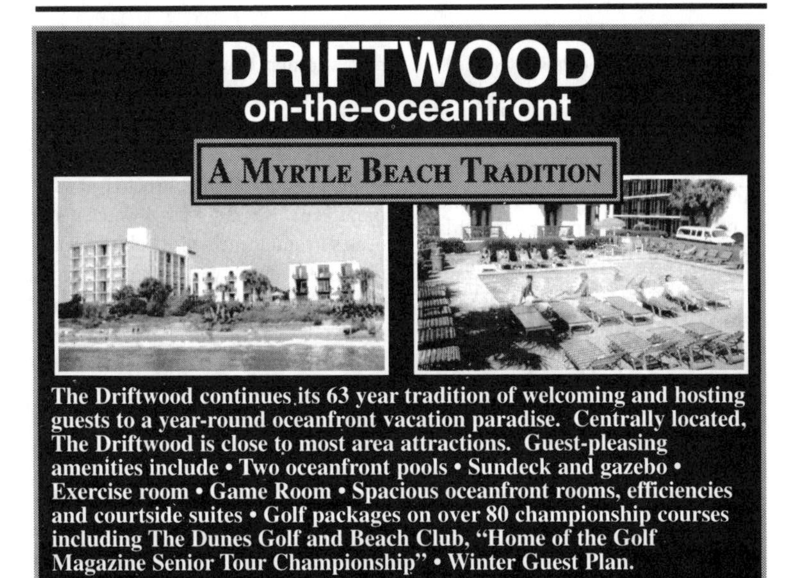

restaurant. Golf specials are offered from Labor Day through June 1.

Buccaneer Motel

401 S. Ocean Blvd. *249-1466*
North Myrtle Beach *(800) 548-7552*
$ *All major credit cards*

Ahoy mates, you've landed at the Buccaneer Motel, a very affordable place for families looking for one-room efficiencies or two-room apartments on the beach. If the ocean isn't for you, then splash around in the pool.

Colonial Inn

1630 U.S. 17
Little River *249-9894*
$ *MC, VISA*

The Colonial Inn is a family-owned and operated property that takes pride in adding their personal touch. Generations of families have been vacationing here and enjoying the year-round amenities, like swimming pools and king-size beds. If you're looking for alternative recreation from the beach, charter a boat at one of the nearby marinas or ask about the golf packages.

Days Inn North

1321 S. Ocean Blvd *272-5131*
North Myrtle Beach *(800) 845-0605*
$ *All major credit cards*

The Days Inn North has been completely remodeled and, in fact, is quite lovely. With 75 oceanfront units, guests enjoy affordable rates and a beautiful stretch of beach. Breakfast is offered daily in the on-site cafe. Guests have access to an outdoor swimming pool and laundry facilities. Golf packages are also available.

Helms Vista Family Motel and Apartments

300 N. Ocean Blvd. *249-2521*
North Myrtle Beach *(800) 968-8986*
$ *All major credit cards*

This small, friendly looking property offers oceanfront rooms, suites and apartments to guests looking for an affordable place to lay their heads. Special package deals include golf, deep sea fishing and dinner cruises. Amenities include two kiddie pools, a hot tub and a refrigerator in every room. The Helms Vista is within walking distance of North Myrtle Beach's finest restaurants and dance clubs.

Ocean Creek Plantation Resort & Conference Center

10600 U.S. 17 N. *272-7724*
North Myrtle Beach *(800) 845-0353*
$$ *All major credit cards*

This is one of the grandest resorts along the beach. The luxurious accommodations include studios, one-, two- and three-bedroom condominiums in six separate complexes. The resort's oceanfront beach club features a large outdoor pool, sun decks and poolside bar. Guests can enjoy fine dining at the Four Seasons restaurant if they don't want to leave the property. Supervised activities for the kids are available in summer months, freeing parents for a little private vacation time. The resort also features 10 on-site lighted tennis courts and extends guest privileges at a majority of area golf courses. Ocean Creek considers the finest detail whether hosting a family of four or a conference for hundreds.

San-A-Bel Resort

1709 S. Ocean Blvd. *272-2079*
North Myrtle Beach *(800) 272-2079*
$$$ *No American Express cards*

San-A-Bel, a fairly new property in the North Myrtle Beach section, offers 90 two-bath condominiums. Each unit comes equipped with a full kitchen, complete with a microwave, dishwasher and washer and dryer. The beautiful indoor heated pool features expansive skylights and glass walls for unobstructed views of the ocean. Outside, a large wooden sun deck surrounds the whirlpool — a relaxing haven after a workout in the fitness room. Golf packages are available. San-A-Bel rents rooms on a weekly basis only.

Sea Captain Motor Lodge

608 West St.
Southport, N.C. *(800) 554-5205*
$ *All major credit cards*

This out-of-the-way but quaint lodge is the largest motel in Brunswick County and is located near the Small Boat Harbor and attractions of the Cape Fear coast. All 95 two-bedroom efficiencies are modern, and all units come equipped with refrigerators. As you dine in the lodge's charming restaurant, watch the fishing charters return with their catch of the day. A diner is also open for breakfast and lunch. Guests enjoy drinks in the Harbourside Lounge and soak in the casual atmosphere and picturesque setting. An Olympic-size pool is just one of the many features available to guests.

Sea Trail Plantation

211 Clubhouse Rd. *272-2185*
Sunset Beach, N.C. *(800) 654-6601*
$ *All major credit cards*

Not many resorts in the coastal region can offer three golf courses in their backyards . . . Sea Trail offers this and much more. Located between Myrtle Beach and Wilmington, North Carolina, Sea Trail welcomes guests looking for exclusive living at affordable prices. Mini-suites feature one bedroom with two double beds and a kitchenette for as low as $59 a night in the off-season. You can rent one-, two-, three- and four-bedroom villas, complete with two full bathrooms, a fully equipped kitchen, living and dining areas and a balcony overlooking the fairways. Scenic trails are perfect for biking, jogging and nature walks. The swim and tennis club provides swimming pools, a sauna, whirlpool spas, a fitness room and lighted tennis courts. This off-the-beaten-path getaway spans over 2,000 acres. Golf packages are also available.

The Seaside Inn

2301 S. Ocean Blvd. — *272-5166*
North Myrtle Beach — *(800) 433-5710*
$ — *All major credit cards*

The Seaside Inn provides about 50 oceanfront units. The rooms are clean and modest but provide all the comforts of home — microwaves, sleeper sofas, refrigerators and card tables. Golf packages are available, and here's a bonus for golfing groups: If a group leader brings 10 players, he/she gets free lodging; if he/she brings along 20 players, his/her golf package is also free. By the way, there are about 25 golf courses within a 15-minute drive. Other features include a pool and hot tub, both of which are covered for comfortable use during the cooler temperatures of winter.

Myrtle Beach

Anderson Inn

2600 N. Ocean Blvd. — *448-1535*
Myrtle Beach — *(800) 437-7376*
$$ — *All major credit cards*

You'll enjoy a stay at the Anderson Inn, a family-owned and operated property. Located on the oceanfront, it houses 112 units ranging from efficiency rooms to suites and singles. Rooms with fully equipped kitchens are available. The children will be amazed at the custom-built kiddie pool — the largest of its kind in the area. Other features include two more oceanfront pools, an indoor Jacuzzi and exercise room. An indoor heated pool is a new addition for '95. Anderson Inn is conveniently located in the center of Myrtle Beach close to grocery stores, malls, entertainment and restaurants. If you'd rather not venture out, don't worry: You won't go hungry with the Magnolia Cafe on the premises. The staff at the Anderson Inn also coordinate golf packages. Handicapped facilities are available.

Atlantic Paradise Inn

1401 S. Ocean Blvd. 444-0346
Myrtle Beach (800) 992-0269
$ All major credit cards

Nothing fancy, but the one- and two-room units of Atlantic Paradise offer your family an affordable vacation at the beach. Amenities include an outdoor pool, kiddie pool and indoor whirlpool. Golf and country music packages are available.

Beach Colony Resort

5308 N. Ocean Blvd. 449-4010
Myrtle Beach (800) 222-2141
$$ All major credit cards

This resort has everything you'll need for a great vacation. Rooms include oceanfront executive suites, two-, three- and four-bedroom condominiums and efficiency apartments. Guests may dine in the restaurant or relax in the lounge. In addition to a kiddie pool, two outdoor pools, an indoor pool and an indoor and outdoor whirlpool for winding down, an exercise room and saunas offer you many ways to work up a sweat. Beach Colony Resort also provides an on-site racquetball center, and guests have privileges at the Myrtle Beach Tennis Club. Beach Colony has begun constructing another tower that will feature 77 two-bedroom condominiums. While they were at it, they added an outdoor Lazy River and an arcade. Beach Colony Resort is the home of Fusco's, one the area's best Italian restaurants, and one of the area's only Sunday brunch buffets.

Breakers Resort & North Tower

2700 N. Ocean Blvd. 626-5000
Myrtle Beach (800) 845-0688
$$ All major credit cards

Staying at the Breakers has been a family tradition for generations, and now the owners have added the North Tower to accommodate even more vacationing families and golfers. There are more than 350 units on this property and more than 20 room plans to choose from. Typical rooms feature two beds facing the ocean, or you can choose from two-room or three-room suites with fully equipped kitchens. Honeymoon, golf and family packages are specialties of the house. During the summer season, kids can take part in various planned activities while their parents enjoy oceanfront dining or drinks in the Top-of-the-Green Lounge. Located near downtown Myrtle Beach, the Breakers is accessible to numerous shops, restaurants and attractions. Ample parking is available, and that's hard to come by at most places. Handicapped facilities are provided in the main tower only.

Cadillac Court

2202 N. Ocean Blvd. 448-5143
Myrtle Beach (800) 525-1371
$ All major credit cards

There is an array of units to choose from at the Cadillac, including one- and two-bedroom efficiencies, two-room suites and three- or four-bedroom apartments. A small cafe on the premises opens at 9 AM for breakfast and stays open until the last appetite of the night is satisfied. Amenities include an outdoor oceanfront pool, a kiddie pool and a rooftop pool and Jacuzzi. Exercise and game rooms are open to all guests, and a game of shuffleboard can be scared up across the street.

Captain's Quarters Resort

901 S. Ocean Blvd. 448-1404
Myrtle Beach (800) 843-3561
$$$ No Discover Cards

Although the Captain's Quarters Resort has been around for many years, the management continues to keep up with the times by expanding and renovating the property when needed. (Many of the newer hotels should look this good on their opening day!) There are 328 units, either efficiency apartments or one-bedroom suites. The family can splash about in the large oceanfront outdoor pool, indoor pool or one of the three whirlpools. The on-site recreation center features an extra-large arcade, so bring lots of quarters. The Captain's Restaurant can serve you up a meal. Guests also have access to laundry facilities. Golf privileges are offered at more than 70 championship courses in the area, so pack your clubs.

Caravelle Resort Hotel & Villas

6900 N. Ocean Blvd. — *449-3331*
Myrtle Beach — *(800) 845-0893*
$$$ — *All major credit cards*

To accommodate the ever-increasing demand for places to stay, the Caravelle added the Villas tower about five years ago. The main hotel offers about 100 units, and the tower has 56 efficiencies. The Caravelle has recently added two-room oceanfront executive suites to its accommodations roster. Rooms feature queen-size beds and refrigerators. Efficiencies feature full kitchens with microwaves and queen-size or king-size beds. Amenities featured between both buildings include several pools, game room, exercise room, restaurant, snack bar and men's and ladies' saunas. Adults and children love the Lazy River pool where you grab an oversized inner tube and glide along the course of the ride. Golf packages are available.

Carolina Winds

200 76th Ave. N. — *449-2477*
Myrtle Beach — *(800) 523-4027*
$$$ — *All major credit cards*

Carolina Winds is known for its fine condominiums and guest suites. There are 145 units in all. The oceanfront property is located away from the hustle and bustle of the downtown hype and features everything you'll need for a luxurious visit. Guests can take a dip in the 120-foot oceanfront pool and wind down in the Lazy River. Staying fit is no problem in the on-site sauna or exercise room. Jacuzzi and hot tubs are a featured attraction, in addition to golf packages.

Chesterfield Inn & Motor Lodge

700 N. Ocean Blvd. — *448-3177*
Myrtle Beach — *(800) 392-3869*
$ — *All major credit cards*

Located just one block from the Myrtle Beach Pavilion, the Chesterfield Inn has maintained a certain tradition that comes with being one of the oldest hotels along the beach. For more than 60 years the same family has owned and operated this property of vintage elegance. A rarity these days, guests have the option of including breakfast and dinner in the price of the room. The charming and inviting dining room yields a perfect view of the ocean. There are 57 units on the property featuring various floor plans. Unfortunately, the Chesterfield Inn closes for a short time in the winter, but plenty of repeat guests plan their vacation around the closings. Golf and entertainment packages are available.

Coral Beach Resort

1105 S. Ocean Blvd. — *448-8421*
Myrtle Beach — *(800) 843-2684*
$$$ — *All major credit cards*

With more than 300 units and plenty of features, Coral Beach is definitely one of the trendiest and largest resorts on the beach. Accommodations include rooms, efficiencies and two-room suites. It's also probably one of the only resorts on the beach that houses a game arcade with a bowling alley. Other amenities include in-room safes, complete kitchens in all efficiencies and suites, steam room, saunas and three whirlpools. Did we say pools? How about two outdoor heated swimming pools, kiddie pools, a Lazy River Ride and a pool bar. The exercise room and suntanning beds might give you an excuse not to set foot on the beach, but go ahead just to say you did. In addition to a full-service restaurant, guests may enjoy cocktails and entertainment in MacDivot's Clubhouse lounge.

Court Capri

2610 N. Ocean Blvd. *448-6119*
Myrtle Beach *(800) 533-1338*
$$ *All major credit cards*

If for no other reason, we had to include this motel since it's the only one along the Grand Strand with a rooftop heart-shaped whirlpool! Needless to say, Court Capri offers honeymoon packages. Rooms and one- or two-bedroom efficiencies can be booked as well as extensive golf packages. The Capri treats guests to an indoor pool, indoor whirlpool, kiddie pool, exercise facilities and has recently added a full-service restaurant. Free in-room movies are another perk.

Crown Reef Resort

2913 S. Ocean Blvd. *626-8077*
Myrtle Beach *(800) 405-7333*
$$$ *All major credit cards*

The Crown Reef is brand new to the area and looks beautiful. All units in this motel are oceanfront with balconies overlooking 125 feet of the Atlantic beach. Efficiencies and rooms are for let and the property offers a pool, fitness center, 275 feet of Lazy River, Jacuzzis, an express restaurant and a game room. Look for the gushing waterfall out front.

Dayton House Best Western

2400 N. Ocean Blvd. *448-2441*
Myrtle Beach *(800) 258-7963*
$ *All major credit cards*

For more than 30 years, the Thomas family has been rolling out the red carpet for families, senior citizens and vacationing couples. In the last four years, three new building have been added to the property, now offering more than 250 units. Amenities include a large indoor spa, an oceanfront lawn and sunning area, indoor and outdoor pools and whirlpools, a sauna and exercise room and golf packages at more than 60 courses.

Driftwood Lodge

1600 N. Ocean Blvd. *448-1544*
Myrtle Beach *(800) 942-3456*
$$ *All major credit cards*

All of the 90 accommodations at Driftwood have refrigerators, whether you're staying in a room or efficiency unit. Conveniently located just six blocks (a 10-minute walk) from the downtown Pavilion area, this hotel offers an on-site game room, fitness room and two outdoor pools.

Dunes Village Resort

5200 N. Ocean Blvd. *449-5275*
Myrtle Beach *(800) 648-3539*
$$ *No American Express Cards*

The Dunes Village was torn down and rebuilt about five years ago. Once a rustic two-story building, this eight-story resort features about 100 units, indoor and outdoor pools and a coffee shop. The rooms and efficiencies are oceanfront and beautifully decorated. On-site tennis courts are offered free to guests, and golf packages can be arranged at any one of 80 courses.

Firebird Motor Inn

2007 S. Ocean Blvd. *448-7032*
Myrtle Beach *(800) 852-7032*
$ *All major credit cards*

The Firebird Motor Inn specializes in two-bedroom apartments for families. There are also single rooms and efficiencies available on the oceanfront, poolside or along the sideview. Children will love the Lazy River, the video game room and supervised summer activities. There is even a cook-out area if you want to fire up the grill. Located just south of the busy downtown area, the Firebird is still close to restaurants and attractions. Golf and entertainment packages are available.

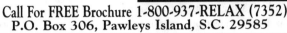

Forest Dunes Resort

5511 N. Ocean Blvd. — *449-0864*
Myrtle Beach — *(800) 845-7787*
$$$ — *No Discover Cards*

This resort, across the boulevard from the beach in the "Cabana" section, houses 134 units including one-bedroom suites and three-bedroom condominiums. Once you've unpacked, take advantage of the wide sandy beach in front of this resort, or float along the Lazy River. The Lazy River is enclosed during the winter months, so its always available to guests. Other features include indoor and outdoor pools, a kiddie pool, whirlpool, exercise room, video game room and restaurant. Comforts of home include laundry facilities and spacious rooms. Golf and entertainment packages are available.

Four Seasons Beach Resort

5801 N. Ocean Blvd. — *449-6441*
Myrtle Beach — *(800) 277-7562*
$$ — *All major credit cards*

Located in the "Cabana"section, the Four Seasons Beach Resort offers both single and double rooms and fully equipped condominiums. Winter rates are outrageously low for the caliber of accommodations and amenities offered at Four Seasons, thus it's an especially appealing lodging option to many senior citizens. The resort is across the street from the beach with an unobstructed view of beachfront cabanas. Monthly winter rental rates start at $375.

Hampton Inn

4709 N. Kings Hwy. — *449-5231*
Myrtle Beach — *(800) 833-1360*
$$ — *All major credit cards*

The Hampton Inn is a family-oriented hotel where children stay free with parents. Located a couple of blocks from the ocean, the Hampton Inn is somewhat of a landmark around these parts and is a favorite of local seniors. There are 152 units. Everyone starts the day with a free continental breakfast served from 6 AM to 11 AM, and then you're on your own to explore the area.

Holiday Inn Downtown

415 S. Ocean Blvd. 448-4481
Myrtle Beach (800) 845-0313
$$$ All major credit cards

Right in the middle of all the action, this Holiday Inn hosts one of the liveliest, continuous pool bar parties all season long. All 311 rooms boast private balconies to watch the poolside happenings or the ocean. Amenities include a second bar in the lobby, indoor and outdoor pools, sauna, Jacuzzi, video game room, exercise room, full service restaurant and gift shop.

Holiday Inn Express

9203 N. Kings Hwy.
(Restaurant Row area) 449-5348
Myrtle Beach (800) 222-5783
$ All major credit cards

Recently voted the "Best Budget Hotel Chain" by *Entrepreneur* magazine, the "Express" hits on some unique concepts: It offers guests a free continental breakfast each morning and special dining rates in cooperation with fine eating establishments along Restaurant Row. In fact, let the hotel staff make dinner reservations for you. There are 85 rooms here, plus five Jacuzzi suites and an outdoor heated pool. Special packages include golf, entertainment, romance, Christmas and New Year's. Room rates are considered low during the tourist season but are higher during the winter months as the hotel aims for consistent pricing rather than extreme fluctuations from one season to another. This hotel is several blocks from the beach.

The Inn At Myrtle Beach

7300 N. Ocean Blvd. 449-3361
Myrtle Beach (800) 845-0664
$$ All major credit cards

This is where the "inn" crowd goes, but the crowds don't get "inn." Well, to put it another way, the Inn's 124 rooms and suites are spacious and upscale but located away from the crowded downtown area. Full kitchens in the suites and an on-site laundry facility provide a home-away-from-home atmosphere. But you're here for a vacation, so relax in the hot tub while the kids play in a pool custom-built for little people. Golf packages are available also.

Jonathan Harbour

2611 S. Ocean Blvd. 448-1948
Myrtle Beach (800) 448-1948
$$ All major credit cards

Two- and three-room efficiency units with fully equipped kitchens and laundry facilities are what you'll find here. Recreate in either the indoor or outdoor pool, one of two whirlpools, the kiddie pool, an exercise room, sauna and steam room. Guests have ample parking facilities across the street.

Landmark Best Western Resort Hotel

1501 S. Ocean Blvd. 448-9441
Myrtle Beach (800) 845-0658
$$$ All major credit cards

Everything you need for a great vacation is found right here at this oceanfront property. The accommodations include 327 units ranging from single and double rooms to penthouse suites. Entertainment includes the Landmark's legendary poolside parties on the Yellowbird deck, the Coquina night club, an English-style pub and dining in the Gazebo restaurant. Families can play in the video game room, relax in the sauna or splash about in the outdoor covered pool. The Landmark also specializes in hosting group tours and conferences. Golf packages are available. Small pets are accepted.

Meridian Plaza Resort

2310 N. Ocean Blvd. *626-4734*
Myrtle Beach *(800) 323-3011*
$$$ *All major credit cards*

The Meridian Plaza is a tall, sleek building housing more than 90 ultramodern one-bedroom suites with fully equipped kitchens. Each suite has a balcony that overlooks the ocean. Parking in the downtown area would normally be crowded; however, the Plaza provides garage parking spaces for its guests. Amenities include indoor and outdoor pools and whirlpools, an exercise room and video arcade. Special golf packages are available from September through May.

Myrtle Beach Martinique Resort and Conference Center

7100 N. Ocean Blvd. *449-4441*
Myrtle Beach *(800) 542-0048*
$$$ *All major credit cards*

The motif may be "Come to the island, mon," but the beach is definitely Myrtle. All 203 units face the ocean, and each has a private balcony with a view of the Grand Strand. Located near the northern end of a Myrtle Beach residential section, the Martinique exudes a sense of exclusivity. The resort features an oceanfront swimming pool, sun deck whirlpool, exercise room and an oceanfront restaurant and lounge. Banquet and meeting facilities are large enough to accommodate 400 people. Golf packages are coordinated through the staff.

Ocean Dunes/Sand Dunes Resort

201 74th Ave. N. *449-7441*
Myrtle Beach *(800) 845-0635*
$$$ *All major credit cards*

The twin towers of this huge resort provide more than 600 rooms, suites and one-, two- and three-bedroom villas. On-site features include oceanfront pools with bars, indoor pools and whirlpools, steam room, saunas, indoor lap pool, weight room, game room and convenience store. Wait . . . there's more. Entertainment includes restaurants, a lounge, deli, raw bar, pizza parlor and sports bar. During the summer, supervised programs are offered for children, and they get a free T-shirt and identification bracelet (see our Kid Code sidebar in the Kidstuff chapter). Children younger than 18 also stay free in the same room with an adult. Golf packages are available, as are tennis privileges at a nearby tennis club.

The Palace Suite Resort

1605 S. Ocean Blvd. — 448-4300
Myrtle Beach — (800) 334-1397
$$ — All major credit cards

The Palace Suite Resort condominiums are fit for kings and queens. You'll feel like royalty staying at any of the 298 suites in this plush resort that towers over the ocean. Featured amenities include Jacuzzis, hot tubs and covered pools. While many of the condominiums are privately owned, there are numerous units available for weekly rentals — call 448-7959.

Patricia Grand Hotel

2710 N. Ocean Blvd. — 448-8453
Myrtle Beach — (800) 255-4763
$$ — All major credit cards

From the moment you step into the plush setting of the Patricia Grand, you'll feel like royalty. Luxurious accommodations include double rooms, efficiency apartments and executive suites designed to pamper those with the most discriminating tastes. The oceanfront restaurant and lounge provide relaxing retreats when you've had enough of the decadent pool, whirlpool or Lazy River. For those who must mix business with pleasure, meeting rooms are available. When it's time to have fun, arrange a golf outing through the front desk or set up a tennis match. The downtown location puts shopping malls, attractions and restaurants within easy reach.

The Radisson Resort at Kingston Plantation

9800 Lake Dr. — 449-0006
Myrtle Beach — (800) 333-3333
$$$$$ — All major credit cards

The Radisson is a multimillion dollar resort outside of downtown with more than 600 rooms and condominiums set in a richly designed atmosphere. The grounds alone span 145 oceanfront acres east of Restaurant Row. The resort features conference centers, several pool decks, two bars, restaurants and lush surrounding foliage. A visit to the Radisson is not complete if you don't take advantage of the $4 million Sport and Health Club that includes racquetball courts, aerobic classes and state-of-the-art tennis courts, cardiovascular and weight machines and massage. With their own golf department, arranging a round is easy. This is more than a place to store your

Insiders' Tips

Low winter rental rates used to begin on October 1 and run through April 1. But, since music theaters, golf and spectacular entertainment have drawn more and more visitors year round, most hotels no longer offer those low monthly rates in October or March. This has been a real blow to some of our snowbirds, but you can't stop progress!

luggage; this is a vacation destination and group meeting attraction.

The Reef Resort Hotel

2101 S. Ocean Blvd. *448-1765*
Myrtle Beach *(800) 845-1212*
$$$ *All major credit cards*

Located south of the downtown traffic is The Reef, an all-suite family resort of 122 units. Oceanfront features include a large outdoor pool, kiddie pool and Lazy River Ride. Inside, there is another pool and game room. The staff organizes golf packages and supervised activities for children.

Sands Ocean Club Resort

9550 Shore Dr. *449-6461*
(Near Restaurant Row) *(800) 845-2202*
Myrtle Beach
$$ *All major credit cards*

Treat yourself to a lavish one-, two- or three-bedroom suite or efficiency along the oceanfront at the Sands Ocean Club Resort. This upscale facility near Restaurant Row offers numerous on-site amenities including several pools, lounges, Ocean Annie's Beach Bar, restaurants and golf privileges at more than 70 courses.

Sea Crest Resort

803 S. Ocean Blvd. *626-3515*
Myrtle Beach *(800) 845-1112*
$$ *All major credit cards*

You would think with eight oceanfront pools and a Lazy River Ride, all you'd have to do is splish and splash all day. But at the Sea Crest, near the heart of downtown Myrtle Beach, there's much more. The rooms are very affordable considering its location and modern design. You can't go wrong here. Golf packages are offered to guests.

Sea Mist Resort

1200 S. Ocean Blvd. *448-1551*
Myrtle Beach *(800) 732-6478*
$$ *All major credit cards*

The Sea Mist is a complete world within itself, sprawling along both sides of Ocean Boulevard. It houses more than 800 rooms, efficiencies, suites, townhouses and bungalows for families and group tours. And if you stay six paid nights, the seventh night is free. The expansive complex features eight adult swimming pools, six kiddie pools and a large on-site water park with an inner tube slide, activity pool and a Lazy River that stretches more than 500 feet. That's not

Beautiful sunsets can be viewed along the Intracoastal

'aterway, as seen here from the dock at Barefoot Landing.

all. Guests can putt on the resort's miniature golf course, play on the private tennis courts, work out in the health club or dine in one of several restaurants. The kids really seem to go for the ice cream parlor and donut shop, too. Organized activities focus on the children and keeping them occupied. Adults can enjoy golf privileges and the glorious Carolina sunshine. The Sea Mist is located in the very middle of downtown Myrtle Beach, and parking and traffic are hectic. But once you've parked the car, there really isn't any need to leave until it's time to pack up and go home; everything you'll need is found in the resort complex.

SHERATON MYRTLE BEACH RESORT

2701 S. Ocean Blvd. *448-2518*
Myrtle Beach *(800) 842-1871*
$$$$$ *All major credit cards*

The Sheraton continues its tradition of quality service at its Myrtle Beach Resort. More than 200 rooms overlook the ocean and include family suites and efficiencies. Geared more to the adults, Kokomos' oceanfront bar and restaurant attracts guests from the pool deck during the summer season and provides a lot of fun for everyone. Other amenities include an exercise room and sauna. Honeymoon, golf and entertainment packages are available.

SWAMP FOX OCEAN RESORT

2311 S. Ocean Blvd. *448-8373*
Myrtle Beach *(800) 228-9894*
$$ *All major credit cards*

The Swamp Fox Ocean Resort is a spacious complex that overlooks the ocean. It features 377 units, seven indoor and outdoor pools, a Jacuzzi, sauna and a restaurant and lounge. Its central location gives guests convenient access to area attractions. An added bonus for the budget-conscious family is that children under 14 stay free with parents. Golf packages are also available.

THE YACHTSMAN RESORT

1400 N. Ocean Blvd. *448-1441*
Myrtle Beach *(800) 868-8886*
$$$$ *All major credit cards*

The Yachtsman's twin towers house more than 140 all-suite units in the very heart of the downtown area. Exclusive packages cater to golfers, honeymooners and tour groups. One of the closest attractions to the resort is Pier 14, a restaurant that extends over the ocean. The studio and one-bedroom suites feature garden-size whirlpool baths and fully equipped kitchens. Inside, you'll find one pool and outside, two pools, Jacuzzis, hot tubs and a miniature golf course. The Yachtsman was voted one of the area's favorite getaways by *The State* newspaper.

South Strand

BARNACLE INN

115 S. Waccamaw Dr. *651-2828*
Garden City Beach *(800) 272-1222*
$ *No Discover Cards*

Families with small pets are welcome (from September through March) at the Barnacle Inn, located in quiet Garden City. This quaint motel has 30 modest units for folks looking for an affordable beach vacation. Guests can access an onsite swimming pool and laundry facilities. Golf packages are also available.

DAYS INN SURFSIDE PIER HOTEL

15 S. Ocean Blvd. *238-4444*
Surfside Beach *(800) 533-7599*
$$$ *All major credit cards*

This Days Inn offers the same affordable rates as most area Days Inns. This one overlooks the Surfside Pier, which was recently restored after sustaining severe damage during a recent storm. This area tends

All Aboard A Boat and Breakfast

As Neptune's Pleasures' motto states: "If you don't have your own toy, you can play with ours!" Coming up with a uniquely different concept in accommodations, this company has acquired a select fleet of yachts that offers boat and breakfast stays, meeting facilities and party plans. The professional staff is willing to coordinate menus for any occasion, including full weddings. A couple can now arrange a wedding ceremony, reception and honeymoon stay on one of the yachts with the Atlantic Ocean or Intracoastal Waterway as the backdrop. Golf and entertainment packages are available, and special winter rates are offered October through February. The staff will arrange deep water charters, cruises and fishing expeditions, and also rents water sports equipment. You can contact Neptune's Pleasures by calling Patty Dombrowski at 280-4100 or (800) 805-4379.

to be more crowded than others in the South Strand because of the pier. Guests enjoy sampling the restaurant's homestyle cuisine and sipping their favorite beverages on the deck at Scotty's Lounge, located on the property's oceanfront. All 158 units face the ocean for a panoramic view of Surfside Beach.

Litchfield By The Sea Resort Hotel & Country Club

U.S. 17 S. — *237-3000*
Litchfield — *(800) 845-1897*
$$$$$ — *All major credit cards*

There is no other resort in the historic Lowcountry that compares to Litchfield By The Sea. Spanning 4,500 acres of marshlands and oceanfront property, the complex features an array of accommodations including villas, condominiums and cottages. The grounds are enhanced with avenues of century-old oaks, flowering gardens and uncrowded beaches. Although the resort is about 15 minutes from Myrtle Beach, there is no hint of either neon or a hectic pace. Ranked one of the top 50 tennis vacation destinations in the country by *Tennis* magazine, Litchfield's 26 on-site courts attract tennis lovers from far and wide. Guests also receive privileges at the exclusive Litchfield Country Club. A comprehensive summer children's program appeals to many families looking for accommodations a cut above those of traditional resorts. In addition to the spa, indoor and outdoor pools and racquetball courts, the resort offers a sauna, beauty salon and a popular restaurant and lounge.

Royal Garden Resort

1210 N. Waccamaw Dr. — *651-1929*
Garden City Beach — *(800) 446-4010*
$$$$ — *All major credit cards*

In the midst of the weather-worn beach houses and cottages of Garden City is the Royal Garden Resort, with more than 100 condominium units and suites. The oceanfront property features golf packages and poolside activities for families and couples. Restaurants and attractions are within walking distance.

Water's Edge Resort

1012 N. Waccamaw Dr. — *651-0002*
Garden City Beach — *(800) 255-5554*
$$$$ — *All major credit cards*

With 145 spacious one-, two- and three-bedroom condominiums, this resort is a

Photo: Cecelia Konyn, The Sun News

During the summer you'll almost always find a child playing in the sand. This family was a little more creative than most.

little larger than its neighbor, the Royal Garden Resort, but offers basically the same features including pools, and an oceanfront lounge and deck with a perfect view of the Garden City beach. Golf, entertainment and honeymoon packages are offered.

Bed and Breakfasts

Although not plentiful in number, these bed and breakfast accommodations offer a charming alternative to hotel rooms or condominium suites. With the exception of two located in the Myrtle Beach area, bed and breakfasts tend to be found on beautiful, grand properties near Georgetown. All are known for their superb decor and luscious fare.

1790 House Bed and Breakfast

630 Highmarket St. *546-4821*
Georgetown *(800) 890-7432*
$ *All major credit cards*

Yes, this home was built over 200 years ago and boasts historical and architectural significance. A member of the National Historic Register, this West Indies-style post-Revolutionary War home was Georgetown's social center in the late 1700s and early 1800s when rice plantation culture was at its peak. Six lovely guest rooms with private baths are turned out in early Colonial furnishings. Three of the rooms are adorned with fireplaces. Public rooms include a large drawing room with fireplace, dining room, parlor/game room and large wraparound veranda facing other historic homes and gardens. A gourmet breakfast is served daily on the veranda or in the dining room, as well as afternoon refreshments. Bicycles, games and Ping-Pong are available to guests. Smoking is permitted on the veranda and patio only.

The Brustman House

400 25th Ave. N. *448-7699*
Myrtle Beach *(800) 448-7699*
$ *All major credit cards*

Although the Brustman House's ar-

DAVID'S LANDING

2708 S. Ocean Boulevard
Myrtle Beach, SC 29577
1-803-626-8845
Call Collect For Reservation

- All Units Face South Ocean Boulevard and Atlantic Ocean
- Easy Beach Access
- All Units Are For Sale
- On Site Parking
- Private Balconies
- Completely Remodeled
- Sales Rep. By Wellons Properties, Inc.

2611 South Ocean Boulevard,
Myrtle Beach, SC 29577
1-803-448-1948
TOLL FREE RESERVATIONS ONLY
1-800--448-1948 U.S. & Canada

- All Units Two-Room Suites
- Indoor Pool
- Oceanfront Outdoor Pool
- Large Kiddie Pool
- Bubbling Whirlpool
- Steam Room and Sauna
- Spa and Exercise Equipment
- Free Cable TV with Showtime and Disney Channel
- VCR Player in All Units
- Close-by Driving Range, Par 3 Golf, Amusements, Movies, Tennis and Shopping
- Major Credit Cards Accepted

In the heart of Myrtle Beach,
The Palace features...
All Oceanfront Condominium Units

Beach Rentals
P.O. Box 3523, Myrtle Beach, SC 29578
(803) 448-7959
TOLL FREE 1-800-952-8580
• Not Sole Rental Agent for The Palace

All Condos Have

- Full Size Kitchen
- Affordable Rates
- Free Tennis (2 blks)
- 10 Screen Theatres (2 blks)
- 5 Hot Tubs
- Steam Room 7 Sauna
- Exercise Room
- Free Parking
- Restaurant
- Large Pool Decks
- 2 Outdoor Pools
- 1 Indoor Pool
- Game Room

chitecture is Colonial, its decor is Scandinavian. This bed and breakfast has three guest rooms and one suite with separate entrance and cooking facilities to accommodate a group or family. Dr. Brustman has created the breakfast recipes that include a stack of 10-grain pancakes and vegetarian delights. Guests are served high tea from 4 PM to 6 PM daily consisting of sweets, ciders and gourmet coffees and teas. The house is 200 yards from the beach. For a special occasion — and a onetime fee of $35 — the folks at Brustman House will bedeck your room with champagne, chocolates and flowers and serve you breakfast in bed.

King's Inn at Georgetown Bed & Breakfast

230 Broad St.
Georgetown *527-6937*
$ *MC, VISA*

The King's Inn, a Federal mansion built in 1825, knows a long political history that innkeepers Marilyn and Jerry Burkhardt enjoy talking about. Seven designer-decorated rooms with private baths are available, along with several parlors and nine fireplaces. The outside of King's Inn is graced with porches and piazzas. Enjoy breakfast with china and linens in the garden room overlooking the pool and gardens. Afternoon tea and sherry, plush terry robes, croquet and airport shuttle service add special touches to your stay. Smoking is limited to outdoor porches and piazzas.

Litchfield Plantation Manor House

Pawleys Island *237-9121, (800) 869-1410*
$$$ *All major credit cards*

At the end of a ¼-mile avenue lined with live oaks draped in Spanish moss, you'll find the stately Plantation Manor House (c.1750). The home overlooks fields where Carolina long grain rice flourished in the early 1800s. The Inn tariff includes lodging in one of the four gracious rooms, a daily continental breakfast, use of the private pool and cabana, a private Beach Club at Pawleys Island and on-site tennis courts. The plantation also has retreat cottages on the property to accommodate groups.

Sea Island Inn

6000 N. Ocean Blvd.
Myrtle Beach *449-6406, (800) 548-0767*
$$$ ($$$$ w/ two meals) All major credit cards

Sea Island looks like a regular oceanfront hotel from the outside, but inside its ambiance and food plans made us consider it as a bed and breakfast. There are 113 oceanfront units here, ranging from full rooms to efficiencies to deluxe suites in Colonial decor. Guests may partake of a full breakfast and a five-course dinner in the quaint dining room. Chefs change the menu daily to keep palates pleasantly surprised, never bored. Sea Island also offers two outdoor swimming pools and two kiddie pools.

Sea View Inn

414 Myrtle Ave.
Pawleys Island *237-4253*
$$$$ *No credit cards*

This place is a Pawleys Island tradition. Sea View's 18 rooms overlook the ocean and the salt marshes of the inlet. As bed and breakfasts go, this is among the most rustic. For more than 40 years, families have dined on authentic Lowcountry cuisine and have relaxed in the privacy of the traditional wraparound porch. This is the ideal vacation destination for anyone who wants to get away from it all and have it all at the same time. In addition to your swimsuit, shorts and T-shirts, the only other things you'll need are a good book and a fishing pole. Your stay includes three meals daily.

Group Accommodations

If you plan to vacation along the Grand Strand with five or more friends, you may want to consider renting a larger condominium or beach house. They're great for larger parties and events like family reunions and are often more affordable than resort hotels once the cost is divided. The problem is finding them. Group accommodations tend to be rather elusive since most are under the thumb of property management companies or real estate firms. We've tried to uncover a few that may be worth looking into.

Booe Realty

7728 N. Kings Hwy. 449-4477
Myrtle Beach (800) 845-0647

Booe's inventory of 130 rental properties consists of condominiums and townhomes that will sleep four to eight persons and beach houses that will accommodate nine to 14 guests. None of these include swimming pools, but keep in mind that most beach houses are oceanfront or just across the street from the blue Atlantic Ocean. In the middle of July, condos and townhouses will start at $150 per day and beach houses will run $186 to $357. Reservations are accepted by Visa, MasterCard or Discover Card only.

Compass Vacations

1610 U.S. 17 S. 272-2073
North Myrtle Beach (800) 624-6418

Compass deals exclusively with vacation condominium rentals that are usually found in high-rise oceanfront motels. They can help you find three- and four-bedroom units that would comfort-

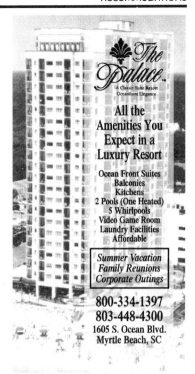

ably accommodate six guests or more. Daily rates in mid-July start at $185.

Dunes Realty

Atlantic Ave. 651-2116
Garden City (800) 845-8191

All up and down the Grand Strand and along canals, inlets and channels, Dunes Realty manages a large inventory of condominiums, cottages and beach houses. Some of the beach houses — high atop stilts — are so large that 20 people could stay together and you'd still have a hard time running into someone! Call for details and rates.

Pawleys Island Realty

U.S. 17 & N. Causeway 237-2431
Pawleys Island (800) 937-7352

These properties are concentrated in the Pawleys Island and Litchfield Beach areas. Choose from two-bedroom duplexes from about $350 per week to a four-bedroom home for $800 per week. If you have a really large group, ask about the $3,000 per week beach house rentals. On the average, Pawleys Island Realty handles accommodations for groups of about eight people.

Plantation Resort

1250 U.S. 17 N. *238-3556*
Surfside Beach *(800) 845-5039*

Although a little way from the beach, this resort is nestled among the 36 championship fairways of Deer Track Golf Course. Three-bedroom villas are available with three bathrooms, fully equipped kitchens, towels and linens, and washer and dryer. Staying here entitles you to free summertime shuttle to and from the beach and access to a 16,000-square-foot health and swim club. The club — a $1 million facility — includes a heated pool, sauna, steam rooms, weights and aerobics. The staff can arrange great golf and show packages. Mid-July rates run approximately $152 per night.

Regency Towers

2511 S. Ocean Blvd. *448-8516*
Myrtle Beach *(800) 494-5055*

The Regency is a condominium property offering two- and three-bedroom units with two full baths, completely outfitted kitchens and washers and dryers. Enjoy the sauna, exercise room, child's wading pool, arcade and outdoor swimming pool. The condos are rented by the week only and start at $1,035 plus tax. Credit cards are not accepted.

RV and Camping Facilities

The Myrtle Beach area campgrounds offer more than 9,000 individual campsites with all the comforts of home for a perfect family vacation. Each campground offers basic services plus a variety of recreational activities.

Summer is the area's most popular camping season; most children are out of school, and families can plan their vacations together. However, camping is quickly becoming a year-round activity along the Grand Strand, so don't roll into town during October through March and expect to find accommodations easily. The fall and winter seasons attract many campers due to the mild climate and off-season rates.

All of the campgrounds are within walking distance of grocery stores, restaurants and attractions.

Apache Family Campground

9700 Kings Rd. *449-7323*
Myrtle Beach *(800) 553-1749*

You can select from more than 700 spacious campsites at Apache Family Campground — some overlooking the dunes to the Atlantic Ocean and others nestled beneath towering pines and oaks.

All sites have utility hookups, free cable and picnic tables. Amenities include a large swimming pool, laundry facilities and fully stocked trading post. Apache Campground is now home to the longest and widest fishing pier in the Southeast, complete with a restaurant.

Depending on site location, the summer daily rate is about $29.

Barefoot RV Resort

U.S. 17 and 48th Ave. S. *272-1790*
North Myrtle Beach *(800) 272-1790*

Barefoot RV Resort is fairly new and offers 250 recreational vehicle campsites for a more intimate camping adventure on the oceanfront. Although smaller than most campgrounds in the Myrtle Beach area, the Barefoot RV Resort still offers all the comforts of the larger campgrounds including utility hookups, bathhouses, laundry facilities and a convenience store. The resort boasts a new clubhouse complete with a game room, whirlpool, fitness center and outdoor pool.

The Park Model rentals are equipped for up to six people, with two bedrooms and a sofa-sleeper. Bring your own sheets, pillow cases, wash cloths and towels. Also pack your own lawn chairs and outdoor grill to take advantage of the "back-to-nature" setting.

Depending on site location, the summer daily rate is $78.

Huntington Beach State Park

U.S. 17 S.
Murrells Inlet *237-4440*

Huntington State Park is a nature lover's dream come true. Located about 3 miles south of Murrells Inlet, this diverse natural environment of the South Carolina coast can be observed at the freshwater lagoon, salt marsh and nature trail. The view of the beach from Huntington Beach State Park is one of the most breathtaking you'll find along the Grand Strand. The park is also the site of the historic castle Atalaya, the former winter home and studio of the American sculptress Anna Hyatt Huntington.

Park facilities include about 130 campsites, 40 of which can be reserved in advance; the rest are rented on a first-come, first-serve basis. There are picnic areas with shelters, a boardwalk, a park store and nature programs directed by park staff. Each site has water and electrical hookups and is convenient to hot showers and restrooms.

The summer daily rate is $17.12.

KOA Kampground

5th Ave. S. *448-3421*
Myrtle Beach *(800) 255-7614*

Nestled in this densely wooded area, campers at the KOA will have trouble believing that the heart of Myrtle Beach is just 700 yards away.

More than 500 campsites are available in this 60-acre complex that offers log cabin-style rentals — called Kamping Kabins — in addition to its large, shaded tent sites. Free cable TV is included with utility hookups, and KOA provides bathhouses with showers. You and the family can splash about the two pools or rent a bike for recreation.

Depending on site location and hookups, the summer daily rate is $25.

Lakewood Camping Resort

5901 U.S. 17 S. *238-5161*
Surfside Beach *(800) 258-8309*

Lakewood is among the largest oceanfront campgrounds in the area, with more than 1,900 campsites complete with utility hookups. It is also home of the *High Steppin' Country* musical and variety show featuring professionally trained local talent. Each summer, from June to August, the entertainers perform a couple of nights a week before a packed house, singing and dancing country favorites mixed with a few contemporary numbers.

The three-acre recreation complex provides a variety of activities and also offers an 18-hole miniature golf course. Four freshwater lakes are stocked with fish just begging for a hook. When it's time to cool down, kids of all ages will love rushing into the Olympic-size pool from the sliding board built into a tropical rock formation. Campers can also enjoy a heated pool and Jacuzzi.

Beach Villa rentals are available in addition to camper storage and annual leases.

Depending on site location, the summer daily rate is $30.

Myrtle Beach State Park

4401 S. Kings Hwy.
Myrtle Beach *238-5325*

The Myrtle Beach State Park is just 3 miles south of the city limits and is one of the most popular public beaches in the area. It was the first state park opened to the public in South Carolina, and it was also the first campground and fishing pier on the Grand Strand.

The park offers more than 350 campsites, picnic areas with shelters, a swimming pool, nature trails, playground equipment, a park store and snack bar. Campsites are rented on a first-come, first-serve basis. Only 40 sites are available each year for advance reservation. Each site has water and electrical hookups and is convenient to hot showers and restrooms.

The summer daily rate is $17.12 or $18.19 for reserved spots.

Myrtle Beach Travel Park

10108 Kings Rd. *449-3714*
Myrtle Beach *(800) 255-3568*

Located only 10 miles north of downtown Myrtle Beach, the Travel Park offers more than 1,100 campsites in a variety of locations: oceanfront, wooded or lakeside. Furnished villas and 35-foot travel trailers are also available for rent. Campers can enjoy a variety of swimming activities, rent paddleboats or fish freshwater game from surrounding lakes. A Putt-Putt golf course is also on the property.

The summer daily rate starts at $24.

Ocean Lakes Family Campground

6001 U.S. 17 S. *238-5636*
Surfside Beach *(800) 722-1451*

Like many of the other campgrounds, Ocean Lakes is a world within itself, providing campers with everything from convenient shopping, meeting rooms and laundry facilities to a chapel, a book-exchange library and a post office.

Offering 3,500 campsites, Ocean Lakes is the largest campground property in the area. However, only about 1,000 are considered "transient" sites — the rest are occupied by permanent residents.

Depending on site location, the summer daily rate starts at $29.50.

PirateLand Family Campground

5401 U.S. 17 S. *238-5155*
Surfside Beach *(800) 443-CAMP*

Set among 140 acres of stately oak

trees, private lagoons and oceanfront property, PirateLand is a real treasure. More than 25 years of business has garnered PirateLand several generations of family vacationers whose visits turn into neighborhood block parties.

Each of the 1,100 oceanfront and lakeside campsites is fully equipped with a picnic table and hookups for utilities and free cable TV. Trailer storage space is also available. Keep in mind that you don't have to be a camper to enjoy the surroundings at PirateLand. The campground also offers fully furnished, two-bedroom Lakeview Villas for weekly and monthly rentals.

Campground amenities include a new heated indoor pool and spa, playgrounds, tennis courts, a miniature golf course and an arcade. The staff organizes activities that range from beach volleyball, deep sea fishing and golf to Bible School, arts and crafts and "neighborhood" cookouts. The campground's general store is stocked with practically everything you can imagine or forgot to pack. There is also a coin-operated laundry facility for campers' convenience.

Depending on site location, the summer daily rate starts at $28.

Inside **Nightlife**

Like the song says, "There's no use in sitting alone in your room; come to the cabaret." With the happening nightlife this area has to offer, there is absolutely no excuse for entertaining your own company, lamenting that there is nothing to do. When the sun sinks below the horizon, the lights come up around the Grand Strand, alive with the buzz of animated conversation, laughter and the beat of a variety of musical genres. Locals who can "hang" with the best of them all night long and rested vacationers congregate until the wee hours of the morning in too many nightspots to mention. Besides those included in this chapter, many restaurants double as late-night spots, and most resort hotels provide lounges with live entertainment.

Now, we'll get into some of the rules and regulations about night stalking so you can avoid any possible trouble or surprises.

The legal drinking age in South Carolina is 21, and that is a strict order around here. Some clubs allow underage patrons to enter with a clearly marked hand stamp — they can purchase only soft drinks at the bar. You'll find that Grand Strand club bouncers are fastidious ID checkers, so make sure you have a form of photo identification.

South Carolina is still a mini-bottle state when it comes to serving alcohol. You won't see a shot glass used by a bartender in these parts! Each mini-bottle contains nearly two ounces of liquor, so you're getting a double compared to most free-pour bars. If you prefer mixed drinks containing more than one liquor, like Long Island iced teas or fuzzy navels, keep in mind that you must pay for each separate liquor that is opened and poured. More than one unsuspecting mixed cocktail imbiber has nearly fainted when presented with the tab at the end of the evening!

Local patrol officers show no mercy to drunken motorists, and if you're picked up for driving while impaired, you will spend the night in jail before facing charges. Luckily, some clubs around town sponsor SoberRide — *free* taxi service to your hotel or home. All you have to do is call 238-HOME, and a Coastal Cab will pick you up. They're really nice guys . . . they don't laugh in your presence, even when you slur your destination.

Nightlife really picks during the spring and summer months, so consult the Friday "kicks!" section of *The Sun News* for the most up-to-date profile on the entertainment scene.

Dancing the Night Away

2001 VIP Entertainment

920 Lake Arrowhead Rd.
Myrtle Beach *449-9434*

2001 is an upscale entertainment complex with two separate dance floors and a sing-along piano bar.

Photo: The Sun News

Darius Rucker and his band Hootie and the Blowfish play in Myrtle Beach regularly.

Pulsations Dance Club features Top 40 music pumped into a high-tech sound system by DJs and live bands. The spacious dance floor is always crowded, so watch your step. In the next room, you'll find **Razzies Beach Club,** where folks shag to beach music oldies and other tunes from the '50s and '60s, played nightly by the house band T.K.O. Razzies just added a new DJ, Crazy George, who not only spins records but acts out skits (they seem funnier with every drink!) to songs. The newest addition to 2001 is **Yakety Yak's Piano Saloon** where everyone is fair game. Performers on dueling baby grand pianos lead the audience in sing-alongs and zany antics, whether or not they want to be included. This provides great fun for groups celebrating special occasions, birthdays or anniversaries. Make sure that every member of your party can handle bawdy humor: There are a number of songs performed that could make even your drunken cousin blush.

Several bars are set up throughout the club and professionally trained bartenders can whip up specialty cocktails and any kind of shooter. Valet parking at 2001 adds a touch of class and convenience for patrons. The decor is finished in brass fixtures and accessories. A high ceiling provides lots of air circulation. The club is open year round Monday through Friday, 8 PM to well after midnight. Last call is at 2 AM on Saturdays. Locals are admitted free, but cover charge applies to all others, and the exact price is contingent upon special nights and entertainment. Call ahead for details.

Atlantis Nightlife

U.S. 501
Myrtle Beach *448-4200*

Atlantis is three clubs in one, for three times the fun. The first area you'll enter features a stage on which live entertainment is performed nightly. There are plenty of tables and chairs if you wish to sit down and enjoy the music, most of which is rock 'n' roll. If you feel the need to move to the beat of DJ Alex A's high-energy music, make your way to the 4,000-gallon aquarium dance floor filled with tropical fish. Honest . . . real fish swim beneath your feet. This gives a whole new meaning to "walking on water!" Finally, to wind down, you can sit under the stars at the Patio Paradise, a wooden deck built around a huge volcano-like fountain. There is also a game room with several pool tables and pinball machines.

Atlantis is open year round Monday to Friday from 8 PM until after 4 AM and Saturday and Sunday from 8 PM to 2 AM. The club also offers special theme nights continuously, so keep your eyes and ears open.

Coquina Club

1501 S. Ocean Blvd. (Landmark Resort Hotel)
Myrtle Beach *448-9441*

It would be safe to say generations of beach music lovers have shagged at the Coquina Club. Bands like Chairmen of the Board, The Band of Oz, The Fantastik Shakers, The Original Drifters and The Catalinas have entertained at the Coquina Club for years and continue to draw a large following. The club is on the fourth floor of the Landmark Resort Hotel and is open year round.

Crazy Zack's

221 Hillside Dr. and Second Ave.
North Myrtle Beach *249-2404*

Welcome to the re-enactment of the movie *Animal House*. It looks like an old beach house with wooden floors (easier

Photo: Cecelia Konyn, The Sun News

Two shaggers compete in the National Shag Dance Championship, held annually at Studebaker's in Myrtle Beach.

The Shag

Some people have a hard time recapturing those special, carefree days of youth. But people who grew up along the South Carolina coast need only put on a little beach music and dance a few steps of the shag to return to those warm, humid Carolina summer nights when life was simple, but oh so exciting.

Nobody is exactly sure how the shag got started, although most people point to the Ocean Drive section of North Myrtle Beach as its place of origin. One story claims a group of dancers in Ocean Drive in the 1940s attempted to do the jitterbug but slowed it down because they had a little too much to drink. Spectators liked what they saw, and the shag was born.

Some people say the shag is the Lowcountry version of the jitterbug, Lindy hop, boogie-woogie and quickstep. It's danced to beach music — rhythm and blues mixed with sea spray, sun and sand.

It was during the 1950s and '60s that shagging really flourished along the beaches. Most shaggers wore alligator belts, Bass weejuns (good for sliding over sandy floors) and Gant shirts. Others, barefooted and in bathing suits, turned their radios up and danced right on the Strand.

The nice thing about the shag is that anybody who can count to eight can do it, although it took hours of practice on Saturday afternoons for serious shaggers to synchronize their fancy footwork with their partner's.

The bellyroll, sugarfoot, boogie walk and pivot separated the polished pros from the once-a-year hoofers.

Kids lined up to hear the Tams tell them to "Be Young, Be Foolish and Be Happy." But with or without the Tams' instructions, kids got lost night after night in the music, the kicks and the turns and their favorite shagging partner. They flocked to the old Beach Club to see The Drifters, The Intruders, The Four Tops, Maurice Williams and the Zodiacs, Billy Stewart, Jackie Wilson and Major Lance.

Beach Music was synonymous with being young, having fun and being at the beach with your friends — not a care in the world.

Those times were so great the kids refused to give up shagging. Now, many of them in their 40s and 50s can bellyroll even better than they could when they were young. The interesting thing about the shag is that kids don't make fun of their parents' weird, outdated dance. Instead, they have joined in, and the dance is bigger than ever.

Photo: The Sun News

North Myrtle Beach is home to the shag, which some folks call a slow jitterbug.

One South Carolina legislator, John James "Bubba" Snow, had such fond memories of his dancing days on the Grand Strand that he convinced his fellow legislators in 1984 to make the shag the official state dance.

For the past two years, the State Museum in Columbia has depended on a huge shag party to raise funds. The first party drew about 1,500 people from North Carolina, South Carolina and Georgia. It was such a success, museum officials plan to hold the party every year in May, usually the second Friday.

For 10 years, the Myrtle Beach Area Chamber of Commerce has hosted the National Shag Dance Championships in conjunction with Canadian-American Days in March.

The 1993 competition drew 70 couples for three categories: professionals, new dancers and juniors.

Contestants pay $40 to enter. They get a complimentary room for three nights at a hotel that belongs to the Myrtle Beach Area Chamber of Commerce, a free dinner and hors d'oeuvres. The competition is held at Studebaker's in Myrtle Beach.

The national competition was created by Barry Thigpen — longtime shagger turned shag instructor. Thigpen was called on in 1987 to train dancers for the movie *Shag*, filmed in part in the Grand Strand area. The film didn't do much at the box office when it was released in 1989, but it did put even more focus on the dance so many Stranders already loved.

Thigpen calls the shag a sensuous, slow dance and said lots of people like it because it doesn't require much upper-body movement.

Nine of the first 10 years, the competition was won by the same Atlanta couple, Charlie Womble and Jackie McGee.

The competition has gotten national attention through two spots on "Good Morning America" and one on NBC's "Today Show." Winners of the shag championship performed before 2,000 people at the Beach Ball Classic in Socastee and 24,000 at the halftime of the Charlotte Hornets-New Jersey Nets basketball game.

In the past, the shag and beach music were limited to the South Carolina Strand. Grand Stranders recognized folks from home in other states when they'd spot them doing the unusual dance.

Thigpen believes people across the country will soon be shagging the night away. The past two years, the National Shag Championship has drawn dance instructors from New York to California, Texas and Louisiana. Once a few of their students get hooked on shagging, people everywhere will be doing it.

Old shaggers are keeping their craft alive through a group called S.O.S. (Society of Stranders). The shaggers have what they call fall and spring migrations to the Grand Strand where they shag their hearts out morning, noon and night for five days, just the way they did when they were young, foolish and happy.

Norfleet Jones of Ducks in North Myrtle Beach said S.O.S. was born in 1980 while a group of "old beach bums" sat around playing "Do you remember?" They talked about old times and wondered aloud what had happened to the friends with whom they'd worked summers lifeguarding or selling snow cones.

The group began compiling a list of all the people they knew how to find and invited them to the beach for a reunion. They were amazed when several thousand people showed up.

The word spread, and now about 12,000 people show up in North Myrtle Beach in April and again in September of each year to renew acquaintances, lose themselves in the music and brush up on their shagging.

Older, but still avid, shaggers pay $25 for a yearlong S.O.S. ticket. Four Ocean Drive clubs participate: Ducks, 229 Main Street, 249-3858; Fat Harold's Beach Club, 210 Main Street, 249-5779; O.D. Arcade and Lounge,

100 South Ocean Boulevard, 249-6460; and The Spanish Galleon, 100 Main Street, 249-1047.

With one ticket, a Strander can get into all four clubs as many times a day as he or she likes. So, Stranders tend to wander from club to club looking for as many old friends as they can find.

Since 1980, the S.O.S. reunion has attracted people from all 50 states and seven foreign countries. Most of the attendees grew up along the beaches or at least visited for a week here and there. Some people come just to see this curious dance, and others just like the music.

It isn't just a dance being perpetuated, Jones explained. . . . It's a lifestyle.

Many area clubs now offer shag and line dance lessons, so even if you didn't spend your teenage years along the Grand Strand, it's not too late to join the fun.

Thigpen and his wife teach a five-week series on Tuesday nights at Studebaker's before the club opens. If you're going to be in the area long enough, call ahead, 448-2287, and sign up for the classes.

Ducks offers free classes on Wednesday nights. Call 249-3858.

If you don't have time for classes, but you still want to learn, just look around the popular shagging haunts until you spot a couple doing it and ask them to show you how. There's nothing a shagger likes better than a new convert.

to wash away all the spilled beer). If you're into fraternity and sorority mixers, Crazy Zack's is like a homecoming dance. DJs spin Top 40 hits nightly. Zack's serves great drink specials, especially the Bucket of Beer that holds a quart. This is mostly a summertime hangout for college students. It's open every day from 7 PM until 6 AM. Cover charges range from $3 to $5 per person.

H.E.A.D. Room

Magnolia Plaza (Restaurant Row area)
9714 U.S.17 N.
Myrtle Beach *497-0100*

H.E.A.D. stands for "High Energy Alternative Dance;" if you want to work up a sweat on three levels of dancefloors, check this place out for an evening. DJs pump tunes through a state-of-the-art sound and coordinated laser and light show system. The H.E.A.D. Room also features live alternative bands on a staggered schedule. Past performers include Tesla, Danzig, Marilyn Mason, The Ramones, The Smithereens and Drivin' n' Cryin'. The club is open seven days a week from 9 PM until the wee hours of the morning. Anyone 18 and older is admitted. Call ahead for entertainment information.

Jamaica Joe's

U.S. 17 N. (Restaurant Row area)
Myrtle Beach *449-6456*

Although Jamaica Joe's is a private social club, memberships are sold at the door. Locals consider it an after-hours spot, so it really gets shaking when most of the other clubs close for the night. If you're a late starter or just haven't had enough fun and dancing by about 2 AM, this is a great place to pop into. The decor is classy and cozy. Top 40 hits blast into the early morning.

The Attic

812 N. Ocean Blvd.
Myrtle Beach 448-7477

Located above the Myrtle Beach Pavilion, The Attic is the area's only teen nightclub. It's well supervised and no alcoholic beverages are sold — just soft drinks and munchies. For decades, teenagers have danced at The Attic to live bands and their favorite Top 40 hits during their summer vacations. The club is open 7 PM to midnight. Oh, to be young again!

Mother Fletcher's

Eighth Ave. N. and Ocean Blvd.
Myrtle Beach 626-7959

A girl could make a living just entering the contests held at Mother Fletcher's. Each night, between the sets of pumping dance tunes, girls compete in such skill-events as the wet T-shirt contest, the skirt flirt contest and the legs contest, cajoled by testosterone-induced howling and clapping. The other breathtaking view offered by Mother Fletcher's is from the double oceanfront deck. The club is open daily in the summer until 2 AM. Cover charge is $8 for non-locals. Locals are admitted free of charge.

NightMoods

Magnolia Plaza (Restaurant Row area)
9714 U.S. 17 N.
Myrtle Beach 449-1888

Live bands kick in the sounds of contemporary jazz and Billy Holliday-style blues at Night Moods. It's a place where you can "dress up" to "get down." The atmosphere always seems to be friendly and gentle, with a crowd that ranges from 20-something to senior citizens. The club is open nightly from 5 PM to 4 AM, Monday through Friday and 5 PM to 2 AM on Saturday and Sunday. It is a private club; however, memberships are sold at the door.

Sandpipers

4883 U.S. 17
Murrells Inlet 651-1050

Driving around town, especially in the South Strand area, you're likely to see this bumper sticker: "Meet Me At The Pipe!" — that means Sandpipers. From the highway, the Pipe looks like a rundown beach house with a screened-in porch. Funny, it looks just like that from the inside too! Rocking chairs and a table made out of a 1960s surfboard are all the furniture you'll find in the Pipe, except for bar stools, of course. Live bands play on a newly renovated stage to crowds of new generation hippies and the real McCoys. There is also a volleyball net set up out back for Sunday afternoon tournaments. Sandpipers is a private social club that sells memberships at the door. It's open seven days a week, Monday through Friday from 7 PM into the morning and Saturday and Sunday from 7 PM until 2 AM

Spanish Galleon

100 Main St.
North Myrtle Beach 249-1047

The Galleon has been a favorite dance club for years. The club actually houses several dance floors under one roof to appeal to a variety of musical interests, including beach music and high-energy dance music. Live beach music bands entertain Galleon customers throughout the year, and an oceanfront grill keeps everyone from going hungry. Although you can wear T-shirts and shorts, most people tend to turn a night at the Galleon into a fashion show. It's open nightly in the summer and several nights a week in the winter. Call ahead for hours and admission prices.

Studebaker's

2000 N. Kings Hwy.
Myrtle Beach *448-9747*

The motif of Studebaker's is straight from the '50s and, as you might already have guessed, so is the music. Actually, the music ranges from the '50s to the early '70s. It's a real blast from the past. Studebaker's is also home of the National Shag Dance Championship, which is held annually in March. Don't miss the Stude-a-boppers (bartenders and waitresses) and DJ Jumpin' Jack Flash, the self-proclaimed "oldest living brain donor," plus a floor show and line dances that are very entertaining. Dress is casual but neat, and the club is open nightly in the summer from 8 PM until 2 AM. During the off-season, Studebaker's opens several nights a week, and the club hosts an "After Work Attitude Adjustment Happy Hour" for locals on Thursday nights. Studebaker's is open from 5:30 PM to 2 AM on Thursdays and from 8 PM to 2 AM every other night except Sunday. Locals are admitted free, and there is a cover charge ranging from $5 to $10 for all others.

The Afterdeck

9719 U.S. 17 N. (Restaurant Row area)
Myrtle Beach *449-1550*

The Afterdeck used to be a completely open concept, but when an unusually rainy summer dampened business, the owners prudently enclosed the decking areas and dance floor. The new, clear polymer enclosure protects patrons from inclement weather while maintaining the club's starlight view and scenic panorama of the Intracoastal Waterway. The Afterdeck always has scheduled live entertainment and holds headliner concerts with the likes of Hootie and the Blowfish, Fleetwood Mac and Joan Jett. The club also books comedy acts.

Dress casually and comfortably for the hot, humid temperatures — you wouldn't want to wilt during the height of the evening. The club opens full-time for the season just before Easter and stays open through October — it's open for special events only the rest of the year. Operating hours are Monday through Friday from 8 PM to the wee hours of the morning. The club closes at midnight on Saturday.

Xanadu

1900 N. Kings Hwy.
Myrtle Beach *448-7241*

Funk and Top 40 played on an awesome sound system draw huge crowds of dancers from the younger generation. Xanadu hosts numerous contests including the beach's only men's bikini contest. Ladies flock to the Xanadu All Male Review featuring male burlesque dancers. The neon-flashing fun begins around 9 PM nightly and winds down well after 2 AM.

Insiders' Tips

Especially during the winter months, locals take advantage of the wonderful Happy Hour specials throughout the area that usually include a full buffet of free food.

Kickin' Country Nightlife

Beach Wagon

906 S. Kings Hwy.
Myrtle Beach *448-5918*

Country music fans come here for live concerts and all-night two-steppin'. The club itself is a big, long dance hall with little neon but big rootin' tootin' fun. Names like Marty Stuart, John Anderson, Sweethearts of the Rodeo, Aaron Tippin and McBride & The Ride all played the Beach Wagon just before their careers took off. It just goes to show, the performers you see at this club today might be the country music stars of tomorrow. The house band, Silver, plays Tuesday through Saturday nights from 7 PM to 2 AM. Ladies are admitted free, and everyone else pays a cover charge of $5 each.

Charlie's Nite Life

4345 Wesley Rd.
Murrells Inlet *651-4286*

Speaking of rising stars . . . Charlie Floyd, homespun talent from Horry County, is the owner of Charlie's Nite Life. The country-crooning hunk has recently signed a record deal in Nashville and is expected to follow the footsteps of Billy Ray Cyrus. The small two-story club with wooden floors and no real decor to speak of is not for the claustrophobic, especially when jam-packed with hundreds of adoring young female fans and Garth Brooks-wanna-be cowboys. But the music of Charlie and Southern Express is worth a little bump and push in the crowd, especially with an ice-cold long neck in your hand. Charlie's is open Wednesday through Friday from 8 PM until at least 2 or 3 AM. The bar closes at midnight on Saturday.

Sportsbars

Sometimes you just wanna hang out somewhere, have a brew, watch a game and play a few rounds of pool or darts. If that's how you feel one night, we have a sportsbar lineup here that should satisfy. While a number of places in town hail themselves as such establishments, we came up with some guidelines to ensure the full "sportsbar experience." By our criteria, a bar was only given mention in this section if it had at least four televisions locked on sporting events and at least two games to play. If there's anything else that should have been factored in, like critical mass male-bonding or frontal lobe-induced competitiveness . . . hey, there was no way to measure it! Unless otherwise noted, find the following sportsbars in Myrtle Beach.

Carrick's Cafe

5101 N. Kings Hwy. *449-1664*

Six televisions, two pool tables and two electronic darts games are the fare du jour, everyday at Carrick's. Sandwiches and appetizers are also served daily and throughout most of the night. Carrick's is open from 2:30 PM until 4 AM seven days a week and hosts live bands on Wednesday and Friday nights; folks younger than 21 must pay a $5 cover charge on band nights.

Foster's Cafe & Bar

6307-A N. Kings Hwy. *449-7945*

Foster's just made it into the sportsbar category by one television and a game called Foozeball. This bar also sports one pool table and a full menu. While this place is very small, its rough-hewn wood decor exudes a certain coziness. Foster's is open Monday through Friday from 11:30 AM until 4 AM and Saturday and

Sunday from 11:30 AM to 2 AM. The kitchen closes 1 hour before the bar.

Magoo's Fine Food and Spirits

905 Oak St. *946-6683*

Magoo's is the newest bar of this genre to have sprouted up along the Grand Strand. View one of six televisions or head to the back room, chalk up a cue stick and shoot some pool, or try electronic darts. Under the category of "fine food," Magoo's serves up fabulous hamburgers and fries and also offers low-fat and fat-free menu items to help you stave off that armchair athlete's figure. Magoo's is open Monday through Friday from 11:30 AM until the last sports fan leaves and Saturday from 11:30 AM to 2 AM; it's closed on Sunday.

Mulligan's Sports Bar & Grill

Surfwood Shopping Center
North Myrtle Beach *249-9700*

Just to make sure, one of Mulligan's bartenders patiently counted all the TVs here to make sure we had accurate information. Here, 22 televisions broadcast (you guessed it!) all sports, all the time. If the myriad TVs don't keep you busy, test your skills on one of six pool tables or two dart boards. And, as a little added perk, the juke box is free; keep your quarters for the games. Mulligan's is open every day from 11:30 AM to 2 AM.

Murphy's Law Sports Bar

405 S. Kings Hwy. *448-6021*

Patrons of Murphy's Law enjoy two pool tables — positioned smack dab in the middle of tables and chairs — electronic darts and golf, along with 15 television sets. Murphy's sells draft beer for 50¢ a glass or by the pitcher — an exciting prospect if not for the ice cubes floating around the headless, apparently watered down brew. Murphy's Law is open seven days a week from noon to 2 AM.

Oscar's

4101 U.S. 17 N.
North Myrtle Beach *272-0707*

Oscar's is the proud owner of the only L-shaped pool table in town. This sportsbar is a continuous arena of action, with 23 TVs and an array of electronic games including basketball, golf and trivia. You're likely to work up an appetite, so it's a good thing Oscar's serves sandwiches until 1 AM. Oscar's is open seven days a week from 11:30 AM to 2 AM.

Player's

9600 U.S. 17 N. (Restaurant Row area)
Magnolia Plaza *449-8660*

With its beautiful brass decor, this is probably the glitziest sportsbar you'll ever encounter. Player's tunes in 25 televisions, including three big-screen versions. Not only does it have about 18 pool tables but a dance floor to boot! Player's is open from 4 PM until 2 AM, Monday through Friday and from noon to 2 AM on Saturday and Sunday.

Spectators Sports Bar and Grill

9200 N. Kings Hwy.
(Restaurant Row area) *449-2658*

Spectators is brand new to the area (and to the sportsbar concept). Among the 26 TVs, four are installed in booths so your party can watch whatever game you choose privately. Inside, this sportsbar offers two pool tables, an electronic dart board and a pingpong table; outside, the fun continues with a regulation basketball hoop (ask the bartender for the ball) and a shuffleboard game. Spectators is open seven days a week from noon to 2 AM; food can be ordered until 1 AM. On the other side of this sports-a-rama is Coconuts Comedy Club, newly relocated and hosting top name comedians for a night of hilarity. As of March 1995, Coconuts was booking acts Wednesday through Saturday nights, but promised to add evenings as the season progressed. Shows start promptly at 9:30 PM and typically last 2 hours. Call 448-JOKE for schedules and prices.

Karaoke

We've included karaoke houses in this chapter in case you get an overwhelming urge to put all of those singing lessons your mother made you take to the test. Actually, karaoke has become serious entertainment business. The places we've included feature some tone-deaf singers who can't seem to focus on the words to the song; but you'll be amazed at the majority of everyday "Joes" with incredible singing talent. Karaoke seems to have developed a veritable cult-following. Picture this: Someone gets up on stage with the microphone to belt out his or her selected tune and is met with the same audience reaction as if he or she had just blown away a panel of Broadway casting directors at a walk-on audition. The best karaoke performers pick just the right time to perform and, when finished, are met with tears, hugs and the inimitable Hollywood-style alternate cheek kissing. Hey, it's a lot of fun and, who knows, there may be an incredible crooner hidden in those vocal chords of yours! OK, now it's criteria time. There are a number of local clubs and restaurants that bring in karaoke at one time or another. For our purposes, an establishment had to offer this entertainment at least two nights per week to qualify for mention in this chapter. All listings are in Myrtle Beach.

The Original Steak House

2801 N. Kings Hwy. *448-0391*

Chip Bellamy and his Karaoke Sounds Ltd. take over the lounge of this steakhouse every night from 9 PM 'til closing. Sandwiches and appetizers are available until 10 PM to satisfy performers' appetites.

Warren's Restaurant

1108 Third Ave. S. *448-3110*

This place is about as local-yokel as it gets. J.W. & the Karaoke Party are on hand every night from 8 PM to 2 AM. This is a serious karaoke venue with a mind-boggling number of terrific singers performing regularly.

Adult Entertainment

The Grand Strand region has its fair share of adult entertainment establishments, even though area authorities and courts seem to be constantly debating club locations and what constitutes the appropriate amount of nakedness displayed therein. We won't list the clubs here, because all you have to do is consult the Yellow Pages or ask almost anyone — after a wink and a nod, you'll be set in the right direction. Besides, isn't half the fun just getting there? Sort of like a fleshy version of a treasure hunt? There is even one club devoted to the female sector, featuring perfect samplings of the primal male species, dancing and sweating pretty in cages . . . things that make you go "hmmmm."

Inside Shopping

To say that the Grand Strand boasts terrific shopping is a terrific understatement. From stem to stern, this 60-mile stretch of real estate is jam-packed with retail establishments from the warehouse-size to the quaint and oh-so-small, offering a bit of everything: books and food, flowers and clothes, antiques and art supplies, handmade goodies, high-tech gadgetry and collectibles galore. Little wonder "golf" and "shopping" are tied for second just behind "beaches" when folks explain why they choose the Myrtle Beach area for their vacations — year after year. In fact, truth be told, lots of people come here for no other reason than the shopping. Completely oblivious to sunshine, surfboards, waterparks and rollercoasters, these folks fritter away every waking hour wandering from store to shop to mall — and back again. They know what you're about to learn: Very few places offer so much variety, so many bargains and scads of fun to boot.

When shopping is the subject of discussion, the question is never where to start but where to stop. From bargain-packed flea markets filled with secret surprises to swanky boutiques sporting well-dressed windows, there's absolutely nothing you can't find here. The selection will probably spoil you. Before you launch into a browse-and-buy frenzy, slip on your most comfortable shopping shoes, rest your trigger finger on your Gold Card, and . . . well, what are you waiting for?!

On a serious note, shopping here can be an overwhelming experience. You'll find some, but not many, of the big-name department stores you left back in your big city. There is no Saks, no Neiman-Marcus, no Williams-Sonoma, no Sharper Image and no FAO Swartz. But, there are more than a few dozen extraordinary outlet stores: **Eddie Bauer**, **J. Crew**, **Laura Ashley**, **Jones New York**, **Johnston & Murphy** and **Geoffrey Beene**, to name a scant few. **Belk**, a wonderful department store (though less recognizable to Northerners) can be found in each of the area's three malls. (Belk in Briarcliffe Mall is the newest and best.) There's also a veritable treasure trove of lesser-known but charming stores and shops where you'll discover treasures you might never have happened upon anywhere else.

It goes without saying that this chapter can't begin to discuss the finer details of every shopping excursion. Even as locals, we find ourselves divvying the area into delicious geographic slices to savor over several weekends, at least. We'll focus on several areas that have respectable concentrations and varieties of stores. We will also list a handful of personal favorites we feel are worth mentioning because of price, quality or uniqueness. Naturally, as a "shopper-extraordinaire," you'll discover your own favorites in the course of your shopping safari. Keep your eyes open; 'round every curve in the crowded high-

Photo: The Sun News

Readers of The Sun News have voted Barefoot Landing as the best place to take out-of-towners.

way there's yet another clutch of shops to burrow through. Most places are open seven days a week, although Sunday hours are frequently abbreviated — if you shop between 1 PM and 6 PM, you should find most of what you're looking for.

The entire Myrtle Beach area is growing by leaps and bounds, and there are lots of shopping facilities on the drawing board even as we struggle to produce a comprehensive overview. Unfortunately, it's tough to recommend or detail the joys of shopping in stores we've never seen — let alone shopped in. So make a note to look for shopping surprises that could not be included here (but will probably be included in next edition's update). Specifically, you should definitely research the retail options at **Broadway at the Beach** on the U.S. 17 Bypass at 21st Avenue North. This brand new shopping and entertainment complex plans to offer more than 75 unique shops and boutiques. Rumor has it that they'll offer something for everyone, from delicate pewter and holiday decorations to sports equipment and fine collectibles. Also up-and-coming are the **Myrtle Beach Factory Stores** on U.S. 501, west of Myrtle Beach. The first phase of their construction is expected to house as many as 55 retail tenants. Phases II and III will bring the center to a whopping 398,000 square feet and will include up to 100 tenants.

As for the basics, we've already mentioned Belk, our finest department store, which can be found at any one of three area malls. There's also a **Belk Outlet Store** at Outlet Park at Waccamaw. Other department stores with more than one location include **JCPenney**, **Sears** and **Peebles** — similar to but smaller than Belk. Several discount "chain" stores pepper the Strand, including **Wal-Mart**, **Kmart**, and a single **Roses** location in the Windy Hill area of North Myrtle Beach.

The larger supermarket chains include Food Lion, Harris Teeter, Kroger,

A&P and Winn-Dixie. **Kroger**, open 24 hours a day, is absolutely unparalleled for late night shopping. Impulse buyers will relish the general merchandise section that includes everything from cosmetics and hair coloring to auto and pet supplies. **Harris Teeter** boasts the cleanest and best-maintained stores, as well as the finest inventories of gourmet items. **A&P** generally has nice selections of fresh-cut flowers. The **A&P Super Store**, on the north end of Myrtle Beach, is brightly lit, has impressive selections of produce, fresh bakery goods and meats and even features a user-friendly computer that will help you find what you're looking for — fast. Over the past few years, **Winn-Dixie** has opened several new facilities, and we all know there's nothing better than shopping at a brand new grocery store. And, if you're a resident sprucing up your yard, they tend to have better-than-ordinary landscaping plants too. **Food Lion** wins the best-all-around award. They typically have the best prices; their stores are well-stocked, bright and clean, and their locations seem to be the most convenient.

It would be unjust to write a section on shopping without mentioning our beachwear stores — **Eagles, Wings**, etc. As residents, we don't frequent them often and tend to resent their garishly bright lights and every-other-block locations. Still, visitors love them — and rightfully so. Their inventories are skewed to the needs and wants of the tourist crowd: swimsuits and sun tan products, sun shades, beach chairs, rafts, umbrellas, souvenir items, beach toys, T-shirts and summer sportswear of the most casual sort. They are definitely worth a gander. Exercise your courage and negotiate with the sales staff for the very best prices.

Major Malls and Outlets

Inlet Square Mall

U.S. 17 Bus. and U.S. 17 Bypass
Murrells Inlet *651-5500*

Anchored by **Belk**, **Kmart** and **JCPenney**, Inlet Square is the newest of the area's three shopping malls. It offers most of what you'd expect from a mall: plenty of apparel shops, a bookstore, electronics, jewelry, shoes, a cinema and more. Additionally, there's **Foxy Lady**, a fine women's boutique that stocks some of the area's finest evening and daywear. Its inventory tends toward extravagant — lots of sequins, hand-beading, scarves, fitted silhouettes, flashy accessories — but it speaks to those who prefer understated elegance as well. There's also **The Stork Club**, the best maternity store on the Strand, featuring attire for professional moms and moms with classic tastes; there's not much of the cookie-cutter, "fru-fru" stuff you find at so many places. And they have a few really adorable things for infants that make perfect shower gifts.

Although not particularly large, the **Oasis Food Court** at Inlet Square is bet-

Insiders' Tips

Divide the area into geographic slices and take a day to cover each area. We suggest: North Strand, Myrtle Beach, South Strand and west of the Intracoastal Waterway.

ter than adequate. **Spinnakers**, a cheerful restaurant bedecked in nautical attire, is great for lunch, afternoon drinks or dinner. The warm cashew chicken salad, marvelously high in cholesterol, makes for a perfect meal. If the flowerpot bread isn't included with your selection, order it on the side. Baked in small, terra-cotta pots, it's warm, soft and delicious. Butter makes it better. **Chick-fil-A** is a fast food place you can always count on. **Big Dave's** has great burgers, and the **Mandarine Express** makes a mean egg roll.

Myrtle Square Mall

2501 N. Kings Hwy.
Myrtle Beach *448-2513*

With more than 84 stores and attractions, Myrtle Square is the area's oldest and most centrally located mall. Anchored by **Sears**, **Peebles** and **Belk**, it offers a nice combination of specialty shops, apparel stores, food, electronics, books, health products, music and more. This mall originally opened in the late '70s, in a beachside community just beginning to explode. But don't be fooled into thinking it's outdated. The recently remodeled facade is quite appealing and very modern.

Some of the better-known retail establishments include: **Blockbuster Music** (they actually let you listen to your music before you buy it), **Things Remembered, D.A. Kelly's** and **Radio Shack**. Some of the better-loved shops include: **The Mole Hole**, a charming gift shop with a staggering inventory of collectibles; the **Miss-Master Children's Shop**, for pricey and precious clothes; **Gingham Peddler**, an upscale women's boutique that tends toward classic; **Gentry House**, a men's clothing store; and **Scents Unlimited**, a business that specializes in "knock-off" colognes (you cannot tell the difference) and pretty niceties like perfume bottles and bath items. **Crafts Unlimited** is one of the area's only remaining craft stores, and it's quite nice.

Myrtle Square boasts the area's only indoor carousel, with 20 high-steppin' horses, tigers, giraffes, spinning lights and old-fashioned music. The world's largest clock, a 60-foot-diameter timepiece that combines ultramodern technology, high-tech graphics, playful sculptural forms and special "time-triggered" fountains, is located in the mall's center court. (A great distraction for antsy spouses.)

The **Food Court** at Myrtle Square is a locals hangout, particularly with business folks on lunch hour. A delightful collection of restaurants is situated in a gigantic, sky-lit dining area that combines palm trees, water sculptures, bubbling towers and sparkling waves of fabric and neon. **Hamburger Joe's, The Steak & Fries Grill, Lotsa Pasta** and **Good Times** are personal favorites.

Briarcliffe Mall

U.S. 17 N. (North of Restaurant Row)
Myrtle Beach *272-4040*

Like all the area's malls, Briarcliffe is a one-level facility. Since opening in 1986, it has been anchored by the area's biggest **Belk** department store (recently expanded), as well as **Kmart, JCPenney** and a state-of-the-art cinema. Other stores have names that are currently quite popular throughout the nation: **Lane Bryant, Limited Express, The Limited, Structure, Paul Harris, Earth Friendly** and **Victoria's Secret**. If you're a petite woman (that falls beneath the height of 5'4") make time to drop by **Little Women**. Just a bit pricey, the clothes are beautiful, well-made and classic in design. **Christmas Joy**, aptly named, sells Christmas paraphernalia year round. They stock holiday stuff that is definitely a cut above the selection you'd be forced to contend with come November.

While Briarcliffe's lineup of stores seems to outdo the other malls', their **Food Court** is not so comprehensive. But, that's not necessarily a liability. The choices are really good: **Spinnaker's, Chick-fil-A, Taco Bell, Great Steak and Fry,** and **Sadie's Buffet** are a few.

Barefoot Landing

U.S. 17 N.
North Myrtle Beach *272-8349*

Barefoot Landing bills itself as "the East Coast's most exciting waterfront shopping, dining and entertainment destination center," and we think they're probably right. A vibrant complex of shopping, dining, entertainment and attractions, Barefoot was recently honored as one of South Carolina's Most Outstanding Tourism Attractions. Little wonder! In a single year, Barefoot Landing plays host to more than 7 million visitors! Its restaurants, shops and attractions have been featured in magazines, newspapers and television clips throughout the nation. *Southern Living*, *The Wall Street Journal*, *USA Today*, *Barron's Investment*, *Forbes* and *Country America* are just a few of the biggest media names that know and love Barefoot Landing. In 1993 and 1994, in a readership poll sponsored by *The Sun News*, locals voted this shopping mecca the "Best Place to Take Out-of-Towners." We think that's an unbeatable vote of confidence.

Built around a 20-acre freshwater lake, fronted by U.S. 17 N. and bordered in back by the beautiful Intracoastal Waterway, Barefoot has more than 1,000 feet of floating dock on the waterway, as well as miles of rocking-chair-peppered boardwalks and bridges. This development, a rare marriage between commerce and preservation, prides itself on environmental sensitivity. While strolling among the more than 100 shops, restaurants and attractions, you can enjoy seagulls swooping over the lakes, alligators swimming stealthily and all manner of water birds including swans, geese, blue heron, snowy egrets, ducks and pelicans; you can even feed the fish from many of the boardwalks. And, if you keep your eyes peeled, you stand a good chance of glimpsing turtles and a beaver or two.

With a Lowcountry seaport village theme, Barefoot Landing's eclectic assortment of shops and restaurants is housed in quaint, cedar shake buildings with bright green awnings. Specialty stores feature everything from resort wear, jewelry, designer fashions, western wear, and accessories to handmade gifts and unusual collectibles. Variety is the order of the day. Thirteen factory-direct stores are wonderful finds with merchandise priced at 20 percent to 50 percent below retail. There's **Geoffrey Beene, Capezio, London Fog, Outer Banks, S&K Famous Brands, Bass, Van Heusen, Westport, Cape Isle Knitters, Rack Room, Megan O'Neal, Hinkle Brothers,** and **Fox Bags, Belts, Etc.**

The Boardwalk Shops — Barefoot Landing's core — opened in 1988. You can find brightly colored flags, banners and wind socks at **Klig's Kites**, the best kite store we've seen anywhere. If you're from "up north," **The Sweater Connection** offers an outstanding collection of Peruvian sweaters. The **Shirley Pewter Shop** is a great place to pick up a memorable keepsake for someone you love. And **Scents Unlimited**, a dramatically successful shop that specializes in "knock-off" fragrances, is an absolute must-stop shop.

The signature floating bridge leads to two more clusters of shops: **Dockside Vil-**

lage and **Barefoot Factory Stores**. You'll find wood carvings at **David Blackwell's Studio**, unusual clothing at **Barefoot Republic**, **Carolyn's Unique Fashions** and **Spoiled Rotten**. Vintage rock music pours from **Wound 'N Around**, where the checkout counter sits atop a 1964 Ford Falcon. Other stores specialize in jewelry, comic books, candles, crystal tableware and Broadway posters.

The **Carousel Courtyard** offers shops of educational toys, games and children's apparel and features an old-fashioned European carousel that delights the young and young-at-heart. Seasonal musicians, magicians, jugglers, clowns, mimes and other entertainers add to the festive spirit. For a real thrill, you might hop on the Barefoot Simulator with your kids. This virtual reality theater pod features roller coaster rides, jet fighting, motocross racing, downhill skiing and more. There's also an arcade with plenty of electronic and video fun and frolic.

Entertainment ranges from magicians performing on the boardwalk to live music in some restaurants to excursions on the ***Barefoot Princess*** riverboat. The **Alabama Theatre**, namesake of the country music group, features 2,200 seats. Alabama performs there during the year and also books fellow country stars such as Charlie Daniels, Lorrie Morgan, Pam Tillis and Confederate Railroad. A resident variety show fills other nights with country, gospel, rock, pop and comedy.

Twelve waterfront restaurants feature menus with something for everyone — fresh seafood, steaks, ribs, chicken, Italian, Mexican and more. It's estimated that this lineup of a dozen restaurants serves well over a million meals every year! Among the award-winning establishments are **T-Bonz Gill and Grill**, **Umberto's Italian Trattoria**, **Damon's - The Place for Ribs**, **Fuddrucker's**, **Knickerbocker On The Water** and **Porter's Coffee House Cafe**. (See our Restaurants chapter for more detailed listings.) Fresh-baked goods, homemade ice cream, candies and freshly squeezed juices are favorite treats you'll find along the boardwalks.

In a nutshell, here's what *Southern Living* had to say about Barefoot Landing: "Shorebirds, concerts, fragrances, fashions, rare finds, and good eats — not bad for a mall. That is, not bad for a nature-friendly shopping, dining and entertainment complex." This is easily a full-day excursion, and you'll be disappointed if you don't allow ample time for moseying through all the unusual stuff.

Waccamaw Pottery

U.S. 501 (West of the Intracoastal Waterway)
Myrtle Beach *236-1100*

The Outlet Park at Waccamaw

U.S. 501 (West of the Intracoastal Waterway)
Myrtle Beach *236-1400*

No description of Grand Strand shopping would be complete without bestowing accolades on Waccamaw Pottery and Outlet Park. Shoppers literally come by the busloads, and many couldn't care less about the ocean, the restaurants, the golf courses or any of the other attractions we all know and love. If you fall into this category, there's a Holiday Inn next door that overlooks the Intracoastal Waterway. (Of course, the view won't matter to you.) You can start early, shop late, catch a few winks and start all over again the following day. A free tram runs from mall to mall, and we suggest you use it liberally; this place is the Energizer® Bunny's outpost for shopping — it keeps going and going . . .

"The Pottery," as locals call it, was Myrtle Beach's original purveyor of shopping fame. It is immense, to say the least. Comparable to three football fields in size, its inventory of housewares and home decor is as staggering as its capacity. Everything is priced 20 percent to 50 percent below regular department store prices. Waccamaw Pottery stocks name brand china, glassware, wicker, silk flowers and trees, cookware, lamps, candles, picture frames, kitchen items, gourmet food selections, cookware, selected pieces of furniture, flower pots, delicately etched glassware, even a Christmas shop. **Waccamaw Linen**, the Pottery's next door neighbor, will overwhelm you with bedroom and bathroom accessories, rugs of all shapes and sizes, kitchen linens, pillows and a craft shop.

Outlet Park at Waccamaw has literally grown up around Waccamaw Pottery. If you like name brands and bargains, this is the be-all and end-all of your dreams. With three enclosed malls covering 750,000 square feet, Outlet Park is the largest manufacturers' outlet shopping center on the East Coast. At last count, there were more than 125 stores! You'll recognize popular names like **Oshkosh B'Gosh** and **Polly Flinders** for the kids; **Anne Klein, Jones New York** and **Laura Ashley** for discriminating ladies; **S&K Famous Menswear, Van Heusen** and **Geoffrey Beene** for the men; and **Hanes, Swank, London Fog, MagnaVox** and **Rack Room Shoes** for the whole family. There are stores for books, jewelry, records, ribbons, rugs and silver.

In Mall One, you'll enjoy **Duck Head's Factory Store, Leslie Fay, Jonathan Logan, Umbro** and **American**

Insiders' Tips

Instead of weekends, schedule your shopping excursions for weekdays — when the locals are at work and the tourists crowd is at its lowest ebb.

Eagle Outfitters. There's also a **Dollar Tree**, a neat place to give the kids $5 and see what they come out with. **Fancy Free Kids** is a great place to discover bargains in children's wear. In Mall Two, **Acme Boot** and **Ducks Unlimited** have a lot of fans. **Casual Corner** is a real favorite among fashion-conscious women, as is the **Dress Barn**. **Genuine Kids** is worth a stop. **Carolina Clock and Rugs** is filled with tempting things for your home. **The Children's Outlet** in Mall Three is one of our personal favorites. If you have a little one you like to dress up and show off, this is just the place to find unusual things that you'd rarely stumble upon in a department store. They have tiny sunshades, tiny hats, tiny sandals and tiny denims. Other favorites in Mall Three include **Eddie Bauer, Laura Ashley**, a **Belk Outlet, Bass, Johnston & Murphy, Jones New York** and **J. Crew**. There's also a **Music 4 Less** store that offers a great selection of cassettes and CDs at more reasonable prices than you'd find uptown at the mall.

The Hammock Shops

U.S. 17, Pawleys Island *237-8448*

In 1889, John Joshua Ward, a young riverboat captain who barged rice and other supplies up and down the Waccamaw River from Waverly Mills at Pawleys Island through Winyah Bay to Georgetown and Charleston, created the first Pawleys Island hammock. In an attempt to find relief from the scratchy straw mattresses then used on river barges, he first tried working with canvas, then knotted string, but both were as uncomfortable as the straw. What finally evolved was a hammock of soft cotton rope, woven — rather than knotted — and held open by use of a curved "spreader bar." The new design allowed air to circulate, making the hammock far cooler and more comfortable than the scratchy straw beds. And the spreader bar lent a gentle curve, keeping the soft weave from collapsing inward.

This was the concept of the famous Pawleys Island hammock, a design faithfully retained for more than 100 years. Ward taught the intricacies of the pattern to his brother-in-law, A. H. "Cap't Doc" Lachicotte, and soon the Lachicottes and Wards were busy making hammocks for family members and friends. In the late 1930s, "Doc" set up a small shop on U.S. Highway 17 to sell the hammocks to travelers. And that modest business became the nucleus around which today's famed Hammock Shops at Pawleys Island sprang up.

"Quaint" may be an overused adjective, but it is truly appropriate when applied to The Hammock Shops. This clutch of retail establishments represents the kinds of places you can return to again and again to find something new and uniquely intriguing each time. Nearly two dozen shops, many offering the work of Carolina artists and craftspeople, are now clustered beneath moss-draped trees on the edge of a beautiful salt marsh. Some are located in historic Lowcountry buildings that include an original post office and schoolhouse, but even the newer shops are careful not to compromise the mood of the original architecture; the new buildings feature old beams, used timber and ballast brick. Each shop has been carefully selected for quality, reputation and the appeal of its merchandise. The whole complex provides a welcome complement to the razzle and dazzle of Myrtle Beach. Rocking chairs on open porches, swaying hammocks, and park benches nestled in beautifully landscaped gardens beckon you to linger and aban-

Photo: Cecelia Konyn, The Sun News

Christmas shopping can be done year-round at several stores.

don your worries. The hammock weavers are a special treat. Visitors can pause to enjoy skilled craftspeople transforming 1,000 feet of cotton rope into a world-famous hammock.

Everything from gourmet foods and wildlife prints to contemporary clothes and hand-crafted jewelry can be discovered at The Hammock Shops. **The Audubon Shop**, a wildlife and nature store, features environmentally oriented gifts, gardening books and accessories, celestial and astronomy guides, Audubon prints, and a full line of cassette tapes featuring Mother Nature's soothing sounds. Of particular appeal is the children's room — follow the animal tracks set in the floor — with nature books and games, field guides, puppets and unique plush animals, all displayed at a child's height.

Sporting Life of Pawleys Island is a specialty outdoor store, featuring top clothing lines, accessories and fishing gear. Environmental T-shirts, jewelry and a variety of beach-related items are the specialties of **Options**; and the art, sculpture, weaves and music of our Native Americans celebrate their culture at **Three Feathers**.

Here, too, at **Whitmire's**, are hand-cast gold pendants, charms and bracelets. Fancy footwear abounds at **Island Shoes**. **Annemarie's** features collectibles, antique glassware and dolls, costume jewelry and souvenir gifts. **Creative Candles** specializes in hand-carved candles and accessories. **The Carolina Gourmet** showcases specialty food and cookery items. **Toyland** has served the area for 20 years with unique English garden toys, Playmobil Brio of Sweden and games galore.

At the heart of this beguiling village are the **Hammock Shop General Store** and **The Original Hammock Shop**. Within the General Store, books on local history, customs and legends and a diversity of gift choices including hand-painted birdhouses, wind chimes, salt marsh pottery, and the gnomes of North Carolina artisan Tom Clark facilitate discovery of the Lowcountry lifestyle.

If you're fond of shopping at places that showcase a flair for the distinctive and unusual, you must visit The Hammock Shops. Springtime visits offer the extraordinary beauty of blooming azaleas, dogwoods, tulip trees and more. Around Christmas, the trees are filled with the sparkle of tiny white lights, and all the stores wear holiday finery, making this a particularly enjoyable time to visit.

Other Shopping Stops

South Strand

Hudson's Flea Market

U.S. 17 Bus., Surfside Beach 238-0372

Locally known as Surfside Flea Market, this is a bargain hunter's fantasyland. Snooty folk might raise an eyebrow at the yard sale atmosphere and hodgepodge of merchandise that spills from the back of trucks, vans and cars onto tabletops, dirt floors and wheeled clothing racks. But, if you can abandon pretension for a few hours, the flea market is a world unto its own. There's absolutely no telling what you might stumble across. Here's a sampling: new and used clothes, handmade furniture, kitchen gadgetry, home-baked goodies, homegrown pecans, sunshades, toys, oil paintings, antiques, glassware, books and more books — used and new, personal accessories of all shapes, sizes and purposes, cosmetics, gizmos you often see only on television's infomercials, tools, remarkably priced cassettes, handmade crafts, socks and T-shirts, jewelry, knives, baseball cards, bikes and fresh produce. There . . . that's a start.

The Flea Market is open year round, but hours vary according to season so call ahead for details. A hint: Many of the vendors are moonlighters and only come out on weekends. Consequently, this excursion is best saved for Saturdays and Sundays.

In Murrells Inlet, U.S. 17 S. Business and Bypass unite to become one highway. From this point southward, the roadsides are peppered with a delightful melange of antique shops, boutiques, consignment outlets, galleries, restaurants and more. This strip of the Grand Strand is known for being less developed, more relaxed in atmosphere, brimming with history and full of Lowcountry color. The drive itself is pleasant and pretty. Take your time and stop often.

The Island Shops

U.S. 17, Pawleys Island *No central phone*

Just south and across the highway from The Hammock Shops are The Island Shops. Nestled beneath gnarled, weathered oaks, these shops are filled with one-of-a-kind finds. A ribbon of wooden

Insiders' Tips

For a minimal price, many shopkeepers will ship your merchandise home so you won't have to worry about lugging it around during your vacation.

walkways and bridges amidst a series of small ponds unites the different shops and boutiques. Be sure to pause and enjoy the antics of a friendly population of ducks. Happily splashing in and out of their Lowcountry "swimming hole," they graciously accept tasty tidbits from shoppers. And, if the web-footed friends can't calm your shopping frenzy, cozy benches, oversized rockers and well-placed hammocks will surely do the trick.

If you're curious about what you'll find, here's just a few of the shopping selections: Locals "in-the-know" travel from miles around to visit **The Cricket Shop**. Featuring fine swimwear from leading designers, this fun shop also boasts sportswear and dresses. Meander through the door of **Love, Pawleys** and relish a symphony of smells. Dried flowers and herbs, lavish floral arrangements and oodles of hand crafts make it tough to tuck away the credit card. If the kitchen is your favorite place, head to **Pawleys Pantry** for an absolutely unmatched selection of great gadgets and gourmet cookware. **The Mole Hole** is an infinitely intriguing little gift shop that's become a Pawleys Island landmark. There's no telling what delightful trinket you might discover within! Before you stash the cash, peruse hand-carved birds, whimsical characters, collectibles and framed and unframed prints at **The Wooden Duck**.

Shops at Oak Lea

U.S. 17, Pawleys Island *No central phone*

At this collection of shops, the pace is as slow as honey on biscuits. With so many beautiful things to browse, it's no wonder! The wooden boardwalks, Cape Cod structures and marsh-borne breezes will transport you from the hustle and bustle of a hectic holiday.

A great place to start is the fancy shop called **Eleanor Pitts**. Likely as not, you'll find the elegant Ms. Pitts flitting among her astounding selection of fine gifts, unique jewelry and china. Expect to discover only bounty of the finest quality within these four walls: fine crystal from Baccarat and Waterford, lovely tableware bearing names like Wedgewood and Lenox, and an absolute bevy of beautiful gifts of every size, price and description. Plan to spend plenty of time browsing; there's something unique, delicate and perfect in every nook.

Once you've deposited your packages in the car, pop in at **Pawleys Peddler Shoes** and find footwear and accessories guaranteed to add polish to your latest garment purchases. Women of style drive from "the city" to enjoy one of the area's finest collections of top-quality shoes. Peruse this list of renowned name brands: **Amano**, **Anne Klein**, **Prevata** and **Sesto Meucci**. If you're not impressed, you may need to brush up your fine footwear I.Q.

If you haven't shopped the numbers off the Gold Card, wrap up your shopping excursion at the **Joggling Board**. Featuring fine attire and classic toys, this fun boutique offers a lot more than an adorable array of clothing; you'll find bangles and bows, keepsakes for newborns, unique stuffed toys and oh-so-soft baby blankets. It's a kid-size adventure in good taste!

Also in Pawleys Island is **Harrington Altman Ltd.**, an extraordinary gift shop in a new and larger location on the west side of the highway, just north of The Island Shops. The inventory here leans towards elegant — with more than a touch of cozy tossed in for spice. They feature a rotating selection of tastefully striking furniture: coffee tables, sideboards, china cabinets, bookshelves and dining tables. Many items are hand-painted and one-of-a-kind. They also carry a melange of what your mom might call "knickknacks," or "whatnots" — lovely collectible pieces of tabletop decor that could add a touch of whim or an element of class to an existing display. Harrington Altman showcases some art, flower arrangements, fancy pillows, lots of handmade heirlooms, and an impressive collection of upholstery fabrics.

Across the street, in **Planter's Exchange**, is **The George Pawleys Company, Inc.** Since 1990, owner Michael York has provided his customers with the finest in outdoor furnishings, decorative accessories and practical pieces for the serious birder or gardener. You'll find lots of handmade items of heirloom quality: fountains, furniture, planters, statuary, weathervanes, mailboxes and so much more. All those garden catalogs you covet in the spring come to life at George Pawley. A growing reputation has prompted the store to expand and offer you even more to choose from.

Myrtle Beach

Northwood Plaza

Kings Hwy. at 79th Ave. N.   No central phone

Here, you'll find a few shops we think are worth mentioning. **Bestsellers** is more than a regular bookstore; they carry cards, magazines, custom invitations, puzzles and games, balloons and party supplies. Next door, **Cribb's Cribs** will make every mom wish for the winning number in the Publisher's Clearing House Sweepstakes. Forty or more cribs are on display, featuring coordinated sets of delightfully sweet comforters, shams and bumper pads. Far more than a crib outlet, Cribb's Cribs also carries personalized birth announcements, toys, glider rockers, intercom systems, lamps, "snugglies," dinnerware, bassinets, bibs, chests, bath cushions, mobiles, cradles, strollers, high chairs, car seats, picture frames and a whole slew of items for child-proofing your home.

Just a few doors down, **Ivy's Patio** has everything you need to spruce up your lawn or garden. They stock a unique and beautiful assortment of items from hand-painted flower pots, bird feeders, hanging pots, thermometers, garden tools, wind chimes, decorative mailboxes, vase rooters, outdoor candles, wind socks, garden ornaments and copper faucet covers. If you're not fond of yard work and the great outdoors, Ivy's just might inspire you. And, it's the perfect place to find a thoughtful gift for someone who takes pride in a green thumb.

Across U.S. 17 from Northwood Plaza are a couple of stores you should stop in and browse, if you have the time. **The Jolly Roger**, a time-tested Myrtle Beach favorite, features fine items for the home. **The Wacky Rabbit** is a whimsical gift shop where many items — though certainly not all — feature bunnies. You'll

The best bargains on swimwear can be found at beachwear stores from August to December.

Insiders' Tips

find afghans, wind chimes, nature recordings, mugs, cards, puzzles, clocks, picture frames, stuffed animals, golf memorabilia, toys and gadgets. Best of all, the friendly clerks at Wacky Rabbit usually have a plate of chocolate fudge waiting for weary customers. That in itself makes it worth a stop.

One block down, at 75th Avenue N. on the same side of U.S. 17, is **Joan Crosby's**. A women's wear store, Joan Crosby's is a 40-year-old Myrtle Beach institution and is a particularly nice find for older women seeking traditional clothing styles in sizes that leave Twiggy out in the cold. Again on your left, two blocks south at 73rd Avenue, is **Country Vogue**. This elegant shop recently relocated from Myrtle Square Mall to take advantage of a new and larger location. They feature scads of popular, high quality brands like Lanz, Liz Sport, Liz Claiborne and J.H. Collectibles. Styles lean toward classic more than trendy, and they offer a good selection of petite sizes. The clothes here are top quality . . . the kind of stuff you wear around your country club buddies who recognize designer names.

Old Times Square

Kings Hwy. at 62nd Ave. N. No central phone

Begin your browsing at **Buckles and Bows**, a top-notch children's shoe store. Appropriately located, **The Children's Shoppe** is just next door. They carry top-quality, traditional clothing for "preemies" up to a girl's size 14 and a boy's size 12. You might recognize these brands: Heart Strings, Boston Traitor, Little Me, Feltman Brothers and Strasburg Lace. Many of the girls' fashions feature delicate smocking and the heirloom look. Expect to pay more than you would at a department store, but the clothes are distinctive as well as beautiful. And you'll almost certainly hand them down. This is a great place to find a memorable christening outfit. The Children's Shoppe also stocks dolls of collectible quality, including Madam Alexander, Gotz and Correlle.

Just a footfall from Old Times Square is **Rachel's Plaza**. If there's a bride-to-be or prom queen in your entourage, be sure to find time for a stop at **MiLady's and MiLord's**. Next door is **Barbara's Fine Gifts**, one of the most elegant gift shops in all of Myrtle Beach. Barbara's offers top-quality items from Baccarat, Waterford, Virginia Metalcraft, Mottahedeh, Baldwin Brass, Arthur Court polished aluminum and Miller Rogaska crystal. There is a large selection of silver, lovely picture frames, tassels, wildwood lamps, Beatrix Potter rabbits, yard statutes and bird baths. The back room is filled with china and crystal. Brands from all over the globe include Faberge, Limoges, Wedgewood, Royal Crown Derby, Spode and Royal Doulton. Keep in mind, Barbara's is closed on Sundays.

Insiders' Tips

Don't wear heels, especially if planning a stop at Barefoot Landing; the boardwalks wreak havoc on fine shoes.

Rainbow Harbor

Kings Hwy. at 49th Ave. N. *449-7476*

This clutch of retail options is clearly designed for people who cherish the finer things in life. **Coplon's** has big-name, high-priced American and European fashions for men and women. **Cee Jays** is an exceptionally nice shoe store that stocks sizes 5 through 10 in medium width and sizes 6 through 10 in narrow width. They can special order narrow width in smaller sizes too. Brands include Allure's, J. Renee and Stuart Weitzman. The store also has lots of accessories and a small selection of unusual clothes in sizes 4 to 14. **The Cheryl Newby Gallery** is in its 12th year of specializing in antique prints, engravings and fine art. More than 3,000 prints emphasizing natural history, including collections by John James Audubon, are available for browsing. Also featured is an extensive collection of rare and decorative antique maps and charts. Restoration of fine art and old documents is available here as well.

Pink House Square

4301 N. Kings Hwy. *626-3100, 626-7873*

This complex features seven stores in a natural setting. The centerpiece of this collection of shops is **The Christmas Elegance Park.** When you walk through this Christmas wonderland, you will witness a seemingly endless variety of holiday decorations in addition to items like music boxes, collector dolls, electric trains and even a cutlery shop. **The White Heron** showcases an incredible collection of wind chimes. Other stores carry yard ornaments, fine handmade jewelry, candles, cards and Native American crafts. While most of the shops carry lots of Christmas merchandise, there are gifts for all occasions.

The Tower Shoppes

2701 N. Kings Hwy. *No central phone*

When at The Tower Shoppes, you should pop in at **Victoria's Ragpatch.** This quality women's store features popular brands like David Brooks, Two + Two, Outlander and Karen Kane. The inventory is both unique and traditional with a twist of spirit. A couple of doors over, take a gander at **Ann Lane's Shoes.** Beautiful belts and unusual handbags are displayed along with renowned shoes, including Donald J. Pliner, Anne Klein, Stuart Weitzman and Allure.

Gay Dolphin

Ocean Blvd. at Ninth Ave. N. *448-6550*

No narrative on Grand Strand shopping would be justified in omitting **Gay Dolphin**, a world-famous shopping attraction for more than four decades. Even if you're not interested in shopping, you'll be wowed by an inventory of more than 60,000 items ranging from post cards to collectibles. This gift shop actually has "coves," small shops within the larger store, on both sides of the Boulevard.

Insiders' Tips

Shop on sunny days — when everyone else is at the beach. Traffic is slower and lines are shorter.

Collector's Cove features Hummel figurines, Sebastian and Norman Rockwell, clowns, gnomes, bells and more. In the **Pearl Booth**, you can actually pick your own pearl from genuine South Sea pearl oysters, then watch while experienced staff mount it in jewelry made just for you. More than 50 coves include merchandise like jewelry, stuffed animals, souvenirs, golf memorabilia, shark's teeth, nautical items, toys, swimwear, ceramics and shells.

North Myrtle Beach

Birthday Suits Resort Wear

217 Main St. *249-1110*

If you don't have time to scout around for something unique, this boutique prides itself on an outstanding collection of ladies apparel in sizes six through 24. You'll find shoes, accessories, resort wear, native wear and swimwear from casual to top-drawer ritzy. "Expect the unexpected," is a familiar saying at Birthday Suits: shoes by Onex, Swimwear by Roxanne and Bendigo and designer jewelry galore.

Hidden Village Shops

9904 U.S. 17 N. *No central phone*
(Restaurant Row area)

On the east side of U.S. 17, look for an interesting strip of specialty stores. **Kitchen Capers** has everything any cook could dream up. Expect typical stuff like cookbooks, aprons, oven mitts, pot holders and cookie cutters, as well as unusual things such as bacon presses, expandable trivets, odd kitchen gadgetry you didn't know you needed and decorative ceramics for your counter tops. **Diva's Gift Shop** is a worthwhile stop, too. Try to time your visit so you can enjoy a sandwich or salad at **Taste Buds**, an intimate and friendly little restaurant in Hidden Village. These shops are closed on Sundays.

Magnolia Plaza

U.S. 17 N. (In Restaurant Row) No central phone
(Turn at the stoplight on Chestnut Rd.)

A few blocks south of Hidden Village is Magnolia Plaza. This "strip mall" sits perpendicular to U.S. 17 and is not easily seen. The most recognizable entity is the **A&P Super Store. Kepley's Fine Furniture** is our favorite stop here. This furniture showroom is relatively new to our area and has made a big splash. Featuring substantial discounts on the most respected names in furniture, Kepley's showcases a broad selection of finely crafted furniture in virtually every style imaginable. Here are a few of the names you can expect to see: Henredon, Henry Link, Ficks Reed, American Drew, Weiman, Hickory Chair, Stanley and Pennsylvania House. Savings can climb as high as 50 percent! Even if you're not planning a purchase, the showroom is so beautiful you should stop just to browse!

The Galleria

U.S. 17 and Lake Arrowhead Rd.
(In Restaurant Row) *No central phone*

The Galleria, south of Magnolia Plaza, boasts the wonderful bakery **Toffino's**, as well as **Jerry's Ice Cream Shop, Heavenly Hams** and **Fudge Nut**, a candy store guaranteed to appease the chocolate lovers in your group. At the Galleria, take time to check out **Gothic Accents** and **Frame of Mind**, a frame and print shop.

Inside
The Entertainment Explosion

It all started in 1986 with Calvin Gilmore's Carolina Opry, a family-style opry house in Surfside Beach. Locals clearly remember that the buzz around town was "It'll never make it. . . . There's not enough people to support it year round. . . . This Gilmore guy is crazy." But before long, shows were sold out in advance as throngs of residents, bus tours and visitors vied for tickets to see the countrified, musical/comedy production that was whispered to be "better than anything in Nashville or Branson." If you didn't have your tickets to the Christmas show by June, you were certainly out of luck.

Gilmore was crazy . . . crazy like a fox that is. The former timeshare salesman opened Carolina Opry only after conducting extensive marketing research that indicated the Myrtle Beach area was fertile ground for such grand entertainment. Regardless of most locals' patronage, estimates showed that the opry house could survive on ticket sales from tourists and the ever-growing retirement community. Of course, the rest is a history lesson in success.

Gilmore currently owns and operates three entertainment palaces along the Grand Strand and a television studio that promotes his shows to the masses. Paving the way for live productions, Gilmore and the Carolina Opry are the forerunners of the area's entertainment explosion that now includes Dolly Parton's Dixie Stampede, the Alabama Theatre, the Russian Euro Circus and Magic on Ice. And the list of entertainment options doesn't stop there. As you read on, you'll get information on Coming Explosions that have committed to opening here. As a rule, these variety shows are wholesome and entertaining for the entire family. Tickets are sold by reservation, so call ahead to secure seats. Refreshments are sold before each show and during intermission; however, no alcohol is served on the properties.

Alabama Theatre

Barefoot Landing — 272-1111
North Myrtle Beach — (800) 342-BAMA

With a spectacular red, white and blue grand opening gala during the Fourth of July 1993, the super group Alabama unveiled its $7 million, 2,200-seat theater. Don't let the crystal chandeliers and marble floors fool you; the entertainment is down-home family fun. The theater features four kinds of shows: (1) Alabama performs at least 10 concerts a year; (2) celebrity guests, including stars like George Jones, Diamond Rio, Lee Greenwood and the Oak Ridge Boys, perform at least 20 concerts a year; (3) the house show, "American Pride," features professional entertainers who combine singing, dancing and comedy into a fantastic display of talent; and (4) a special Christmas in Dixie extravaganza is slated to run from November 16 through December 31, 1995. Don't miss the American Pride

Photo: The Sun News

Calvin Gilmore opened the first country music theater, The Carolina Opry, in 1986.

Show, created by Opryland Productions, Inc.

Alabama has been dubbed the Group of the Decade by the American Country Music Association, having sold billions of records during a career that started right here in Myrtle Beach at The Bowery on Ocean Boulevard. The Bowery's notoriety of having Alabama as its house band years ago still brings people through the doors.

Tickets for American Pride run $19 for adults and $7 for children 3 to 16 years of age. The celebrated "Christmas in Dixie" holiday show is $20 a seat for adults and $7 for children. Tickets to the celebrity guests show vary depending on the costs of bringing in particular artists. However, if you book an adult ticket for a celebrity show, you will get $5 off on a seat for either an American Pride or Christmas production. Call in advance for seating reservations. (Note to Alabama junkies: The gift shop sells an assortment of Alabama memorabilia.)

Calvin Gilmore Productions

238-8888 (800) THE-OPRY

The Carolina Opry
N. Kings Hwy. at U.S. 17 Bypass Myrtle Beach

The Dixie Jubilee
701 Main St. North Myrtle Beach

Legends in Concert
Third Ave. S. Surfside Beach

The original Carolina Opry moved into a grand, new state-of-the-art facility with 2,200 seats and a television studio. The newest Gilmore venture opened in March when he replaced the countrified show at Southern Country Nights with a John Stewart production of fine impersonators. The venue is now called Legends in Concert and features impresarios of such stars as Elvis Presley, Cher, Liberace and Frank Sinatra. Tickets for Legends are $19 for adults and $8 for children 3 through 15.

Carolina Opry and Dixie Jubilee still feature a unique blend of country, bluegrass, Big Band, patriotic and toe-tapping tunes. Comedy routines with a Southern drawl and high-kicking dance segments are choreographed into each show. This is a complete evening of great entertainment that will bring you to your feet when the curtain closes. Carolina Opry tickets are $21 for adults and $8 for children 3 through 15. Adult and child seats for Dixie Jubilee shows are $17 and $8, respectively. Call ahead to reserve seats, as they sell quickly weeks ahead of each show. Showtime is 8 PM. Each year, the cast presents a spectacular Christmas show designed to put even Scrooge in the spirit of the season. Many locals reserve seats to the Christmas show as early as June. It's that popular!

Dixie Stampede

N. Kings Hwy. at U.S. 17 Bypass 497-9700
Myrtle Beach (800) 433-4401

Dixie Stampede, a Dollywood Production, is a dinner attraction that combines country cookin' with a rodeo-style show for a rompin,' stompin,' finger lickin' good time. And we're not just whistling Dixie about the finger lickin' part: Don't expect silverware for your four-course dinner of creamy vegetable soup, whole roasted chicken, hickory smoked ribs, corn on the cob, herb-basted potato, homemade bread, dessert and beverage. And just in case you're wondering, the soup is served in a drinking cup. Thankfully, you can wash your hands with warm, wet towels provided by the singing waitrons.

Before dinner, everyone corrals into the Dixie Belle Saloon (no alcohol served) for live musical entertainment, specialty drinks, popcorn and peanuts. Then, the audience is seated in stadium fashion above the arena where the action is held. Country music artist and icon Dolly Parton had a hand in developing this $5 million dinner attraction, so expect Southern belles, glitzy costumes that light up in the dark, cowboys who perform trick riding with some 30 trained horses and audience participation that's downright neighborly. The show's theme is created from the romance of the "Old South" and the North vs. South rivalry of the Civil War. Let's face it, a pig race between Ulysses S. Grunt and Robert E. Lean is pushing the cornball, but it sets the pace for a knee-slapping good time.

Tickets are $24.95 plus tax for adults and $14.95 plus tax for children (11 and younger). The theater seats about 1,000, but call ahead for reservations. Regular shows are held from mid-February through May at 6 PM. Two shows, at 6 PM and 8:30 PM, run mostly from June through August. One show per evening can be seen during September and October, and performances are scheduled for every Wednesday, Friday and Saturday night in November and December. Tickets for the New Year's Eve Extravaganza show are $39.95 plus tax per seat for an adult and $29.95 plus tax for children. Handicapped access and facilities are available.

Fantasy Harbour Entertainment Complex

U.S. 501 *236-8500*
(Behind Waccamaw Pottery) (800) 681-5209

Euro Circus: The Russian Fantasy

Don't expect to see lions, tigers and bears at this cultural event. Instead, a troupe of more than 40 Russian and Ukrainian entertainers enthralls audiences with feats of strength, agility and magic. Apparently, the acts featured in the Cercle Theatre are skills handed down from generations of Russian circus performers. Agile tumblers, power jugglers, high-wire artists, clowns and athletes execute exciting, nail-biting stunts at Euro Circus. Shows are held in a fully air-conditioned, climate-controlled tent that was purchased from The Mirage Hotel & Casino in Las Vegas. The extraordinary tarp was the former home of the Canadian hit show Cirque Du Soleil and seats more than 1,500 spectators comfortably. Tickets to the shows are $14.95 for adults and $7.95 for children 12 and younger.

The Gatlin Brothers Theatre

Known for such hits as "All The Gold in California," "Houston, I Don't Wanna Cry" and the Grammy Award-winning "Broken Lady," The Gatlin Brothers showcase their enormous talent in this state-of-the-art concert hall. This 2,000-seat theater was designed for its customers, with multiple concession and restroom areas and a large gift shop in the lobby. Larry, Steve and Rudy Gatlin perform for six months of the year; guest celebrities round out the calendar. Seats cost $21.95 for adults and $9.95 for children 12 and younger. Showtime is 8 PM from Monday through Saturday; a 3 PM matinee is performed every Wednesday. The theater closes for two weeks in January.

Magic On Ice

Olympic and world-class skaters take to this icy stage to perform a program of precision, fiery explosions and illusions. Considering the Grand Strand's warm climate, the rink itself is a technological marvel, pumping 200 gallons per minute of refrigerant to keep the ice in perfect skating form. Admission for adults is $17.95, and children 12 and younger are seated for $7.95 each. Performances begin at 7 PM from Monday through Saturday; 3 PM matinees are scheduled for every Tuesday, Wednesday and Thursday. Showtimes change frequently between April and September, so call ahead.

Coming Explosions

At the time this Insiders' Guide was published a number of entertainment complexes were announcing their arrival date and are slated for construction. We can't give you a true hands-on sort of insider's scoop on these places, but we can tell you about them and what the public relations people say they will offer.

BROADWAY AT THE BEACH

From 21st Ave. N. to 29th Ave. N.
(Off the U.S. 17 Bypass)
Myrtle Beach No phone available at press time

This 350-acre entertainment complex built around a 23-acre man-made lake will lie in the heart of Myrtle Beach. We locals have been putting up with one-lane driving along the Bypass and dirt clot-flinging-dumptrucks all winter long, but Broadway looks well worth the trouble. This complex of live theaters, nightclubs, restaurants and specialty shops will have cost an estimated $250 million by the time it's complete. The first phase of the project promises to open up in May 1995, including more than 90 stores and 12 restaurants. The multimillion dollar The Palace at Myrtle Beach is scheduled to raise its curtains in summer 1995. Here are a few of the unique attractions Broadway at the Beach has confirmed will open, hopefully in time for your visit!

Celebrity Square developers are busy creating a special nightclub district that will feature a mix of six to eight spots providing wholesome entertainment for the entire family. The square is being fashioned after the popular Church Street Station in Orlando, Florida, and Pleasure Island at Disney World. One cover charge will allow patrons entry to all of the clubs in the Square. Broadway hopes to have a wide variety of live entertainment to include beach and shag music, country, blues, jazz and piano "sing-alongs." A **Hard Rock Cafe** designed to replicate an Egyptian pyramid also will be part of Celebrity Square.

The Coastal Aquarium of the Carolinas

Plans to open a 95,000-square-foot aquatic attraction were unveiled in October 1994. This $30 million aquarium, slated to open in 1997, will be designed by a world-class team of aquatic experts.

Family Amusement Area

A 20,000-square-foot enclosed family amusement center is planned to include Midway games of skill, video games, preschool educational areas and babysitting services. There will also be an 18-hole miniature golf course.

The Dining District

Opening in May 1995, the dining district will be one of the first phases of Broadway at the Beach to open. Located at the northern end of the lake, world-class restaurants will be invited to join the complex, but only after careful screening, according to developers. Here are those hopefuls that have passed the "acid-saliva" test so far. Country musician Mickey Gilley will serve up Southwestern cuisine from his **Gilley's Texas Cafe,** a restaurant designed to show a small airplane crashing into its side. **Liberty Steakhouse and Brewery** will be the Southeast's largest BrewPub, a combination restaurant and micro-brewery. Freshly made beers will be served each day, and visitors will be able to observe brewmeisters at work. The menu for the BrewPub includes specialty cuts of beef and unique appetizers. **Tripps** will be a casual restaurant decorated with photo collages of destinations around the country. Tripps is known for its open and airy decor, fresh seafood dishes, Black Angus steaks and prime rib. A local favorite for years, **The Crab House** will join Broadway and offer its popular "all-u-can-eat salad and raw bar" filled with freshly shucked oysters and clams, cold steamed shrimp and crab. Judged the "best ribs in America" by an international panel at a rib cook-off, **Tony Roma's - A Place For Ribs** will be here to serve up its award-winning baby back ribs. **Key West Grill & Raw Bar** will also join Broadway, bringing specialty fresh seafood, a tropical setting and rave reviews for its daily, "Charter Captain's Catch of the Day." If you have a penchant for the Orient, **Yamato Steak House of Japan** will be on hand with hibachi chefs trained in showmanship as well as Japanese cooking. Yamato's will also have a sushi bar. Featuring authentic artifacts collected from both sides of the border, **Ocho Cafe** is a real South Texas bordertown restaurant with a menu of homemade enchiladas, sizzling fajitas and freshly made chips and salsa. Broadway will be first South Carolina location for **Landry's Seafood House,** a nationally acclaimed restaurant specializing in a wide variety of seafood items and sig-

Insiders' Tips

You should book your tickets for special shows — performed only at Christmas or on other holidays — at least six months in advance.

Photo: Fantasy Harbour

Euro Circus features more than 40 Russian and Urkranian entertainers under the Big Top.

nature sauces. And **Grandma's Saloon & Deli**, known for serving generous portions of food with a distinctly Italian flavor, will offer its award-winning onion rings and will feature surrounding collectibles and a general store. **Benito's Brick Oven Pizza & Pasta** announced plans to join Broadway in March 1995, specializing in traditional Italian dishes with an authentic wood-fired flavor. The Pizza Del Pescatore topped with baby clams, shrimp, garlic, olive oil and mozzarella promises to be a hit.

Medieval Times Dinner & Tournament

Fantasy Harbour (Behind Waccamaw Pottery)

Scheduled to open in late spring or early summer of 1995, Medieval Times is family entertainment from the Middle Ages when the Lord of the castle would invite a thousand friends, neighbors and foes to a feast and royal tournament. Guests should expect to eat without utensils and experience horsemanship, swordplay, falconry, sorcery and romance. The evening's highlight is an authentic jousting match between six brave Knights of the Realm. A cash bar will be available. (See our Kidstuff chapter for more information.)

Ronnie Milsap Theatre

Fantasy Harbour (Behind Waccamaw Pottery)

In January 1995, Fantasy Harbour officials announced that Ronnie Milsap would headline their newest music theater scheduled to open in late August 1995. This venue strays from the mostly country music productions of large theaters in town. Counting on Milsap's true pop-crossover act, the $8.5 million theater will seat 2,000. A six-time Grammy winner, Milsap will hold the fort at his namesake theater about 30 weeks a year; concerts by guest performers will fill the remaining dates.

Photo: The Sun Newsd

In the warm summer months, there's nothing like a trip to an area water park to cool off.

Inside **Attractions**

Life along the Grand Strand has rhythm like fast cars on wide open freeways. Here, your concern will never be what to do, but how to do it all. For as long as you linger along our coast, you'll be amused and entertained and seduced and surprised . . . virtually exhausted with a king-size inventory of possibilities. Attractions include everything you would expect in a bustling resort city as well as some things you might be surprised to discover. There are ever-expanding amusement parks and water parks; there are nature centers, lovely old gardens, museums and zoos; there are acres of razzle-dazzle race car tracks, bumper boats and arcades; there are far more miniature golf, driving ranges and par 3 courses than you could possibly play. If you have kids, or just want to feel like a kid, be sure to peruse the Kidstuff chapter; it's filled with neat stuff we didn't list in this chapter. Here are a few suggestions to get you started. Pick your pleasure.

Amusement Parks

Unlike family entertainment attractions such as Disney World and Six Flags, Myrtle Beach area amusement parks do not impose a "gate fee;" you can hang out with the kids and people-watch to your hearts content. You only pay to ride the rides.

Myrtle Beach Pavilion Amusement Park

812 N. Ocean Blvd.
Myrtle Beach *448-6456*

In the very heart of downtown Myrtle Beach, the Pavilion has been the area's No. 1 family attraction for more than 40 years. In the last few years, the park has spent $10 million on new rides, expansions and renovations. Covering 11 acres, the Pavilion now offers more than 35 rides to delight young and old. An exciting addition is the Hydro Surge, an 1,100-foot whitewater rafting experience that recreates the excitement of rafting down a wild river in an eight-person raft. Another new ride, the Typhoon Plunge, sends you plummeting down 40 feet of hairpin twists, fast turns and heart-in-your-throat drops. A double-looping corkscrew coaster is breathtaking too. The new Pavilion Grand Prix Road Course, a 900-foot-long go-cart course, allows the young and the young-at-heart to test their driving skills on sharp turns and straightaways. Lots of giggles await the littlest family members in two separate kiddie areas, one of which showcases the gentle beasts of a turn-of-the-century Merry-go-round. Food booths abound at every corner, tempting you with all the goodies you loved as a kid — soft drinks, snow cones, hot dogs, corn dogs, hand-dipped ice cream and that wonderfully sticky, sweet-smelling confection called cotton candy.

The Pavilion area includes the amusement park, a much-loved boardwalk along the ocean and an alcohol-free teenagers' dance club, The Attic (see our Nightlife chapter). Recent renovations have doubled the size of the parking deck.

All-day passes are $18.25 for adults

and $11.75 for children shorter than 42 inches. Individual tickets are 50¢, and each ride takes about two to seven tickets. The Pavilion is open from early-March through the end of October. The park is open only on weekends until April and then every day through September. In October, the park is open on weekends. Operating hours are 1 PM to midnight.

Family Kingdom

Third Ave. S. and Ocean Blvd.
Myrtle Beach *626-3447*

Take your pick — South Carolina's largest roller coaster or largest Ferris wheel — Family Kingdom is home to both. The Swamp Fox Roller Coaster is a great wooden classic with an astounding "wish I hadn't eaten that hot dog" 62-foot drop. The view from atop the 100-foot Ferris wheel allows a fantastic view of the coast. The Terminator ride offers a screaming, upside down, 360-degree spin, high above the ground. Children adore a miniature locomotive that chugs placidly around the grounds. Another Family Kingdom highlight is an antique carousel with exquisite hand-carved horses and chariots; it was built in Germantown, Pennsylvania, in 1932. Other attractions include go-carts, bumper cars and the Express Himalaya.

Arcade games include an oceanfront Grand Slam Batting Cage, video machines and carnival-type games. If hunger strikes, you'll enjoy pizza, hamburgers, ice cream and lemonade. At the time of this writing, day passes were $10.95, but call in advance as they are apt to change. Individual tickets are 45¢, and most rides take two to five tickets. Family Kingdom is open March through October or November. Operating hours vary, depending on the season.

Fun Spot Action Park

500 S. Ocean Blvd.
Myrtle Beach *448-5716*

Fun Spot has been billed as "The coast's most exciting Action Park . . . and Myrtle Beach's Maximum Action Attraction." This park will put you in the driver's seat of a custom-designed go-cart on a number of different and exciting tracks. The Super Eight Track, a multi-level, nine-turn course with hairpin curves features Myrtle Beach's only eight-horsepower carts. On the Family Track, two-seater carts allow a parent and child to share a spin. The Road Course doubles over and under. By the way, no formal license is required. The action park also features Bumper Cars, Bumper Boats, a Space Walk, Ferris wheel, carousel, Kiddie Cars and several other attractions for the little ones. Fun Spot rides range from $1 to $5. The action park is open daily from March to November. Operating hours vary, depending on the season.

Garden City Pavilion & Funland Arcade

103 Atlantic Ave.
Garden City *651-2770*

In the relatively quiet section of Garden City is the Garden City Pavilion &

Insiders' Tips

Don't dare miss Brookgreen Gardens during spring when the azaleas and dogwoods and atamasco lilies are blooming. Don't even bother to pack a picnic; they sell pre-made baskets at Brookgreen's Terrace Cafe!

Miniature golf is a treat for the entire family. You'll find dozens of courses along the Strand.

Funland Arcade. Featuring the neon and clamor of more than 100 arcade games, this little gem feels like old-fashioned vacation fun time. Within walking distance, there is a batting cage, other carnival-type games, ice cream, snow cones, popcorn and hot dog booths and several souvenir shops.

Myrtle Beach Grand Prix

3201 S. Kings Hwy.
Myrtle Beach 238-4783

North Myrtle Beach Grand Prix

U.S 17 S., Windy Hill
North Myrtle Beach 272-6010

With two locations on the Grand Strand, The Grand Prixes offer more than 50 acres of family entertainment. From Kiddie rides to Formula 1 race cars, speed racers and go-carts, Grand Prix is a must-see option for most of the Strand's experienced vacationers. An impressive variety of vehicles includes Grand Prix go-carts, mini Ferraris, Jeeps and Corvettes that can be maneuvered on a variety of tracks for high performance fun. A few of the most challenging tracks require licensed drivers; however, there is plenty of racing excitement available for all ages. Both parks also offer miniature golf courses and water race parks with bumper boats. The south park boasts speed boats and the East Coast's only Hydro-Fighter. The North location has a complete Kiddie Park with rides that include Dinosaurs, a Car Carrousel and a merry-go-round. Air-conditioned arcades and snack bars are provided at both locations. Tickets range from $2 to $5.50 per ride. Parking is free. In summer, the gates are open from 10 AM until about 11 PM or midnight. Hours vary during other seasons, so call ahead for details.

Water Parks

Leave the sand-scrubbed beach behind and mosey along to a wild and wicked collection of waterpark rides and slides. Food concessions are available at all parks, as are lockers and clean facilities.

Myrtle Waves

1001 10th N. (off U.S. 17 Bypass)
Myrtle Beach *448-1026*

As they're fond of saying at Myrtle Waves, "Get set to get wet" on 20 acres of water rides and slides. The Carolinas' largest water park is also the tallest; Turbo Twisters is a 10-story, lightening-fast ride that plunges through the dark . . . an experience that's nothing shy of awesome. With 30 rides and attractions, Myrtle Waves is proudly staffed by professionally certified lifeguards. Let's wade through a couple of additional features: The just-for-kids Tadpool, only 18 inches deep, includes a Little Dipper Slide and the Magic Mushroom water fountain. The Lazy River serves up a cool and relaxing opportunity to float along a designated course and soak up a little Carolina sunshine. Picking up the pace is no problem on Snake Mountain, Pipeline Plunge or Ricochet Rapids — all heart-in-your-throat water slides. Only the adventuresome venture to the Riptide Rocket, two body flumes that send you blasting.

Myrtle Waves also boasts its own Ocean In Motion Wave Pool. Simulated waves are generated by specially designed wave-making machinery. Alas, no surfing allowed. Food concessions are available, and there's a picnic area too. Footwear is suggested, aqua-shoes or sandals, but not required. Adult admission is $16.49 and $9.99 for children less than 42 inches tall. Senior citizens pay the children's rate. A seven-day pass is $21.99. The park is open from May through mid-September. Operating hours are 10 AM to 5 PM from May 1 to June 4 and August 29 to September 19. From June 5 to August 28 the park is open 10 AM to 7 PM.

Wild Rapids Water Park & Pavilion

301 Third Ave. and S. Ocean Blvd.
Myrtle Beach *448-6065*

In addition to a fabulous oceanfront location in the center of Myrtle Beach, Wild Rapids features several big slides and tube rides for fun that's wet and wild and marvelously refreshing. A children's area is available, as well as an expansive sundeck that overlooks the wide, blue Atlantic. An arcade is underneath the park that looks like a mountain. All-day passes are $10.50 for adults and $7 for children shorter than 48 inches. The park is open daily through the summer from 10 AM to 7 PM.

Wild Water & Wheels

910 U.S. 17 S.
Surfside Beach *238-WILD*

Wally the Walrus, the goofily charming mascot of Wild Water & Wheels, wel-

Insiders' Tips

Head for Gay Dolphin on Ocean Boulevard in Myrtle Beach to find all the shark's teeth you could hope for. No one needs to know you bought them!

comes guests to this treasure chest of wild slides and careening rides. This 16-acre facility is the area's newest waterpark. This park features a tremendous variety of water rides and slides. The Dark Hole, a particularly popular ride that was chosen by *Southern Living* as the Beach's Best Scary Ride, is a fully enclosed tube ride filled with dramatic dips and twists.

A 16-foot wide Lazy River, complete with a tropical rainforest and cascading waterfalls, meanders throughout the park. The Sidewinder and Serpentine will have you twisting and turning down body flumes at truly thrilling speeds. The enclosed Twin Twisters will spin you round and round in a tunnel of water. The 65-foot-high Free Fall Cliff Dive, along with the 65-foot high Triple Dip Speed Slide, will send you scampering to the Lazy River for a rest. Wild Water & Wheels also offers Wally's Wee-Kids World, a wonderful kiddies' park with a pool, a "shipwreck," slides and more. Grownups will love the Lounge Pool; in-water lounge chairs are snooze approved, and island music is upbeat and plentiful.

Brand new for the coming summer is the Strand's first computerized, state-of-the-art Wipeout Wave Pool. This technologically advanced wave pool produces eight different kinds of waves. Boogie boarding is available. The Park also boasts six age-scaled race tracks allowing participation from toddlers to adults. An arcade, bumper boats, numerous kiddie rides, an 18-hole miniature golf course and a live Polynesian Luau & Revue round out the recreational opportunities. Admission is $15.95 per adult, $10.95 for children shorter than 42 inches; children younger than 3 are admitted free. The park opens for the season in early April and closes in mid-September. Operating hours vary until after Easter when the park is open on a daily basis from 10 AM to 7 PM.

Nature Centers

Bellefield Nature Center

U.S. 17
South of Pawleys Island *546-4623*

The Bellefield Nature Center, at the entrance to Hobcaw Barony, is operated by the Belle W. Baruch Foundation. (Bernard Baruch, famous stockbroker and confidante to famous folks like Winston Churchill and Franklin D. Roosevelt,

Brookgreen Gardens features more than 500 pieces of American figurative sculpture.

once called Hobcaw home.) The Center features displays and audiovisual programs on Hobcaw's history, coastal environments, local wildlife and the teaching and research programs of the Baruch Institutes. If you want to get a real "feel" for the animals that call our area home, stop by the center and visit the saltwater touchtank and snake displays. Audiovisual programs are also shown daily. There are no walking trails or self-guided tours, and advanced reservations are required for guided tours and special programs. The center is open year round, and admission is free. Operating hours are 10 AM to 5 PM, Monday through Friday, 1 to 5 PM on Saturday.

Waccatee Zoo

8500 Enterprise Rd. (Socastee Community)
Myrtle Beach *650-8500*

The Waccatee Zoo Farm began roughly 15 years ago as a private collection of exotic and domestic animals. Today, on a 500-acre farm in the Socastee community west of Surfside Beach, Waccatee Zoo contains more than 100 species of animals. Including a herd of miniature horses and deer; a variety of big cats such as a black leopard, a lion, cougars and tigers; a long-necked llama; long-necked ostriches; a rainbow of exotic birds; and a menagerie of monkeys, the Waccatee Zoo is a wonderful off-the-beaten-path treat for the family. The zoo has a petting area that is ideal for introducing small children to animals. Adult admission is $3. Children between the ages of 1 and 12 are admitted for $2.

Brookgreen Gardens

U.S. 17 S.
Murrells Inlet *237-4218*

There is something for everyone at Brookgreen Gardens. South of Murrells Inlet, this 9,000-acre slice of the Lowcountry is home to the finest public sculpture garden in America. Stately oaks and formal gardens provide a breathtaking backdrop for more than 500 pieces of American figurative sculpture. Brookgreen is home to a Wildlife Park that protects an abundance of native animals, and Brookgreen is a botanical garden too! A variety of distinctive gardens blend into a collection of landscapes with delights around every bend.

The property that comprises Brookgreen Gardens once flourished as rice plantations. Designated a National Historic Landmark, Brookgreen's history is awash in famous faces. "Swamp Fox," Francis Marion, the South's much-loved and legendary guerrilla leader, plied its waterways during the American Revolution. Washington Allston, celebrated painter of the Romantic period, was born on Brookgreen Plantation in 1779. In April of 1791, George Washington enjoyed an overnight stay at Brookgreen. Theodosia Alston, daughter of Aaron Burr and wife of South Carolina Governor Joseph Alston, made her home at The Oaks Plantation until her tragic disappearance at sea in 1813. Carolina Golden Big Grain rice, which played a central role in early Southern economy, was discovered and cultivated at Brookgreen. And, the Pulitzer Prize-winning author Julia Peterkin used the plantations as a backdrop for several of the novels she published in the 1920s.

Brookgreen Gardens' visionary founders, Archer and Anna Hyatt Huntington, first visited the property in 1929. They were captivated by the Carolina Lowcountry's undulating rivers and shadowy swamplands, sandy pine forests, sweeping marsh vistas and stately moss-scarved oaks. And so, the railroad magnate and his beloved sculptress wife bought Brookgreen and three adjoining plantations, amassing nearly 10,000 acres of forest, swamp, ricefields and beachfront. Originally, their plan was simply to establish a winter home overlooking the Atlantic, but the beauty and history of the land quickly transformed their modest intention into something far more grand. And in 1931 they organized a nonprofit institution with a lofty mission — preserving habitats for native plants and animals while providing an outdoor showcase for American figurative sculpture.

Among the most impressive features of the gardens is an avenue of massive 225-year-old oak trees with branches that drip Spanish moss. The antebellum home, which stood at the end of this avenue, burned in 1901. The original kitchen has been restored as a small museum displaying plantation tools and utensils.

Adjacent to the gardens, a wildlife park thrives, home to many animals native to the region. An aviary provides visitors an opportunity to see egrets, herons, ducks and other waterfowl in their natural habitat.

You can drive your car to Brookgreen's brand new visitors' center and then walk through the gardens. A 10-minute orientation film is available and is definitely worth seeing. Sandwiches and other light lunch items are available at The Terrace Cafe. A new gift shop, showcasing its own greenhouse, is a veritable treasure chest of unique items.

Picnic areas are available for family outings. Brookgreen Gardens is completely accessible to handicapped individuals; wheelchairs are provided. Brookgreen Gardens is open daily (except Christmas Day) from 9:30 AM to 5:30 PM. Admission is $6.50 for adults and $3 for children. Children younger than 6 are admitted free.

Museums

Hopsewee Plantation

U.S. 17 S.
South of Georgetown 546-7891

As you climb the steps to this stately Georgian house, you might be struck by the urge to ask for a Mint Julep or to inquire about the "mighty wharam weather." The house, c. 1740, is the birthplace of Thomas Lynch Jr. who signed the Declaration of Independence. The house is open to the public early March through early November on Tuesday, Wednesday, Thursday and Friday from 10 AM to 4 PM. Other times are available by appointment. A nominal admission fee is charged, $5 for adults and $2 for children between the ages of 5 and 17.

Horry County Museum

438 Main St. 248-1542
Conway 626-1282

The name of the Horry County Mu-

Insiders' Tips

One of the most interesting "attractions" on the entire Strand is "people-watching" on Ocean Boulevard near the Myrtle Beach Pavilion.

seum is a bit misleading in that it showcases not only Horry County history but much of the surrounding area's history as well. You'll find a variety of informative displays, interesting artifacts, old photographs, life-size animal specimens, scale models and memorabilia galore.

Originally a post office, the building stands on what was formerly the grounds of a historic home. Just outside the museum, the twisted arms of the stately old Wade Hampton oak welcomes visitors. A plaque on the oak commemorates the day in 1876 when Confederate Gen. Wade Hampton brought his campaign for the governorship to Conway and addressed the residents from beneath the tree. Many years later, when construction of a railroad threatened the historic oak, a spirited local lady, Mary Beaty, brandished a loaded shotgun and ordered workers, "Touch not a single bough." Her defiance inspired other residents to actively protect the town's magnificent live oaks.

Start your self-guided museum tour by ambling among display cases filled with wildlife specimens. One fascinating display, a favorite of young and old, offers the opportunity to stand face to face with an incredible black bear family. Papa bear, tipping the scale at 300 pounds, was actually hit by a car on U.S. 501 many years ago. Papa represents an estimated population of 400 black bears that still call the less developed areas of Horry County home. How's that for learning something new!?

Other exhibits feature birds of prey such as owls, hawks, osprey and heron, as well as a 400-pound, 11-foot alligator. A Bats of South Carolina display showcases striking color photos, informative write-ups and lots of interesting trivia about how these often maligned creatures are portrayed in folklore and mythology. Did you know, for example, that African folklore teaches that bats are vehicles for the souls of witches?

The area that now flourishes with tourist-related activities was once a major supplier of the turpentine, rosin, tar and pitch that was so vital to the colonies burgeoning ship-building industry. Resources of the Land, a three-dimensional exhibit, brims with photos and scale models of naval stores produced in the area in the 1700s. Loggers and Locomotive boasts nearly life-size images of loggers, wagons and other lumber-related subjects. Antiquated logging equipment is also on display. It's truly fascinating to see how much life has changed.

For another surprise, be sure to peruse the exhibit on Native Americans of the Coastal Plains. Displays feature tools, arrowheads and other artifacts, along with models that recreate the intricacies of the Indians' daily existence.

There is no admission charge, and the museum is open 10 AM to 5 PM, Monday through Saturday.

Myrtle Beach National Wax Museum

1000 N. Ocean Blvd.
Myrtle Beach *448-9921*

The museum houses about 30 life-size scenes ranging from historical events recreating the Last Supper and the war in Vietnam to figures that immortalize the likes of Elvis and Abraham Lincoln. The self-guided tour takes about 30 minutes and includes a haunted house segment for a scary finish. Call ahead for prices and hours of operation.

Rice Museum

Front St.
Georgetown *546-7423*

The Rice Museum, in a beautifully renovated section of downtown Georgetown, offers a concise and fascinating overview of the society that flourished around the cultivation of rice. Old maps, dioramas, artifacts and a 17-minute video give the visitor an intriguing glimpse into the past . . . into a history that literally changed the face of this country. A changing exhibit gallery provides topical exhibits of art and history on a revolving basis.

The building itself was erected as a two-story structure in 1842 and is known locally as the "Town Clock" because of the clock faces on all four sides of its bell tower. Over a century and a half the building that originally served as a hardware store has evolved from two to three stories. In 1878, a rear addition was added, and the facade of the building was remodeled. In 1989, a renovation to the first floor earned The Rice Museum the coveted Superior Renovation Award presented by the American Institute of Architects. And the evolution continues. Currently renovations are under way on the second and third floors. When complete, the second floor will include a small theater, rice exhibits and an area dedicated to African-American history. On the third floor, the actual frame of a ship built in the early 1700s, the Browns Ferry Vessel, will be exhibited.

Tickets are $2 for adults. Students and children are admitted free. It's open Monday through Saturday from 9:30 AM to 4:30 PM and is closed on major holidays.

Ripley's Believe It or Not! Museum

901 N. Ocean Blvd.
Myrtle Beach *626-2168*

Explorer and cartoonist Robert Ripley has put together a bizarre collection of human oddities, amazing artifacts and displays of the unbelievable, including a two-headed calf, shrunken heads from Ecuador and a man who could put three golf balls in his mouth and whistle at the same time. Check out the replica of Cleopatra's barge made entirely out of confectioners sugar — the ship's detailing is incredibly "delicious." You can take your time on a self-guided tour of the more than 500 exhibits situtated throughout the two-story museum. By the way, don't let the outward appearance of the building's "cracked" structure fool you; though the building looks as if an earthquake has wreaked havoc, it's just part of the decor. Adult tickets are $7; tickets for children ages

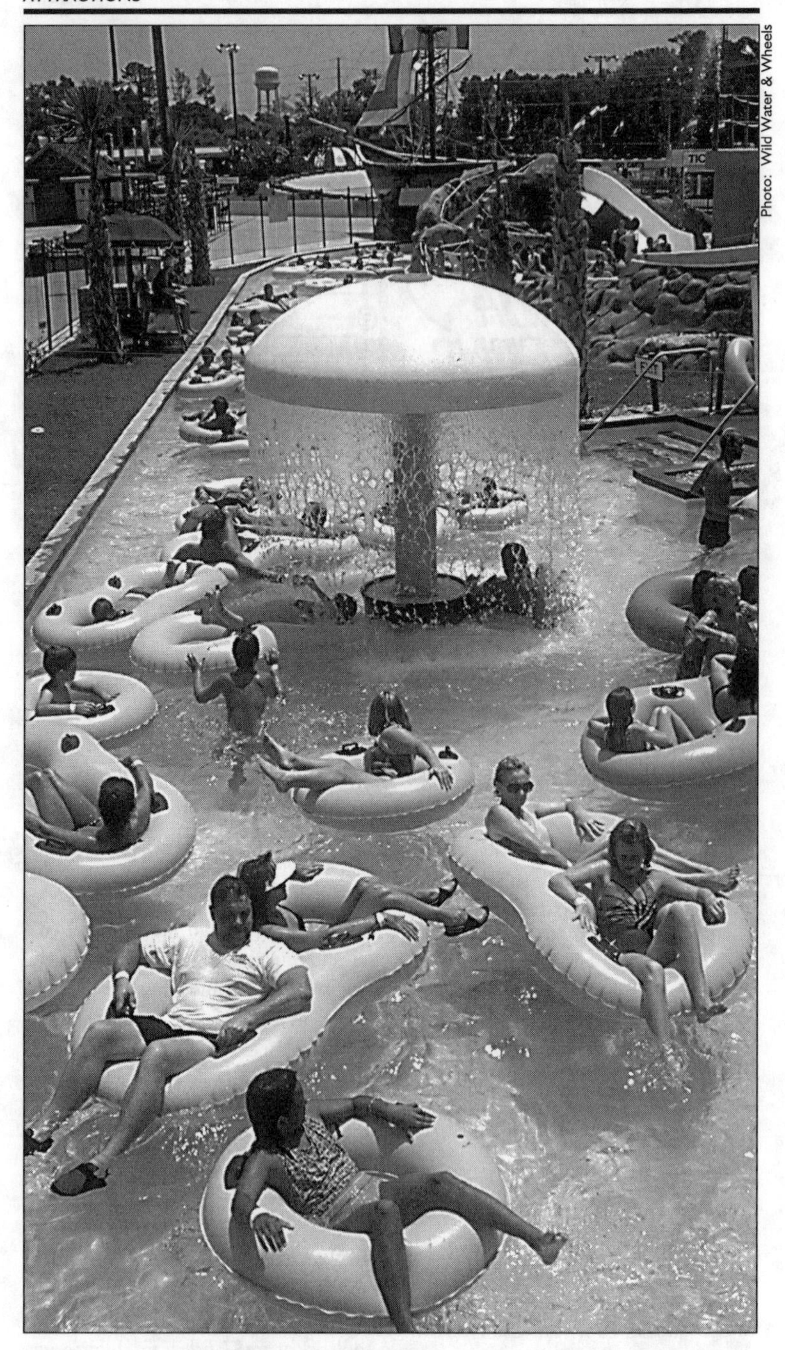

Photo: Wild Water & Wheels

Floating in the Lazy River is a popular way to spend a sunny day on the Strand.

6 to 12 are $4.50 each; children 5 and younger are admitted free. Ripley's is open year round. In the summer, hours are 10 AM to 10 PM. Off-season hours vary, so call ahead for specifics.

South Carolina Hall of Fame

21st Ave. N. and Oak St. at Convention Center
Myrtle Beach *448-4021*

History buffs will find the South Carolina Hall of Fame very interesting. Located within the Myrtle Beach Convention Center is an area designated for honoring South Carolinians who achieved greatness, as well as people who were born elsewhere but made significant contributions to the Palmetto state. The first induction ceremony was held in 1973. Each year, the selection committee honors one deceased and one contemporary nominee. Enshrined are famous patriots, distinguished statesmen, eight signers of the Declaration of Independence and Constitution of the United States, a Nobel Prize-winning physicist who fathered the laser beam, an astronaut who walked on the surface of the moon, a teacher who spent a lifetime trying to overcome ignorance and illiteracy and a doctor noted for his fighting of public apathy to the plight of the mentally ill. Portraits of each inductee are accompanied by a written biography.

Admission is free, and the Convention Center is open Monday through Friday 9 AM to 5 PM.

Whaling Wall

21st Ave. N. and Oak St. at Convention Center
Myrtle Beach *448-4021*

Internationally acclaimed environmental artist Wyland chose Myrtle Beach to paint one of his famous "Whaling Walls." On the Convention Center's exterior northeast wall, the breathtaking painting measures 240-feet wide by 36-feet high. The mural features life-size renderings of whales and other marine species within the beauty of their own habitat. The blue hues are indescribable. It's a delight to see, and there's no admission fee!

Miniature Golf

Forget about tee-times, golf cart fees and buckets of lost balls! By playing any one of dozens of miniature golf courses, driving ranges or par 3 courses along the Grand Strand, you can enjoy spirited competition and the joy of sinking a hole-in-one without breaking the budget or slicing away a five-hour chunk of daylight. Actually, playing miniature golf might be even more challenging than a professional course. After all, how many long-necked llamas, bearded pirates or spooky caves have you tripped over on a fairway lately?

Several miniature courses are already listed with amusement parks as complete properties. Most courses are open from 9 AM to midnight and have snack bars or cold drink machines. Admission ranges from $3 to $7 per putter. Special prices are offered for all-day play, which means you can play for a while and then come back later to play some more.

North Strand

Aladdin's Magic Springs

U.S. 17 and 43rd Ave. S., Windy Hill
North Myrtle Beach *272-0952*

This course setting is filled with oversize animal statues and waterfalls. Aladdin's has 27 holes on two courses and offers discounts to children, senior citizens and groups. All-day play ends at 6 PM.

Bermuda Greens

601 Main St.
North Myrtle Beach *249-9848*

This course is for golfers who really

want to work on their putting. You won't find any dinosaurs, giraffes or windmills here, but there are plenty of sand traps, grass bunkers and water hazards. Two par-70 18-hole courses feature Bermuda putting greens, just like you'd find on regulation golf courses. All-day play ends at 6 PM.

Pelican Point

4600 U.S. 17 S., Windy Hill
North Myrtle Beach *272-8247*

Natural shading from trees and waterfalls provides a nice setting for this 18-hole course. All-day play ends at 6 PM.

River Country

Sea Mountain Hwy. (S.C. 9)
North Myrtle Beach *249-82273*

Animals "roam" on this 18-hole course. All-day play is available until 6 PM.

Rainbow Falls

9850 U.S. 17 (Restaurant Row area)
Myrtle Beach *497-2557*

Tricky corners, animal caves and fairytale castles make up 36 holes of these two courses. One or two uphill holes could throw your game. Special rates are offered to groups and children 3 and younger. All-day play is available until 5 PM.

Myrtle Beach

Captain Hook

21st Ave. N. and Kings Hwy.
Myrtle Beach *626-1430*

Marked by a haunting Skull Cave, waterfalls, lagoons and swinging bridges, this 36-hole course is one of the newest additions to the area's miniature golf lineup. Players can choose the Lost Boys' Course or the more challenging Hook's Course, which has uphill shots and includes water holes and sand traps.

Jungle Golf

71st Ave. N. and Kings Hwy.
Myrtle Beach *449-4831*

True to its name, this 18-hole course is themed with jungle objects. Its most distinctive feature is live animals. Don't panic, there's nothing like lions and tigers and big black bears, but there are miniature horses, pygmy goats, African gray geese and a monkey. The kids will love it. Senior citizen discounts are available. All-day play ends at 6 PM.

Jungle Lagoon

Fifth Ave. S. and Kings Hwy.
Myrtle Beach *626-7894*

In this tropical jungle setting you may wish you had a machete instead of a putter. There are lots of uphill shots and fast downhill curves and angles on two courses that feature a total of 36 holes. Special rates are offered for children 5 and younger. All-day play is available.

Noah's Ark Golf

29th Ave. S. and Kings Hwy.
Myrtle Beach *448-2116*

You guessed it — oodles of animals, two by two. Choose from two

Insiders' Tips

To avoid the crowds at off-ocean amusements, go early in the morning while most folks are sleeping or sunning.

18-hole courses. Discounts are offered to children 5 and younger. All day play ends at 5 PM.

Pirates Watch

1500 S. Kings Hwy.
Myrtle Beach *448-8600*

Enjoy 36 holes brimming with action-packed waterfalls, scary pirates, water traps and lagoons. All-day play is offered until 5 PM.

SpyGlass

3800 17 N. Kings Hwy.
Myrtle Beach *626-9309*

This 18-hole course has a fun degree of difficulty and offers discounts to senior citizens, children and groups. Waterfalls, uphill holes and those bloody pirates are the main obstacles. All day play ends at 6 PM.

Treasure Island

48th Ave. N.
Myrtle Beach *449-4754*

A hole-in-one is not easy to come by on this 18-hole course, but the play at Treasure Island is definitely worth the challenge. Discounts are available for senior citizens, children and groups. All-day play ends at 6 PM.

South Strand

Adventure Falls

735 U.S. 17
Surfside Beach *238-0168*

Animals and castles overlook the 36 holes of two courses. Groups and children are offered discounts, and all-day play ends at 5 PM.

Buccaneer Bay

6001 U.S. 17 S.
Surfside Beach *238-3811*

Two courses — 36 holes, filled with pirates and big boats — will make you ache to walk the plank. Several holes feature difficult angles and tricky obstacles. All-day play ends at 5 PM.

Inlet Adventure

3215 U.S. 17 S.
Murrells Inlet *651-0048*

Easy angles and slopes make the 18 holes at this course very pleasurable to play. Discounts are available, and all-day play ends at 6 PM.

Golf Driving Ranges

Cane Patch

72nd Ave. N.
Myrtle Beach *449-2732*

Practice your swing year round starting at 8 AM. The range is also lighted for night practice. All you need is a club and putter, which are furnished. Buckets are $3 for 45 golf balls, $4 for 75 and $6 for 115.

Gator Hole

U.S. 17
North Myrtle Beach *249-6583*

Golfers will need drivers and irons for this range, which is also lighted for night play. It's open from 8 AM until. Buckets are $2.50 for 35 golf balls and $3.50 for 55.

Harbor Light

701 U.S. 17 N.
Surfside Beach *238-8978*

The tees at Harbor Light are covered. Buckets are $5 for about 70 to 75 golf balls. The range is lighted for night practice. During the summer season the range is open 8 AM to 11 PM but closes earlier in the winter.

Midway

29th Ave. S. and Ocean Blvd.
Myrtle Beach *448-6137*

Buckets are $3 for 45 golf balls, $4 for 75 and $6 for 115. The range is also lighted for night practice, and it is open from 8 AM until . . . depending on the season.

Par 3 Courses

Cane Patch

72nd Ave. N.
Myrtle Beach *449-2732*

Three nine-hole courses are available. For nine holes the cost is $6, and 18 holes is $9.

Golf Hill

4600 U.S. 17 S.
North Myrtle Beach *272-8505*

This course offers nine lighted holes and is open year round. The cost is $7 per player. At certain times of the year, all-day rates are available.

Midway

29th Ave. S. and Ocean Blvd.
Myrtle Beach *448-4713*

This 27-hole course is open year round. Costs vary, depending on the time of year, but are comparable to other par 3s in the area.

Inside Kidstuff

Pardon us for stating the obvious, but our sun-splashed shoreline is still the Strand's first and finest lure for the kid in all of us. What faster track to vacation paradise than spending long lazy days shaping castles of sand, collecting shells, riding waves warmed by the sun or watching a family of dolphins frolic on the horizon? Sleeping 'neath a hypnotizing flood of sunlight is a delicious option too, as is renting a jet ski or a big canvas float, initiating a game of paddleball, perfecting a Frisbee toss or simply enjoying the feel of sand between your toes. No doubt about it, for your kids and for the kid in you, the beach itself offers more than a handful of wonderful ways to while away a holiday.

And away from the ocean, life holds one sweet, unpredictable choice after another. Make a big splash with the family at one of a splendid array of water parks. While there are several to choose from, each boasts a bevy of thrill-a-minute wet-and-wild rides and slides. For other "watery" options, consider the inky ribbon of the Intracoastal Waterway and the Waccamaw River, scores of mystery-shrouded, serpentine creeks and wide, open marshes. (See our Watersports chapter.) Mosey to the Myrtle Beach Pavilion or any one of the area's theme parks. We've got race car tracks, bumper boats, roller coasters, fast rides, slow rides, tried-and-true to inventive and brand new. (See our Attractions chapter.) Stroll Ocean Boulevard and squirrel away the kids in a shady arcade; watch them revel in tests of eye-hand coordination at one of a jillion games. The boulevard is perfect, too, for stocking up on souvenirs and watching candymakers at work; for eating ice cream, cotton candy and hot dogs; for personalizing a T-shirt; for touring a wacky museum and more . . . much more.

There's bowling and movies and miniature golf. There's skating and dancing and racing and diving. It's plain to see, for kids of all ages, Myrtle Beach and the entire Grand Strand is certain to serve up a vacation that will be everything you imagined.

Be sure to scan the Watersports, Attractions and Parks and Recreation chapters for cool stuff we didn't list or detail here.

For additional information about amusement and water parks, see our Attractions chapter.

Amusements

Aggie Gray

8500 Enterprise Rd.
Myrtle Beach *238-0168*

See the beautiful South Carolina Lowcountry and enjoy a narrated historical tour of the Waccamaw River aboard the 51-foot aluminum riverboat *Aggie Gray*. Spend a few fun-filled hours at the Waccatee Zoo (see the subsequent listing in this chapter, as well as our Attractions chapter) before boarding and heading south. The tour lasts about 50 minutes and covers approximately 6 miles. The *Aggie Gray* is licensed by the Coast Guard to carry 49 passengers — the open upper deck seats up to 29, while the enclosed lower deck is adequate for all 49 passengers in case of inclement weather. It's equipped with a restroom, and soft drinks are available. Rates are $6 for adults and $3 for children 6 through 16. Children younger than 6 are admitted free. Please call ahead for schedules.

Aladdin's Bankshot Basketball

4205 U.S. 17 S.
North Myrtle Beach 272-0952

Bankshot Basketball is a fast-growing family sport that originated in Israel. The game involves neither running or contact, and players need not be equivalent in ability to play together. It can be played solo or in groups, competitively or just for fun, by absolutely everyone, even handicapped individuals. No specialized equipment is necessary.

The game is similar in concept to miniature golf. Played with a conventional basketball and rims, Bankshot Basketball uses unconventionally configured backboards at 19 different stations with a number of opportunities to make each goal. Each station requires its own shooting "strategy," and each player shoots a total of 111 times. The cost is $3 per game.

Beamers

1101 N. Ocean Blvd.
Myrtle Beach 448-1900

This high-tech, futuristic interpretation of "Tag, you're out!" is the area's only laser tag game, one that has enjoyed huge success for a number of years. Armed only with a laser gun, from two to 60 participants at a time dodge and zap each other in a 5,000-square-foot playing arena that's illuminated by black light. The object is to make it to the enemy line without being hit. Glow-in-the-dark shields provide protection while players implement their strategies for eliminating opponents. Wear comfortable clothing and rubber-soled shoes (also for comfort). Tickets are $6.50 per person for 20 minutes of play. Beamers is open 10 AM to 2 AM every day of the week from June to September. From March through June, hours depend on Boulevard traffic. Call ahead for specific times.

Euro Circus

U.S. 501 (at Fantasy Harbour)
Myrtle Beach 236-3876

Euro Circus spotlights 45 Russian and Ukrainian superstars from the Moscow Circus. (See our Entertainment Explosion chapter.) The show also includes 10 charming and amazingly talented Russian children. Since unlocking the doors for the very first time, these circus professionals have roused crowds with a variety

Insiders' Tips

Check vacation guide magazines for coupons to lots of restaurants and attractions.

Photo: The Sun News

Building sandcastles is a favorite activity for many vacationers. Myrtle Beach once held the record for the longest sand castle.

of fun-filled and gravity-defying acts. Talent on parade includes the requisite funny-faced clowns, as well as acrobats, aerialists, muscle-bound jugglers, quick-change artists, one of the most accomplished teeter board acts in the entire circus world and an unusual performance by a dog and cat team. Truly "fantasy-like" . . . complete with music and lights and breathtaking demonstrations of talent and bravado, Euro Circus is held in an enormous and beautiful, climate-controlled "big top" reminiscent of childhood circus fantasies. Far cooler and more comfortable than the circus tents of yesteryear, this tent was purchased from the Mirage Hotel and Casino in Las Vegas, where it housed the famed Cirque du Soleil. The $1.4 million vinyl structure is flameproof and strong enough to withstand hurricane-force winds. Admission is $14.95 for adults and $12.95 for children 12 and younger.

Fant-A-Sea Wheels

700 U.S. 17 N.
Surfside Beach *238-0409*

Nothing like a good ole skating rink to bring out the kid in all of us! This one's new and better than anything you can remember. Circle the floor on traditional roller skates or — if you're a bit more hip — the in-line skates that are currently all the rage. While skating, pause for a moment to peer into one of the seven 125-gallon aquariums that take center stage. When you get tired, there's a snack bar and an arcade for refueling. This place is fun. Really fun. And we think it's high time skating made a comeback! There are a variety of special sessions like Thursday's Adult Night. Family day is Sunday, when a family of four can get in for just $6. Now that's value! Costs vary per session, but it's usually around $5. Call ahead if you'd like more information.

Photo: Fantasy Harbour

Euro Circus opened in 1994 and has been delighting crowds ever since.

SKATE ESCAPE

3800 N. Kings Hwy.
Myrtle Beach *448-7465*

We are delighted that skating's back in style. Escape showcases a 9,000-square-foot rink, a snack bar and a to-die-for arcade with more than 30 of the latest games. Skate equipment, speed, in-line and traditional skates, can be rented at reasonable prices, and skating lessons are available. If you're a local, you might want to sign up for a roller hockey league. A skate shop sells equipment and skate memorabilia. There are all kinds of special sessions from "Mom's Morning Skate" (great exercise!) to "Matinee Skate." Depending on the session you choose, rates vary from $3.25 to $5.

GAMEMASTER USA

Between Fifth and Sixth Aves. S.
and Ocean Blvd.
Myrtle Beach *946-6641*

Kids over 12 are going to love Paintball 2000! Paintball, for those of you who don't know, is billed as the fastest growing sport in the world. Paintball combines Hide & Seek with Tag! to create a game that is much more challenging and sophisticated. Players "tag" each other with a paint-filled gelatin ball (much like a bath oil bead) fired from a CO_2-powered gun. The paint is a non-toxic, water soluble mixture of food coloring and vegetable oil.

GAMEMASTER showcases Myrtle Beach's only indoor paintball arena complete with special lighting and sound effects, fog, barricades to hide behind and a glass-enclosed viewing area. The pace is fast, and the music is loud! Choose from two exciting playing fields (comprised of more than 16,000 square feet) and a target range for those who want to play around with the guns without engaging in warfare. Don't worry about the kid's clothes; they will be provided with clothing, masks, cover-ups and paint guns.

This new sport is played in more than two dozen countries by millions of men, women and children of all professions and lifestyles. Physical size and strength are not as important as intelligence, wit and determination, so anyone can compete. As a quick aside, mommies and daddies take note: This has been called "the ultimate grudge match," so you might want to sneak in with the spouse and blow off some steam. Please call for rates.

MAYHEM MANOR

204 Ninth Ave. N.
Myrtle Beach *626-4413*

Briefly put, Mayhem Manor is a high-tech take on the ever-popular haunted house. Dr. Morphious Mayhem is reputed to have performed murderous experiments on unsuspecting beach visitors, and the mansion is said to be haunted by the doctor's many victims. High-tech twists utilize robotics that'll startle the starch out of your shirt. While this voyage into the scary unknown is loads of fun, it may be too intense for very young children. Please call ahead for rates and times.

MAZE MANIA

U.S. 17 S.
Garden City *651-1641*

Talk about a rat race! This maze is loads of fun for the whole family. Take your time card and "punch in," scurry through the mind-blowing network of paths, find the "cheese," get out quickly and "punch" the clock again. If you beat the posted time on your first attempt, you'll win a Maze Mania T-shirt. Take care not to get too confident; you can't memorize the maze because it's modified at least once a day. An outdoor course constructed on three-fourths of an acre, Maze Mania has a spacious observation deck where you can root for family and friends. There's also an arcade and a refreshment stand. Admission is $4.95 for adults and $3.95 for children 12 and younger. A ticket is good for the day, so if you get frustrated you can leave and come back later to try again. During summer, Maze Mania is open daily 10 AM to midnight. Call ahead for a schedule during other times of the year.

Motion Master Moving Theater

917 N. Ocean Blvd.
Myrtle Beach *448-2331*

As implied by its name, Motion Master is a theater that literally thrusts participants into film adventures with seats that move in eight different directions! Seats are motion-synchronized with the giant-screen action for realism that's heart-pounding, nonstop fun. Brought to you by the folks of Ripley's Believe It or Not! fame, you can be sure this pastime will keep your attention from start to finish. The cost is $5 for one ride or $8 for two rides. Take note: Your little one must be 43" tall to climb aboard.

The Railroad Crossing Toy Train Museum

835 N. Kings Hwy.
(Across from Myrtle Beach Pavilion)
Myrtle Beach *448-7330*

In the Myrtle Beach area, railroad intersections have long since been hidden beneath blankets of asphalt . . . or so we thought. Then along comes The Railroad Crossing, a delightful toy train museum and gift shop, bearing fond childhood memories and the long lost sense of wonder that was part and parcel of those old-fashioned toy trains. Featuring more than 100 model trains, The Railroad Crossing is an attraction that appeals to all ages. Bright-faced children will light up at the sight of scaled-down villages sporting fully operational trains. And grown-up kids seem softened and transformed by the reminiscent sounds and wonders of the railroad-in-miniature.

In addition to a charming gift shop, this 1,250-square-foot museum is filled with scads of railroad-related memorabilia. Antique trains dating to the early 1900s are showcased in displays that outline associated historical tidbits. Two elaborate running layouts are especially interesting. Plasticville, U.S.A., brings a 1950s town back to life. Complete with its own railroad system, grocery store, church and more, it's a bit like stepping back in time to a real city of the same name. A second layout called Mountain City, staged in the 1930s, is also decorated with handmade buildings, old-model cars and tiny human figures.

A stop at The Railroad Crossing should round out any itinerary to the Strand. The pace is decidedly slower here . . . it's a laid-back kind of fun. There is a small admission fee to the museum. Seniors get in for $3. Admission for other adults is $3.50. Children between the ages of 3 and 11 can get in for just $2.50, and wee ones younger than 3 get in for free.

Places to Eat

Since the Myrtle Beach area is famous as a family beach, the place is nearly overrun with great places to feed your hungry tykes. Nearly all restaurants cater to the younger set with special menus. Here are two kid-tested choices, and one for all ages, deemed especially likely to make everyone smile.

• Kid Code • Kid Code • Kid Code • Kid Code •

What is Kid Code?

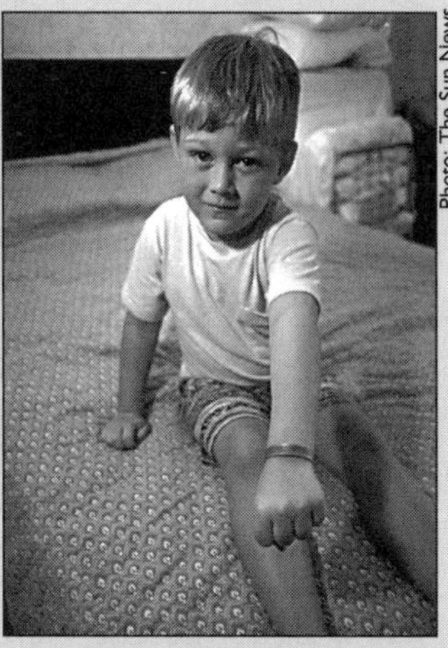

Photo: The Sun News

Kid Code uses plastic wristbands to ensure that lost kids will be able to find their hotel.

The Kid Code Program offers an ingenious system for tracking lost children. Before Kid Code, the Myrtle Beach Police Department grappled with four to 10 "lost child" calls per summer day. That adds up to hundreds of children — and a lot of fear and frustration — in a single summer season!

"A great idea . . . Can't be anything but beneficial to the people working the beaches!" —Wayne Player, Chief of Police, City of Myrtle Beach

Kid Code is a free service offered by select lodging establishments. Upon check-in, plastic wristbands are provided to younger family members. The wristbands have an emergency telephone number and a Motel ID number. If a child is lost or involved in an emergency situation, a single phone call will inform local authorities of the parents' whereabouts.

"Kid Code came through! . . . Next time we come to the beach, we will choose a hotel with Kid Code!" —Mr. & Mrs. Mike Cross, parents of the program's first lost child

For safety's sake, the information on the wrist band does not identify your child or your lodging by name. If someone other than a member of the local authorities calls, Kid Code will not interpret the Motel ID number on your child's bracelet but will contact the lodging establishment directly to advise them of your child's current location. Additionally, Kid Code will apprise the local authorities of your child's location, as well as the identity of your lodging establishment. So, if you and your child are separated, you should immediately contact your lodging establishment.

"I really believe in Kid Code. We know it works." —Marianne Smith, General Manager, Cherokee Motor Inn

Although Kid Code offers a clever system for tracking your lost child, it does not promise miracles. It is your responsibility, not the hotel's, to be sure the Kid Code ID bracelet is securely fastened to your child's wrist or ankle. Fit your child with the Kid Code bracelet as soon as you arrive, and wait until you return home to remove the band.

"Kid Code is a concept that should have been initiated a long time ago!" —Diane DeVaugh-Stokes, Cox Cable

• Kid Code • Kid Code • Kid Code • Kid Code •

Dixie Stampede

North Kings Hwy. at U.S. 17 Bypass
Myrtle Beach *497-9700*

It's always wise to pencil-in Dixie Stampede (see the Entertainment Explosion chapter) on your vacation agenda. Created by a league of talented planners, performers and all-star dreamers, Dixie Stampede is brought to you by the Dollywood Theme Park Association. For one all-inclusive admission ($24.95 for adults and $14.95 for children 4 to 11), this unique dinner attraction serves up scads of food, unlimited beverages and as much rib-ticklin' recreation as a body can stand. Even if they're too young to understand the context, kids will love the thrilling re-enactment of the North/South rivalry, complete with prancing horses, handsome heroes and fair maidens. The spectacular finale showcases no fewer than 15,000 sparkling lights. Little ones 3 and younger can enjoy the fun for free if they sit on an adult's lap and share the grown-up's meal.

Chuck E. Cheese's Pizza

615 Lake Arrowhead Rd. (Restaurant Row area)
Myrtle Beach *449-1459*

This is a longtime favorite of locals and tourists. Kids love the game room that features skill games, skee-ball, kiddie rides and other offerings that make up the more than 40 available games and attractions. Parents love the outstanding pizza, as well as sandwiches and salads. An animated show stars Mr. Cheese and Munch's Make-Believe Band. If you're visiting during the summer, don't miss the all-you-can-eat lunch buffet. For kids, this is a must-stop . . . maybe more than once.

Medieval Times

U.S. 501 (at Fantasy Harbour)
Myrtle Beach *236-8080*

Imagine the year is 1093 A.D., and you are a noble guest of the Spanish kingdom's Royal Family. The Lord of the Castle has invited more than 1,000 of his friends, neighbors and foes to enjoy the sport and splendor of a royal tournament. As you step back in time nearly a millenium, you will feast on a hearty four-course meal. You'll marvel as spirited stallions perform intricate equestrian drills, and you'll gaze in awe as fearless knights compete in daring tournament games, jousting matches and sword fights. Sound intriguing? You bet it is! In North America, there are currently six Medieval Times castles in locations from Florida to Ontario to California; all operate within the same program format, and all have been tremendously successful.

At Medieval Times (see our Entertainment Explosion chapter), the evening of quality family entertainment begins as you cross a drawbridge into the 11th century castle. Once inside, you are personally greeted by the Count and Countess of Perelada who invite you to share in a sumptuous banquet while cheering for brave knights on horseback.

Festivities begin as trumpeters herald the guests into the Grand Ceremonial Arena. Gracious serfs and wenches scurry to fill glasses and attend to the Count's honored guests who feast on succulent roasted chicken, tasty spare ribs and castle pastries. An awe-inspiring thunder of hooves fills the arena as the Master of Ceremonies leads a talented cast through a truly spectacular array of equestrian skills and medieval pageantry. Sitting proudly astride colorfully attired Andalusian horses, the valiant knights of yore face their competitors in breathtaking and authentic tournament games, including the ring pierce, the flag toss and the javelin throw.

The one-price admission includes

show, dinner and two rounds of beverages. Sales tax and gratuity are extra. Although Medieval Times was not open at press time, admission was set at $26.20 for adults and $15.70 for children 3 to 12. Tiny tots younger than 3 get in free. Reservations are suggested.

Educational Choices

Shhh! Don't tell the kids and they'll never notice! These options offer marvelously entertaining ways to marry playtime and learning.

Captain Dick's Educational Cruises

4123 U.S. 17 Bus.
Murrells Inlet *651-3676*

If you're looking for a fun and unusual activity to spice up your vacation repertoire, add "educational cruises" to your calendar. It's a painless way to include a little schooling in the typical funfest holiday. These anything-but-boring boat trips offer firsthand exposure to the vast array of plants and animals that make the salt marshes of Murrells Inlet their home. Narrated by a marine biologist, these cruises last up to 2½ hours and are restricted to the calm waters of the inlet. (No need to worry about getting seasick.) Using crab traps, bottom dredges, plankton nets and rods and reels, a collection of marsh plants and animals is produced for up-close looks and touches. During the last portion of the trip, participants can fish for samples of inlet dwellers like spot, croaker and pinfish. Cruises operate from late spring through early fall. Please call Captain Dick's Marina for current rates and schedules.

Captain Sandy's Tours

117½ Harborwalk
Georgetown *527-4106*

History, mystery and the incomparable lure of the Old South . . . the delightful Captain Sandy offers tours that are guaranteed to leave you smarter than when you arrived. Three-hour plantation tours combine fascinating historical lore with wildlife tales, as well as a ghost story or two. Shell-lovers should take the 5-hour trip to undeveloped, off-the-beaten-path Shell Island, where the selection is far removed from anything you'd find on the mainland. These tours are a perfect way to introduce the children to a beautiful, slower side of the Grand Strand. Tours are generally scheduled based on demand, and rates depend on the tour you choose, so call ahead for hours and prices. And since you'll be boarding and departing the tour along the Front Street docks in Georgetown, why not round out the day with some shopping in this shady little city on The Strand's southernmost tip?

Waccatee Zoological Farm

8500 Enterprise Rd., (Socastee Community)
Myrtle Beach *650-8500*

For kids and animal lovers, this is a not-to-be-missed opportunity to view myriad unusual animals. For more information, please see our Attractions chapter.

Carolina Safari Jeep Tours

606 65th Ave.
North Myrtle Beach *497-5330*

These tours are the first of their kind in the Lowcountry. Tour Director Virgil Graham is a magazine photographer and a naturalist, so you can look forward to more than a few unique and beautiful sites. Each specially designed tour vehicle seats 10 to 13 passengers and a tour guide "safari-style," allowing for an extensive and personalized overview of area history and local lore, as well as tons of narrative information. The itinerary includes natural coastal attractions, historic areas, old plantation homes, two islands and an unexpected abundance of natural beauty; until you've seen the natural side of the Grand Strand, you're missing something extraordinary. You'll see Atalaya, an imposing Spanish-styled castle at Huntington Beach State Park; the lovely old homes of Pawleys Island, the oldest resort area in the United States; a maritime forest, mystery-shrouded marshes, historic grave sites, nesting bald eagles and more. Binoculars are provided, but you're welcome to bring cameras; you'll likely encounter lots of photo opportunities for the vacation scrapbook. Don't worry about inclement weather; the jeeps have covers. Carolina Safari will even pick you up for one of three daily tours. Call for rates and reservations.

Brookgreen Gardens

U.S. 17 Bypass
Murrells Inlet *237-4218*

This Grand Strand landmark melds nature and history in an incomparable way. An absolute must for families with kids (and without), Brookgreen Gardens is an unequalled picnic spot. See our Attractions chapter for full details.

Inside Annual Events

With all of the entertainment options available along the Grand Strand, you will probably be amazed at this lineup of annual events, festivals, tournaments and shows. And you can well believe that even though there are 101 things for you to see and do here, these events are very well received and attended. Myrtle Beach Convention Center hosts a number of these and, while we don't provide the center's address in respective listings, we won't leave you in the dark as to its whereabouts — Oak Street and 21st Avenue N. in Myrtle Beach. Since plans can vary at any given time when coordinating such large programs, we cannot guarantee that dates, places, times and prices won't change. Keep your eyes and ears tuned to the news for current information or call the number listed to verify details. So, come on, let's get in the game and join in the fun!

January

Annual Myrtle Beach Wildlife Exposition

Late January
Myrtle Beach Convention Center 449-7272

Families can enjoy a wide variety of activities at this show. Past events have included a Buckmaster archery competition, gem mining for kids, a snake safety program led by Okefenokee Joe, live animal exhibits and fine artists and craftspeople. Proceeds from the exposition benefit the Harry R.E. Hampton Memorial Wildlife Fund to support wildlife and marine resource projects within South Carolina. Admission is $5 per day. Seniors 65 years and older and young folks 13 to 18 are eligible for a 50 percent discount. Children 12 and younger are admitted free.

Annual North Myrtle Beach Winter Run

Last Saturday in January
North Myrtle Beach 280-5570

This is the 5K and 15K road race for the Southeastern Region. Sponsored by the North Myrtle Beach Recreation Department, this competition attracts 350 to 400 entrants each year. Following the grueling race, an awards ceremony is held to recognize the top-5 overall runners and the best in each age category — up to 60 years of age! Registration is $12 to $15 and is open until the day of the race.

February

Dog Show

First weekend in February
(Friday through Sunday)
Myrtle Beach Convention Center 293-2479

More than 2,100 pooches, hailing and howling from all over the United States, were entered into this canine extravaganza last year. Three days of showing determine the appearance and standard

Photo: Charles Slate, The Sun News

The watermelon eating contest is popular during the annual Sun Fun Festival.

for each particular breed; judges select the winners and "Best in Show." Competitions start each day at 8:30 AM and continue until 6:30 PM or later. There is no cover charge to attend.

South Carolina Hall of Fame Induction Ceremony

Early February
Myrtle Beach Convention Center 626-7444

Two notable South Carolinians are inducted into this hall of fame each year, representing a gallant procession of statesmen, scientists, artists, soldiers and teachers. Inductees include President Andrew Jackson, jazz legend Dizzy Gillespie, painter Jasper Johns, General William C. Westmoreland, author Elizabeth Boatwright Coker and more than 30 others. The South Carolina flag taken to the moon by NASA astronaut Charles M. Duke Jr. is also on display. The hall is open from 9 AM to 5 PM, Monday through Friday, and admission is free.

Myrtle Beach Stamp Show

Mid-February
Holiday Inn West (Next to Waccamaw Pottery)
Myrtle Beach 347-0087

Children receive a free pack of stamps and an album to begin their stamp collecting careers at the Stamp Show. Ten dealers participate from the Southeastern region and display goods from beginner status to advanced. The United States Post Office is on hand to sell current stamps. Collections are appraised free of charge. About 600 philatelists and other enthusiasts join the fun every year. Admission is free.

KidsFest '95

Mid-February
Myrtle Beach Convention Center 449-6616

A fun-filled weekend of educational, cultural and safety-related presentations and exhibits for children and their families is the fare of KidsFest. More than 120 booths provide interactive or educational presentations. Continuous entertainment includes dancers, tumbling acts, magicians, singers and storytellers. Children are given the opportunity to take part in various contests on stage. The 1995 event witnessed a special star appearance by Walter Jones — a.k.a. Zach the Black Ranger — from the hit show "Mighty Morphin Power Rangers." Admission is $5 for children, free for infants and $1 for adults with a parent pass ($3 without a pass).

Grand Strand Boat Show

Late February
Myrtle Beach Convention Center 448-1629

The Boat Show attracts up to 10,000 boating enthusiasts and 112 exhibitors displaying motor boats, fishing equipment, pontoon boats, sailboats, watersports gear including scuba diving equipment and much more. Safety instruction is offered, and the U.S. Coast Guard is represented. Admission is $5.50 for adults and $3 for children 12 to 16 years of age.

March

Carolina Woman's Show

Mid-March (800) 868-SHOW
Myrtle Beach Convention Center

This show must be put on your agenda if you ever suffer from "consumer fever." Exhibits include bridalwear, fashion, fitness, makeup, jewelry, health and home decor. Fashion shows are featured every hour with special events announced each half-hour. The focus for 1995 is centered around a Health Forum that addresses issues particular to women. Admission is $5.

Annual Canadian-American Days Festival

Mid-March
Throughout Horry County 626-7444

Coinciding with the March school-break in the Canadian Province of Ontario, Can-Am Days is a festival that attracts about 100,000 visitors from both countries every year. It's definitely more fun than you could ever imagine; with so many events going on in so many places, we suggest you consult *The Sun News* or the Chamber of Commerce each day to keep up with the happenings.

Lifestyles Expo

Mid-March
Myrtle Beach Convention Center (800) 476-5429

This shindig is dedicated to our senior citizens, snowbirds escaping the harsh winter at home and more than 4,000 Senior Adult Baptists. Coinciding with Canadian-American Days, the Lifestyles Expo usually attracts more than 10,000 people each year. More than 150 booths offer senior consulting and planning, health screenings, demonstrations and a host of educational items. Continuous entertainment and speakers fill the agenda. We suggest you plan to spend the whole day at the Lifestyles Expo. An admission fee is charged.

Annual Doll Show & Sale

Mid-March
Myrtle Beach Convention Center 248-5643

Doll dealers from 15 states and more than 200 tables of related goods are on hand at this show. Items includes antique dolls, collectibles, modern artists' dolls, accessories, doll-making supplies, replacement parts and molds. Special exhibits and demonstrations are scheduled, and a raffle is held to raise money for a number of area charities. A one-day ticket for adults is $3, or you can purchase a two-day admission for $4. Children 6 to 12 years can enter for only $1.

Bridge Bottom South

Late March *No phone listing*
Georgetown

Right at the bottom of the bridge that takes you into Georgetown, you'll find this arts, crafts and antique cars festival. Local church groups have pitched in for 1995 to hold a garage sale alongside exhibitors. There is no fee to attend.

Annual Spring Art Show

Late March to early April
Horry-Georgetown Tech. College Auditorium
904 65th Ave. N.
Myrtle Beach 626-4210

Sponsored by the Waccamaw Arts & Crafts Guild, this is a juried art showing. Artists, craftspeople and photographers enter their original creations in the categories of water media paintings, easel paintings, graphics, drawings, photography and 3-D works. Exhibitors must register to enter and must follow certain criteria in order to have work judged and be eligible for awards.

Annual Georgetown Plantation Tours

Late March to early April
Georgetown 546-2292

A must-see for history buffs, these plantation homes and Colonial townhouses are only open to the public once a year for this 48-year-old tour. All the homes are privately owned, and several are on the National Register of Historic Places. A different group of properties is open to tours each day. Histories and maps are provided, box lunches are for sale and afternoon tea is served. Advance tickets go on sale in early February and cost $20 for one day or $35 for both days.

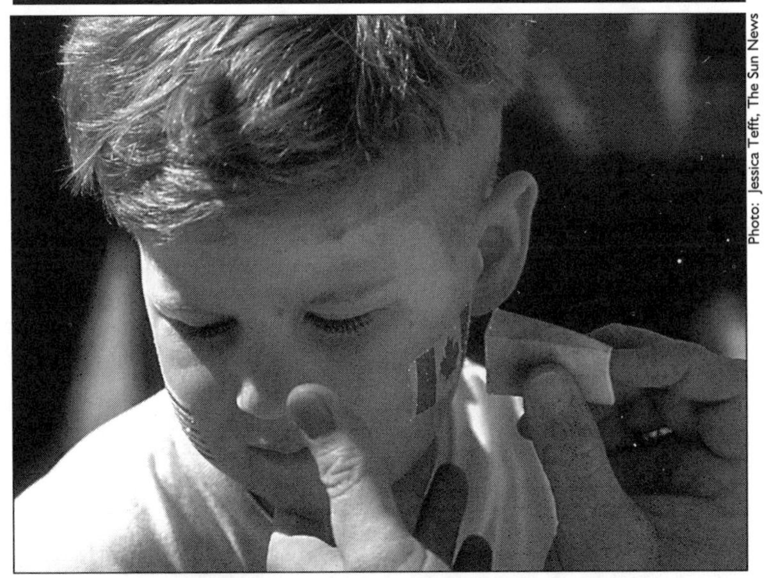

Photo: Jessica Tefft, The Sun News

The Canadian-American Days Festival is held every year in March.

April

Spring Games Kite Flying Contest

Mid-April

Myrtle Beach *449-2856*

This high flying competition takes place in the empty field across U.S. 17 Bypass at 10th Avenue N. in Myrtle Beach. Exhibitions will be on hand as participants vie for first place in the categories of highest-flying, most artistic or unique and most kites on one string — by the way, the record is 144 kites attached to a single string! About 500 people normally enter the contest that includes two-string flying and stunt kites. Admission is free, and sponsor Klig's Kites gives away a good number of flyers to those who drop by.

March of Dimes Walk America

Early April

Myrtle Beach Pavilion *347-2320*

It's a sight to behold. Thousands of people walk along the beach en masse for 4 miles to raise money to aid in the prevention of birth defects and infant mortality. The 1995 Walk America marked this project's Silver Anniversary. In 1994, the combined efforts of 31,000 South Carolina walkers pulled in more than $2 million! The staff of Coastal Federal Savings Bank usually leads the Grand Strand pack in the March of Dimes fundraising commitment — they show up early, announced by a marching band.

S.O.S. Spring Safari

Late April

North Myrtle Beach *782-7582*

This is the world's largest Spring Break for mature adults. More than 8,000 shaggers, members of the Society of Standers and lovers of the beach gather in North Myrtle Beach for an annual rite of spring. Ten full days and nights of beach music and things-to-do are all part of this riotous ritual.

Senior Games

Mid-April
Myrtle Beach *448-8578*

Endorsed by the S.C. Senior Sports Classic, this competitive athletic Olympic-style event seeks to promote fitness to citizens 55 years of age and older. First-, second- and third-place finishers are recognized at a wrap-up awards ceremony for excellence in such categories as track and field events, swimming, tennis matches, 3-on-3 basketball and bowling. This sports gala is complete with a welcoming ceremony, and all participants proudly march in The Parade of Athletes.

Annual Murrells Inlet Seafood Festival

Mid- to late April
Public Boat Landing (Beside Behlin Methodist Church)
Murrells Inlet *651-2044*

More than 10,000 seafood lovers join in the fun to sample the area's fish specialties, Mexican, Italian and Cajun cuisine. All dishes are prepared by the restaurants of Murrells Inlet and cost anywhere from 50¢ to $2.50 for a mouthwatering taste. Other features include arts and crafts exhibits, clowns, pirates, children's games and musical entertainment. The infamous Waiter and Waitress Race is also held; professional service staff are timed opening and pouring wine and make salads while running through an obstacle course. Admission is free.

S.C. Crawfish Festival & Aquaculture Fair

Late April
Pawleys Island/Litchfield Beach *237-3563*

The crawfish festival, which essentially celebrates the indigenous little crawfish, is one of the most beloved events to locals. If you have never witnessed crawfish eating before, we should warn you that sucking the brains and munching the tail is the connoisseur's preferred method. Area restaurants set up food booths, showcasing a "crawdad" dish and their most patronized menu items. The best crawfish recipe of the day receives a prize and big recognition. Listen to music all day long from 10 AM until about 7 PM, examine arts and crafts on display and check out the children's activities that, of course, include a crawfish race. Admission is $4 for adults and $2 for children.

Myrtle Gras

Late April
Chapin Park, Kings Hwy. at 16th Ave. N.
Myrtle Beach *448-8578*

Billed as "the Grand Strand's Cajun celebration," Myrtle Gras is basically a simple festival in the park that offers Cajun and local cuisine for sale, arts and crafts and a variety of musical entertainment. If you're at a loss as to what to do for the day, it's worth stopping by for an hour to two. Admission is free.

May

Brown Bag Days Lunchtime Concert Series

Every Wednesday in May, noon to 2 PM
Chapin Park, Kings Hwy. at 16th Ave. N.
Myrtle Beach

Bring your lunch and a lawn chair to the park and enjoy the warm weather and fine entertainment. If you forgot to pack food, chili dogs and beverages are on sale. This is a great break from work for locals who want to kick off their shoes and clear their heads for an hour or so.

Annual Blue Crab Festival

Mid to late May
Little River Waterfront *249-6604*

In 1994, 50,000 people flocked to the

waterfront streets of this historic fishing village to attend the Blue Crab Festival. More than 135 judged arts and crafts booths are featured, as well as food booths boasting everything from steamed crabs to grilled tenderloin to pizza. The children's area includes a petting zoo, pony rides, face painting and puppets. Entertainment promises widespread appeal, with performances of jazz, country, bluegrass and gospel. Admission is $3 for folks 9 and older ($2 in advance); kids 8 and younger get in free. Just come as you are.

Omar Shrine Temple Parade

Mid-May
Myrtle Beach *651-5675*

This is your chance to see grown men ride around in miniature cars! Yes, the ceremonial parade includes 50 to 60 Shrine units who delight the annual crowds with go-carts, clowns, floats and motorcycles. The parade gets started between 10 AM and 10:30 AM at Fifth Avenue N. in Myrtle Beach, travels to Ocean Boulevard and then moves north to Chapin Park at 16th Avenue N.

June

Annual Sun Fun Festival

Early June
Throughout the Grand Strand *626-7444*

To a Grand Strand local, summer officially begins with Sun Fun. The largest annual festival of its kind in either North or South Carolina, it usually attracts about 300,000 people to the beach each year. A parade along Ocean Boulevard kicks off the festival and rings in the summer season. From bikini contests to sand sculpture competitions to hog-calling yell-offs, Sun Fun hosts a multitude of activities that seldom miss the cameras of national television networks. Consult *The Sun News* or contact the Chamber of Commerce to keep abreast of daily goings-on.

Art in the Park

Mid-June
Chapin Park, Kings Hwy. at 16th Ave. N.
Myrtle Beach *249-4937*

Art in the Park is really a mini-festival held three times during the summer months in Chapin Park. Local artisans show and sell fine art pieces and handmade crafts. Food and beverages are always available and admission for the art show is free. Art in the Park is also held in early July and again in mid-August.

July

Fourth of July Concert Series

Early July
Myrtle Beach Memorial Stadium
Oak St. at 33rd Ave. N. *448-3189*

A concert, a dazzling fireworks display and food is why more than 8,000 people flock to the stadium every Fourth of July weekend. The local Long Bay Symphony orchestra is the lead act for the 1995 celebration. Bring your own lawn chair or blanket if you want to be close to the stage; bleacher seating is available farther back. Admission is free, and participants are allowed to bring their own coolers onto the grounds.

Murrells Inlet Fourth of July Boat Parade

July 4
Murrells Inlet *651-5675*

For 11 years now, more than 100 boats have gussied up for the Fourth of July and entertained multitudes who watch from and picnic on the shores. From 14-foot fishing boats to 40-foot yachts, participating watercraft start the aquatic caravan at high tide at the jetties of Garden City and proceed to Murrells Inlet. Trophies are given to the three best-decorated boats and to the three most-adorned docks along the route.

August

By the Sea Storytelling Festival

Early August
Fourth Ave. S. and Ocean Blvd.
Surfside Beach 248-1543

Remember as a kid laying in the dark or around a bonfire while you and your friends told scary tales? Well, this festival celebrates the great art of storytelling in concert! From 10 AM to 4 PM each day of this event, tales are continuously told by professionals in the field. At 7 PM the Swapping Ground begins where anyone in the audience who is inspired to relate a story can take the stage. During the evening, featured tellers get you shaking with ghost stories. This festival is sponsored by the Horry County Memorial Library and the Town of Surfside Beach. Coordinators are concerned about funding for 1995, so it's probably best to call ahead to ensure it is taking place. Admission is usually free.

11th Annual DuPont World Amateur Handicap Championship

Late August to early September
Grand Strand golf courses (800) 833-8798

Golf Digest called it the "Everyman Open," and *Golf World* referred to this tournament as the "mother of all golf tournaments." Each year thousands of amateur golfers the world over come to Myrtle Beach to play in this four-day, 72-hole championship. Players tee up for more than $200,000 in awards and prizes. Everyone has a chance to win at their skill level, whether it be scratch or 40. The top 10 players in each handicap flight win prizes and trophies. This year's sponsors are Glenlivet, Rosenbluth International, LaMode, Datrik, Lincoln Mercury, USAir, Pinnacle, Olympus and Golf Training Systems. The 1995 entry fee is $375 per golfer, and participants must sign up at the Myrtle Beach Convention Center by 7 PM on August 27th.

Carolina Craftsmen's Summer Classic

Early August
Myrtle Beach Convention Center (919) 274-5550

Collectors and unique gift-givers alike will be surrounded by a smorgasbord of authentic, handcrafted items at this arts and crafts show. Original designs include pottery, wood, fine art, toys, jewelry, baskets, stained glass, leather, tin, weaving, sculpture, musical instruments and furniture. Although prices have not been set yet, there will be advance ticket and group rates and an admission charge at the door.

The Bragging Rights 3-on-3 Tournament of Champions

Myrtle Square Mall
2501 N. Kings Hwy., Myrtle Beach
Mid-August 448-7305

For one whole day, the parking lot of Myrtle Square Mall in Myrtle Beach is not full of cars, but hoops and basketballs to accommodate this annual tournament. Seventy-two three-player teams from around the Carolinas vied last fall (1994) for the "bragging rights" to boast about how they stacked up against their peers. After the round-robin event, trophies and merchandise are awarded, but no money is involved. A $80 per team entry fee applies.

September

Afrofest

Labor Day Weekend
Atlantic Beach 272-5287

Atlantic Beach hosts this annual fes-

Photo: The Sun News

Andre Agassi participated in the 1989 GTE Tennis Festival, held annually at the Kingston Plantation Sport & Health Club.

tival of the arts and humanities that draws thousands of participants and features concerts, story-telling, arts and crafts and various contests.

S.O.S. Fall Migration

Mid-September
North Myrtle Beach *782-7582*

The Society of Stranders calls its thousands of active members to return to North Myrtle Beach for one last big party before winter sets in. Days and nights are filled with activities, shagging and sightseeing. Eight clubs around the Ocean Drive section pitch in to make sure that every evening resounds with non-stop beach music.

South Carolina's Largest Garage Sale

Mid-September, 8 AM to 1 PM
Myrtle Beach Pavilion Parking Garage

A bargain hunter's paradise, this sale is held in a huge covered garage, with hundreds of wares hocked from every parking space, on every level! Come as early as you can, since most things are well picked over by 10 AM.

The GTE Tennis Festival of Myrtle Beach

Mid-September
Kingston Plantation Sport & Health Club
9760 Kings Rd., Myrtle Beach *(800) 876-0010*

Included in this fast-paced and well attended festival is the GTE Southern Pro Classic, the USAir Junior Tournament, the 2001 Adult Tournament, the Atlantic Legends Classic, Rosa Linda's Club Pro Challenge, a mixed doubles event, seminars and clinics. The festival usually features a celebrity player, and John McEnroe delighted the crowd in 1994. Ticket prices vary for each event, seminar and clinic. Please see our Parks and Recreation chapter for details about facilities.

South Atlantic Shrine Parade

Late September
Myrtle Beach *651-5675*

This 4½-hour procession features Shrine Temple representatives from six states: West Virginia, Virginia, North and South Carolina, Tennessee and Kentucky. Expect wacky go-carts, clowns and floats to abound as they travel along Ocean Boulevard from Sixth Avenue S. to 11th Avenue N. in Myrtle Beach. This event brings approximately 9,000 Shrine families to the area each year.

Annual Atalaya Arts and Crafts Festival

Late September (Friday through Sunday)
Huntington Beach State Park *734-0517*

The site for this festival is Atalaya, a castle in the sand that was once the winter home of Archibald Huntington and acclaimed sculptress, Anna Hyatt Huntington. In honor of Ms. Huntington's contribution to the art world, the Spanish castle has been transformed into a showcase of fine arts and crafts for three days every year. More than 100 artisans from all over the country exhibit an inspiring diversity of work, ranging from rustic baskets to delicate glasswork. Live entertainment enhances the atmosphere, and food and drink are available. Admission is $3 for adults and $1 for children.

October

BrookgreenFest

Date to be announced
Brookgreen Gardens *237-4218*

A celebration of the culinary, performing and visual arts, this festival is Brookgreen Gardens' annual fall event. Interesting family activities include puppet shows, Lowcountry storytelling, magic, various music, ice carving, Middle

Photo: The Sun News

"The Crook & Chase Show" was broadcast during past Sun Fun Festivals.

Eastern dance and a food court. BrookgreenFest runs from 10 AM to 5 PM. Admission is $6.50 for adults and $3 for children ages 6 to 12.

Taste of the Town

Early October
Myrtle Beach Convention Center 249-4885

If you would like to sample foods from a variety of Grand Strand restaurants, this is an event you will not want to miss. More than 30 restaurants participate each year, serving up the very best they have to offer. Taste of the Town has become so popular that two rooms of the Convention Center are currently booked for the 1995 event (more than 5,000 attended in 1994). This is a fundraising project for St. Andrews Catholic School. Admission is $7 for a family and $3 for individuals with food tickets sold for 50¢ each.

Carolina Aviation Festival

Early October
Airway ramp at the old
Myrtle Beach Air Force Base 238-3378

The proceeds from this three-day public event go toward the new Carolina Aviation Museum. Coordinators expect to have 400 to 500 general aircraft such as Cesnas and Pipers flying in for the festival, along with planes that were used in combat: P-51 Mustangs, P-47 Thunderbolts and Warbirds. Air shows are conducted every afternoon. A Piper Aerostar convention dovetails with the event, as well as a reunion of the 352nd Fighter Group who flew Mustangs during World War II and were affectionately known as the "Blue Nose Bastards." There is an admission charge. Food and souvenirs are sold.

Oktoberfest

Early October
Chapin Park, Kings Hwy. at 16th Ave. N.
Myrtle Beach *448-8578*

Beer and bratwurst are the favorites at this celebration of the harvest season. Authentic oom-pah music is played in the park, and arts and crafts are on display. There is no admission charge.

Surfside Beach Family Festival

Early October
One block off Surfside Dr. *238-4131*

What started out as a little ole family picnic in 1985 has now grown into a full-fledged festival for more than 10,000 people a year! It's a whole day affair with plenty of food and arts and crafts for sale, plus informational booths.

Bayfest

Mid-October
East Bay Park
Georgetown *546-2481*

Since the days of rice planters and antebellum life, Georgetown County has been intricately tied to its coastal resources. Bayfest celebrates the community's timeless link to the sea and its sense of pride. This theme is woven throughout all the festival activities that include arts and crafts, boat tours of Winyah Bay, educational exhibits and the annual fish stew cook-off. A shuttle is provided between the park and marina to help you take in all the events. There is a $25 entry fee to compete in the fish stew cook-off.

Ghost Hunt

Late October
Self-guided tour throughout
Georgetown County *546-8437*

If you're a fan of ghost stories and would like to see the better part of historic Georgetown, this spirit hunt will certainly turn your crank. Participants are armed with tickets and a map, and a fully costumed interpreter greets them at each site to relate the folklore. There is time to tour the grounds of each point of interest after the ghost story has unfolded. The Ghost Hunt runs from 10 AM to 5 PM. Tickets are $10 for adults and $6 for children younger than 12.

Annual Haunted Trail

October 24 - 31
The Myrtle Beach Jaycees' grounds
Oak St. at 13th Ave. N.
Myrtle Beach *448-7305*

For an entire week leading up to Halloween, you'll hear nothing but screams and howling as hundreds of people walk through the wooded Haunted Trail expressly to scare themselves silly. Flashlight-wielding, ghoulish guides take the unsuspecting, knee-trembling crowds along the trail, encountering something terrifying at every bend. Not for the weak of heart, this excursion has caused some to shake for hours afterwards. Admission is usually $4 per person, and proceeds go to charity.

November

ACBL Sectional Bridge Tournament

First week of November
Sites to be announced *249-1316*

In this tournament, 1,200 duplicate bridge players play for four days around and about town. Eighty tables are set up per day, and entrants must pay $6 per session. A championship match is also played during Can-Am Days in mid-March.

12th Annual Dickens Christmas Show & Festival

Mid-November
Myrtle Beach Convention Center *448-9483*

You know that Christmas is just

Photo: Jessica Tefft, The Sun News

Seniors over age 55 can compete in various events during April's Senior Games.

around the corner when the Dickens show is at the convention center. And what a charming way to get in the holiday spirit. Grand Stranders spend hours decorating the trees on display at this show, and the adornments are a sight to behold. The beautifully trimmed tannenbaums are usually auctioned off by the end of the festival, and hundreds of holiday gifts and ornaments are for show and sale. The 1995 admission price has not been set.

Annual South Carolina State Bluegrass Festival

Late November
Myrtle Beach Convention Center 448-7166

The Johnson Mountain Boys will head the talent-rich lineup for this bluegrass festival, touted as "the Palmetto state's oldest, largest and best bluegrass event." Drawing fans from throughout the eastern United States and Canada, promoters are proud to say that the festival will be a "who's who" of traditional bluegrass performers, including The Osborne Brothers, The Lewis Family, Doyle Lawson & Quicksilver, Jim & Jesse, IIIrd Tyme Out, Ralph Stanley & The Clinch Mtn. Boys and Raymond Fairchild. Entertainment begins Thursday at 1 PM and goes until 11 PM. On Friday and Saturday, guitars and fiddles go strong from noon 'til midnight. Tickets are available at the gate and are sold at the Convention Center box office during the festival. Depending upon seating and number of days you wish to attend, prices range from $20 to $58 for adults and $10 to $28 for children 13 and younger.

December

Christmas Tour of Homes

Early December
Throughout Georgetown County 546-8100

This tour will get you in the Christmas spirit while providing some of the most beautiful Yuletide decorating ideas. A number of gracious historic homes and bed and breakfast establishments in Georgetown are opened to the public for this program, resplendent with holiday adornments. This is an annual fundraising project to benefit the Georgetown County Mental Health Association. Tickets are $15 each, including admission into each homesite and a map of the tour.

North-South All-Star Football Game

Mid-December
Memorial Stadium
Myrtle Beach 448-2214

As the name implies, this game showcases the best young players from the northern and southern portions of South Carolina. The teams battle it out on the field while college scouts get a good look

Insiders' Tips

When visiting open houses, always ask to see utility bills, so that over time you can judge what constitutes a "high" bill and what is "low" for a given area.

at potential recruits. Last year, head coaches and representatives from Clemson University, University of North Carolina and Wake Forest University were on hand to assess players' skills. Ticket prices for the big game will be set late in 1995.

Beach Ball Classic

Late December
Myrtle Beach Convention Center   650-7222

Sponsored by Belk department store and McDonald's, the Beach Ball Classic is always an exciting showcase of this country's best high school basketball talent. Teams are rated and selected to play in this tournament before standing-room-only crowds of cheering fans, basketball enthusiasts and college scouts. Games start each day at 3:30 PM and culminate around 10 PM. There is an admission fee to be announced closer to tournament time.

Photo: Bill Scroggins, The Sun News

Rees Jones stands overlooking the 12th and 13th fairways of the Falcon course at Wild Wing Plantation. Jones designed the course.

Inside Golf

Nobody *needs* to play golf. Just like nobody needs Super Bowl tickets, a flair for remembering names or a bowl of homemade ice cream on the hottest day of August. Nobody needs chocolate, either. So, forget about golf. Drink virgin Margaritas. Sans salt. And, above all else, consider your cholesterol.

On the other hand, life is short and need is a very subjective concept. Conclusion? Throw sensibility to the wind and leap into the wonderful world of Grand Strand golf.

And what a wonderful world it is! Next to the captivating expanse of the blue Atlantic and its wide, white ribbon of shoreline, the Strand's most abundant recreational resource is glorious, glorious golf. There are currently 83 public courses and three private courses, and two additional courses are scheduled for completion by the end of 1995. And, by the year 2000, more than 100 courses are projected to be in operation!

While the sheer abundance of courses is staggering, perhaps more impressive than the quantity is the quality. This 60-mile stretch of real estate boasts a collection of the country's finest course layouts. Creations of golf-great architects like Jones, Player, Nicklaus, Fazio, Palmer, Maples and Dye, these courses offer a lot more than what you might expect . . . they're everything golf fantasies are made of!

Something you may not know about the Grand Strand: The topography of our countryside is delightfully diverse. If you're a beachgoer, you may know and love our salt-scrubbed beaches, sand castles, sailboats, sea oats and little else. But, wander inland just a bit and you'll discover bountiful secrets in the corners of our counties. You'll find undulating river bluffs and panoramic river vistas, shadowy swamplands, stately old oaks weeping silver moss, sandy pine forests and seemingly unchanging marshlands. The titillating assortment of ecosystems continues to provide golf architects with some of the richest natural resources in the world.

And, not only has Mother Nature given us an abundance of beautiful real estate, she's blessed us with a subtropical climate that make the outdoors pleasant almost every day of the year. Crisp days and aqua-blue skies make autumn and spring the favored seasons of many golfers. Still, lots of folks are learning a local secret — outrageous bargains abound during the summer and winter months. Since our weather is governed by cool Gulf Stream breezes when temperatures rise and warm Gulf Stream breezes when temperatures dip, golfing is a year-round delight.

Like everything else in our neck of the woods, golf offerings are eclectic, electric and just plain fun. Provocative and dazzling new courses flourish along with the vintage, time-tested courses graced with history and tradition. Pine Lakes Country Club, a semiprivate layout designed by Robert White in 1927, launched golf's popularity in this area and is appropriately known as "The Granddaddy." The highly regarded Dunes Golf & Beach Club, designed in 1948 by Robert Trent Jones, carried on the tradition. In the decades following, a parade of splendid designs have come to maturation along the Strand. As the number of courses spirals upward, the area's reputation blossoms accordingly. Today, the amount of golf played on the Grand Strand (well in excess of three million rounds per year!) is astounding, as is the fact that the tally shows no sign of slowing down.

One of the oldest and biggest golfing events along South Carolina's Grand Strand is the DuPont World Amateur Handicap Championship, billed as the world's largest on-site championship. *Golf Digest* dubbed the August event the "Everyman Open," and *Golf World* crowned it the "mother of all golf tournaments." In 1994, it received South Carolina's annual award for the most outstanding tourism event. Little wonder: Over the past 11 years, more than 30,000 golfers from all over the world have participated in the four-day, matched handicap competition.

One of the newest and biggest golfing events along the Grand Strand is the Senior Tour Championship, held in Myrtle Beach for the first time in November of 1994. (An estimated 90,000 people attended!) The Senior PGA Tour's decision to name The Dunes Golf & Beach Club as host for the Championship for the next five years met with a groundswell of excitement and support not only from the local community, but from the entire region. "This is the one we've been working for," said Cecil Brandon, Executive Director of Myrtle Beach Golf Holiday. "Few opportunities to secure a tournament of this stature present themselves."

It would be unfair to talk about golf on the Grand Strand without some mention of Myrtle Beach Golf Holiday. Founded in 1967, Myrtle Beach Golf Holiday is a nonprofit association of accommodations and golf courses along "The Carolinas' Golden Golf Coast," from Georgetown, South Carolina, to Southport, North Carolina. The organization's mission is to increase consumer awareness of the advantages of a Myrtle Beach-area golf vacation, and make it as easy as possible for a golfer to reserve accommodations of a preferred level of luxury or economy. Prospective vacationing golfers and travel agents can call (800) 845-4653 to receive a free 152-page vacation planner complete with golf package rates for 92 different accommodations, details on 77 golf courses, travel tips and information on how to directly book a golf vacation with a member accommodation.

In addition to the Senior Tour Championship and the DuPont World Amateur, Myrtle Beach Golf Holiday also hosts 55 International Summer Family Golf Tournaments, the PING Myrtle Beach Junior Classic and the Annual Golf Writers Association of America Tournament. Given this lineup, it's easy to see the enormous value of Myrtle Beach Golf Holiday's efforts to encourage the growth of area tourism via golf.

For the inside scoop regarding golf on the Strand, refer to *The Sun News'* monthly magazine ***Myrtle Beach Golf.*** You will enjoy scads of interesting editorial, dining and entertainment tips, a directory of courses, maps and much more.

A subscription costs a modest $9 per 12 issues or $18 for 24 issues. Write to: Myrtle Beach Golf, Box 406, Myrtle Beach 29578-0406 or call (800)568-1800.

Of course, there are far and away too many golf courses for us to tell you about more than a fraction. Nonetheless, here's a representative assortment featuring different styles, prices and locales. Rates change seasonally, so call ahead for exact prices. Remember, too, that despite the fact that there are oodles of courses to choose from, tee times are precious — especially during peak seasons. Call well in advance — three months or more — to book reservations.

Arcadian Shores

701 Hilton Rd. *449-5217*
Myrtle Beach *(800) 248-9228*

Rees Jones designed this delightful course which opened in 1974. It features standard Bermuda fairways and lush bent grass greens. Surrounding the greens and sprinkled along the fairways, you'll find no fewer than 64 sand bunkers — just so you'll know you're at the beach! A variety of picturesque natural lakes adds to the challenge. In 1993, the course was listed among *Golf Digest's* "Top 50 Resort Courses." *Golf Magazine*, too, has noted Arcadian Shores' outstanding design.

Arrowhead

1201 Burcale Rd. *236-3243*
Myrtle Beach *(800) 236-3243*

This brand new Raymond Floyd-designed course is already meeting with rave reviews. Eighteen holes are currently open for play, but there will eventually be a total of 27. Each nine-hole course has its own name. The appropriately named Lakes Course travels through a pristine pine forest and features striking undulations in the fairways, numerous bright white bunkers and abundant lakes. The Cypress Course, in contrast, is set amid a beautiful stand of hardwoods, unique to the Myrtle Beach area. Arrowhead's design, masterminded in collaboration with Tom Jackson, offers the feeling of playing golf in the Carolina foothills. A beautiful clubhouse, large practice facility and a well-stocked pro shop add to the quality of this beautiful new course.

Caledonia Golf & Fish Club

King River Rd. *237-3675*
Pawleys Island *(800) 483-6800*

Like Arrowhead, Caledonia is one of the area's newest courses, and we'd like to say it's been well worth the wait. Constructed on the site of a former rice plantation, along the black ribbon of the Waccamaw River, Caledonia is dazzling. The oak-lined drive to the antebellum-style clubhouse sets the tone for the experience. It won't take you long to realize that expense has not been spared — even the bridges that connect one hole to another feature old Charleston brick.

This beautiful course, designed by up-and-coming architect Mike Strantz, is highlighted by huge oaks, shimmering natural lakes, broad expanses of long abandoned rice fields and more than an occasional glimpse of the area's rich wildlife. *Golf Digest* voted Caledonia "5th Best Public Course in America" in 1994, and *Golf Magazine* voted it one of the 10 best public courses in 1994. (What a debut, Mike!) When you've finished your round, take some time to hang around the clubhouse — an actual replica of an 18th-century colonial plantation home. With its rocking chair-studded wraparound porch, old brick fireplace, soaring ceilings and delicious food, it's a great place to reflect on your game . . . and watch the sun set. Don't miss this one.

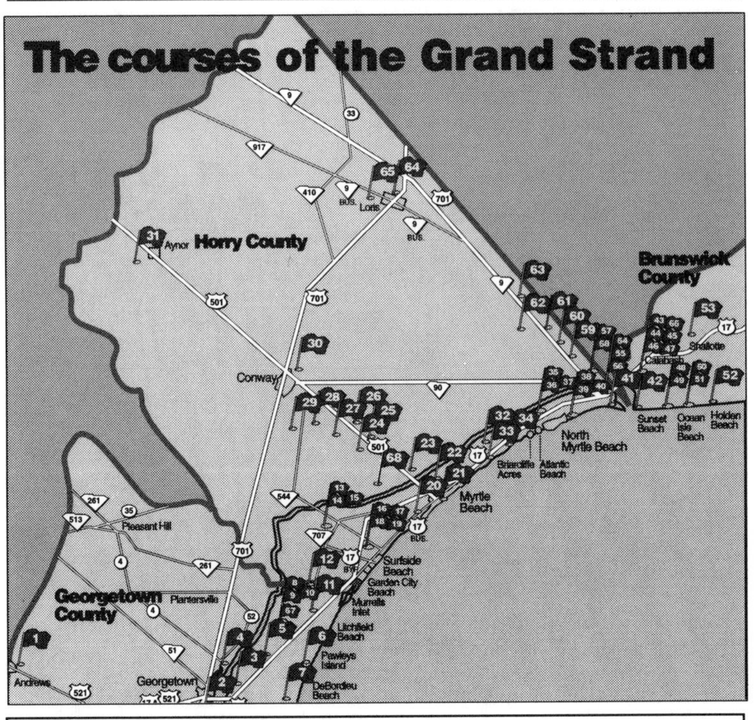

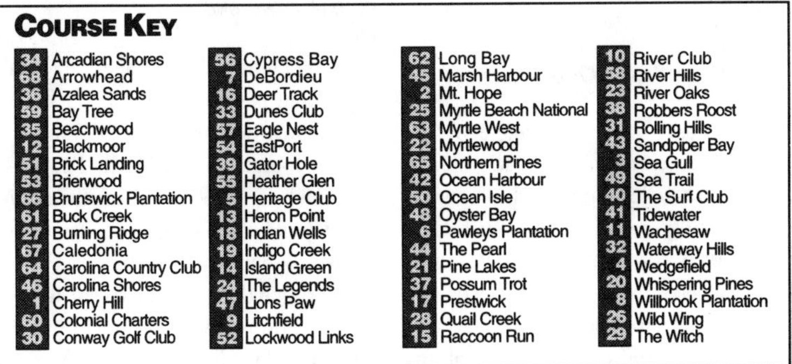

DeBordieu

Pawleys Island *546-1525*

Without a doubt, DeBordieu is one of the finest courses along the Grand Strand. Designed by Pete and P.B. Dye, it offers a fair challenge, a good variety of holes and true beauty. DeBordieu is located in one of the area's most expensive and exclusive neighborhoods. Unfortunately for "outsiders," this club is private, and there are only a few ways to wrangle yourself a round: accompany a member, be sponsored by a member or lease a villa owned by a member. The club still grants memberships, but only to DeBordieu property-owners — a pricey proposition, but worth it if you can swing it. For more information, contact the sales office at

Photo: Bill Scroggins, The Sun News

One of South Carolina's leading golf course architects, Tom Jackson, designed the water-filled River Oaks.

546-4176 or drop by; no appointment is required.

Deer Track Golf Resort

U.S. 17 *650-2146*
Surfside Beach *(800) 548-9186*

Deer Track, a time-tested favorite, offers two 18-hole championship courses. The carefully crafted North Course, a par 72 layout, offers wide tree-lined Bermuda fairways, elevated bent grass greens and picturesque landscaping to make this course a fun and enjoyable part of any golf outing. The more modern par 71 South Course features sculpted sand bunkers, dramatic bent greens and spectacular lakes and ponds. Home of the **Classic Swing Golf School**, Deer Track has a natural turf driving range and putting greens. A bit of trivia for you golf fanatics: Deer Track is owned and operated by Gary Schaal, former president of the PGA of America.

The Dunes Golf & Beach Club

9000 N. Ocean Blvd.
Myrtle Beach *449-5914*

The Dunes Club is one of the area's oldest and best-loved courses. A Robert Trent Jones design, Dunes was only the second course built in Myrtle Beach — way back in 1949. Recent renovations make it one of a handful of courses with PennLink Bent grass greens.

Through the years, the course has become world-renowned. The 13th hole, rated one of the best 18 holes in America by *Sports Illustrated*, is particularly popular. *Golf Magazine* included the 13th hole in its "100 Best Holes in America," and *Southern Living* named it one of the "18 Ultimate Golf Holes of the South," proclaiming: "If a single golf hole can be given credit for popularizing Myrtle Beach golf, this is it. Its crescent-shaped fairway winds around the former Singleton Swash, now a lake. A monstrous drive

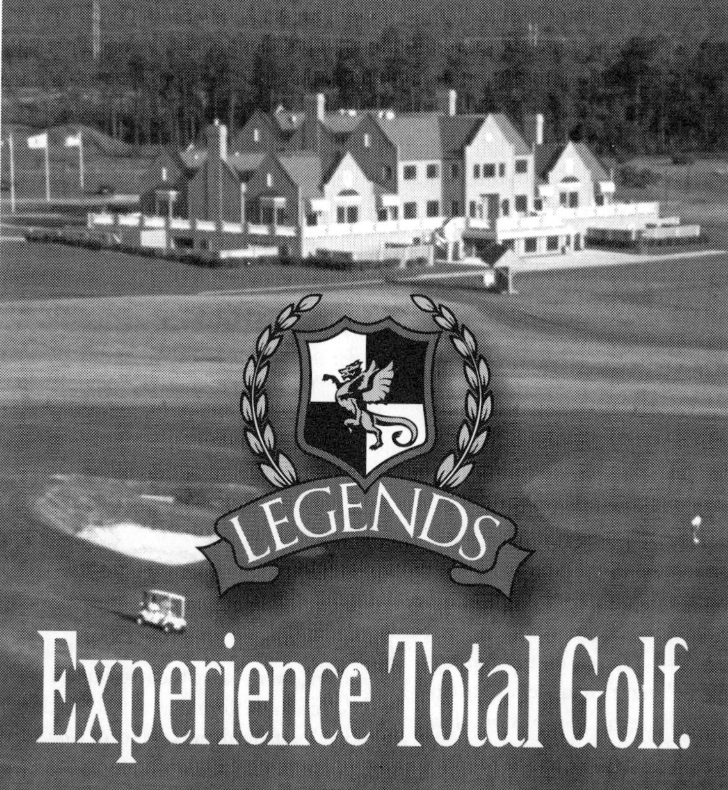
LEGENDS

is advised, to be followed by a monstrous 3-wood, and you're still a strong iron from a round green. It's a par 6 for most of us." So few people have reached the 13th green in two shots that those who have are noted in The Dunes Club's history. The hole is known as Waterloo — don't let it be yours.

The rest of the course is pretty traditional, with wide open fairways, deep bunkers and elevated greens. The course's beauty is anything but ordinary. The Atlantic Ocean is the backdrop for several holes, while others wind around and through the marsh. Understandably, this course has a maturity that other Grand Strand courses envy. Rest assured, when you wrap up at No. 18, you will have used every club in your bag. There's a grill for a quick bite or an elegant dining room with a panoramic view of the beach.

The Dunes remains one of the Strand's most exclusive private clubs and is available to the guests of a few select member hotels: The Breakers, The Caravelle, The Caribbean, The Driftwood, The Dunes Village and The South Wind. Tee times are scheduled through the hotels.

Heather Glen

2111 U.S. 17 N. *249-9000*
North Myrtle Beach *(800) 868-4536*

Timeless oaks and stately pines stud the 400-acre historic setting of Heather Glen, a course reminiscent of the best Scotland has to offer. Designed by Willard Byrd and Clyde Johnston, this course was pegged a masterpiece as quickly as it opened for play. *Golf Digest* named it 1987's "Best New Public Course in America" and one of the "50 Best Public Courses in America" in 1990.

Heather Glen made a great thing better when it expanded from 18 to 27 holes. This allows golfers to personally design their rounds by picking two of three stellar sets of nine holes.

Back at the 18th-century-style clubhouse, cap off your round in an authentic pub.

The Heritage Club

King River Rd. *236-9318*
Pawleys Island *(800) 552-2660*

The Heritage course, designed by Dan Maples, is built on the site of not one, but two historic rice plantations. Here, overlooking the inky waters of the Waccamaw River, you'll feel a little like you've stepped onto the set of *Gone with the Wind*. The majestic tree-lined approach to the plantation-style clubhouse sets the stage. This grand avenue of 300-year-old oaks would impress even Rhett and Scarlett.

While you play, enjoy not only the captivating hole designs but breathtaking views of the scenic Waccamaw River, endless marshes, freshwater lakes and towering oaks and magnolias. Take

Insiders' Tips

With so many courses to play, you may think tee times come easy, but it "just ain't so." Our golf courses do brisk businesses, and you'd be wise to call well in advance to book your round. In fact, the most popular courses encourage their customers to book next year's tee times on this year's vacation!

Photo: Charles Slate, The Sun News

More than 90,000 people attended the Senior Tour Championship, held for the first time in Myrtle Beach in November 1994.

Senior Tour Championship Heralds A New Era

When the Senior Tour Championship, the Senior PGA's most prestigious competition, kicked off in November of 1994, Myrtle Beach attained a whole new level of credibility in the collective eye of the world. "This is the one we have been working for," said Cecil Brandon, Executive Director of Myrtle Beach Golf Holiday. "Few opportunities to secure a tournament of this stature present themselves. Our years of negotiations with the Tour have paid off."

No doubt about it, Myrtle Beach has struggled for too many years to overcome the perception that it doesn't belong in the "top drawer" of golf resorts. The Senior Tour's decision to bring the championship to Myrtle Beach is nothing short of a tribute to the whole region — the caliber of golf, the caliber of restaurants and the caliber of accommodations.

In October before the tournament, the Senior PGA announced that Myrtle Beach Golf Holiday would host five consecutive annual tournaments. A collective intake of breath, almost audible, was heard from Georgetown, South Carolina, to Southport, North Carolina. Everyone in the golf industry, and nearly everyone else in the region, immediately recognized the value that coverage of this one event could bring its host community. The excitement was well-founded; an estimated 90,000 people spilled into the area for the Tour's week of festivities.

Myrtle Beach Golf Holiday proved the area was more than ready for major league golf. They organized a tournament to rival anything on the eastern seaboard and, in so doing, put Myrtle Beach "on the map." Through four days of play, ESPN's live coverage, the MetLife blimp's aerial footage and the major networks' daily news updates showed the nation a captivating corner of the world that many had only heard of. They showed dolphins frolicking offshore; they showed miles of sandy beach; they showed our restaurants and our theaters; and they showed our golf. Boy, did they ever! If folks didn't know it before, they sure know now: The Grand Strand offers some of the best golf and golf values this country has to offer. Plus, we have a beautiful ribbon of shoreline, dazzling entertainment, first-class dining options and amusements galore.

The Dunes Golf & Beach Club was chosen to host the tournament in 1994, and no better example of the spectacular Myrtle Beach area courses could have been selected. The 45-year-old Dunes, with its oceanfront setting and legendary reputation, offered the whole world a glimpse of what they'd find on the Grand Strand.

Without a doubt, the "Carolinas' Golden Golf Coast" has come of age.

heed! The Heritage demands accuracy off the tee.

The pro shop, bar and dining room are exquisitely appointed with dark, rich wood paneling. Before your round, loosen up at the driving range or practice putting green. Lessons and rental equipment are available.

The Legends Complex

U.S. 501 — *236-9318*
Myrtle Beach — *(800) 552-2660*

Since 1990, the Legends Complex has offered three of the finest and most distinctive courses along the Grand Strand. The newest, and arguably the best, of the three courses is Parkland. When members of the Carolina's PGA held a championship here, the pros pointed out similarities to New Jersey's highly acclaimed Pine Valley course. Parkland requires the ability to draw or fade the ball, and accuracy is an absolute must. Don't try this course unless you're up to the challenge; you'll only get frustrated and slow down play.

Heathland is one of the most unusual courses along the Grand Strand; it would seem more at home in the Scottish landscape. Heathland is known for its lack of trees, menacing winds and rolling fairways. Pot bunkers appear more ominous than they are, so don't be intimidated. One of the more interesting holes requires male golfers to drive straight over a grove of trees; ladies can bypass them and hit from the other side. Upon opening in 1990, this Tom Doak design was immediately selected as one of *Golf Magazine's* "Top 10 New Courses for 1990."

Rounding out The Legends Complex is Moorland, which features many of the most feared holes in Myrtle Beach — you'll either love or hate this P.B. Dye course. When Legends' owner Larry

This 72-hole golf reserve provides four distinctly different golfing choices. The common denominator is PennLinks bent grass greens... voted "Best Greens on the Grand Strand" in 1991.

AVOCET

The 33,000 sq. ft. clubhouse has exceptional dining a warm ambience and a golf shop revered as having the best, most diverse selection of apparel and equipment in the area.

Highway 501,
Myrtle Beach,
South Carolina

1-803-347-1900
or Toll Free
1-800-736-WING

The golf course architects of Wild Wing Plantation are diverse. Willard Byrd, the team of Larry Nelson and Jeff Brauer, and Rees Jones have given their all to provide both variety, quality and challenge in their course designs.

FALCON

Come experience the serene setting and GREAT GOLF of Wild Wing Plantation, located just minutes from everything. Myrtle Beach's "must play" golf reserve.

Young hired the renowned Dye to design the course, his instruction was simple: "Make it as hard as you can." And Dye did! It's very difficult in places, especially the short par 4 called "Hell's Half-Acre," but when the tees are placed forward, it isn't an impossible challenge even for average golfers. Ironically, the higher a player's handicap, the more he/she seems to enjoy Moorland.

The Legends has one of the most impressive clubhouses we've ever seen. It climbs skyward from the undulating green terrain like a Scottish castle. Inside, the tradition of elegance continues with an upscale pro shop, comfortable pub and dining room. There is also a state-of-the-art driving range with greens and flags as targets, instead of the usual wide open space with distance markers.

You can also book tee times at The Heritage, Marsh Harbor and Oyster Bay by calling the telephone numbers listed above.

Litchfield Plantation

U.S. 17 — *448-3331*
South Pawleys Island — *(800) 845-1897*

Litchfield Plantation, sculpted from yet another former rice plantation, was one of the first dozen courses built along the Grand Strand. Time has given the course a seldom-found maturity. Litchfield Plantation meanders lazily around an upscale neighborhood and, though private, the club allows a limited number of visiting golfers. Because the course isn't noted for its difficulty, your round here should provide a pleasant memory.

The antebellum-style clubhouse, the tree and flower-lined approach — the entire ambiance of the club — will make you feel like you're "walking in high cotton." In fact, you are. So, why not continue the self-indulgence after your round? Stay for "supper" in the dining room and sample the fare that locals love.

Marsh Harbour

Marsh Harbor Rd. — *236-9318*
Calabash, N.C. — *(800) 552-2660*

This Dan Maples course has an interesting claim to fame — some holes are in South Carolina and some are in North Carolina. Marsh Harbour is located on wetland along an inlet and the Intracoastal Waterway, making the course every bit as enjoyable to look at as it is to play. The combination of manicured turf and sparkling water creates a green and blue backdrop that's nothing shy of spectacular. Upon opening in 1980, Marsh Harbour was rated among *Golf Digest's* "Top 25 Public Courses in America."

The course's signature hole is the 570-yard 17th. Marvelously terrifying, this par 5 has three landing areas — two sport water on three sides. No one leaves Marsh Harbour without talking about No. 17.

Insiders' Tips

With few exceptions, all Grand Strand courses insist you use golf carts — instead of walking. If the hike is part of the game's attraction for you, course managers are more receptive to letting you stroll during the summer and winter seasons.

Myrtle Beach National

U.S. 501 — *448-2308*
Conway — *(800) 344-5590*

You'll find an outstanding trio of impeccably conditioned courses at Myrtle Beach National, each one bearing that special Arnold Palmer touch — all three courses were designed by Frank Duane with input from the master himself.

If you can take your pick, choose the North Course, one of the oldest and most requested on the beach. The signature hole is No. 3, thanks to distinctive sand traps shaped like the letters "SC" — this may be the most recognizable hole on the entire Strand. No. 3 also features an island green.

If you can't get on the North course, don't despair; you'll enjoy playing the SouthCreek or West courses, too. West is probably the easiest of the three. All three offer gently rolling fairways, towering pines and a few perilous lakes. Myrtle Beach National serves up the perfect opportunity for a multi-round day.

Oyster Bay

Lakeshore Dr. — *236-9318*
Sunset Beach, N.C. — *(800) 552-2660*

Yet another Dan Maples design, Oyster Bay really does have it all — pretty lakes, sweeping marshes, the Intracoastal Waterway and abundant wildlife. Expect to see all sorts of shore birds, and don't be surprised if you glimpse an alligator basking in the Carolina sunshine. This course was rated the "Best New Resort Course in America in 1983" by *Golf Digest*. In 1990, the magazine sang its praises again, rating it one of the "Best 50 Public Courses in America."

Pawleys Plantation

U.S. 17, Pawleys Island — *237-1736*

Pawleys Plantation is an upscale residential community and golf course. You

Golf Specialty Shops

Nearly as prolific as beachwear stores, golf specialty shops abound in the Myrtle Beach area. Pardon the cliché but, if you're a golfer, you'll feel like a "kid in a candy store." Some shops are small and some are warehouse-sized, but all are filled with golf supplies, active wear, shoes, clubs and more; many feature tennis equipment too. Most carry used golf balls — an excellent option if you're really good at finding water traps! Some names to look for include **Martin's Golf and Tennis**, serving four locations, and **Golf and Tennis World**, a mainstay since 1971.

And don't miss **Scottish Pride** on 1500 U.S. 501 in Myrtle Beach. Far and wide, this retail store is known for custom built Scottish golf clubs — the only place in this country where you can buy them. Best of all, you can get the clubs at wholesale prices — below the pro's cost! If you have questions, call 946-9464 and ask to speak with Bob O'Day.

can play this Jack Nicklaus signature course only if you're staying at one of its affiliated hotels — Sand Dunes, Ocean Dunes, Sands Ocean Club, Sands Beach Club and Ocean Forest — unless, of course, you're "tight" with a member who owns real estate on the Plantation.

Built around the timeless beauty of the marsh, pictures of Pawleys Plantation frequently land in reputable magazines. Among the most unforgettable features are a tremendous double green, a dramatic split fairway, lovely lake views and, of course, the marsh itself. There's an elegant clubhouse with a grill room that's ideal for a little 19th-hole relaxation.

Pine Lakes Country Club

Woodside Dr. *449-6459*
Myrtle Beach *(800) 446-6817*

Affectionately hailed as "The Granddaddy," this is quite literally where Myrtle Beach golf began. This course, the oldest in the area, was constructed in 1927 and was originally called the Ocean Forest Club. Course architect Robert White, first PGA President and a native of St. Andrews, endowed the layout with a unique Scottish flair.

Today, as always, golfers are greeted by kilted starters, welcomed with hot chocolate or a cooled mimosa on the first tee, refreshed with a cup of Lowcountry clam chowder near the turn and comforted with a "crying towel" at the finish. "Granddaddy" can be tough, but being a part of the legend is worth the heartache.

Prestwick Country Club

S.C. 544 *293-4100*
Surfside Beach *(800) 521-8522*

Prestwick, a semiprivate course, is another jewel designed by Pete and P.B. Dye. A 20-acre man-made lake, dramatically situated between the 9th and 18th holes, highlights the natural beauty of this masterful layout. An assortment of winding streams and ponds bring water directly into play on eight of the course's 18 holes. Each hole has six different sets of tees offering challenges for every skill level. Dye-inspired features abound: undulating greens, seemingly bottomless pot bunkers and railroad ties galore. A brand-

new clubhouse is scheduled to open in the fall of 1995.

River Oaks Golf Plantation

831 River Oaks Dr. *236-2222*
Myrtle Beach *(800) 762-8813*

Ranked in the Top 5 on the Grand Strand by Golf Course Rankings of America, this course has something for everyone. You can't help but enjoy 27 holes of undulating greens, mounded fairways, large lakes and finger-shaped bunkers.

In addition, the natural beauty and abundance of wildlife makes every golf experience a mini-adventure. A professional staff, excellent practice areas and beautifully manicured fairways, greens and tees have made River Oaks a popular choice. Its convenient location across from Waccamaw Pottery and Outlet Park is also appealing.

Sea Trail Plantation

211 Clubhouse Rd. *272-2185, (919) 579-4350*
Sunset Beach, N.C. *(800) 624-6601*

Sea Trail Plantation has three courses, all designed by notable architects Dan Maples, Rees Jones and Willard Byrd. (With those names, how could you go wrong?!) Each course offers an enjoyable round — not too easy and not too tough — the kind you'll remember fondly once you've returned home. Even so, the traditional design of the Rees Jones course stands out to golf afficianados: Wide fairways, elevated greens, large mounds, swales, pot bunkers and freshwater lakes add to its aesthetic beauty. But, rest assured, its beauty hasn't softened its challenge.

Tidewater Golf Club and Plantation

4901 Little River Neck Rd.
North Myrtle Beach *(800) 446-5363*

If scenic vistas showcasing water are what you like, you'll fall in love with Tidewater in a hurry. Truly incredible views of the Intracoastal Waterway, saltwater marshes and the Atlantic Ocean abound. At least one hole plays alongside Hog Inlet (a popular fishing area for Cherry Grove residents), so you can watch fishermen reel in a few as you plan your next shot. This fabulous course is the only one along the Grand Strand to be named one of the best new public courses by both *Golf Digest* and *Golf Magazine* in 1990.

Situated on 560 acres of seaside peninsula, Tidewater gives you plenty of elbow room and privacy. The only hole you can see at any given time is the one you're playing, creating the feeling of absolute solitude. The course has five sets of tees, so golfers can select those that best suit their individual games. Depending on tee selection, you can stretch this course from 4,765 to 7,020 yards.

Tidewater has the dubious honor of being the Grand Strand's most expensive golf course, but when you see it, you'll

Insiders' Tips

Suitable attire is required to play on most area courses. Cutoffs and bathing suits are generally prohibited. Tank tops are discouraged, and shirts with collars are preferred. Jeans aren't smiled upon, either.

understand why. Hale Irwin, three-time U.S. Open Champion, called Tidewater "one of the finest and most spectacular courses on the East Coast." This course is definitely not to be missed.

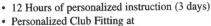

Wild Wing Plantation

1000 Wild Wing Blvd. (off U.S. 501)
Conway 347-9464, (800) 736-WING

Wild Wing Plantation is a highly acclaimed, multi-course golf reserve that delivers world-class golf in a world-class setting. Comprised of four award-winning courses covering more than 1,000 acres, Wild Wing has gone to great lengths to preserve the property's natural beauty.

A special distinction at Wild Wing is computerized golf carts, available on the Avocet and the Falcon courses. These computers give exact yardages from the ball, wherever it lies, to the center of the green. The computers also offer helpful hints like, "bunker on left," and "green slopes to the right." (Sounds a little like cheating, but you gotta live with your conscience.)

The Falcon Course, a favorite among locals, was designed by Rees Jones. With mounding, narrow fairways and small greens, the Falcon specializes in diversity and visual excitement. There are two 20-plus-acre lakes on this 18-hole course, and a 500-yard bunker that'll haunt your memory for a long time to come. In 1994, *The Sun News* named the Falcon the best new course in Myrtle Beach. Locals frequently call it a favorite.

The Sun News named the Avocet "Best New Course in Myrtle Beach" in 1993. Designed as a signature course by Jeff Brauer and two-time PGA Champion Larry Nelson, the Avocet will keep you seeing double; creative contouring presents a host of elevated tees and greens,

Photo: The Sun News

The Dunes Golf & Beach Club features this famed hole, No. 13, dubbed the Waterloo.

double fairways, grass bunkers . . . even a double green. *Golf Digest* named the Avocet one of the "Top 10 New Courses in America" in 1994.

The Wood Stork, Wild Wing's first course, has been open for play since 1991 and has had time to garner even more praise than her sister courses. *Southern Links Magazine* called it "Best in the South" for course conditioning and presentation. *Golf Digest* listed Wood Stork in its "Top 100 Great Value Courses in America" and in its "Top 3 Value Courses in Myrtle Beach." On this course, Willard Byrd paid special attention to preserving the lay of the land, the natural vegetation and water resources. The first eight holes play through pristine wetlands, and the remaining 10 wind through the shade of a stately pine forest.

Willard Byrd also designed the Hummingbird Course. Here, wetlands showcase stands of love grass and other native grasses that form the course's perimeter. Lush bermuda fairways, strategically placed lakes and an array of pot bunkers and waste areas create excitement and an undeniable challenge. It's little wonder the Hummingbird has racked up all the same awards as her sister, the Wood Stork.

Don't miss WishBones, Wild Wing's restaurant, in the 33,000-square-foot clubhouse. ("Wows" are in order.) It's a favorite hangout for golfing and non-golfing locals alike. A 45,000-square-foot putting green, a practice green with a 138-yard practice hole and a huge pro shop round out the amenities at this outstanding development.

Willbrook Plantation Golf Club

U.S. 17 S. — *237-4900*
Pawleys Island — *(800) 324-5590*

Dan Maples carved Willbrook Plantation from the fertile forests and wet-

lands of two historic rice plantations. He calls the course, "one of my best," — quite a statement considering his résumé. The scenery, design and inherent challenge make this course captivating, as does its history. The ruins of an old plantation home are visible from No. 5, and historic markers along the course signify a slave cemetery near the 8th hole, as well as an old slave settlement near the 4th green. You don't have to play great to score well here — easy in spots and tough in others, it's an ideal course for golfers of mixed abilities.

Photo: Cecelia Knoyn, The Sun News

Running with your pooch on the beach can be great exercise; just make sure you observe the beach rules concerning animals.

Inside Water Sports

Oh, boy have we got fun for you! Blessed with the drama of the Atlantic Ocean, marshy inlets, rivers and a gaping Intracoastal Waterway, the Grand Strand offers a soaking amount of options when it comes to water sports. We have also included surfwalking and sunbathing because . . . well . . . you do get your feet wet, right?

Depending upon your personal preferences, daring and nerve threshold, you can skid, sail and ski across ocean waves or leisurely cast fishing lines from a local pier or deep sea vessel.

To help you enjoy all of the natural wonders of the beach, access points are marked all along the coastline off Ocean Boulevard. When you see the sky-blue and yellow signs that proclaim, "Public Access," it's a good spot to park your car and walk to the beach.

Sunbathing and Surfwalking

There are few things in life easier to get and more painful to live with than a bad sunburn, and around here you can turn a good stinging shade of pink in just 30 minutes to an hour. Longer doses of sun can send sunbathers to the hospital with blisters, nausea and excruciating pain.

Don't be fooled by clouds or cool air; you can get a bad burn even on a day when you can't see the sun. Before you hit the strand, pick up some good suntan lotion with a high sun protection factor (SPF). We suggest an SPF of 15 to begin the suntan process. Apply it before you start swimming, walking or bicycling, and remember to reapply it after swimming or if you're perspiring, even if it's waterproof. Most experts recommend avoiding the sun during the hottest part of the day, between 1 PM and 3 PM. Even under the shade of an umbrella, the sun can reflect off the water and sand, so you can still get a burn.

Be sure to wear something on your head. A visor is good to protect your face, but to shield your head and hair, a full hat is best. Good sunglasses that filter out ultraviolet rays should also be part of your standard beach attire. If you've got young children or a baby with you, be sure to take extra care to protect their tender skin. Make them wear hats and reapply sunscreen every few minutes. If kids are determined to stay in the ocean for hours, put T-shirts on them. Some rafts and boogie boards will give them mild rashes on their stomachs anyway, so the T-shirts will serve two purposes.

Beach wheelchairs are now available for use for free by handicapped persons in the Myrtle Beach area. The chairs are designed with oversized rubber wheels that make rolling on a sandy surface easy. The following beach services are responsible for the distribution and storage of the wheelchairs at the following locations:

Myrtle Beach Lifeguards, 76th Avenue

Photo: The Sun News

These beach-going wheelchairs now provide accessibility to the beach for everyone.

N. to 69th Avenue N.; John's Beach Service, 63rd Avenue N. to 23rd Avenue N.; Boardwalk Beach Service, Ninth Avenue N. to the Myrtle Beach Pavilion; Huggins Beach Service, Seventh Avenue N. to Third Avenue N.; and Lack's Beach Service, 20th Avenue S. to 29th Avenue S.

Members of the handicapped public who wish to use one of the beach-going wheelchairs can either contact the beach service of their choice, or go to one of the locations indicated in the previous list. If it's the off-season, call the police department for assistance. Although there is no fee for using the wheelchair, there is a 1-hour limit, unless no one else wishes to use it. The beach-going wheelchairs are of a type that must be pushed by a second party.

Beach Rules

Alcohol

All of the beaches forbid alcohol consumption and possession. All open containers with alcohol are forbidden.

Motorized Watercraft

In North Myrtle Beach, motorized craft cannot be launched from the beach between 9 AM and 5 PM from May 15 through September 15. Vehicles must be kept at least 50 yards away from swimmers. Motorized craft must be at least 50 yards beyond bathers in Myrtle Beach, except jet skis, which must be at least 100 yards away. No motorized boats are allowed at Surfside Beach. All boats must be registered with a permit secured from the lifeguard. Boats can't be left unattended between 8 PM and 8 AM. In Horry County, boaters cannot endanger swimmers and must be at least 400 feet from the shore.

Fireworks

The Horry County ordinance is the only one that allows fireworks. Their use is restricted to private property between the hours of 10 AM and 10 PM.

Sleeping on the Beach

Myrtle Beach, North Myrtle Beach and Horry County forbid sleeping on the beach between 9 PM and sunrise. In Surfside Beach, people can't sleep in or around automobiles or motor vehicles, on the street, alleyway or at public accesses.

Pets

Pets are not allowed east of Kings Highway between 21st Avenue N. and 13th Avenue S. during the period from March 1 through September 30 in Myrtle Beach. In North Myrtle Beach, pets are not allowed on the strand between 9 AM and 5 PM from May 15 through September 15. In Surfside Beach, pets are not allowed at all on the beach from May 15 through September 15. In areas under the jurisdiction of Horry County (Garden City, South Strand campgrounds and Shore Drive area between Myrtle Beach and North Myrtle Beach), pets are not allowed on the beach between 9 AM and 4 PM from June 1 through September 1.

Horses

Horses are not allowed on the strand in North Myrtle Beach. Riders in Myrtle Beach must have a permit from the city clerk. In Surfside, horses are banned from the beach April 1 through November 1, and in Horry County, horses are banned from beaches March 1 through October 31.

Rafts and Floats

In Myrtle Beach and in Horry County areas, rafts must be covered with fabric and have 360-degree ropes attached to them.

Thong Bathing Suits

It is illegal to wear a thong bathing suit in North Myrtle Beach, Myrtle Beach and Surfside Beach.

Cars on the Beach

Only North Myrtle Beach and Horry County allow driving a car on the beach. In North Myrtle Beach, cars are allowed on the strand between December 1 and February 28 from 8 AM to 5 PM. The speed limit is 15 miles per hour.

Ingress and egress are at:

Cherry Grove
59th Avenue N.
50th Avenue N.
Sea Mountain Highway
Ocean Drive
Main Street
Sixth Avenue S.
Ninth Avenue S.
Crescent Beach
16th Avenue S.
25th Avenue S.
Windy Hill
39th Avenue S.
45th Avenue S.

Cars are allowed in Horry County from November 1 through February 28. Drivers must use public accesses or private property to get to the beaches.

Swimming

Swimming in the ocean isn't the same as swimming in a lake, river or pool, so don't expect it to be. Veteran ocean swimmers don't fear the ocean, its waves or currents, but they have a healthy respect for it. Caution and common sense are the keys.

One of the most important things to remember is that the lifeguard, young and good looking though he or she may be, has trained rigorously for this job. Listen to the lifeguard.

All Grand Strand beaches set shoulder deep and 50 yards from shore as the limit for swimmers, but the lifeguard has the authority to keep you in closer if he or she believes conditions warrant it. Disobeying the lifeguard can result in an arrest and charges. Fines can run from $25 to $200.

Safety Tips for Swimmers

1. Never swim alone.

2. Don't swim if you've been drinking alcohol.

3. Swim only in guarded areas. Almost all of the drownings at Grand Strand beaches in recent years have happened when the lifeguards were off duty.

Photo: The Sun News

When swimming in the ocean, make sure to obey the instructions of lifeguards.

4. Watch your children carefully when they get in the ocean.

5. If you get caught by an undertow, the pull of a wave as it pulls back from the shore, don't panic or try to fight it. The undertow may pull you out toward sea, but it will stop eventually. You'll be able to come in, or you can tread water or float until someone can come get you. Some days the undertow is worse than others. One rule of thumb is the bigger the waves, the stronger the undertow. When you get in the ocean, notice how strong the undertow is before you go out. If the undertow is especially bad, stay in shallower water.

6. If you get caught in a riptide, the pull of a wave between sand bars, don't panic. React the same as you would to undertow. You may choose to swim parallel to the shore until you swim out of the riptide. Then, head for shore.

7. Before you get in the ocean, check with the lifeguard about the conditions. Lifeguards fly flags that tell you at a glance what to expect; kinda like traffic signals for the ocean. As you might expect, a green flag means "go ahead." A yellow flag means you'll need to use extra caution while swimming. And a red flag . . . NO SWIMMING!

8. Jelly fish stings usually aren't serious and amount to little more than a brief stinging sensation. If you get stung, there are two health tips you need to remember — don't rub it, and don't put fresh water on it. Some old home remedies you might want to try include sprinkling a little meat tenderizer on it, dabbing it with diluted ammonia, putting a poultice of tobacco on it, covering it with Crest toothpaste or toothpaste mixed with baking soda. Most lifeguards are armed with an aerosol spray that takes the sting out quickly. If a tentacle has come loose from the sea creature, it can still sting you. If a tentacle wraps around a part of your body, don't try to pull it off. Grab a shell, comb or other device and try to lift it off.

Surfing

South Carolina waters are not especially good for surfing except when there's a hurricane or other storm approaching. Still, the Grand Strand has its share of avid surfers. Just about any day, you'll see crowds of young people waxing their boards and rushing to the water to ride the wall or hit the lip.

Surfing is restricted to certain areas and times on all Grand Strand beaches. All surfers are required to wear leashes. In North Myrtle Beach, surfing and skim boarding are forbidden between 9 AM and 4 PM from May 15 through September 15, except for these four areas: near Cherry Grove Pier, 13th Avenue S., 28th Avenue S. and 38th Avenue S. Surfboards are not allowed in Myrtle Beach between 9 AM and 5 PM March 16 through September 15, except in these four locations: 29th Avenue S., 41st Avenue N. through 47th Avenue N., 82nd Avenue N. to the city limits line and on the south side of Eighth Avenue N. to the north end of the public boardwalk.

In Surfside Beach, surfing is not allowed from 9 AM to 5 PM except in the 12th Avenue N. to 14th Avenue N. area. For more regulations, call 650-4131. In Horry County, surfers must not endanger swimmers and must not surf within 400 feet of a fishing pier.

Surfer Lingo

Goofy: Most surfers stand on their boards with their right foot back and control the board with that foot. Some surfers prefer to put their left foot back. It apparently works for them but puts them in the category of being goofy.

Kook: A kook, in olden days called a poser, is a nonsurfer who dresses like a surfer and puts surf racks on his car so everyone will think he's a surfer.

Bust or **Get Slammed**: This is when a wave "slams" a surfer, throwing him off his board. You'll know it when you see it.

Shoot the pier: Some surfers play a game similar to chicken, trying to see who will come the closest to the pier before pulling out. This is called shooting the pier.

Hit the Lip: A surfer hits the lip when he moves up the side of a swell that he's riding and his board touches the tip of the curl.

Floater: A ride is called a floater when the surfer rides on the top of a breaking wave.

Riding the Wall: A surfer rides the wall when he rides the inside of a swell, also called a clean face.

Fishing

Within the 60 miles of beaches, inlets and rivers that make up the Grand Strand, there exists an angler's paradise.

Surfcasting

Surfcasting is the most "fishing friendly" form of the sport, since you only need to bring reel and rod to the edge of the Atlantic Ocean. With year-round access to the beach, common catches from the surf of bluefish, flounder, whiting, spot, pompano and channel bass are plentiful.

For those who prefer solitary fishing, the South Strand region offers salt marshes, inlets and tidal creeks. Flounder, blues, croakers, spots, shrimp, clams, oysters and blueclaw crabs can be caught using a small boat, wading or with a net.

Fishing Charters

When casting into the world of deep-sea fishing, we feel the need to give you fair warning. If you have never been on this type of a boating trip, take medication the night before you leave for the relief of seasickness. Even some experienced sailors have been found writhing around the deck, begging for a quick and merciful death. Once a deep-sea fishing vessel is out on an excursion, it will not turn back to shore early for the sake of one or two heaving passengers who have turned green from the pitching motion. Most local pharmacies carry motion sickness pills available over the counter and patches that affix behind the ear.

Capt. Bill's Fleet

Capt. Dick's Marina
Murrells Inlet *651-3676*

Enjoy deep sea bottom fishing all day from 7 AM to 6 PM aboard the *Capt. Bill*, *New Capt. Bill*, *Capt. Bill III* and the new *Inlet Princess*. Bait and tackle are furnished. Electric reels are available. Air conditioned snack bars are aboard. Fishing excursions run anywhere from $27 to $60 per person.

Insiders' Tips

Don't bring valuables to the beach. In fact, police recommend that you not bring any more valuables than necessary with you on your vacation because jewelry, for instance, isn't really safe, even in your motel room. If you bring along electronics, write down the serial number. Police say most of these items, if stolen, end up in pawn shops, and if you have the serial numbers, you have a chance of getting them back.

Hurricane Fishing Fleet

Vereen's Marina
North Myrtle Beach 249-3571
Capt. Juel II Dock
Little River 249-3571
Capt. Jim's Marina
Calabash 249-3571

Trips depart daily, March through December, from Vereen's Marina in North Myrtle Beach, Capt. Juel II Dock in Little River and Capt. Jim's Marina in Calabash. Expect the best in bottom fishing and sport fishing. Half-day, full day, Gulf Stream, night, shark and offshore trips are available. The vessels, the 110-foot *Hurricane*, 78-foot *Capt. Juel II*, 50-foot *Southwind* and 45-foot *Cyclone,* are U.S. Coast Guard-approved and are staffed with qualified, experienced captains and crews. All equipment, bait and mate service is included. Breakfast is served aboard the *Hurricane* prior to her half-day trips. Snack bars are on each vessel. The Hurricane Fleet also offers a wide variety of other excursions such as charters and cruises that feature dinner, scenery or dances. Reservations are recommended. Costs range from $24 to $60 a person.

The Pride of the Carolinas

Little River Plantation Marina
Little River 249-1100

Half-day and Gulf Stream fishing are offered in addition to scenic cruises and Gulf Stream charters. Boats, fuel, bait, tackle and ice are available for your convenience. Dockage is also provided for small and large boats. Costs are $22 per adult, $11 for children.

Runnin' Wild Surf, Inlet and Offshore Fishing Excursions

Myrtle Beach 449-5483

Enjoy the Grand Strand's surf, inlet and offshore fishing at its best with one of the pros, Grigsby Arnette, who has more than 30 years of experience in and around these waters. Excursions include a guide, a boat, transportation to and from the necessary fishing spot and all tackle and bait. You'll learn about effective casting, proper equipment, reading inlet and beach, best times to fish, best baits to use and best places to fish. Inquire about photo safaris and freshwater excursions.

Voyager's View Marina

U.S. 17 Bus.
Murrells Inlet 651-7033

Sportfishing charters can be booked here aboard the 45-foot *Point Runner*, the *Hats Off*, *Adventurer*, the *Jane Carroll* or *Super Suds*. Half-, three-quarter and full-day and Gulf Stream adventures are available. Each one of the boats is privately owned, and each captain sets his or her price for trips. Voyager's View is a full-service marina offering slip rentals, fuel, bait, fishing supplies and dry storage of boats.

Georgetown

Landing Marina
Marina Dr. and U.S. 17
Georgetown 546-1776

An inshore and offshore sportfishing vessel can be chartered from here, from May 1 to November 1. The inshore boat costs a party of four people $350 to $550 for the day, and an offshore fishing trip will run six passengers $750 to $950. The marina does not take individual reservations, you must organize your own party.

Marshall Truluck manages this 120-slip, deep-water marina with floating and fixed docks. In addition to charter fishing boats, fuel, a ship's store, showers, restrooms and a laundromat are available. It is open year round. Hours are spring, summer and fall 8 AM to 8 PM, winter 9 AM to 5 PM.

1995 TIDE TABLES

JANUARY

	LOW A.M	LOW PM	HIGH A.M	HIGH PM
Sun. 1	12:45	1:27	7:16	7:32
Mon. 2	1:37	2:17	8:08	8:24
Tue. 3	2:27	3:05	8:58	9:15
Wed. 4	3:16	3:52	9:46	10:06
Thu. 5	4:06	4:38	10:34	10:55
Fri. 6	4:55	5:25	-----	11:21
Sat. 7	5:47	6:14	11:46	12:09
Sun. 8	6:41	7:04	12:37	12:59
Mon. 9	7:37	7:56	1:29	1:50
Tue. 10	8:34	8:49	2:22	2:43
Wed. 11	9:30	9:41	3:15	3:35
Thu. 12	10:23	10:31	4:06	4:26
Fri. 13	11:12	11:18	4:54	5:14
Sat. 14	11:57	-----	5:40	5:59
Sun. 15	12:35	12:39	6:22	6:41
Mon. 16	12:44	1:19	7:02	7:20
Tues. 17	1:25	1:58	7:39	7:58
Wed. 18	2:05	2:36	8:16	8:36
Thu. 19	2:46	3:14	8:53	9:16
Fri. 20	3:29	3:54	9:32	9:59
Sat. 21	4:15	4:37	10:15	10:49
Sun. 22	5:06	5:26	-----	11:03
Mon. 23	6:04	6:22	11:46	11:59
Tue. 24	7:09	7:25	12:49	1:02
Wed. 25	8:17	8:32	1:57	2:10
Thu. 26	9:24	9:38	3:05	3:19
Fri. 27	10:27	10:40	4:10	4:25
Sat. 28	-----	11:25	5:11	5:26
Sun. 29	11:37	12:18	6:08	6:23
Mon. 30	12:30	1:07	7:00	7:16
Tue. 31	1:21	1:54	7:49	8:05

FEBRUARY

	LOW A.M	LOW PM	HIGH A.M	HIGH PM
Wed. 1	2:08	2:38	8:35	8:52
Thu. 2	2:54	3:21	9:19	9:37
Fri. 3	3:39	4:04	10:02	10:21
Sat. 4	4:24	4:46	10:44	11:05
Sun. 5	5:10	5:31	11:27	11:51
Mon. 6	5:59	6:18	—	12:12
Tue. 7	6:51	7:10	12:40	1:02
Wed. 8	7:49	8:05	1:32	1:56
Thu. 9	8:48	9:01	2:28	2:52
Fri. 10	9:44	9:56	3:23	3:47
Sat. 11	10:37	10:47	4:16	4:39
Sun. 12	11:25	11:34	5:05	5:38
Mon. 13	—	12:09	5:51	6:12
Tue. 14	12:20	12:50	6:33	6:54
Wed. 15	1:03	1:30	7:14	7:35
Thu. 16	1:46	2:10	7:53	8:16
Fri. 17	2:29	2:49	8:33	8:59
Sat. 18	3:14	3:31	9:14	9:45
Sun. 19	4:01	4:16	10:00	10:35
Mon. 20	4:53	5:06	10:50	11:32
Tue. 21	5:50	6:03	—	11:47
Wed. 22	6:54	7:08	12:35	12:51
Thu. 23	8:01	8:16	1:43	2:00
Fri. 24	9:08	9:24	2:51	3:09
Sat. 25	10:10	10:26	3:56	4:14
Sun. 26	11:06	11:23	4:56	5:14
Mon. 27	11:57	—	5:51	6:08
Tue. 28	12:15	12:44	6:41	6:57

MARCH

	LOW A.M	LOW PM	HIGH A.M	HIGH PM
Wed. 1	1:03	1:27	7:27	7:42
Thu. 2	1:48	2:09	8:10	8:25
Fri. 3	2:31	2:49	8:50	9:05
Sat. 4	3:12	3:28	9:29	9:45
Sun. 5	3:53	4:08	10:07	10:24
Mon. 6	4:35	4:49	10:46	11:05
Tue. 7	5:19	5:34	11:28	11:50
Wed. 8	6:08	6:24	—	12:15
Thu. 9	7:03	7:19	2:41	1:08
Fri. 10	8:02	8:19	1:37	2:07
Sat. 11	9:01	9:18	2:35	3:06
Sun. 12	9:57	10:13	3:32	4:01
Mon. 13	10:47	11:05	4:25	4:53
Tue. 14	11:34	11:53	5:14	5:41
Wed. 15	—	12:17	6:00	6:26
Thu.16	12:40	1:00	6:44	7:11
Fri. 17	1:26	1:42	7:28	7:55
Sat. 18	2:12	2:25	8:12	8:42
Sun. 19	2:59	3:10	8:58	9:31
Mon. 20	3:48	3:58	9:48	10:23
Tue. 21	4:41	4:51	10:41	11:21
Wed. 22	5:39	5:50	11:41	—
Thu. 23	6:41	6:55	12:24	12:46
Fri. 24	7:46	8:03	1:30	1:53
Sat. 25	8:49	9:10	2:35	3:00
Sun. 26	9:49	10:11	3:38	4:02
Mon. 27	10:43	11:07	4:36	4:58
Tue. 28	11:32	11:57	5:29	5:49
Wed. 29	—	12:16	6:17	6:35
Thu. 30	12:43	12:58	7:01	7:17
Fri. 31	1:26	1:38	7:42	7:57

APRIL

	LOW A.M	LOW PM	HIGH A.M	HIGH PM
Sat. 1	2:06	2:17	8:20	8:34
Sun. 2	3:46	3:54	9:57	10:11
Mon. 3	4:25	4:32	10:33	10:47
Tue. 4	5:04	5:12	11:09	11:25
Wed. 5	5:45	5:54	11:48	—
Thu. 6	6:31	5:42	12:06	12:33
Fri. 7	7:21	7:36	12:53	1:24
Sat. 8	8:17	8:36	1:47	2:23
Sun. 9	9:15	9:38	2:44	3:23
Mon. 10	10:12	10:37	3:43	4:21
Tue. 11	11:05	11:33	4:39	5:16
Wed. 12	11:55	—	5:33	6:08
Thu.13	12:25	12:43	6:24	6:57
Fri. 14	1:16	1:29	7:14	7:46
Sat. 15	2:05	2:15	8:03	8:35
Sun. 16	2:54	3:02	8:53	9:26
Mon. 17	3:44	3:51	9:44	10:18
Tue. 18	4:35	4:42	10:37	11:12
Wed. 19	5:29	5:37	11:34	—
Thu .20	6:26	6:37	12:10	12:34
Fri. 21	7:25	7:41	1:11	1:38
Sat. 22	8:26	8:47	2:13	2:42
Sun. 23	10:26	10:52	4:15	4:45
Tue. 24	10:23	10:52	4:15	4:43
Tue. 25	11:15	11:46	5:11	5:37
Wed. 26	—	12:02	6:02	6:25
Thu. 27	12:35	12:46	6:49	7:09
Fri. 28	1:20	1:28	7:32	7:50
Sat. 29	2:02	2:07	8:12	8:29
Sun. 30	2:42	2:46	8:51	9:05

MAY

	LOW A.M	LOW PM	HIGH A.M	HIGH PM
Mon. 1	3:21	3:24	9:27	9:41
Tues. 2	3:59	4:01	10:03	10:16
Wed. 3	4:37	4:40	10:38	10:51
Thu. 4	5:17	5:21	11:16	11:30
Fri. 5	5:59	6:06	11:58	—
Sat. 6	6:45	6:57	12:13	12:47
Sun. 7	7:35	7:55	1:02	1:42
Mon. 8	8:30	8:58	1:57	2:42
Tue. 9	9:27	10:01	2:55	3:42
Wed. 10	10:23	11:01	3:54	4:40
Thu. 11	11:17	11:58	4:53	5:37
Fri. 12	—	12:09	5:50	6:31
Sat. 13	12:53	1:01	6:45	7:24
Sun. 14	1:45	1:51	7:40	8:17
Mon. 15	2:37	2:42	8:34	9:10
Tue. 16	3:29	3:34	9:29	10:04
Wed. 17	4:21	4:27	10:26	10:59
Thu. 18	5:14	5:23	11:23	11:55
Fri. 19	6:09	6:21	—	12:23
Sat. 20	7:05	7:22	12:53	1:23
Sun. 21	8:02	8:26	1:51	2:23
Mon. 22	8:58	9:28	2:48	3:22
Tue. 23	9:52	10:27	3:45	4:18
Wed. 24	10:42	11:21	4:39	5:09
Thu. 25	11:30	12:10	5:30	5:57
Fri. 26	12:10	12:15	6:17	6:42
Sat. 27	12:55	12:57	7:01	7:23
Sun. 28	1:37	1:38	7:43	8:02
Mon. 29	2:18	2:18	8:22	8:39
Tue. 30	2:57	2:57	9:00	9:15
Wed. 31	3:35	3:35	9:36	9:49

JUNE

	LOW A.M	LOW PM	HIGH A.M	HIGH PM
Thu. 1	4:13	4:14	10:12	10:24
Fri. 2	4:51	4:53	10:49	11:00
Sat. 3	5:30	5:36	11:29	11:39
Sun. 4	6:12	6:25	—	12:15
Mon. 5	6:58	7:21	12:25	1:08
Tue. 6	7:49	8:23	1:16	2:07
Wed. 7	8:46	9:28	2:14	3:08
Thu. 8	9:45	10:32	3:15	4:09
Fri. 9	10:43	11:33	4:18	5:10
Sat. 10	11:41	—	5:20	6:09
Sun. 11	12:31	12:37	6:21	7:06
Mon. 12	1:26	1:31	7:20	8:02
Tue. 13	2:20	2:25	8:18	8:56
Wed. 14	3:12	3:18	9:15	9:49
Thu. 15	4:03	4:11	10:11	10:43
Fri. 16	4:55	5:05	11:07	11:36
Sat. 17	5:46	6:01	—	12:04
Sun. 18	6:38	6:58	12:29	1:00
Mon. 19	7:31	7:57	1:22	1:56
Tue. 20	8:23	8:57	2:16	2:51
Wed. 21	9:16	9:55	3:10	3:45
Thu. 22	10:07	10:50	4:03	4:37
Fri. 23	10:56	11:40	4:54	5:26
Sat. 24	11:43	—	5:43	6:11
Sun. 25	12:27	12:28	6:30	6:55
Mon. 26	1:11	1:11	7:14	7:35
Tue. 27	1:53	1:52	7:55	8:14
Wed. 28	2:32	2:32	8:34	8:50
Thu. 29	3:11	3:11	9:11	9:25
Fri. 30	3:48	3:50	9:47	9:59

1995 TIDE TABLES

JULY

	LOW A.M	LOW PM	HIGH A.M	HIGH PM
Sat. 1	4:25	4:30	10:24	10:34
Sun. 2	5:02	5:12	11:03	11:12
Mon. 3	5:42	6:00	11:48	11:55
Tue. 4	6:25	6:54	——	12:39
Wed. 5	7:15	7:55	12:45	1:38
Thu. 6	8:12	9:01	1:42	2:40
Fri. 7	9:14	10:08	2:46	3:45
Sat. 8	10:17	11:12	3:52	4:49
Sun. 9	11:19	——	4:59	5:51
Mon. 10	12:12	12:18	6:03	6:50
Tue. 11	1:08	1:15	7:05	7:46
Wed. 12	2:01	2:09	8:03	8:40
Thu. 13	2:52	3:02	8:59	9:31
Fri. 14	3:42	3:53	9:53	10:22
Sat. 15	4:30	4:44	10:45	11:11
Sun. 16	5:18	5:36	11:37	——
Mon. 17	6:06	6:29	12:00	12:29
Thu. 18	6:55	7:23	12:49	1:21
Wed. 19	7:45	8:20	1:39	2:14
Thu. 20	8:36	9:17	2:31	3:07
Fri. 21	9:29	10:14	3:23	3:59
Sat. 22	10:21	11:07	4:17	4:50
Sun. 23	11:11	11:56	5:08	5:39
Mon. 24	11:59	——	5:58	6:14
Tue. 25	12:42	12:44	6:44	7:07
Wed. 26	1:25	1:27	7:27	7:47
Thu. 27	2:05	2:08	8:07	8:24
Fri. 28	2:44	2:48	8:46	9:00
Sat. 29	3:21	3:28	9:23	9:34
Sun. 30	3:57	4:09	10:00	10:10
Mon. 31	4:34	4:52	10:40	10:48

AUGUST

	LOW AM	LOW PM	HIGH AM	HIGH PM
Tue. 1	5:14	5:40	11:25	11:32
Wed. 2	5:58	6:33	——	12:17
Thu. 3	6:49	7:34	12:22	1:16
Fri. 4	7:47	8:41	1:21	2:21
Sat. 5	8:52	9:49	2:27	3:28
Sun. 6	9:59	10:54	3:37	4:34
Mon. 7	11:04	11:54	4:46	5:36
Tue. 8	——	12:04	5:51	6:35
Wed. 9	12:50	1:00	6:51	7:30
Thu. 10	1:41	1:53	7:47	8:21
Fri. 11	2:30	2:44	8:40	9:10
Sat. 12	3:16	3:33	9:30	9:57
Sun. 13	4:01	4:20	10:19	10:42
Mon. 14	4:46	5:08	11:06	11:27
Tue. 15	5:30	5:55	11:53	——
Wed. 16	6:15	6:45	12:12	12:41
Thu. 17	7:03	7:39	12:59	1:31
Fri. 18	7:54	8:35	1:49	2:23
Sat. 19	8:48	9:33	2:42	3:17
Sun. 20	9:43	10:30	3:37	4:11
Mon. 21	10:37	11:22	4:32	5:02
Tue. 22	11:28	——	5:24	5:50
Wed. 23	12:09	12:16	6:12	6:34
Thu. 24	12:53	1:01	6:57	7:16
Fri. 25	1:34	1:44	7:38	7:55
Sat. 26	2:13	2:26	8:18	8:32
Sun. 27	2:51	3:07	8:57	9:09
Mon. 28	3:28	3:50	9:37	9:47
Tue. 29	4:07	4:35	10:20	10:29
Wed. 30	4:49	5:24	11:07	11:15
Thu. 31	5:26	6:19	——	12:00

SEPTEMBER

	LOW AM	LOW PM	HIGH AM	HIGH PM
Fri. 1	6:29	7:20	12:09	1:01
Sat. 2	7:30	8:26	1:11	2:07
Sun. 3	8:38	9:33	2:19	3:15
Mon. 4	9:46	10:37	3:30	4:21
Tue. 5	10:52	11:36	4:37	5:22
Wed. 6	11:51	——	5:40	6:19
Thu. 7	12:29	12:46	6:37	7:11
Fri. 8	1:18	1:37	7:30	8:00
Sat. 9	2:05	2:25	8:19	8:46
Sun. 10	2:48	3:11	9:05	9:29
Mon. 11	3:30	3:55	9:49	10:11
Tue. 12	4:12	4:38	10:32	10:52
Wed. 13	4:53	5:22	11:15	11:34
Thu. 14	5:36	6:08	11:58	——
Fri. 15	6:21	6:57	12:17	12:45
Sat. 16	7:11	7:52	1:05	1:36
Sun. 17	8:05	8:50	1:58	2:30
Mon. 18	9:03	9:48	2:55	3:25
Tue. 19	10:00	10:42	3:53	4:19
Wed. 20	10:55	11:31	4:47	5:09
Thu. 21	11:45	——	5:31	5:56
Fri. 22	12:16	12:33	6:23	6:40
Sat. 23	12:59	1:18	7:07	7:22
Sun. 24	1:40	2:03	7:50	8:03
Mon. 25	2:20	2:47	8:32	8:45
Tue. 26	3:01	3:33	9:16	9:28
Wed. 27	3:44	4:20	10:02	10:14
Thu. 28	4:29	5:11	10:53	11:05
Fri. 29	5:19	6:06	11:48	——
Sat. 30	6:15	7:07	12:02	12:50

OCTOBER

	LOW AM	LOW PM	HIGH AM	HIGH PM
Sun. 1	7:18	8:12	1:06	1:55
Mon. 2	8:26	9:17	2:15	3:01
Tue. 3	9:35	10:19	3:23	4:04
Wed. 4	10:39	11:15	4:28	5:05
Thu. 5	11:37	——	5:27	6:00
Fri. 6	12:06	12:30	6:21	6:50
Sat. 7	12:53	1:19	7:11	7:37
Sun. 8	1:37	2:05	7:56	8:20
Mon. 9	2:19	2:48	8:39	9:01
Tues. 10	3:00	3:29	9:20	9:40
Wed. 11	3:39	4:10	9:59	10:18
Thu. 12	4:19	4:50	10:38	10:57
Fri. 13	4:59	5:33	11:18	11:37
Sat. 14	5:42	6:19	——	12:00
Sun. 15	6:29	7:09	12:22	12:47
Mon. 16	7:22	8:04	1:14	1:39
Tue. 17	8:20	9:01	2:11	2:34
Wed. 18	9:19	9:56	3:09	3:30
Thu. 19	10:17	10:48	4:05	4:23
Fri. 20	11:12	11:37	4:58	5:14
Sat. 21	——	12:03	5:48	6:02
Sun. 22	12:22	12:53	6:36	6:49
Mon. 23	1:07	1:40	7:23	7:36
Tues. 24	1:52	2:28	8:10	8:23
Wed. 25	2:37	3:16	8:58	9:11
Thu. 26	3:23	4:06	9:48	10:02
Fri. 27	4:13	4:53	10:41	10:57
Sat. 28	5:05	5:54	11:38	11:56
Sun. 29	5:03	5:53	11:38	——
Mon. 30	6:06	6:54	12:00	12:41
Tues. 31	7:13	7:56	1:06	1:44

NOVEMBER

	LOW AM	LOW PM	HIGH AM	HIGH PM
Wed. 1	8:19	8:55	2:11	2:45
Thu. 2	9:22	9:50	3:13	3:43
Fri. 3	10:10	10:40	4:10	4:37
Sat. 4	11:12	11:26	5:02	5:26
Sun. 5	11:59	——	5:49	6:11
Mon. 6	12:10	12:43	6:33	6:54
Tue. 7	12:51	1:25	7:14	7:34
Wed. 8	1:31	2:05	7:53	8:12
Thu. 9	2:10	2:44	8:30	8:48
Fri. 10	2:48	3:22	9:06	9:25
Sat. 11	3:27	4:02	9:43	10:06
Sun. 12	4:08	4:44	10:21	10:44
Mon. 13	4:52	5:29	11:03	11:31
Tue. 14	5:41	6:19	11:50	——
Wed. 15	6:36	7:12	12:24	12:42
Thu. 16	7:36	8:07	1:22	1:37
Fri. 17	8:38	9:02	2:21	2:34
Sat. 18	9:37	9:56	3:18	3:30
Sun. 19	10:34	10:47	4:13	4:25
Mon. 20	11:27	11:37	5:06	5:18
Tue. 21	——	12:19	5:59	6:11
Wed. 22	12:27	1:10	6:50	7:03
Thu. 23	1:16	2:00	7:42	7:57
Fri. 24	2:07	2:52	8:35	8:51
Sat. 25	2:58	3:44	9:29	9:48
Sun. 26	3:52	4:38	10:25	10:46
Mon. 27	4:49	5:34	11:22	11:47
Tue. 28	5:50	6:31	——	12:21
Wed. 29	6:54	7:30	12:49	1:20
Thu. 30	7:58	8:27	1:51	2:19

DECEMBER

	LOW AM	LOW PM	HIGH AM	HIGH PM
Fri. 1	9:00	9:21	2:51	3:16
Sat. 2	9:57	10:11	3:46	4:09
Sun. 3	10:50	10:58	4:38	4:59
Mon. 4	11:37	11:43	5:25	5:45
Tues. 5	——	12:21	6:09	6:28
Wed. 6	12:25	1:02	6:50	7:08
Thu. 7	1:05	1:41	7:28	7:46
Fri. 8	1:44	2:19	8:05	8:23
Sat. 9	2:23	2:57	8:40	8:58
Sun. 10	3:01	3:35	9:14	9:33
Mon. 11	3:39	4:13	9:49	10:11
Tue. 12	4:20	5:53	10:26	10:53
Wed. 13	5:05	5:36	11:07	11:41
Thu. 14	5:57	6:25	——	11:54
Fri. 15	6:55	7:19	12:37	12:48
Sat. 16	7:59	8:18	1:38	1:48
Sun. 17	9:03	9:17	2:40	2:50
Mon. 18	10:05	10:16	3:41	3:52
Tue. 19	11:03	11:12	4:41	4:52
Wed. 20	11:59	——	5:38	5:51
Thu. 21	12:06	12:52	6:34	6:47
Fri. 22	12:59	1:44	7:28	7:43
Sat. 23	1:52	2:35	8:21	8:39
Sun. 24	2:44	3:26	9:14	9:34
Mon. 25	3:38	4:17	10:07	10:30
Tue. 26	4:32	5:09	11:01	11:27
Wed. 27	5:29	6:03	11:56	——
Thu. 28	6:28	6:57	12:25	12:51
Fri. 29	7:30	7:53	1:23	1:48
Sat. 30	8:31	8:47	2:21	2:44
Sun. 31	9:29	9:40	3:16	3:38

Fishing Piers

Apache Pier

Apache Campground
9700 Kings Rd.
Myrtle Beach *449-7323*

Welcome to the longest pier anywhere along the East Coast, measuring 1,220 feet. Accents include a bait and tackle shop, arcade, restaurant and aquariums full of indigenous fish. Nightly entertainment is also part of the fare from May 30 through Labor Day weekend. It will cost you $4.50 a day to fish from here or 50¢ to partake in the action as a spectator. Hours are 6 AM to midnight during spring and fall seasons and 7 AM to 6 PM all winter.

Cherry Grove Pier

N. Ocean Blvd.
North Myrtle Beach *249-1625*

Daily admission is $4 per rod. Seasonal rates are available. Holiday House Motel guests are admitted for free. This pier is 960 feet long and is lighted for night fishing. You'll enjoy the full line of pier tackle plus a gift shop, arcade and restaurant. Cherry Grove is open from March 1 to December 1, 24-hours a day, except for the restaurant. Admission is 25¢ for spectators.

Myrtle Beach State Park

U.S. 17
Myrtle Beach *238-5326*

Admission is $4 daily, and season passes are available. Tackle, bait, ice and a gift shop are on the premises. The pier is open all year, seven days a week. Since fishing hours fluctuate from season to season, it's a good idea to call ahead.

Second Avenue Pier & Restaurant

110 N. Ocean Blvd.
Myrtle Beach *626-8420*

Admission is $4 for a daily pass; season passes are available. There is a full line of bait, tackle, rod and reels. Enjoy the gift shop, arcade and restaurant (full menu). This lighted pier with a "T" on the end is 905 feet long. Hours are 6 AM to midnight.

Springmaid Pier

S. Ocean Blvd.
Myrtle Beach *238-5212*

Bait and ice are available, and tackle is for rent or sale. Admission is $4.50 with special weekly and year-round rates. Hours are 7 AM to 10 PM in the winter and 7 AM to midnight from spring to fall. Spectators can enjoy the view for free.

Surfside Pier

S. Ocean Blvd.
Surfside Beach *238-0121*

This pier is 850 feet long. Admission is $5. Spectators pay 25¢ for admission. Season passes are available. Inside you'll find tackle, bait, rod and reel rental and a gift shop. The tackle shop and pier are open 24 hours a day from March 1 through December 15.

Insiders' Tips

If you have a lot of time and money invested in your fishing habit, you may be interested in entering some of these tournaments that put your skills to the test and pay off handsomely for the biggest catches.

Photo:Bill Scroggins, The Sun News

Deep-sea fishing can be a fun way to spend the day. Just make sure you take along some seasickness medication.

The Pier at Garden City

Waccamaw Dr. S.
Garden City Beach 651-9700

This is the newest pier on the South Carolina coast. It is open 24 hours a day spring to fall, 7 AM to 10 PM in the winter. Daily admission is $4.50. Spectators are admitted free. Annual and weekly passes are available. Bait and rental rods can be had in the tackle shop. Stop in at the arcade and oceanfront deck at the Pier Cafe.

Boat Fishing Tournaments

Marlin Quay Invitational Billfish Tournament

Mid-May 651-4444

A South Carolina Governor's Cup series tournament, the Marlin Quay involves marinas from North Myrtle Beach to Edisto Beach. Points are gained through six fishing events for the biggest billfish caught or released. Entry is $1,000 per boat, and the first place purse is $10,000, plus winners are invited to the Governor's mansion for a celebratory dinner.

Natural Light King Mackerel Fishing Tournament

Early June 238-0485

This tournament starts off with a "multi-inlet kickoff" where boats are launched from Murrells Inlet, Little River and Georgetown. Anglers are competing for the biggest King Mackerel they can catch since the biggest of this species will net $10,000. This is a $160,000 all cash tournament. Entry fees are $300 per boat.

Pier Fishing Tournaments

Annual Grand Strand Fishing Rodeo

April 1 through October 31 626-7444

If you would rather just cast from one of the Grand Strand's piers, this tournament is for you since more than $10,000

Lost Children

One of the most common problems lifeguards face is finding the parents of lost children. Children get involved in swimming or chasing sea gulls, and they don't realize they've drifted so far away. The beach looks pretty much the same from one spot to another, and the crowds of people all blend together. When someone spots a lost child and wants to help him or her, the child frequently doesn't even know which direction he or she came from.

Before you go on the beach, instruct your child to go to the nearest lifeguard and ask for help if he or she becomes lost. As soon as you check into your accommodations, tell your child, "You're staying at the Holiday Inn, or Landmark or Patricia Grand." Make your child repeat it back to you. In Surfside, there is a sign system that helps children know where they came from. If you're sunning near the sign with the dragon, for instance, point it out: "You're a dragon."

in cash and prizes are given out over six months for catching the biggest "fish of the month" in this contest.

Pier King Mackerel Tournaments

Mid-May and Early October 626-7444

These are two other pier tournaments much like the fishing rodeo. Exact locations and prizes have not been set yet.

Scuba Diving

Coastal Wateree Dive Center

Vereen's Marina
North Myrtle Beach 249-9388

Private scuba instruction and full PADI certification can be accomplished here. Daily diving charters are at your disposal for half or whole days. Costs of diving charters range from $50 to $80 per person, depending on how long you want to spend and how far out you want to go. Their boats will travel anywhere from 6 to 55 miles out from shore. Complete PADI certification will average $200 to $225, which includes all equipment, air and training materials.

Island Scuba, Inc.

#4 Pawleys Station
Pawleys Island 237-1317

Island Scuba clients are restricted to those 12 years of age and older. Basic tuition for diving lessons is $99 per person; complete PADI certification is available. Half- and full-day charters can be had for $45 to $75, while diving trips to the Florida Keys or Bahamas will run $199 and up per person, double occupancy. Equipment rental is also available.

Scuba Syndrome

2718 U.S. 501
Myrtle Beach 626-6740

Certified divers can plunder the Grand Strand's offshore for $50 to $90 a day depending on how far out you want to go. Rental for a full set of gear is $29 to $35. The certification course, a $100 investment, lasts two weeks plus two extra days of training.

Under Sea Adventures

Garden City 651-1290

Under Sea specializes in custom diving packages. They serve up lobster hunting excursions, multiple deep-site dives

Photo: Bill Scroggins, The Sun News

When it's high tide, you're bound to find someone trying to "catch a wave."

and underwater tours of World War II wrecks. Be prepared to stay aboard overnight since a number of these exciting trips last one-and-a-half to two days. Depending on what you choose, costs start at $45 and run up to $100 a person. PADI certification and equipment rentals are also available.

Sailing and Wind Surfing

Whether or not you're nautically inclined, you shouldn't miss experiencing the incredible feeling of gliding across the waves and taking in the salty ocean spray.

Downwind Sails

29th Ave. S.
Myrtle Beach *448-7245*

Rentals, rides and lessons for Wave Runners, windsurfers, sailboats, a 50-foot catamaran and banana boats are available here. Downwind Sails is open from April to September and is right on the beach. This is a great spot to hang out during the summer with all of the boating action plus regular beach volleyball tournaments.

Driftwood Cruising

Myrtle Beach Yacht Club
Coquina Harbor *249-8036*

Leave the driving to the crew of the 38-foot sailboat *Blue Chip* for a 2.5-hour ride along the Intracoastal Waterway to Long Bay, Waties and Bird Islands. The cost is $20 per person, with a four-person minimum per cruise. From mid-May through mid-October, dinner cruises launch from here, lasting an hour and catered by the Down Under Australian Restaurant. A dinner cruise runs $25 per person.

North Myrtle Beach Water Sports, Inc.

Coquina Harbour *249-4333*

Jet ski and pontoon boat rentals are available here from 9 AM to 7 PM, seven days a week during the spring and summer months. Call ahead for rates and reservations.

Parasailing/Wave Running

So you can't sit still. You want to try "walking on water." Well, then, parasailing or riding a Wave Runner is for you.

Family Kingdom Parasailing

Third Ave. S. and Ocean Blvd.
Myrtle Beach *626-9172*

With Family Kingdom's parasailing ride you'll be suspended about 200 feet in the air for approximately 15 minutes. The ride is $50 per person and the view is priceless.

Intracoastal Water Sports, Inc.

2200 Little River Neck
North Myrtle Beach *249-5387*

Wave Runners are rented by the half-hour, and for the half-day, but only for use in the Intracoastal Waterway. The hourly rate averages around $45.

Kayaking

The Great Outdoors

626-2348

Like the natives of our Lowcountry, the rivers are laid back and easygoing. Kayaking here means you don't have to worry about rushing whitewater rapids or rocks. These guided tours include an introductory instructional clinic and roomy, stable boats. There is a half-day tour paddling the dark waters of the Old Waccamaw River, gliding under moss-draped giant cypress trees, for $30 per person or $40 per couple. The same prices apply for another half-day tour through the salt marshes of Murrells Inlet. Group rates and specialty tours are available, plus discounts for church, civic or school organizations. Kayaks are available on site for sale or rent.

Inside Parks and Recreation

During sky-blue summers, Carolina sunshine is hot and plentiful. The water is cool — and equally plentiful. Autumn is brilliant . . . crisp mornings and breezy afternoons perfect for beach walks and surf fishing. Winter comes in bite-sized pieces... a string of snappy days with long warm stretches in between. And, when spring arrives — quickly — bearing wisteria, daffodils and bright-faced college kids, it's hard to believe another year has passed. This deliciously temperate climate enables tourists and residents to enjoy the great outdoors for most of the year. So, head for the parks and take advantage of our enviable climate. And while there are myriad parks to choose from, this overview should set you in a direction that's perfect for you.

Parks

State Parks

Myrtle Beach State Park

U.S. 17 S. *238-5325*
Between Myrtle and Surfside beaches

Situated in the heart of the Grand Strand, Myrtle Beach State Park boasts one of the most popular public beaches along the Carolina coast. This 312-acre oceanfront park is one of the last remaining natural areas along the northern shores of South Carolina. Natural beauty reigns here and gives visitors a glimpse of the way the entire Strand looked long ago — before its development as a resort mecca.

Myrtle Beach State Park was developed by the Civilian Conservation Corps, a New Deal program created by President Franklin D. Roosevelt to provide employment during the Great Depression. During World War II, the U.S. military took over the park as a coastal defense staging area. In March of 1945, the park was returned to the citizens of the state. It was the first state park opened to the public in South Carolina, and it also holds the distinction of having the first campground and fishing pier on the Grand Strand.

Park facilities include 350 camping sites, rented on a first-come, first-serve basis. (See our Accommodations chapter.) The park also offers five cabins, two apartments and picnic areas with shelters. In addition to the 730-foot pier, there's a nature trail and nature center. A park naturalist conducts activities year round and interprets the natural history of the coast. Surf fishing and pier fishing are allowed. Swimmers can splash about in the ocean or in the park's pool. The park also provides a snack bar and playground equipment.

Park hours are 6 AM to 10 PM year round. Office hours are 9 AM to 5 PM, Monday through Friday and 11 AM to

Photo: The Sun News

There are plenty of tennis courts along the Grand Strand to practice your serve and volley.

noon and 4 PM to 5 PM on Saturday and Sunday.

Huntington Beach State Park

U.S. 17 S. (Across from Brookgreen Gardens)
Murrells Inlet 237-4440

Huntington Beach State Park, a personal favorite, offers the best preserved beach on the Grand Strand. Observe the diverse coastal environment at the freshwater lagoon, salt marsh, nature trail and along the wide, beautiful beach.

The park is also the site of the imposing Spanish-style castle Atalaya, the former winter home and studio of noted American sculptress Anna Hyatt Huntington. Mrs. Huntington and her husband, Archer, were the visionary founders of Brookgreen Gardens. Seasonal tours of Atalaya are available. (See this chapter's sidebar as well as our Accommodations and Annual Events chapters.)

Park facilities include 127 camping sites, picnic areas with shelters, a boardwalk and a general store. Activities such as surf fishing, swimming and crabbing are encouraged, and the park offers one of the finest birdwatching sites on the East Coast. Nature programs and playground equipment are available for the young and young-at-heart. Atalaya Arts & Crafts Festival, a prestigious juried arts and crafts show, attracts thousands of visitors to the park every fall.

Park hours are 6 AM to 9 PM April through September, and 6 AM to 6 PM October through March. Office hours are 9 AM to 5 PM, Monday through Friday and 11 AM to noon on Saturday and Sunday.

Hampton Plantation State Park

1950 Rutledge Rd.
McClellanville 546-9361

Located southwest of Georgetown, Hampton Plantation is not technically a part of the stretch of real estate we call the Grand Strand. However, Hampton offers a peek at one of the most impressive restored plantation homes in South Carolina and, therefore, is well worth the short drive.

Adjacent to the Santee River, this 322-acre property was once a coastal rice plantation and last served as the home of Archibald Rutledge, noted writer and South Carolina poet laureate. The state purchased the property from Mr. Rutledge in 1971.

A National Historic Landmark, the Hampton mansion stands as the centerpiece of the park and a monument to the state's glorious rice empire. The mansion's colossal Adam-style portico is one of the finest and earliest examples of its kind in all of North America, while its interior, purposely unfurnished, highlights the structure's design and construction. Cutaway sections of walls and ceilings exhibit the building's evolution from a simple farmhouse to a grand mansion. Exposed timber framing, hand-carved mantels and delicately wrought hinges and hardware reveal the 18th-century builder's craft.

The grounds surrounding the mansion offer a unique opportunity to examine the wildlife of the Carolina Lowcountry. Cypress swamps, abandoned rice fields and pine and hardwood forests are home to a staggering variety of flora and fauna. From the massive live oaks to the wild flowers and shrubs, Hampton Plantation is a naturalist's and photographer's delight in every season.

In addition to the beautiful home, the park includes a picnic area and marked nature trails.

The park is open 9 AM to 6 PM, Thursday through Monday, and office hours are 11 AM to noon, Thursday through Monday, year round. The mansion is open between 1 PM and 4 PM on Saturdays and Sundays from Labor Day to April 1, and between 1 PM and 4 PM, Thursday through Monday the rest of the year.

City Parks

City parks pepper the Strand and are perfect for a little rest and relaxation. Several parks provide playground equipment, basketball courts and running tracks — others offer serene picnic areas complete with tables and restrooms. There is no admission fee to any of the following parks.

Central Park

1030 Possum Trot Rd.
North Myrtle Beach *280-5570*

This park is a kind of sportsman's track and field course. It features four tennis courts, four baseball/softball fields, a soccer field and a ¼-mile running track, a paved basketball court, two playground areas and a picnic area.

Hill Street Park

Hill St.
North Myrtle Beach *280-5570*

This park showcases what may be the North Strand's best lighted tennis court. There's cool playground equipment, too.

McLean Park

2nd Ave. S.
North Myrtle Beach *280-5570*

McLean Park is a couple of blocks from the ocean and is sometimes used for outdoor concerts, Easter egg hunts and small festivals. In addition to two tennis courts, a paved basketball court and playground equipment, the park features a picnic area, small lake and a baseball field.

Yow Park

Windy Hill Rd.
North Myrtle Beach *280-5570*

This is a quaint little park with a basketball court, playground and picnic area.

Chapin Park

16th Ave. N. and Kings Hwy.
Myrtle Beach

Located in the very hub of downtown traffic, everybody's favorite Chapin Park offers an unbelievably tranquil setting featuring a beautiful arbor area, picnic tables and garden swings. Local business folk seeking to escape the rat race frequent Chapin during lunch — especially in the spring and fall. The swings are ideal for reading the paper and eating a homemade sandwich. Weekends bring a variety of activities to Chapin, including art shows, outdoor concerts and small festivals. Also, more than a few couples have exchanged wedding vows in the two-story gazebo that sits in the heart of this pretty park. The playground, favored by local parents, features wooden equipment and lots of sand.

Hurl Rock Park

20th Ave. S. and Ocean Blvd.
Myrtle Beach

Wooden decks create a lovely trail through Hurl Rock Park, which features a spectacular view of the beach. This park is great for photo opportunities, hand-holding and people watching.

Midway Park

19th Ave. S. and Kings Hwy.

Tennis is the name of the game at Midway, with six lighted courts. But that's not all. There's a lighted basketball court with two goals, as well as a rest area and bathroom facilities.

Fuller Park

Surfside and Myrtle Drs.
Surfside Beach

Fuller Park is a nice family destination with three tennis courts, two paved basketball courts, a playground and a picnic area with bathroom facilities. You'll also find shuffleboard courts and horseshoe pits — amenities not common to other area parks.

Lakeside Park

Lakeside Dr. and 8th Ave. S.
Surfside Beach

A great place for a family reunion, Lakeside Park features a large picnic area and the Floral Clubhouse, which may be rented by contacting the Town of Surfside Recreation Department, 238-2590.

All Children's Park

10th Ave. S. and Hollywood Dr.
Surfside Beach

This innovative playground, designed and equipped to accommodate both able-bodied and handicapped children — hence its name — has set a nationwide example.

At this unique park, you'll discover "standard" equipment modified to suit the singular needs of challenged youngsters — without separating them from their peers. Traditional playgrounds are usually unsatisfactory for kids with physical disabilities; sand limits mobility and equipment is not properly structured. At All Children's Park, the main platform is a specially designed ramp that offers a view of the entire playground. The slide has a tiered ramp along its side, so parents can walk down as they help their children slide. Mesh-net swings make it easier to accommodate handicapped children. An elevated tic-tac-toe board and sandbox make it possible for children in wheelchairs to scoop up and play. A land-

scaped, shaded area with picnic tables and an adult swing adjoins the park. All Children's Park is more than a mere recreational structure: Over time, facilities like this will create invaluable bonds of understanding and acceptance among all people. Don't miss it.

Residential Parks

The following parks are public residential facilities maintained by the City of Myrtle Beach. Carefully manicured landscapes and multicolored blooms create a delightful series of green sanctuaries — retreats from the hustle and bustle of resort living. Read a book; take a nap; ponder the mysteries of life.

Pinner Place Park
Pinner Pl. and Pridgen Rd.

Withers Park
Second Ave. S. and Myrtle St.

Loblolly Park
Loblolly Cir. in the Dunes section

Gray Park
45th Ave. N. and Burchap Dr.

Memorial Park
Porcher Ave. and Haskell Cir.

McMillan Park
Haskell Cir. and Ocean Blvd.

Cameron Park
28th Ave. N. and Ocean Blvd.

Springs Park
Springs Ave. and Hampton Cir. at Ocean Blvd.

McLeod Park
61st Ave. N.

Health Clubs

As the country's fitness I.Q. continues its steady climb, health clubs have become increasingly popular — particularly here in a land of hard bodies, teeny bikinis and nearly eternal summer. Kingston Plantation's Sport & Health Club on the north end of Myrtle Beach and the Plantation Resort Health & Swim Club in Surfside Beach's Deerfield Plantation are two of the area's most successful fitness forums.

The Sport & Health Club, located in the renowned resort community of Kingston Plantation, 9760 Kings Road, is a $4.5 million, 40,000-square-foot facility that is open seven days a week. Outdoor facilities include nine lighted tennis courts (four clay and five hard) and an Olympic-size pool. Indoors, the list of offerings is staggering: three racquetball courts, an aerobics studio, a pool and whirlpool, a sauna, more than 30 pieces of cardiovascular equipment, two weight rooms, tanning facilities, a pro shop and more. Classes and clinics include gymnastics for kids, aerobics, yoga, aquacise, racquetball and tennis. Massage therapy is available too! For details on different offerings and class times, call 497-2444.

The Plantation Resort Health & Swim Club, 1250 U.S. 17 N. in Surfside Beach, is also located in the residential community of Deerfield Plantation. Featuring a 70-foot swimming pool complex that's fully enclosed and heated, this club offers aerobics, water aerobics, weight programs and babysitters.

If you're looking to work up a sweat, here are a few other health clubs; one's bound to be convenient for you.

GOLD'S GYM OF MYRTLE BEACH

951 Jason Blvd.
Myrtle Beach *448-3939*

ELITE FITNESS

523 U.S. 17 N.
North Myrtle Beach *249-5820*

OCEAN DUNES RESORT

75th Ave. N.(On Ocean Blvd.)
Myrtle Beach *449-7441*

AMERICAN HEALTH AND RACQUET

4125 S.C. 544
Socastee *650-0271*

Tennis

If spirited competition on the courts is what you love, you can slam an ace or volley for fun on any one of numerous tennis courts along the length of the Grand Strand. We'll start with the freebies, available on a first-come, first-serve (pardon the pun) basis. Pay-as-you-play courts require reservations, so call in advance.

Photo: The Sun News

From the marsh at Huntington Beach State Park you can see all types of wildlife, including alligators.

Myrtle Beach Public Courts

3200 Oak St.
Myrtle Beach

These three outdoor, asphalt-surfaced courts are next door to the Myrtle Beach Recreation Center. Lights allow you to play all night; however, when the center closes, so do the restroom facilities.

Myrtle Beach Public Courts

U.S. 17 and 19th Ave. S.
Myrtle Beach

This complex has six lighted courts, along with restrooms and outdoor water fountains. All courts are asphalt treated.

Central Park

1030 Possum Trot Rd.
(Between 13th and 15th Ave. S.)
North Myrtle Beach *280-5570*

Central Park offers four outdoor, lighted asphalt courts. Lights-out is 11 PM.

Hill Street Park

Hill St. (off Sea Mountain Hwy.)
North Myrtle Beach *280-5570*

Be the first to grab the one lighted asphalt court. The lights go out at 11 PM.

McLean Park

First Ave. S.
North Myrtle Beach

McLean offers two outdoor, lighted asphalt courts. Lights-out at 11 PM.

Surfside Beach Public Courts

Surfside Dr.
Surfside Beach *650-4131*

All three of these outdoor lighted courts are treated with asphalt. Restroom facilities and water fountains are nearby.

Kingston Plantation Sport & Health Club

9760 Kings Rd.
Myrtle Beach *497-2444*

Home of the annual **GTE Tennis Festival**, which has hosted pro players such as Pete Sampras, Michael Chang, Andre Aggasi and Jimmy Connors, this $4.5 million health club offers four outdoor clay courts and five Har-tru courts. All courts are lighted and cost about $15.75 per hour. Nonmembers pay a guest fee of $12 per person.

Litchfield Racquet Club

Cypress Dr.
Litchfield Beach *237-3411*

Two public indoor courts are available for $20 per hour. The club also maintains 17 Har-tru clay courts and one outdoor Rubico stadium court. Three lighted courts are available; hourly fees are $16, and instruction is available from two full-time professionals. Ball machines are also available.

Myrtle Beach Tennis & Swim Club

U.S. 17 Bypass (Across from Dixie Stampede)
Myrtle Beach *449-4486*

Two of the 10 composition courts are lighted. You can practice with the ball machines or at the free backboard area. Full-time tennis professionals offer adult and junior programs year round. Courts cost $6 per player per hour for singles and $4 per player per hour for doubles. A match setup service and racquet stringing are available. There's also a pro shop.

Ocean Creek Tennis Center

U.S. 17, Windy Hill
North Myrtle Beach *272-7724, Ext. 1011*

The center offers seven Tru-Flex courts, one practice court and two lighted courts at $12 per hour, per court. Lessons are available through the United States Professional Tennis Association (USPTA).

Pan-American Resort Motor Inn

5300 N. Ocean Blvd.
Myrtle Beach *449-7411*

Guests of the Pan-American can play any of the five outdoor cushion-tex courts for free. Others pay $8 per hour for singles or $10 per hour for doubles.

Dunes Village

5200 N. Ocean Blvd.
Myrtle Beach *449-5275*

Guests of Dunes Village can play any of the five outdoor cushion-tex courts for free. Others pay $8 per hour for singles or $10 per hour for doubles.

Prestwick Health & Tennis Club

1375 McMaster Dr.
Myrtle Beach *828-1000*

Prestwick offers 11 clay courts, one lighted stadium court and two lighted hard surface courts. Nonmembers pay $15 an hour per court. Private lessons are available for $32 an hour from the head pro. If you're really in top form, you can have a video tape made of your match.

Recreation Centers

North Myrtle Beach Community Center

Possum Trot Rd.
North Myrtle Beach *280-5570*

Serving the community for decades, the North Myrtle Beach Community Center offers four meeting rooms and a gymnasium/auditorium. Activities include classes for the young and young-at-heart. Just a few of the offerings include arts and crafts, clogging, sign language, karate, drama and creative dance. Team sports include basketball, T-ball, softball, baseball and volleyball. Other activities offered at the center are aerobics, seniors' toning classes, introduction to bridge and bridge games. Fees are nominal, and the center is open Monday through Friday. Operating hours hinge on activities, so please call for details.

Atalaya: Fortress By The Sea

South of Myrtle Beach is the castle Atalaya, meaning "watchtower" in Spanish. Empty now, save the hushed footfalls of old ghosts, this silent sentinel of the wide, blue Atlantic captivates visitors.

Photo: The Sun News

Once home to Archer and Anna Hyatt Huntington, Atlaya is not to be missed on your trip to Huntington Beach State Park.

Atalaya's construction began in 1931. Archer and Anna Hyatt Huntington, new owners of a vast track of land that included four Colonial plantations, orchestrated the plans for their winter home. Mr. Huntington was a scholar of Spanish history and culture, so it is not surprising his new home was fashioned after the 8th-century Moorish fortresses along the Mediterranean coast of Spain.

Eager to provide work for depression-poor community residents, the Huntingtons insisted on using local labor to construct Atalaya. Mr. Huntington brought in craftsmen to teach the unskilled area residents. Atalaya was quite a boon to the impoverished community. Working only on oral instruction (there were no written plans), grateful laborers were known to lay 2,000 bricks a day.

Atalaya's layout is a three-sided "square" with 33 rooms around an interior courtyard. The building is dominated by a square tower stretching nearly 40 feet into the air. In its glory days, the cleverly designed tower held a 3,000-gallon, cypress water tank. The height of the tank gave the water enough pressure to flow throughout the house. Ingenious indeed!

Don't miss out on this intriguing slice of coastal history. Visit Atalaya in Huntington Beach State Park on U.S. 17, just across from the world famous Brookgreen Gardens.

Pepper Geddings Recreation Center

3205 Oak St.
Myrtle Beach — *448-8575*

Otherwise known as the Frank M. Beckham Complex, Pepper Geddings Recreation Center is the most complete recreation center in the area. This facility features a 25-yard heated indoor swimming pool that is fully accessible to the physically challenged. Programs include American Red Cross swimming lessons for all ages and abilities, a variety of water exercise programs and a swim team, as well as lifeguard certification and water safety classes. You can pump up in the weight room with free weights and Nautilus equipment under the supervision of a professional trainer. Instructional classes include arts and crafts, a variety of dances like clogging, shag and tap, and bridge and other card games. The Parks and Recreation Department also offers after-school care and a summer day camp.

City-sponsored team sports, including basketball, aerobics and swimming, are coordinated through this center. In addition to meeting rooms and a game room, the complex is surrounded by softball fields, baseball fields, football fields, three lighted tennis courts and a picnic shelter with a grill and tables.

Fees for most classes are nominal, and annual passes for the weight room and swimming pool are available. The center is open six days a week: Monday through Thursday, 6 AM to 9 PM; Friday, 6 AM to 6:30 PM; and Saturday, 10 AM to 5 PM.

Surfside Beach Recreation Department

H. Blue Huckabee Recreation Complex
Spanish Oak Dr. and Glenns Bay Rd.
Surfside Beach *238-4131*

Dick M. Johnson Civic Center
Pine Dr.
Surfside Beach *238-4131*

The Surfside Beach Recreation Department provides year-round recreational programs for all ages. Many of the sports activities are held at the H. Blue Huckabee complex, surrounded by three ball fields and a large picnic area. Instructional courses and seminars, held at the Dick M. Johnson Civic Center, include arts and crafts, dance, aerobics and more. Special events include Easter egg hunts, an Old-Fashioned Family Festival, a Christmas Tree Lighting Ceremony and a Santa Hotline.

Grand Strand YMCA

904 65th Ave. N.
Myrtle Beach *449-9622*

Our local YMCA actively sponsors community events, many geared toward children. Kids enjoy T-ball, baseball, soccer and swim classes, preschool full- and half-day classes and day camp. Adults can enjoy coed volleyball, basketball, shag and ballroom dancing, softball and health enhancement workshops. The center features a Nautilus and free weights center, as well as a selection of cardiovascular equipment. Fees are moderately low.

Spectator Sports

During the academic year, Coastal Carolina University fields men's and women's teams that compete in a handful of sporting events, all of which can be watched by the general public. As members of the NCAA's Division I Big South Conference, men and women participate in such sports as soccer and tennis in autumn and spring, basketball and volleyball during the winter months and golf and baseball in spring. For specific details, the sports section of *The Sun News* is a comprehensive resource. Or you may want to contact the athletic department at Coastal Carolina University, 448-1481.

Beach volleyball is a favored activity during the summer season. From May through August, various annual tournaments are sponsored by nationally known entities such as Jose Cuervo, Native Sons and Sets. At the time this book went to print, tournament dates had not been established. As with other spectator sports, we suggest you read *The Sun News* to keep abreast of the latest happenings. If it's summertime, head for Downwind Sails (on the south end of Myrtle Beach) or the strip of shore in front of the Radisson in Kingston Plantation (on the north end of Myrtle Beach). Chances are you'll run into spirited competition; these two areas boast public volleyball nets and, even if what's happening is not a professional tournament, something's always in the works.

Finally, the Grand Strand has established itself as a veritable golfing mecca, and numerous big-name tournaments, including the DuPont World Amateur Handicap Championship and the Senior Tour Championship, call this area home. For more information see our Golf chapter.

Auto Racing

Myrtle Beach Speedway

4300 U.S. 501 W.
Myrtle Beach *236-0500*

Amateur and professional drivers thrill racing fans as the roar of engines ricochets off the asphalt of the Myrtle Beach Speedway. With each wave of the checkered flag, this spectator sport draws increasingly larger crowds.

Races are held on Saturday nights from March to September and feature five divisions: ministock, late model stock, street stock, chargers and late model sportsman.

The local racing season is highlighted by **The Winston Racing Series** and also includes the All-Pro, NASCAR Dash, Open Wheel Modified and Busch Grand National touring series. Each year the Speedway staff coordinates special events including pre-race concerts featuring big-name entertainers.

The roots of stock car racing in this area can be traced back more than three decades when dirt tracks were carved out of remote forests near modern-day downtown. The present speedway facility was built in 1958 and was known as the Racing Association of Myrtle Beach Inc. (RAMBI) Raceway. At that time, racing fans were following the budding careers of Richard Petty, Ralph Earnhardt, Ned Jarrett and David Pearson. After a decade of dirt track racing, the speedway was paved in 1969.

The popularity of auto racing fell during the '70s but produced a name to be reckoned with — Dale Earnhardt. In 1978, Dale won the late model sportsman championship at Myrtle Beach Speedway. A year later he joined the Winston Cup roster and won Rookie of the Year honors. Since the mid '80s, auto racing has gained momentum. It's not unusual that hot racers at Myrtle Beach Speedway become future stars.

Gates open at 5 PM, and drivers take practice laps before the green flag drops on the first of five heats at 7:30 PM.

Concession items are available, including beer, soft drinks and snack food like hot dogs, chips and candy. Spectators are permitted to bring small handheld coolers.

Seating is stadium-style, so you might want to bring a blanket or a cushioned seat for comfort. Admission is $10 per person, and children 9 and younger cruise in for free.

Photo: Bill Scroggins, The Sun News

Beautiful Georgetown is a must-see for those vacationing in the Lowcountry.

Inside **Daytrips**

On the Grand Strand, there's more to do than you ever imagined. But, if your tan's a bit overdone and you'd like to take your sunburn somewhere different . . . keep reading. You can set aside a single day of your vacation to examine a plethora of treasures waiting just a short drive beyond the beach.

We're offering four suggestions for daytrips. All will give you a close-up look at Southern culture and the extraordinary beauty and history of the coastal region. Zip to Conway, Georgetown or Charleston in South Carolina or Wilmington just above the North Carolina line, spend a day enjoying the sights and return — cozy in your bed before lights out. We've listed our suggestions according to distance. Conway, the closest, is first.

Conway

Conway is one of the prettiest little towns you'll ever stumble upon, and it's filled with friendly folks who can teach you the very meaning of Southern hospitality. A mere 14 miles from Myrtle Beach, most people are introduced to Conway as they drive through it to Myrtle Beach. What many people don't know is that a few blocks east of the congested U.S. 501 Bypass, just beyond the blare of car horns, lies Conway's historic section. Fact is, Conway's one of the most historic towns in South Carolina. Additionally, based on the extensive planting and protection of trees, Conway is a Tree City, USA. However, the newest trees aren't those that most impress visitors; the enormous oaks are what Conwayites and tourists love best. The local residents have gone to great lengths to preserve and protect their oaks. In some cases, they have even constructed roads around the majestic old trees! They've been rewarded with a canopy of shade over streets where lovely old homes date back a century and more.

One of the first and finest oaks you'll see as you drive down Conway's Main Street is the Wade Hampton Oak in front of the Horry County Museum. A plaque on the oak commemorates the day in 1876 when Confederate Gen. Wade Hampton brought his campaign for the governorship to Conway and addressed a crowd from beneath the tree. Many years later, when construction of a railroad threatened the historic oak, a spirited local lady, Mary Beaty, brandished a loaded shotgun and ordered workers, "Touch not a single bough."

Just across the street from the Horry County Museum, another stately oak spills shade in the yard of the First Methodist Church. Its gnarled branches stretch over the historic graves in the cemetery. Don't miss the oak on Elm Street at Fifth Avenue where motorists have to maneuver their cars around the tree. On Sixth Avenue, near Elm Street, the road literally divides and goes around another tree.

Photo: The Sun Newsd

Stately oak trees add to Conway's charm. This tree is dedicated to the Confederate soldiers who died.

A monument at the foot of this tree was erected in honor of soldiers who died defending the Confederacy. The blacktop makes way for another oak at the intersection of Seventh Avenue and Beaty Street. Wind in and out of the nearby streets and enjoy a veritable parade of the beautiful old trees that typify the South at its finest.

But, before you take off to amble beneath the trees, stop for a enlightening tour of the **Horry County Museum**. Open from 10 AM through 5 PM, Monday through Saturday, one of the museum's most popular exhibits includes a variety of Lowcountry animals. Sadly, burgeoning development in the area has endangered many animals. The ones on display were accidentally killed. In addition to birds, an alligator and more, you can see everybody's favorite, a 300-pound black bear that was actually hit by a car on Highway 501 many years ago. The central theme underlying all of the exhibits is the wide range of environmental conditions found in Horry County and how its inhabitants, from prehistoric to the present, have adapted to these local conditions.

If your's is a spring vacation, Conway is a not-to-be-missed excursion. Flowers begin blooming as early as the beginning of March and usually flourish through most of April. Tulip trees and Japanese magnolias are particular favorites. They're complemented by quince, daffodils, narcissus, goldenrod, white and purple wisteria, crape myrtle, flowering cherry trees, Bradford pear trees, pink and white dogwoods and thousands of azaleas in vivid, delicious colors.

Conway is the county seat of Horry County. Plans for the town, originally known as Kingston Township, were drawn up around 1734. The first settlers arrived a few years later. (It wasn't until the early 1900s that Conway residents began to build cottages at New Town, the new summer retreat now known as Myrtle Beach.) As the area's primary method of transportation, early life in Conway literally depended on the Waccamaw River. For many, many years, the town's economy centered on by-products from surrounding pine forests. Many a businessman found his wealth selling lumber, tar, pitch and turpentine.

Your best bet is to enter Conway over the Main Street Bridge. (The bridge has been restored to look as it did when it was first erected.) The Conway Chamber of Commerce, 203 Main Street, will be the first building on the left. Do yourself a favor; stop and ask questions. And get a copy of "Conway's Historic Tour" brochure so you won't miss a single one of the city's many beautiful and significant buildings, many of which are on the National Register of Historic Buildings. The tour will also treat you to a number of distinctive homes including Snow Hill, at the corner of Kingston Lake Drive and Lakeside Drive, and the Arthur Burroughs home just across the street.

Conway City Hall, on the left at the foot of the bridge, was designed by Robert Mills, who also designed the Washington Monument and several other public buildings in our nation's capital. The building was constructed in 1824 or 1825 as the area's first courthouse. The city clock, which has become a Conway trademark, was added more than a century later in 1939. In recent years, since the city became part of the Main Street USA program, Conway's once-sleepy downtown has been transformed by extensive renovations. Buildings, most of which were built in the early 1900s, have been restored to their original appearances. Numerous businesses have opened and flourished since the restoration began six years ago. A host of department stores, speciality shops and antique markets now line the historic streets.

For a town of its size, Conway has a surprising number of excellent restaurants. A popular spot with locals is **The Trestle**, 308 Main Street. Lunchtime fare includes stuffed potatoes, chicken salad and a delectable club sandwich made extraordinary by fresh-baked sourdough bread. Fresh pastries are featured every morning. A doughnut or a cinnamon twist with a cup of coffee will start your Historic Tour off right. Other lunch suggestions include the **Rivertown Bistro**, 1111 Third Avenue, **The Sidewheeler**, 110 Main on the Riverfront, **Chan's Garden**, 1117 Third Avenue, and **Ski's Deli**, corner of Third Avenue and Elm Street. **Wayne's Restaurant**, 1127 Third Avenue, a local's longtime favorite, will serve up a samplin' of the South's finest . . . Southern fried chicken, chicken bog (also known as chicken pilau — pronounced "per-low"), corn bread, Southern-style vegetables, collards and creamy banana pudding. And, believe it or not, Conway's list of eateries is still growing.

Conway began development of its riverfront area several years ago, and the improvement has been phenomenal. For a change of pace, check out the boats at the city-owned Conway Marina at the end of Elm Street. Have lunch at the marina's charming cafe, and take a stroll along the scenic riverwalk. For a uniquely tranquil day, rent a canoe or a pontoon boat at the marina and disappear down the river or into the swamp off Kingston Lake. Canoes and pontoons can be rented for a half-day or a full day. If you can, talk marina operator Dick Davis into serving as your guide. He also rents fishing boats and might be willing to show you where to go to catch "the big one." Call 248-4033 to set up your river adventure.

Conway is the heart of Horry County's thriving tobacco industry. Each year, in a little more than three months, the Conway market pumps about $40 million into the economy. Many visitors to Conway enjoy the unique experience of a tobacco auction. The tobacco market typically opens in mid-July and closes toward the end of October. Conway's warehouses are Horry on Second Avenue between Laurel Street and Elm Street, Coastal Farmer's on Cultra Road, off U.S. Highway 501 W. at El Bethel, and New Farmers at 2401 Main Street. Tobacco isn't sold every day during marketing season, and the order of the sale rotates. Get a sales schedule from the Conway Chamber of Commerce before you head for the warehouses.The prattle of the auctioneer sounds like a strange language to the uninitiated, but any of the friendly farmers will be glad to give you a lesson in growing, grading, stabilization regulations and "turning the tag."

Conway boasts several popular annual events. The Rivertown Jazz Festival, sponsored by the Conway Main Street program, draws thousands to the riverfront under the Main Street bridge. Usually scheduled in May or early June, this event showcases plenty of food, upbeat music and pretty river scenery. The festival is free and appropriate for all ages, so bring a lawn chair or a big blanket, stretch out comfortably and abandon your cares to another day.

Riverfest is another of the much-anticipated annual events. Best wear your swimsuit; to truly enjoy this festival, you have to get wet. Events include Waccamaw raft races for all ages, concerts, lunch and scads of children's games. The day's most unusual event is undoubtedly the Jell-O Jump. Adventuresome kids actually leap into a chilled vat of Jell-O to recover marked golf balls. Ball markings determine what prizes can be won, including things such as soft drinks and free passes to area attractions. But the grand prize winner gets cold, hard cash. Riverfest is typically held on the Saturday closest to the Fourth of July and features an explosive fireworks finale.

On the first Saturday in December, one of the season's first daytime parades kicks off Christmas. The riverfront is the focus of another colorful event that same weekend — the **Christmas Boat Parade**. In 1992, Conway had its first nighttime boat parade. The parade features boats of all sizes ablaze in Christmas lights. The 1992 occasion was such a hit, it has become a much-loved annual event.

The Conway Area Chamber of Commerce offers popular bus tours of Conway's historical areas each year in conjunction with **Canadian-American Days** in March. Call 248-2273 for more information. Another favorite Canadian-American event is Conway's **Taste of the Town**. Held along the riverfront, eager crowds swarm to sample the best cuisine Conway's restaurant owners can create. Delectable samples of appetizers, entrees and desserts range from about $1 to $3.50.

To get to Conway, take U.S. 501 from Myrtle Beach, S.C. 90 from North Myrtle Beach and S.C. 544 (or U.S. 17 Bypass to S.C. 544) from the South Strand. Or, you might want to ride the Coastal Rapid Public Transit Authority bus. Call 626-9138 for schedules and fares.

Georgetown

On the southernmost end of the Grand Strand, mere miles and whole worlds from fun-filled amusement parks, impressive high-rises and sprawling mega-malls, the history-steeped city of Georgetown has risen from a long era of silence. Today, the oak-lined avenues of this not-so-sleepy town boast vacation treasures guaranteed to please. A completely renovated riverfront teems with activity the whole year. Overlooking waters where Blackbeard once headed for the open seas, history, shopping and scenery reign supreme.

On Winyah Bay, where four beautiful rivers spill into the Atlantic Ocean, Georgetown was settled as a seaport more than 250 years ago. South Carolina's magnificent rice plantations flourished throughout the surrounding countryside, and the port of Georgetown was one of the busiest in the entire nation. Front Street was the indisputable hub of commerce. For roughly 200 years, the waterfront prevailed as the dynamic heart of the city. In the 1960s, when shopping centers started springing up outside city limits, the merchants followed the crowds; downtown began a sad, slow decline.

Several years ago, in the interest of preserving a remarkable history and jump-starting the local economy, Georgetown embarked on an ambitious multimillion-dollar main street and riverfront redevelopment plan. The visionary project, called Streetscape, is now complete, and the discriminating public — locals and tourists alike — are singing songs of praise. Streetscape's winning combination of contemporary convenience and carefully preserved history is drawing happy crowds, and Georgetown has a new lease on life.

HarborWalk is a charming waterfront boardwalk that spans a four-block area between two of Georgetown's most historically significant buildings, the **Kaminski House** (c. 1760) and the **Rice Museum** (originally the Old Market Building, c. 1842). Overlooking the Sampit River Harbor, the boardwalk is lined with restaurants, galleries, antique shops and speciality stores. If you're going to eat in town, every one of the eateries along the boardwalk is memorable. **Frogmore's** is fun; the **River Room's** shrimp and grits is exquisite; **Pink Magnolia** is excellent too. In fact, there are just too many fine restaurants to list. Whatever you do, don't miss **Kudzu Bakery**. The fresh selections are nothing short of heavenly. If you can't decide, settle for an anything-but-basic chocolate chip cookie, and take home a loaf of black pepper bread.

Shoppers who visit Georgetown's revitalized business district have more than 30 specialty shops to browse. From name-brand department stores to quaint shops with Lowcountry names, the selection is a treasure trove of alternatives boasting books, clothes, fine art, jewelry, crafts and antiques. The list goes on and on!

There are several ways to see the rest of Georgetown. And see it you must. Historic attractions such as the Kaminski House and Rice Museum complement a staggering concentration of 50-plus antebellum mansions, a few of which are operated as charming bed and breakfast inns. Historical tours are readily available. Based on supply and demand, new ones are being developed all the time, so stop off at the Chamber of Commerce on the corner of Front and Broad for current information.

Native Georgetonian Nell Morris Cribb will take you on a personal walking tour of the historic district and downtown area. You can walk with **Miss Nell** for about 30 minutes for $4, an hour for $6 and 90 minutes for $8. Tours are available Tuesday through Thursday at 10:30

AM and 2:30 PM and on Saturday and Sunday at 2:30 PM. Other times can be scheduled by appointment. Tours begin and end at 723 Front Street at the Mark Twain Bookstore. Call 546-3975 for more information.

Georgetown Tour Company offers a tram tour of the historic district. The tram stops at two of the area's historic churches. Lasting approximately 45 to 55 minutes, this educational tour features interesting commentary. Cost is $7.50 for adults, $6.50 for seniors and $4 for children. During most times of the year, tours run daily from 10:30 AM until 2:30 PM. For details and schedules call 546-9812.

One of our favorite ways to see Georgetown is by boat with **Captain Sandy's Tours**. These tours take you around Winyah Bay and the surrounding rivers past plantation mansions and long-abandoned rice fields. You can even go to a remote barrier island for shell collecting. Believe us, you'll find it very different from the beach you know. These tours board on HarborWalk, near Colonial Florist. Call 527-4106 or 527-8486 for information.

Points of interest in Georgetown are far too numerous to mention each one individually. Georgetown's Chamber offers a **Guide to Historic Sites** that is indispensable. All in all, Georgetown's historic district lists 44 points of interest including houses and churches. Here are just a few highlights: The **Rice Museum**, 546-7423, at the intersection of Front and Screven streets, uses maps, dioramas, artifacts and other exhibits to help visitors understand the crop that shaped a society.

The **Kaminski House Museum** is a pre-Revolutionary landmark at 1003 Front Street. Built in the 1700s, the home still has many of its original floors and moldings. The most impressive feature of the Kaminski House Museum is its staggering collection of antiques. Visitors are invited to picnic on the lawn where there is a great view of the Sampit River. The house is open Monday through Friday from 10 AM to 4 PM. Guided tours begin on the hour, except at 1 PM. For more information, call 546-7706. The **Man-Doyle House** is another pre-Revolutionary home and is maintained as a private residence. The owner offers tours several times a day, Monday through Friday, from March until October. Call the Georgetown Chamber for more information, 546-8436 or (800) 777-7705.

Billing itself "The Real South," Georgetown really does have a capacity for transporting its guests back to the antebellum era. In fact, there are more than a few plantations for you to see. **Hopsewee** is a favorite. Hopsewee is off of U.S. 17 S., 12 miles south of Georgetown. The plantation, featuring a view of the North Santee River, is open to the public early March through early November on Tuesday, Wednesday, Thursday and Friday from 10 AM to 4 PM. Other times are available by appointment. The plantation mansion, which was once the home of Thomas Lynch Jr., a signer of the Declaration of Independence, is surprisingly elegant in its simplicity. An admission fee is charged, $5 for adults and $2 for children between the ages of 5 and 17. Grounds and cabins can be seen year round at any time for $2 per carload.

Georgetown is an easy drive south of Myrtle Beach on U.S. 17. Depending on traffic, you may be able to make it in about 40 minutes.

Wilmington, N.C.

Wilmington is a beautiful and historic seaport that affords its residents and

The Hot and Hot Fish Club

In the 17th and 18th centuries, wealthy Lowcountry rice planters disposed of their enviable incomes with secondary homes, expanded land holdings and distinguished educations for their offspring. They enjoyed an abundance of leisure time, too, which they spent traveling, collecting fine wines, hunting . . . and socializing at the Hot and Hot Fish Club.

Established sometime before the War of 1812, the sole purpose of the Hot and Hot was social interaction among a group of successful, ambitious and fun-loving friends. The club did not have a written list of policies until 1845. In 1860, members of the Hot and Hot decided to publish a social history of the club, thus the *Rules and History of the Hot and Hot Fish Club* came into being. This booklet, the original of which is stored in the Brookgreen Garden Archives, contained a preface of reminiscent musings from former South Carolina governor R.F.W. Allston — one of the club's oldest members — along with 16 rules and a distinguished membership roster including many of the period's most prominent names: Col. Joshua John Ward, John La Bruce, Dr. Henry M. Tucker, Joseph Alston, Jr., Dr. Allard B. and Arthur B. Flagg, and many others.

The name for the Hot and Hot Fish Club was derived from the two separate courses of fresh, hot fish that were served at monthly meetings, thus "hot and hot." According to the rule book, members met at or around noon "each Friday from the first Friday in June, to the last Friday, but one, in October" when planters could take time away from their crops. The club initially met in a clubhouse on Drunken Jack Island, a small, scrubby patch of land in Murrells Inlet near today's Huntington Beach State Park. Some say the island was named for a pirate abandoned there (with several kegs of rum for comfort) by his captain, the infamous Edward Teach — better known as Blackbeard. Others believe that the island was named for John "Jack" Green, an original club member who could "eat a peck of fish at a meal . . . and drink a quart of brandy."

When the clubhouse on Drunken Jack Island was irreparably damaged by storm, a new structure was built on the mainland "on the clam bank at Major Ward's salt vats," in what is currently Huntington Beach State Park. Other sites were used through the years until a 10-acre land grant for a parcel on Midway seashore was obtained from Col. T. Pinckney Alston around 1860. A comfortable two room house was constructed there, complete with an adjoining bowling alley. The house featured a "good chimney" and a "substantial kitchen," as well as "a billiard table and its appurtenances." It was in this house that club rules were framed and adopted, requisite member signatures were obtained and a $50 fee (a significant sum in 1860!) was established.

R.F.W. Allston's rule book preface includes colorful verbal sketches of parish residents and club members and provides valuable information about the Club. The following is an abbreviated excerpt from his writings:

"My earliest knowledge of the Hot and Hot Fish Club was when, as a boy of fifteen, I went occasionally to the upper beach on a visit to my excellent and very dear sister (Elizabeth) Mrs. Tucker. Mr. John H. Tucker, a keen and successful sportsman all his life, was as ready for the fishing, when the day came round, as for a deer drive. There was no one, not even 'big uncle,' Jack Green, to surpass him in deep-water fishing. I was always glad when my visit to his home included a club-day. I had a place and line in his boat, and contributed, according to my own estimation, in no mean degree, to its success. . . . The other gentlemen, with only an occasional exception, dropped their anchors in the creeks, or a little further removed from the inlet —their object being sheep-head, and the varieties of pan-fish, in all which the Club dinner abounded. There was but one salt dish (beef or ham) and one of fresh meat (generally game) on table, and these were furnished, together with rice, by rule, in turns. For the rest, every member caught his own dinner and enough for his boat hands, each contributing some kind of bread, and such condiments as he liked. . . . At one o'clock the President repaired to his post, and raised a flag to call in the boats; the fish taken by each boat was surveyed, and each variety in turn duly discussed. . . . Certain hands from each boat being detailed to clean these fish, (the rule was, after scaling, to wash the fish in three waters, the last to be fresh,) the boats dropped off into the stream, within two or three hundred yards, and recommenced fishing, coming in one by one to fetch whatever was choice, during dinner. Thus, not infrequently, the best of the fish came last, and there were not wanting several at table whose experienced palates taught them to reserve a vacant place for the fish coming in second course, 'hot and hot.' "

Some of the rules of the Hot and Hot were as follows: New members were nominated by the president and elected by a majority. For each meeting, members were required to contribute one "substantial dish for dinner, one bottle of wine . . . and not less than two forks, two tumblers, two wine glasses, two plates and one dish." Individuals took turns providing sugar for the Club's use. Unmarried members were "permitted" to furnish a "pudding, in lieu of" the substantial dish requirement. Any man who announced an engagement was "complimented" by other unmarried members with a basket of champagne. Any member who became the parent of twins furnished a basket of champagne to the Club, as did any member who was elected or appointed to a distinguished state office. A "contingent fund" was established to which each member paid $5 on the second Friday in June.

All members, "in rotation, and in order of residences," assumed the role of president. The president was responsible for furnishing a ham and rice and for making certain dinner was prepared and on the table by 2 PM, "or not later than half past two." Along with the vice-president, the president chose sides for playing games. Absence did not relieve the president of his ham and rice requirement; by rule, he sent it along even if he could not attend.

The vice-president brought, along with his own supper and wine, water and ice for the other club members. He also attended to the games and announced whether or not champagne would be brought to the next meeting. In the president's absence, he presided over the meeting and had his next neighbor officiate for him.

It is unfortunate we cannot rescue from history clearer, more colorful details about the Hot and Hot Fish Club. Like much social history, many of the facts can only be theorized, and the gaps filled by the imagination. How fascinating the conversations and camaraderie of those powerful men would be today! Next time you are strolling Huntington's long, blond beach, gaze northward and try to single out Drunken Jack Island. Visualize fishing boats peppering the surrounding waters. Listen for the sounds of fish flopping on wooden decks, men laughing and fresh catch frying. Imagine how it might have been to be a member of this decades-old fellowship.

Ah . . . the magic of imagination . . . the next best thing to being there.

visitors the very finest opportunities for shopping, dining, culture and art. The city's symbol — appropriately — is a beehive. There is much to do, see and study. In fact, there's far too much for a single day; but if you choose carefully and plan your trip before leaving the Grand Strand, you can cover a lot of interesting territory in a short period of time. For a complete guide to this beautiful Southern city, read *The Insiders' Guide to Wilmington and The Cape Fear Coast*.

Wilmington boasts the largest urban registered historic district in the entire state of North Carolina. Indeed, it boasts one of the largest districts on the National Historic Registry, with homes dating from as early as the middle 1700s. Meticulously restored Victorian, Georgian, Italianate and antebellum homes, from grand mansions to cottages, attest to the perseverance of Wilmingtonians. The area considered historically significant covers 200 city blocks, but much of the fun and captivating charm of Wilmington is concentrated on and near the riverfront. An architecturally unique historic district highlights the downtown area with a scenic riverfront park overlooking the Battleship *North Carolina*.

Follow U.S. 17 N. all the way from the Grand Strand to Wilmington. Follow signs to downtown where a deep harbor, restaurants, shops and impressive homes await you. The harbor itself offers surprises. With a little luck, a Coast Guard ship or other vessels will be docked there, allowing visitors to board and browse.

As in many historic Southern cities, a good way to start your Wilmington adventure is with a horse-drawn carriage tour along the riverfront past stately mansions and beautifully restored homes. Various tours, including walking and boat tours, are available for nominal fees at the foot of Market Street by the river. They are well worth the reasonable prices as they provide lively narratives of the area's history and point out attractions you might want to return to on your own. Two popular boat tours on the Cape Fear River are *The Captain J.M. Maffitt* and the *Henrietta II*. The *Henrietta II* bills itself as North Carolina's only true sternwheel paddleboat. Sightseeing cruises offer opportunities to view real plantations. The *Maffitt* also offers sightseeing cruises on the Cape Fear River. Special fall cruises are a real treat. During the summer months, the Maffitt serves as a river taxi to take people to the Battleship *North Carolina*. The ship, once the most powerful battleship in the world, sits majestically in the harbor and is easily seen from River Street; but to drive to it, you have to go to U.S. 17 and circle the city. (If you save the battleship for your last stop before heading back to the Grand Strand, it will be right on the way home.) If you want to stay downtown for shopping and supper, take the *Maffitt* instead of driving. For more information call (800) 676-0162.

The **Battleship *North Carolina***, a 15-story ship that is two city blocks long, is Wilmington's most popular attraction. Dedicated to the 10,000 North Carolinians who gave their lives during World War II, the Battleship *North Carolina* participated in every major naval offensive in the Pacific. But, here's a word of warning. If you have a physical handicap, claustrophobia or any kind of vertigo, tuck your bills back in your pocket and move on. Only the main deck is handicapped accessible. There are five-to six-inch ledges to step over at every door and staircases one after another to maneuver. There are some tight spots. You don't have to climb into the turrets, but if you take the tour of the lower deck, once you get down into the tight spots, it's too late to turn back. The brave souls who decide to go ahead will enjoy a wonderful history lesson.

The self-guided tour begins with an orientation film about the battleship and its escapades during WWII. Then, there are two self-guided tours to choose from. One tour can take as much as two hours. As you wind through a maze in the ship's bowels, you'll see the cobbler shop, sailors' quarters, officers' quarters, galley, bake shop, kitchen, dining areas, engine room, laundry, print shop, dark room, a doctor's office, a dispensary, an operating room, an isolation area, a financial section, a supply office and more. It's awesome! A second tour eliminates much of the climbing and takes in fewer decks; it takes approximately an hour.

The ship is open daily from 8 AM until sunset. Cost is $6 for adults and $3 for children 6 to 11. Children younger than 6 get in free. From the first Friday in June through Labor Day, there's a spectacular light and sound show each night. Music, lights, sound effects and the voices of Roosevelt, Churchill, Hitler and Truman come together to re-create highlights of the battleship's glorious career. Tickets are $3.50 for adults and $1.75 for children 6 to 11.

Let's head back downtown for some shopping. In most cases, downtown stores are independent specialty stores that brim with surprises from upscale to whimsical. One of Wilmington's brightest stars is the recently revived **City Market**. (You can enter on S. Front Street or Water Street.) The city market has fresh fruit and vegetables, all kinds of tempting home-baked treats, jellies, honey and plenty of homemade crafts. The **Cotton Exchange** is another not-to-be-missed shopping stop on the northern end of the riverfront. It is at the corner of Water and Grace streets. You can also enter at 313 N. Front. An old cotton warehouse that's been converted into a mall of sorts, The Cotton Exchange houses more than 30 businesses on three levels. Even if you don't like to shop, it's worth the stop to see the displays of cotton bales, weighing equipment and photographs that recount the building's evolution. At last count, there were four restaurants at the Cotton Exchange, so don't worry when hunger assails you. **Chandler's Wharf**, an equally charming but smaller shopping complex is on the extreme southern end of the

International arts festival Spoleto is held annually in Charleston.

riverfront. It, too, is definitely a worthwhile stop.

If there's any time left in your day, other attractions include **St. John's Museum of Art**, 114 Orange Street; **Orton Plantation**, an old rice plantation where the gardens are open to the public; and the **Wilmington Railroad Museum**, a kind of fun house for folks fascinated by trains and train culture.

Wilmington's biggest shindig of the year is the **Azalea Festival**. It's held in April. For more information, about the area or the festival, call the Cape Fear Coast Convention and Visitors Bureau at (800) 222-4757.

And, one last note, you might want to call ahead to see if **The Thalian Hall Center for the Performing Arts** has a performance scheduled during your visit. Full-scale musicals, light opera and internationally renowned dance companies are part of Thalian's consistently high-quality programming. Thalian Hall is the only surviving theater designed by John Montague Trumble, one of America's foremost 19th-century theater designers. Historic tours are available for a nominal fee. Call (910) 343-3660.

Charleston

Charleston, the very name of this beautiful old city conjures up images of fine plantations, fair-skinned Southern belles and the scent of magnolia, wisteria and azaleas. (En masse, azaleas smell heavenly.) Charleston, both charming and cosmopolitan, is steeped in a history so rich it's beyond description. Arguably more distinctive than any other Southern city, Charleston has found its way into operas, novels, movies and soap operas. Simply put, there's no place like it, and you don't dare get as close as Myrtle Beach and miss it.

It will come as no surprise to you that Charleston has far too many enticements to mention even a respectable fraction. If you want to know more, pick up a copy of *The Insiders' Guide to Greater Charleston*.

Any time is a great time to visit the area, but spring, as a whole, is remarkable. Warm days, crisp nights and flowers galore. In May, **Spoleto**, an international arts festival, exacts a welcome grip on the city. Spoleto is a two-week celebration of opera, jazz, theater, dance and visual arts, sometimes classical and sometimes so modern as to cause controversy. By any standard, it is always a huge success. People from all over the globe return year after year, and the numbers keep growing. You can get more information on the festival by writing P.O. Box 157, Charleston 29402 or calling 722-2764. In September, **The Charleston Preservation Society** opens many of the city's privately owned homes and gardens to visitors during its annual candlelight tour series. This is the second of our two favorite times to visit. Many of the tours include chamber music and champagne receptions. Learn more by calling 722-4630.

Many of Charleston's legendary plantations are open to the public. The gardens are all memorable; some are outright unforgettable. The most popular and well known of the lineup are **Drayton Hall, Middleton Place, Magnolia Plantation and Gardens, Cypress Gardens,** which was once part of Dean Hall Plantation, and **Boone Hall**. Admission to the plantations and gardens usually amounts to less than $10.

Charles Towne Landing, a South Carolina State Park, is also a former plantation. Today this beautiful park is dedicated to recreating and interpreting the first permanent English settlement in the Carolinas that occurred on this plantation site in 1670. There's a film about the history of the Lowcountry, an animal forest, a reproduction of a 17th-century trading vessel, and a colonial area where visitors can see candlemaking, open fire cooking, woodworking and even the colony's first printing press. Bicycles are available for rent, and we think it's the best way to get around. Hours are 9 AM to 5 PM, except during June, July and August when the park stays open until 6 PM. Admission is $5 for adults, $2.50 for children 6 through 14, and $2.50 for seniors. Handicapped visitors and children younger than 6 are admitted free.

Nearly every school child in South Carolina has been to the **Fort Sumter National Monument** in Charleston Harbor at least once. Many know the story by heart. In 1861, Confederate soldiers fired on the Union forces stationed at the fort, and the Civil War began. You can only get to Fort Sumter by boat, but that's a big part of the fun. Catch the tour at Charleston's City Marina on Lockwood Boulevard or at Patriots Point in Mount Pleasant. Call 722-1691 for more information.

Charleston is home to **The Citadel**, a military college that has recently been the center of much controversy regarding the admittance of women. If you're headed to Charleston, plan your trip to include a Friday so you can watch the weekly dress parade. It starts at 3:45 PM.

Charleston is chock-full of museums and carefully preserved historic homes, many of which are open to the public. **The Frances R. Edmunds Center for Historic Preservation**, 108 Meeting Street, is a good place to start your visit. You can buy tickets here to most area attractions, and they'll offer lots of friendly tourist advice. The center is open Monday through Saturday from 10 AM through 5 PM, and Sunday from 2 PM through 5 PM.

Charleston also sports excellent shopping alternatives, so if your daytrip isn't full to overflowing, at least check out **King Street** and the **Old Market** area. The selections are overwhelming — old shops, new shops, food shops, open air shops. You'll have to experience it to understand.

If you don't feel like trying to find your way around Charleston by yourself, take a daytrip through **Unique Tours**. The bus leaves Myrtle Beach every morning and returns every afternoon. The trip includes Boone Hall Plantation, lunch at the Colony House Restaurant at the Charleston Waterfront Park, sightseeing along Rainbow Row and the Harbour of History with a view of Fort Sumter. There is also an hour of free time to shop or browse. The bus heads back to Myrtle Beach at about 3 PM. Cost is $50 per person. You can make reservations by calling 280-1450. If you're going to drive yourself, take U.S. 17 S. It's an easy two-hour trip.

Photo: Jessica Tefft, The Sun News

You're never too young to be an artist.

Inside Arts and Culture

Once and for all, let's set the record straight: The Myrtle Beach area's artistic reputation as "backward" is an inaccuracy. As is true throughout much of the South, our idea of culture for too long pivoted on teaching our little girls to play the piano and do pirouettes. But today, culture in coastal Carolina is diverse, exciting and far removed from old-fashioned notions. Now, the area takes pride in its very own symphony, a community chorus, a promising opera company, an art museum and several theater groups.

With the 1989 formation of the **Horry Cultural Arts Council** (HCAC), 248-7200, the local arts scene took a giant stride toward credibility. As an umbrella organization for the arts, the Council offers information and assistance to artists, arts-related organizations and Horry County's residents and visitors. HCAC coordinates an arts and cultural events calendar and funds grants for various organizations to help them present top-quality productions. It also funds an Artists-In-Education program that places professional artists in public schools to instruct students in various mediums.

In Georgetown County, The Georgetown County Arts Commission, 546-9449, serves as a catalyst to promote, coordinate and stimulate the cultural, social and economic climate of the arts in the county.

Surprisingly, when summer has packed the beach with tourists, the Grand Strand's arts and culture organizations are slowing down. In fact, most of these organizations' seasons run from September to March or April. Tourists have not traditionally provided large audiences for cultural offerings, and many of the organizations' volunteers are too busy working at their "real jobs" during the summer months to devote more than minimal time to their favorite "artsy" causes.

Four auditoriums in Horry County host the majority of cultural performances. **Wheelwright Auditorium**, on the campus of Coastal Carolina University, roughly 10 miles west of Myrtle Beach off U.S. 501, is a truly elegant facility that seats about 850 people. The **Myrtle Beach High School Auditorium**, 3300 Central Parkway, is the area's largest auditorium, seating 2,000 people. The school district had planned to build a 1,000-seat venue, but Myrtle Beach residents convinced them to enlarge it so their city could attract bigger and better productions. Community-raised funds helped pay for the increased cost of the exceptionally well-equipped if not particularly elegant auditorium. Horry-Georgetown Technical College's Myrtle Beach campus, 904 65th Avenue N., has a 300-seat auditorium. **McCown Auditorium**, on the corner of Ninth Avenue and Main Street in Conway, seats about 350 people. This auditorium was defunct for many years until Horry County bought it and transformed the entire building.

The Strand Theatre, on Front Street in Georgetown, seats 160 people. Home to Georgetown's Swamp Fox Players, it's often called the Swamp Fox Theatre.

Horry County organizations that offer opportunities in the arts are too numerous for us to provide a comprehensive listing. We suggest you check out HCAC's Arts & Cultural Directory; call the Council (see the above-listed number) for additional information.

Wheelwright Council for the Arts

Coastal Carolina University *347-3161*

This organization, comprised of community members and Coastal Carolina University faculty and staff, supervises the use of Wheelwright Auditorium. The group is responsible for coordinating the University's arts program, including a cultural arts series and student plays. The Wheelwright Council's function is to bring to the area high-caliber art performances that other groups are unable to secure. The Council presents a Passport Series that offers experiences in film, dance and the performing arts. Highlights of past performances include Shakespeare's *The Taming of the Shrew*, presented by the North Carolina Shakespeare Festival; *Echos of Africa*, which demonstrated the African roots of contemporary America; and The Troika Organization's 50th anniversary presentation of Rodgers' and Hammerstein's *Oklahoma!* Student productions have included such hits as the 1938 showbiz comedy *Room Service* and the American classic *A Raisin in the Sun*. Season memberships are available.

The Long Bay Symphony

449-2379

This is one of many groups that has wisely capitalized on experienced talent relocating in the area. Many of the group's members have performed with such respected organizations as the Metropolitan Opera in New York and the Radio City Music Hall Orchestra.

The group merges a variety of musical backgrounds, performing selections from classical to pop, as well as full stage productions such as *The Nutcracker*. The Symphony presents four concerts each season in addition to performing at the City of Myrtle Beach's annual Fourth of July Celebration. The Symphony recently accompanied legendary recording artist Ray Charles at a concert in the Myrtle Beach Convention Center. Musicians range from high school students to retirees, from points all along the Grand Strand. For concert information or season memberships, call 449-2379.

Long Bay Youth Symphony

449-2115

The Long Bay Symphony promotes its approximately 40-member youth symphony to spark youngsters' interest in serious music and to train older members for the "big" symphony. Adults who haven't played in years, as well as those who are just learning, can hone their skills with the youth symphony; the addition of adults has prompted some people to call the Youth Symphony the "Long Bay Orchestra for the Young and Youthful."

The symphony, under the direction of Nan Hudson, performs two or three times a year and holds workshops for interested musicians.

Theatre of the Republic

1319 Riverside Dr.
Conway *236-0383*

Originally known as the Conway Little Theatre, the Theatre of the Re-

Photo: The Sun News

The Community Choral Society performs throughout the year.

public was formed in July of 1969. This represented the county's first venture into the world of culture and entertainment. Today, the group is one of the county's most popular amateur — but not amateurish — stage troupes. Quality family productions have included *Cinderella*, *Oklahoma!*, *The Unsinkable Molly Brown*, *L'il Abner*, *Oliver*, *Annie*, *Anything Goes*, *Finian's Rainbow*, *The Wizard of Oz*, *The Quilters*, *South Pacific*, *Man of LaMancha* and more. This theater group utilizes local talent to train and inspire future generations in the art of dramatic performance and behind-the-scenes participation.

The group performs in McCown and Wheelwright auditoriums and currently is raising funds to rebuild Conway's former Holliday Theatre, currently Main Street Theatre, to use as a performing arts center and home base. Individual and season tickets are available. Please call for prices and schedules.

Grand Strand Seniors For the Performing Arts

1268 21st Ave. N.
Myrtle Beach *626-3991*

In 1991, several Horryites 50 years and older started playing with the idea of forming their own theater group. They decided to give it a try. And when *Send Me No Flowers* attracted 2,000 people over six performances, they figured they were onto something good.

This thespian group produces three shows a year. *Send Me No Flowers*, *Arsenic and Old Lace* and *Prisoner of Second Avenue* are examples of the group's scope. Auditions for each play are publicized, and the cast is selected from the general public and the membership. Volunteers from the general membership handle scenery, publicity, lighting, costuming, makeup, sound, and stage work. Please call for current schedules.

Tricycle Players, Inc.

313C S.C. 15
Myrtle Beach *448-8221*

Tricycle Players, Inc. is another nonprofit, high-quality amateur theater group in the Grand Strand area. The group's specialties are musicals featuring large casts, especially those including children. Since 1989, this group has entertained audiences with productions such as *Pump Boys and Dinettes*, *Peter Pan*, *Alice in Wonderland* and *Nunsense*. *Pump Boys and Dinettes*, their first production, was so successful, the cast was invited to perform in Charleston's Dock Street Theatre. Please call for current information.

Swamp Fox Players, Inc.

P.O. Box 911
Georgetown 295442 *527-2924*

Established in the early 1970s, this amateur theatrical group coordinates at least four productions per year. Since the community seems to be particularly fond of musicals and comedy, many of the Swamp Fox productions are flavored accordingly. It is rumored that this group is comprised of a uniquely fun-loving group of all ages. They call the Strand Theatre, on Front Street in Georgetown, "home." If you're seeking volunteer opportunities, this is your lucky day. The Swamp Fox Players always need help in lots of categories: acting, makeup, costumes, set construction, directing, sales, fundraising and publicity. Annual subscriptions begin at $40 and climb upward depending on the number of performances you want to attend.

Grand Strand Concert Band

2966 Newberry Tr.
Garden City *651-5683*

The Grand Strand Concert Band began in 1976 with the idea of giving high school band members the chance to play with qualified — in some cases professional — musicians. The group has about 25 members, increased seasonally by snowbirds — visitors who flock to this area to enjoy the mild winters. Selections include Big Band pieces from the 1940s and light concert music. They usually offer one performance a year during Can-Am Days (see the Annual Events chapter). If you're interested in keeping your chops sharp, this band has a place for you; they're always looking for new members.

Waccamaw Arts and Crafts Guild

P.O. Box 1595
Myrtle Beach 29577 *626-4210*

The Waccamaw Arts and Crafts Guild, with about 300 members, is dedicated to promoting interest and creativity in the visual arts. Approximately half of the members are artists — painters, print makers, sculptors, etc. The other half are fanciers interested in the programs and goals of the Guild. Monthly meetings include demonstrations, slide presentations, social gatherings exhibiting members' recent works, and panel discussions on topics such as copyrighting.

One of the group's largest events is the annual spring art show — 25 years running — held during Can-Am Days in March in the Horry-Georgetown Technical College Auditorium. (See our Annual Events chapter). Ten years ago, the show drew about 500 people; in 1993, it attracted 2,500 — about half from out of state.

Another popular Guild feature is its summertime Art in the Park series (see also Annual Events). On the second weekends of June, July and August, an impressive parade of artists and craftspeople gather at Chapin Park (behind Chapin Library on 14th Avenue North) in Myrtle Beach for an enormous outdoor show and sale. Shows run from 10 AM to 6 PM and typically draw more than 3,000 people per weekend. There's plenty to eat, and, occasionally, entertainment is offered.

Overture Opera Theatre

449-5201

Upon relocating to The Grand Strand, Martha Bradner Cline didn't lose any time introducing herself to local theater and singing groups. While she enjoyed the performances and the chance to lend a helping hand, it bothered her that nobody ever tackled opera. So in 1992 she formed the nonprofit Overture Opera Theatre. Still young and working hard to get organized, the group has demonstrated tremendous potential, performing not only classical pieces, but modern work as well — part of their conscious effort to avoid being stereotyped as a classical opera company. Overture Opera Theatre organizers envision singers from 12 to 60 years of age performing a range of material from Gianni Schicchi's *Sour (Sister) Angelica* to comedy-opera productions such as Mozart's *Cosi Fan Tutte*, Bizet's *Carmen* and the works of Giacoma Puccini. *Camelot* was one particularly well-received 1994 production.

Coastal Concert Association

P.O. Box 7038
Myrtle Beach 29577 *449-7546*

This group has been bringing wonderful traveling troupes into Horry County since 1971. From the North Carolina Symphony to the San Francisco Pops, diverse performance and cultural events have included the award-winning Broadway musical *Brigadoon*, the off-Broadway hit *Nunsense*, the River City Brass Band, and the original orchestration of the Glenn Miller Band. Concerts are usually held in October, November, January, February and March or April in the Myrtle Beach High School Auditorium. Tickets are available at the door, but annual memberships are encouraged. Please call for a current schedule.

Community Choral Society

P.O. Box 7615
Myrtle Beach 29578 *449-SONG*

Anyone who enjoys singing is welcome to join the Community Choral Society. This avid group of harmonizers, about 80 strong, offers concert performances to residents and visitors throughout the year. Classical choral arrangements have included Rutter's "Magnificat." For the Festival by the Sea — a two-day event, and the group's biggest — the association invites a guest conductor or clinician and choirs from three states and Canada to attend area workshops, culminating with a mass performance for the community. Ticket prices vary, so please call ahead.

The Low Country Chorus of the Grand Strand Chapter of the Society for the Preservation and Encouragement of Barber Shop Quartet Singing in America, Inc. (SPEBSQSA)

2817 Oak St.
Garden City *237-8318*

The traditional art of barber shop singing is alive and well along the Grand Strand, thanks to the active members of SPEBSQSA's Myrtle Beach chapter. Thirty members practice songs like "My Wild Irish Rose," "Bye, Bye Blues" and "Sweet Adeline" every Tuesday evening in the Calhoun Building at Surfside United Methodist Church. The Low Country Chorus performs in four-part harmony at events such as the Little River Blue Crab Festival, the Aynor Harvest Hoe-Down, and Conway Main Street, USA activities. The chorus also sched-

Photo: Danny Chamblee, The Long Bay Symphony

The Long Bay Symphony performs at least four concerts each year.

ules an annual concert at Coastal Carolina University.

Springmaid Villa Art Museum

3200 S. Kings Hwy.
Myrtle Beach *626-2000*

Springmaid Villa, a former two-story Springmaid Beach home donated by Dwight Cox, was the county's first art museum. The original building, which houses 11 galleries — showcasing local and regional artists and numerous traveling events — and a library, will be augmented by three new studios in a planned 7,500-square-foot addition.

Church Concert Series

Several churches along the Strand now offer quality concert series. They include Myrtle Beach's Trinity Episcopal Church, 448-8426, and the First Presbyterian Church, 448-4498, and North Myrtle Beach's Ocean Drive Presbyterian Church, 249-2312. The concert series concept was brought here by Brown Bradley, Minister of Music at First Presbyterian Church, who participated in a successful series in New York before relocating to Myrtle Beach.

Trinity Episcopal Church's Performing Arts Series entertains the community with five quality performances each year. Events include choral concerts, recitals, instrumental ensembles, musical revues, comedies, complete Broadway musical productions and periodic art displays. A recent series opened with the internationally acclaimed Vienna Boys Choir; subsequent events included Peter Schickele of PDQ Bach fame, Moscow's Russian Men's Choir, the musical *Godspell* and *The Fantasticks*. For dates and specific information on upcoming events and season memberships, contact the series director at 448-8426.

At the First Presbyterian Church (FPC), season ticket holders are treated to a variety of featured vocalists and instrumentalists performing classical, pop and Broadway selections. Recent events included the remarkable Dutch classic quartet, Quink. Each year, sellout performances of *The Best of Broadway* are presented. The FPC Players Drama Troupe spotlights local talent in family-oriented presentations such as *Dogs*, and in timeless Broadway hits such as *Bells Are Ringing*. Season memberships are encouraged.

Since 1991, the Ocean Drive Presbyterian Church Concert Series has provided programming such as the Wheaton College Men's Choir and The Palmetto Brass. The North Myrtle Beach Christmas Cantata, featuring members of the Long Bay Symphony, is a part of the series that has become a community favorite during the holiday season. While series memberships are sold for $50 and $100, donations of $5 or more are accepted at the door.

Inside
Day Care and Education

Grand Stranders take great pride in the area's reputation as a family beach. As such, there is a plethora of attractions and activities for the younger set. It's no wonder kids love to visit us. But, imagine the fun of living here! Since children are such an integral part of our resort area, we would like to offer you a little help in meeting their developmental and educational needs at every stage. So, the first portion of this chapter will discuss child care for the youngest of your gang. Then, we'll move on to discuss primary and secondary education options.

Child Care

While word of mouth remains one of the very best ways to zero-in on reliable child care, newcomers may not have an established network of trustworthy parents and other contacts upon whose opinions they can rely. So, if you're new to our area, we suggest you contact the **Family Information Network**, 1316 First Avenue, Conway. This service, a Clemson Extension Service (see the subsequent phone number), is the custodian of a computer database that provides information about day-care centers throughout the state.

The Family Information Network provides data on prices and child-to-staff ratios, as well as information about meals, transportation services and just about anything else you might want to know about a center. It also offers helpful hints on selecting the right center for your child. Get the complete scoop on child-care laws and child-service agencies. If you'd like a shot at using the computer yourself, call for an appointment. If convenience is important to you, just call and ask for County Agent, Debbie Strickland. She will sift through a mountain of information and mail you a printout of the centers in your area along with whatever additional data you request. Best of all, there is absolutely no charge for this service. You can contact the **Clemson Extension Service** directly at (800) 626-1371 or 248-2267.

The **South Carolina Department of Social Services** is responsible for licensing all day-care centers in the state. The Conway office, 365-5565, can provide you a list of approved centers including for-profit and non-profit centers, as well as individuals who are licensed to keep children in their homes. Once you've narrowed your choices, make a visit to each of the caregivers on your list and have a talk with the director about his or her child-care philosophies. Don't be shy . . . ask questions, no matter how trivial you think they may seem. "Better safe than sorry" certainly applies where your child's welfare is concerned. Besides, if you choose your caregiver wisely from the start, you and your children can avoid having to make unsettling changes down the road.

Increasingly popular **AuPairCare** seems especially suited for resort areas where parents are frequently employed by service industries that keep long, erratic hours. AuPairCare matches American families with European child-care providers, ages 18 to 25, who are interested in spending a year in the United States. Au pairs are thoroughly screened, and host families can choose a provider who best suits their personal needs and collective personality. Unlike a paid employee, an au pair essentially becomes a member of the family: They live in your home, participate in household chores, share your meals and your celebrations. In exchange for room, board and a reasonable weekly allowance, the au pair offers stable, loving and constant care for one or more children. During the program year, local AuPairCare counselors provide support to both the families and the au pair. This is a marvelous opportunity for cultural exchange, and we know several two-career couples who wouldn't trade the program for any other child-care option. For more information, call (800) 4AUPAIR.

Be sure to read the Kidstuff and Attractions chapters for fun and educational things to occupy your brood's time.

Education

Public Schools

We think noting a few of the Horry County School District's honors is a great way to begin this portion of this chapter. Three schools have been named National Blue Ribbon Schools of Excellence: Conway Middle (1993), Socastee High (1991) and Conway High (1986). (St. James Middle School is currently being considered for the prestigious Blue Ribbon honor.) In 1992, the U.S. Department of Education selected Myrtle Beach Elementary as one of the nation's 40 Drug-Free Schools. Five of the district's primary, elementary and middle schools have been named Palmetto's Finest, a distinction given to only 36 South Carolina schools in 12 years. And, since 1990, the Horry School District has boasted: the state's outstanding high school principal, distinguished elementary school principal, and middle school assistant principal of the year; the state's top teachers in chemistry, clinical speech, biology, adult education, Spanish, occupational health, American history and autism; and South Carolina's top student council advisor, FHA advisor and speech and hearing program.

The Horry County School District, the fifth-largest of South Carolina's 91 school districts, is a countywide system operating 39 schools with more than 25,030 students. With a staff of more than 3,000, the school system is the county's largest employer. Classroom teachers account for more than half of the the total personnel, and 51 percent of employees hold advanced or professional degrees.

During the last decade, more than 4,000 students have been added to Horry school rosters; another 4,000 are expected by the year 2003. Increases in student enrollment have prompted the use of 255 portable classrooms that line school playgrounds and parking lots.

In an effort to keep pace with student growth, the voters of Horry County recently passed a $60 million bond referendum for new schools. Nine new schools will be built countywide, along with additions and renovations to North Myrtle Beach Primary and Lakewood Elementary. A new attendance zone will be developed between Conway and Myrtle Beach to relieve overcrowding in existing Conway, Socastee and Myrtle Beach attendance areas. The total building program calls for $98 million in construction costs.

Dr. Gary Smith, Superintendent of Schools since 1992, has transformed the Horry County School System. Dr. Smith initiated strategic planning for both the district and individual learning centers. To date, more than 2,500 community members, business leaders, parents, students and teachers have participated in determining the mission, goals and objectives that will guide our schools into the next century. A multi-year technology plan has provided for computers in all classrooms; students and teachers are enjoying access to the training and tools necessary to compete in a worldwide market. Accordingly, in the past two years, the district has gained 31 points in average SAT scores. The combined verbal and math scores were 22 points higher than the state average.

The district is committed to providing professional development opportunities to its faculty and staff. During the summer, Leadership Academy, a week-long intensive staff development program, aids teachers, administrators and staff members in gaining new skills and learning about innovative educational trends.

Year-round education began in Horry County in 1993 and remains an option to the traditional calendar at Myrtle Beach Primary, Elementary and Middle schools. Daisy Elementary, on the western side of the county, offers a total year-round calendar. Students on the year-round calendar attend school the same number of days and receive the same number of holidays as students on the traditional calendar. Simply explained, the days are ar-

Photo: The Sun News

Coastal Carolina University attracts students from across the country and world. The temperate climate and prime location are just a few reasons why.

ranged differently on the calendar to provide for more continuous instruction and decrease the length of summer break.

The school district has a wide range of programs for students, beginning with a program for 4-year-olds with developmental and learning difficulties. Kindergarten for 5-year-olds is a standard part of the statewide school curriculum and is available throughout the district.

Summer Success School is offered to students who need additional help between terms. Summer Success helps students acquire skills they missed during the standard school year and provides additional reading and math instruction to students who need just a little extra help. Oftentimes, this program enables students to advance to the next grade level instead of being retained for an entire year.

Every elementary school offers the **PELICAN** program for gifted and talented students. PELICAN provides enrichment activities one day a week that foster critical-thinking skills and encourage creativity.

Middle schools offer basic classes as well as honor programs. Similarly, all seven Horry high schools provide a basic curriculum plus college preparatory and honors classes. Advanced Placement classes afford students who pass standardized tests possible exemption from certain introductory college classes.

One unusual feature of the Horry district is **Playcard Environmental Center**, a nature preserve located in the western portion of the county. Not only can city kids get a taste of rural life, but the center teaches all children a healthy respect for the earth's resources as well. Students learn about Native American and pioneer cultures and the ecosystems of a thriving black water swamp. The pristine preserve features a collection of farm and domestic animals, a nature trail with labeled flora and fauna, an old rope swing in a forested area and a real beaver dam. School officials assert Playcard is the only natural teaching center of its kind in the United States.

Horry's school district, reflective of a demographically eclectic county, educates an interesting mix of students. Schools along the Grand Strand — North Myrtle Beach, Myrtle Beach and Socastee — and in Conway are growing rapidly to accommodate diverse student populations. Schools in the western part of the county — Aynor, Loris and Green Sea Floyds — are small and somewhat rural with relatively stable student populations.

Conway is the district's largest high school, with 2,093 students. Socastee, the South Strand's high school, comes in second, with an enrollment of 1,627. Having completely recovered from the loss of students resulting from the closure of Myrtle Beach Air Force Base, Socastee remains one of the fastest growing areas in the county. Myrtle Beach High School probably has the greatest physical capacity for growth. The large, modern facility features a 2,000-seat state-of-the-art auditorium capable of supporting high quality performances.

The school district also offers the Aynor/Conway Career Center, the Finklea Career Center and the Academy of Arts, Science and Technology — formerly the Grand Strand Career Center — that collectively provide high school students with vocational, technical, occupational and academic training. The Conway School of Nursing, housed at the Aynor/Conway Career Center, is a two-year program that prepares students for careers as licensed practical nurses (LPNs). The Academy offers instruction in new programs such as graphics, video/audio technology, pre-engineering, golf course technology, dance and hospitality services.

For more information, contact the **Horry County School District** at 248-2206.

Private Schools

With the exception of some day-care centers and preschools, all of Horry's private schools are church-affiliated.

Calvary Christian School

Dick Pond Rd.
Myrtle Beach *650-2829*

A ministry of Calvary Bible Church, Calvary offers preschool programs for youngsters 3 through 5 years of age and regular classes for 1st through 12th graders in a distinctly religious setting. In its second decade of operation, this is the Strand's oldest Christian school, although all denominations are welcome in a student body of approximately 350. The elementary classes are known for their strong phonics program. According to standardized achievement tests, Calvary rates more than a year ahead of national grade-level averages. Similarly, SAT scores rank ahead of state and national averages.

Conway Christian School

1951 Riverside Dr.
Conway *347-7041*

The primary goal of Conway Christian School is to provide quality education with a Biblical perspective in a distinctly Christian atmosphere of loving discipline. The academic goal of Conway Christian is to teach fundamental skills as a priority. An affiliate of Grace Presbyterian Church, Conway Christian offers preschool classes for 4- and 5-year-olds, as well as the A Beka curriculum for students in the 1st through 8th grades.

ATC Christian School

1672 S.C. 905
Conway *365-6800*

An affiliate of The Prayer Center, ATCCS offers A Beka classes for 4-year-olds through 8th graders. A preschool program for 3- and 4-year-olds also is available.

Some graduates begin celebrating even before the ceremonies are officially over.

St. Andrews Catholic School

3601 North Kings Hwy.
Myrtle Beach *448-6062*

St. Andrews is supported by tuition and parish subsidies. Class sizes range from 25 to 30 students and the faculty hovers around 14. The program is enhanced by an active PTO and Mother's Club — parent volunteers contribute significantly to the overall quality of their children's educational experience.

Christian education at St. Andrew's seeks to educate the whole child: intellectually, morally, physically, emotionally and socially. Students interact frequently with teachers and classmates. St. Andrew's strives to develop leadership through classroom activities, school worship, liturgies and curricular activities. The program of studies is designed to foster academic excellence by emphasizing basic skills to build a strong academic foundation; its success is evident in standardized test results and the number of students admitted to advanced placement high school programs. Classes are offered from 5-year-old kindergarten through 8th grade.

Higher Education

Coastal Carolina University

P.O. Box 1954
Conway *347-3161*

Coastal Carolina is a comprehensive liberal arts institution committed to excellence in teaching, research and public service. The university offers baccalaureate degrees in 26 major fields of study.

Located on 242 wooded acres just minutes from Myrtle Beach and the Atlantic Ocean, its campus is home to more than 4,500 students from South Carolina and 40 other states, as well as 26 foreign countries.

Coastal Carolina offers a hands-on, personal educational experience. More than 200 faculty members bring impressive credentials from universities throughout the nation. Select faculty have been awarded Fulbright grants for research projects and study in such countries as Poland, Colombia, Cypress and China. In addition, students interact with worldwide experts on a variety of topical issues through the advanced technologies of long-distance education such as teleconferencing and on-line computer services.

Coastal Carolina's academic programs are often supplemented with field experiences and real-world applications. Each year, students participate in faculty-led travel to study and explore the coastal habitats of a pristine barrier island on the South Carolina coast, the expansive geological formations in the Grand Canyon, archaeological digs in regional historical settings, Fortune 500 companies in Atlanta, the marbled chambers of the United States Supreme Court and, most recently, Oxford University and East Africa.

A student exchange program with Nene College in North Hampton, England, has been established through the Palmetto Partnership for International Exchange, a partnership headed by Coastal Carolina with the College of Charleston, Lander and Winthrop universities.

Coastal Carolina's sports program participates in NCAA Division I and fields 14 varsity teams to compete in the Big South Conference.

The foundation for Coastal Carolina University was laid in 1954 when a group of concerned citizens met in the Horry County Memorial Library to discuss a daring proposal — the creation of a local college. Since then, the institution has been building a tradition of excellence and forging new paths as Coastal Carolina becomes one of the Southeast's notable institutions of higher learning.

Horry-Georgetown Technical College

2050 U.S. 501
East Conway *347-3186*

The Horry-Georgetown Technical Center, established in 1966, continues to grow and prosper in serving Horry and Georgetown counties and surrounding communities. HGTC is a "center of hope" for the more than 2,700 students enrolled in its regular curriculum and the more than 10,000 served annually by a variety of Continuing Education courses and seminars. A comprehensive commuter college with convenient campus sites in Conway, Myrtle Beach and Georgetown, HGTC offers 49 degrees, diplomas and certificates from Associate in Arts and Associate in Science to a varied technical and business curriculum. Its thriving Continuing Education program and intensive on-site industrial training program, serving 12 to 50 businesses and industries each year, round out HGTC's educational opportunities.

HGTC is accredited by the Commission on Colleges of the Southern Association of Colleges and Schools.

North American Institute of Aviation

P.O. Box 680
Conway *(800) 345-6152*

This international institute operates out of the Conway Airport. Students, about 100 at any given time, train to become commercial airline pilots. After a six-month course, pilots return to their home countries to accumulate flight time. Once they have logged 1,500 flight hours, they return to Conway to earn an Airline Transport Pilot designation.

Most of the students come from Scandinavian countries and live in dormitories at the airport.

Babysitting for Visitors

With the heavy influx of families visiting this area, there are frequent inquiries about babysitting services available to nonresidents. Time-starved moms and dads deserve a grown-up break from the family rat-race every now and again! So, if you'd consider leaving your child with a sitting service, call **Resort Baby-sitting Service** at 272-2932.

Resort Baby-sitting, in operation in the Myrtle Beach area since 1982, caters primarily to the tourist market but serves a few locals as well. With approximately 14 or 15 sitters, Resort Baby-sitting can sometimes accommodate parents on short notice. However, especially during the busy summer season, officials suggest calling at least 24 hours in advance. Sitters are thoroughly screened and most are mature women — several in their late 20s, but most older than 30. Sitters provide their own transportation and will accept jobs from North Myrtle Beach to Garden City. The price is $5 per hour for two children, and each additional child is $1.50 per hour. There is a 3-hour minimum service and a $5 transportation charge.

Additionally, some of the area's day-care centers allow drop-ins. A sampling includes: St. Philips Lutheran Church, 6200 N. Kings Highway, Myrtle Beach, 449-5345; Little Angels, 607 17th Avenue N., Myrtle Beach, 626-7337; and Wee Care Day School, 2103 Rosemary Avenue, Myrtle Beach, 448-6290.

A few of the larger hotels and resorts offer sitting and scheduled activities for kids. When you're deciding where to stay, ask if your lodging alternatives have programs to suit your needs.

The school moved to Conway from the Northeast about 15 years ago because officials preferred the area's geography and mild weather.

Webster University

904 65th Ave. N.
Myrtle Beach *497-3677*

Webster University is an independent, comprehensive, nondenominational, multi-campus, international university offering a graduate program at its Myrtle Beach campus. Timothy Groza, senior director of the Myrtle Beach Metropolitan Campus, comments, "We offer degree programs that many other schools in the area do not. We also conveniently schedule classes which attract students from up to two and a half hours away." Class schedules are convenient for working professionals.

All graduate programs are accredited by the North Central Association of Colleges and Schools. Admission to the M.A. and M.B.A. programs is open to all students who hold an undergraduate degree from a regionally accredited college or university.

In a nutshell, Webster offers education tailored to busy professionals. The distinction of Webster's whole approach is that its commitment to education and the community has created distinct advantages for adult students — fulfilling the wish-list of anyone who wants to change careers, retool in the wake of cutbacks or closings, or advance in his or her current situation.

Cathedral Bible College

P.O. Box 2160
Myrtle Beach *946-9134*

Cathedral offers a Bachelor of Theology degree with majors in ministry, missions, secretarial science, counseling, teaching and music. The college enrolls approximately 100 students.

Fortune School of Real Estate

350 Wesley St., Unit 305
Myrtle Beach *236-1131*

Fortune School of Real Estate trains new agents, existing agents and aspiring brokers in preparation for the state licensing exam.

Chris Logan Career College

505 Seventh Ave. N.
Myrtle Beach *448-6302*

The Career College offers students cosmetology and nail technician courses in preparation for the state licensing exam. The college also offers continuing education programs.

Photo: Cecelia Konyn, The Sun News

The Senior Games are held every spring for competitors ages 55 and older.

Inside Retirement

The Grand Strand and retirees have a passionate love affair going. And, this perfect coupling is not only compatible, but seems to be intensifying every year as more and more active seniors come south to embrace the comfortable coastal lifestyle. Between 1980 and 1990, the number of retirees in Horry County alone increased 103 percent. In 1990, Horry County's over-60 population was 26,000 people; the incoming moving vans haven't slowed down. Current projections claim that the county's population will double by the year 2010, with the majority of new citizens being 50 years and older. Who can blame them? They're finished with the workaday world but not with life. They come to get the most out of the golden years under the warm Carolina sunshine. They mostly hail from colder regions to the north where many a winter was spent shoveling snow, wrapping kids in knitted scarves and navigating icy roads. Here, retirees can enjoy the freedom of a temperate climate, partake in the luxury of walking barefoot along a sandy coast and, for the most part, get far more purchasing mileage out of their dollar. In turn, they have wooed and won the hearts of Grand Stranders with the skills and experience they apply to local civic groups, churches, the arts and governmental entities. Retirees have become and will remain an integral part of this community. As one 69-year-old retired widow put it, "I moved to Myrtle Beach four months ago and have a busier schedule than ever before. No one needs to be lonely in Myrtle Beach. There's just too much to do."

Many retired folks volunteer at area schools and hospitals. They serve on boards and councils, operate community projects, head up fund-raising drives and participate in cultural programs. The **Long Bay Symphony** can credit its very existence to retirees who worked in the music business and performed with symphonies in larger cities. The over-55 set has their own acting troupe, the **Grand Strand Seniors for the Performing Arts**, that puts on three productions a year, and their own golf association, the **Senior Golfers Association**, with its own publication, *Senior Golf Journal*. The **Waccamaw Carving Club**, the **Waccamaw Arts and Crafts Guild**, the **Grand Strand Concert Band** and the **Long Bay Photography Club** would all have slim membership rolls without their retirees. The Grand Strand also entices migrant retirees, usually referred to as "snowbirds," who follow the sunshine south to escape the harsh northern winters. They rent houses and apartments or stay in hotels, taking advantage of lower winter rates. Around March or April, when temperatures start to rise, they head home. No one seems to have a good grasp of just how many snowbirds winter along the Grand Strand, although estimates range from 20,000 to 50,000. Horry's seniors have their own newspaper, ***Fifty Plus***; their own magazine, ***Senior Lifestyles***; their own annual trade show, **The Lifestyles Expo**, held in March for 1995 in the Myrtle Beach Convention Center; and, their own production company that puts together a 30-minute program each month for Cox Cable.

Fifty Plus has grown phenomenally since its inception in 1990. The free-circulation paper, which at first averaged about 24 pages, was distributed to 5,000 people. Now, 20,000 newspapers are distributed each month with an average of between 48 and 52 pages. Circulation jumped by 8,000 from 1994 to 1995 alone.

Although there are several very nice residential areas for retirees, many choose to live amidst the regular population. In fact, retirees can be found in just about every Grand Strand neighborhood. And, if the residential community is governed by a homeowners' association, you can bet concerned and conscientious seniors will be involved. Here is a listing we put together of beautiful, safe and active retirement living communities.

WoodLake Village

1904 Starling Ct.
Murrells Inlet *650-1876*

Sales agents at WoodLake Village describe it as the hottest-selling project on the Grand Strand for the past two years. Early in the spring there were about 400 homes located in the subdivision and only two spots left to sell. Of course, with people moving in and out, there is almost always something for sale. The 8-year-old development features a clubhouse, swimming pool and tennis courts. The subdivision isn't restricted but caters mostly to people 50 and older.

These seniors and soon-to-be seniors never lack for something to do. Activities include card games, exercise classes and even oil painting. Developers initially sold lots and provided 10 or 11 floor plans for people to choose from. The homes are neither tremendous nor extravagant, but they're nice. Yards are small, the way most active seniors like them. The sales office is located on site. Homes range from about $89,000 to about $130,000.

Jensen's Inc.

3196 Moonshadow Ln. *651-2520*
Garden City *(800) 238-6565*

In accordance with federal guidelines, Jensen's has restricted its manufactured-housing development to people 55 and older. Initiated in the early 1970s, this development is currently home to about 575 families. While only a dozen or so empty lots are available, existing-home resales account for about 55 contracts per year. At Jensen's, residents lease their lots and buy their own homes. A senior can move into a double-wide abode for between $35,000 and $80,000.

There is also a section of homes closer to traditional mobile units that cost between $15,500 and $27,000. Jensen's is quiet and well-manicured and bubbles with small lakes and canals. Residents plan their own activities through a community council which distributes a monthly newsletter chock full of things to do. There's a sales office on site.

Ocean Lakes

6001 U.S. 17 S.
Surfside Beach *238-3446*

Ocean Lakes is billed as the World's Largest Oceanfront Campground on the East Coast, and although it serves as a typical campground during the tourist season, it also has about 300 year-round

Photo: The Sun Newsd

Friends relax on the beach.

residents — mostly retirees. The campground is on the ocean and has a recreational building where residents can work on crafts or meet for a variety of activities. An activities director makes sure residents stay busy with everything from shopping and trips to miniature golf tournaments. A year-round chaplain works to meet residents' spiritual needs, providing Sunday worship services in an outdoor amphitheater when the weather permits and indoors when it doesn't.

Homes at Ocean Lakes are mostly small mobile homes, some of which have been given a more permanent appearance from added rooms and porches. Ocean Lakes is a guarded community, and security staff stationed at the gate makes sure only residents, their guests, registered campers and people attending worship services get in. As added security, Ocean Lakes instituted a 24-hour patrol of the grounds. Few people use their cars inside Ocean Lakes. Instead, you'll find their transportation much slower and more relaxed — golf carts work just fine, thank you! At any given time, there are about 100 sites for sale, ranging from $20,000 for a mobile home to $225,000 for some oceanfront condominiums.

Myrtle Trace

U.S. 501 *347-6637*
East Conway *(800) 227-0631*

As motorists pass the Myrtle Trace sign on U.S. 501, they don't get a hint about the magnitude of what lies beyond the sign and the wooded area that buffers Myrtle Trace from the highway. But pull in and take a look around, and you'll be stunned to find about 400 homes just off the highway. Myrtle Trace is about 11 years old and has a maturity that some newer developments lack. It is immaculately manicured and features lakes, golf course lots, a clubhouse and swimming pool.

Most of the people who buy at Myrtle Trace move in while they're still in their late 50s or early 60s, and they give new meaning to the words "active retirement." Residents band together to plan activities that range from all kinds of card games to theatrical performances. There is a bowling league and, of course, golf is king. Between 20 and 30 residents work at area golf courses as starters and rangers several days a week to earn a few dollars, but mostly to secure golf privileges. About 50 of Myrtle Trace's women work as volunteers at nearby Conway Hospital.

There are about 100 lots left at Myrtle Trace. Buyers can select a house design from 16 floor plans, and a staff designer is available to adjust the plans to suit the owner. A house and lot ranges from $123,000 to $165,000, depending on the location and the floor plan selected. The sales office is open from 9 AM to 6 PM from Monday through Saturday and from 1 PM to 6 PM on Sunday. Models are open every day.

Covenant Towers

5001 Little River Rd.
Myrtle Beach *449-2484*

Covenant Towers is a new and fabulous idea for retirement living. There are 159 condominiums ranging from efficiencies to a deluxe apartment with two bedrooms, two baths and a full dining room. Ten units are consistently available; the others house 167 people ranging in age from 63 to 97. Covenant Towers is an upscale development with balconies on each unit, a post office, a laundry room on every floor, a library, coffee room, craft room, swimming pool, game room, shuffleboard court, horseshoe pits and beauty shop.

A formal dining room serves dinner each evening for residents who just don't feel like cooking. (Staff members take the residents out to eat lunch at a different restaurant every Friday.) In between, they entertain themselves with sit-ercize during cold weather and water aerobics in the pool during the summer. There are worship services on site, bridge parties, shopping trips, country-western parties, bingo games, waterway cruises and even line dance lessons that residents try out at area clubs.

Each apartment has emergency pull cords that residents can easily activate to summon help within minutes. When residents feel too poorly to stay in their own apartments but aren't sick enough for the hospital, they can stay in Covenant Tower's infirmary. A fully licensed, skilled nursing home is located on the project's second floor, above the lobby and other public areas. The home is licensed for 30 beds, but usually limits its patient load to about 22 to allow for some private rooms.

Residents elect a board of directors to govern the complex. There is a monthly homeowners' fee that includes the cost of the evening meal and maid service every other week. The grounds around Covenant Towers are especially inviting. There's a nice view of the neighboring golf course, a short wooded trail and even a pond with huge goldfish. Unit prices start at $59,900.

Spring Forest

U.S. 17 Bypass
Murrells Inlet *650-8812*

Spring Forest is a charming development dedicated to older residents. Currently, there are only seven building lots available, and takers can choose from eight different home plans to grace their property — all have two or three bedrooms with two bathrooms and an optional attached garage. A resident designer also offers custom services to potential homeowners. The quaint homes are accented by fish-stocked waterways into

Grand Strand Senior Center: A Hub of Activity

The **Horry County Council On Aging** realized the fruits of its labor in 1995 when a brand-spanking new senior center opened at 1268 21st Avenue N. in Myrtle Beach. The $1.4 million project offers seniors 16,000 square feet of space including a full-size auditorium, kitchen, dressing rooms and meeting chambers. A $10 annual membership fee allows access to all of the center's activities plus a monthly newsletter. Honestly, you would have to have the energy of two preteens on summer vacation to partake in all there is to do here! Open Monday through Friday from 9 AM to 4 PM, Grand Strand Senior Center plays host to a schedule of events ranging from line dancing, Tai Chi and language classes to card games, calligraphy and arts and crafts. The **Seniors for the Performing Arts** theatrical troupe performs full-production plays in the auditorium and holds regular luncheons with interesting guest speakers. Membership is open to all senior residents, whether permanent or part-time. For more information, drop by or call, 626-3991.

which residents can cast a fishing line at any time. Spring Forest offers a 5,000-square-foot plantation-style clubhouse with a full kitchen, library, game room, billiards room and library. Outside the clubhouse is a shimmering swimming pool. And, of course, a security gate fronts the development to keep the area private and safe. Homes range from $79,900 to $101,900.

Senior Service Directory

These particular agencies and resources could come in handy for seniors.

American Association of Retired Persons (AARP)

Myrtle Beach 449-4007
South Strand 651-6643
North Strand 249-2940

Devoted to the needs of senior adults, the AARP sponsors an employment program including job training and placement for older workers with limited incomes.

AARP Housing Program

Coastal Carolina University
P.O. Box 1954
Conway 29526 349-2111

In cooperation with the Area Agency on Aging, this program advocates appropriate housing and services to enhance the health, security and independence of senior citizens.

Area Agency on Aging

Coastal Carolina University
P.O. Box 1954
Conway 29526 349-2130

This agency can provide referral services for local seniors and will send you a copy of the Horry County Resource Directory.

Eldercare Locator

(800) 677-1116

This national information system refers families to eldercare providers.

Photo: Cecelia Konyn, The Sun News

Coastal Carolina University offers a variety of courses to seniors over age 50 in its third quarter program.

Elderhostel

Coastal Carolina University
P.O. Box 1954
Conway 29526 *448-1481*

Participants in this exciting program get an opportunity to take up to three non-credit courses in liberal arts and sciences from a host institution in the United States or abroad. This program is offered at more than 1,600 locations internationally.

Fifty-Five Alive Mature Driving

Grand Strand Senior Center
1268 21st Ave. N.
Myrtle Beach *626-3991*

This course consists of eight hours of classroom instruction that stresses safe, defensive driving skills. The program is sponsored by the AARP.

Fifty Plus

314 Bush Dr.
Myrtle Beach *236-3602*

This free newspaper, expressly printed to suit senior citizens and retirees, is published monthly and distributed all along the Grand Strand from the North Carolina border to Georgetown. Subscriptions are also available.

Insiders' Tips

Most Grand Strand businesses cater to retirees by offering discounts and special packages. If you're 55 or older, inquire about any senior perks when making a purchase or reservation of any kind. You'll be pleasantly surprised at your overall savings!

Photo: The Sun News

Myrtle Beach is one of the country's great retirement areas.

GRAND STRAND RETIREMENT CLUB

238-0717

For $5 a year, any permanent and retired resident of the Grand Strand can join this social club, which meets once a month at various locations (call for details). Members perform some charity work each year but primarily meet to network with one another.

HORRY COUNTY COUNCIL ON AGING, INC.

2213 N. Main St.
Conway *248-5523*

The Council on Aging is a busy agency in the area as it acts as an information and referral service for all senior citizens and their families. They can give up-to-date information on everything from home-delivered meals to living wills.

HORRY COUNTY VETERANS AFFAIRS OFFICE

211 Beaty St.
Conway *248-1291*

This agency provides services to veterans, their dependents and a veteran's survivors and operates as an intermediary between veteran patients and the VA hospital.

SENIOR ADVISORY COMMITTEE OF MYRTLE BEACH

10th Ave. N. and Broadway
Myrtle Beach *626-7645*

This committee was organized through the City of Myrtle Beach to address specific needs of senior citizens such as larger print on road signs, longer crosswalk signals and noise ordinances.

SERVICE CORPS OF RETIRED EXECUTIVES (SCORE)

1109 48th Ave. N.
Myrtle Beach *449-8538*

Calling all retired businesspeople and executives. This volunteer corps offers free counsel to individuals who desire to go into business, as well as to businesses experiencing problems.

Senior Golfers Association and Senior Golf Journal

3013 Church St.
Myrtle Beach *448-1569*

The Senior Golfers Association and its publication includes members and subscriptions from every town and city across the United States. It's ironic, but this set of golfers never play along the Grand Strand. Golf tournaments and the journal are coordinated from here, but its interest is national.

Social Security Administration

905 Third Ave. *248-4271*
Conway *(800) 772-2121*
(800) 772-1213

This agency provides information on benefits, including Supplemental Security Income (SSI) and disability.

Third Quarter

Coastal Carolina University
P.O. Box 1954 *347-3161*
Conway 29526 *448-1481*

University faculty and professionals from the community teach a variety of intellectual, cultural and social classes. No formal papers or exams are required of the senior students.

Inside Health Care

For the benefit of any visitor to the Grand Strand, this chapter will give you pertinent information about regional medical services, clinics and hospitals. Health care services listed here should be able to handle anything from a severe sunburn to debilitating pain. If you are about to become a resident, or have just moved into our area, the referral services can quickly put you in touch with a new family doctor or specialist.

Referrals and Free Advice

Ask-A-Nurse

347-8199

Conway Hospital offers this convenient and confidential service 24-hours a day, for people who aren't sure whether or not they need medical care. Qualified nurses will answer your questions and tell you how to handle minor health problems, helping you avoid time-consuming or costly visits to a hospital. There is no charge to you for the call. In its first two years of existence, the program assisted more than 50,000 contacts. Nurses also have a list of area physicians who will take new patients and can refer you to the best possible medical professional.

Physician Referral Source

497-2128

Especially if a medical specialist is needed, this service will give you all the necessary referral information, including a doctor's hours. Physician Referral represents more than 100 of Grand Strand Regional Medical Center's staff and more than 25 medical specialties and sub-specialties. This service is also available 24-hours a day at no cost.

Regional Health Care Facilities

Visitors who need to see a doctor but aren't sick enough to go to a hospital emergency room can save themselves time and money by seeking care at one of the Grand Strand's walk-in medical clinics.

These clinics take patients without appointments, but most of them don't take insurance, Medicaid or Medicare, so be prepared to pay when you go. Costs run anywhere from $55 to $75 for an average visit. Clinic doctors routinely treat sunburn, heat rash, cuts, sprains, broken bones, jellyfish stings and sore throats.

But some offer more serious services, including X-rays and stabilization of patients who have had heart attacks. Here is a listing of walk-in clinics representing each area of the strand.

Walk-in Clinics

ASAP Medical Clinic

27th Ave. N.
Myrtle Beach *946-9690*

ASAP Medical Clinic is probably the

FOR EMERGENCIES.

FOR EVERYTHING ELSE.

When it's a medical emergency, you call 911. But who do you call if you have a high fever, you need a doctor, or you just have a general health question? Keep our number and you'll have a trained registered nurse to call, day or night.

Your Source For Health Care Answers™

Provided as a free community service by:

Conway Hospital

newest walk-in clinic along the Grand Strand. It's open Monday through Saturday from 9 AM through 4:30 PM. Doctors handle minor medical emergencies including sunburn, fire ant stings and cuts. The clinic can also perform drug and alcohol screening. One of the most common services they provide is replacement of prescriptions for travelers who have left their medications at home. Life-threatening emergencies are sent on to a hospital. ASAP accepts credit cards, travelers checks and in-state checks. Costs start from about $45, depending on the services provided. The clinic is also working to develop a local clientele among area industries, providing pre-employment physicals for Workman's Compensation. For this service, they'll accept Medicare, Champus and some city and county insurances.

Convenience Medical Center

108 U.S. 17 N.
North Myrtle Beach *249-0034*

Convenience Medical Center offers minor surgery, physicals, lab work and X-rays. The clinic opens at 8:30 AM on weekdays and tries to have everyone attended to by 7 PM. On Saturdays, the office is open from 9 AM to 2 PM. Office visits are usually around $50 for a noncomplicated treatment. Convenience Medical also has regular patients who are charged $40. Credit cards are accepted.

Access Medical Center

3816 U.S. 17 S.
North Myrtle Beach *272-1411*

Access Medical Care offers minor surgery, X-rays, electrocardiograms and complete laboratory services. The clinic also operates a pharmacy. Insurance is not accepted, but office workers will fill out Medicare and Medicaid papers for people who live in South and North Carolina. The clinic is open Monday through Friday from 8 AM to 6 PM and on Saturday from 9 AM to 1 PM.

Doctor's Care of Myrtle Beach

4701 Oleander Dr.
Myrtle Beach *449-4024*

This Myrtle Beach medical clinic provides primary and urgent care including X-rays, stitches and stabilization of heart attack patients. Doctors also set broken bones. The clinic is open from 8 AM to 6 PM Monday through Friday and on weekends from 9 AM to 5 PM.

Clinic Medical Care

605 N. Kings Hwy., Ste. C
(Beside the Myrtle Beach Post Office)
Myrtle Beach *448-4262*

General medical services, including X-rays and lab work, are provided at Clinic Medical Care. Emergencies are sent to Grand Strand Regional Medical Center. The clinic is open from 9 AM to 6 PM Monday through Friday during the fall, winter and spring. From Easter to Labor Day, the clinic adds Saturday hours from 10 AM to 4 PM. Insurance is accepted in some cases, including Canadian providers.

Doctor's Care At Waccamaw

400 George Bishop Pkwy.
(At Waccamaw Pottery)
Myrtle Beach *236-6000*

The clinic treats a wide array of minor emergencies and offers X-rays and minor lab work. Officials recommend people with chest pains go directly to a hospital. If you're wondering whether Doctor's Care can handle your problem, call ahead and they'll evaluate it for you. The clinic is open Monday through Friday from 8 AM to 4 PM, with extended hours — 8 AM to 8 PM Monday through Friday and 8 Am to 6 PM Saturday and Sunday — kicking in during the summer months. A typical office visit is about $55.

Doctor's Care Surfside Medical Center

1600 U.S. 17 N.
Surfside Beach 238-1461

Doctor's Care Surfside Medical Center treats mostly minor emergencies but can stabilize a heart attack patient pending transport to a hospital. The clinic is open seven days a week from 8 AM to 8 PM, except in January and February when it closes at 6 PM. It's located on the frontage road, just two doors down from the Pizza Hut. An office visit will range from $55 to $65.

Hospitals

It's heart-wrenching to suspect that you, a loved one or friend needs hospital attention, but you can take comfort in the care and professionalism found at the following medical facilities. Scanning through this section, you should be able to get a pretty good idea of the specialty services offered by each, just in case you need to make a quick decision about where to take someone for medical attention.

Conway Hospital

Singleton Ridge Rd.
Conway 347-7111

Conway Hospital, a private, nonprofit institution, was located in downtown Conway for more than a half-century before a large, modern facility was built outside the city limits between Conway and Myrtle Beach.

The hospital opened in 1982, and today more than 80 physicians make rounds among 160 modern, private rooms.

Services include 24-hour emergency and urgent care, one-day surgery, chemotherapy, CT scanning, magnetic resonance imaging, lithotripsy, maternity care, pediatric care, mammography, cardiac rehabilitation, nuclear medicine, cardiac catheterization, physical therapy, respiratory therapy, home health care, surgical care, ultrasound, intensive care, progressive care, echocardiography and angiography. The hospital is also certified as a Level III trauma center and Level II perinatal center. Adjacent to Conway

Your source for local information today!

Shopping. Dining. Golf. Entertainment. Real Estate.

The Sun News is your best source for the best information about the Myrtle Beach area.

And if you're looking for a new house,

make sure you pick up The Sun News on Sunday for Real Estate Plus, your information guide for real estate news along the Grand Strand.

The Sun News and Real Estate Plus are your sources for the best local information!

THE SUN NEWS

Hospital is Kingston Nursing Center, an 88-bed nursing home owned and operated by the hospital. Kingston offers both long-term skilled care and short-term rehabilitative services.

Grand Strand Regional Medical Center

809 82nd Pkwy.
Myrtle Beach *449-4411*

Grand Strand Regional Medical Center, an affiliate of Columbia/Healthcare Corporation of America, is a 172-bed acute-care facility, offering a wide array of medical services on both an inpatient and outpatient basis.

The medical staff covers 25 specialties and sub-specialties. Grand Strand Regional has the county's only cardiac surgery program, with two operating rooms dedicated to open heart surgery, angioplasty and other heart-related procedures. The hospital is noted for its state-of-the-art cardiac catheterization laboratory, cardiac rehabilitation program and its comprehensive obstetrics department. But it also offers highly specialized care, including an on-site dialysis unit, cardiopulmonary services, a comprehensive cancer program including in-house chemotherapy and a tumor registry, and diagnostic SPECT nuclear medicine with three dimensional imaging that enables physicians to view internal organs without the need for surgery.

The Emergency Department was recently expanded, adding electronic technology that includes a hyperbaric chamber commonly used in treating diving accidents, wounds and burns. Emergency also offers Care Express to treat minor injuries and illnesses for anyone without a local physician. Care Express is open to new residents and visitors alike.

For added convenience, an outpatient pharmacy is open to the public from 7 PM to 7 AM, every day of the week.

Hospital officials work especially hard at preventive care and community education through an annual health fair held on the first Saturday in February, and a cardiac wellness program which includes the Mall Walkers' Club, the Cardiac Lifelong Program and ongoing community cholesterol screenings. Other community programs include prostate cancer screening for children and a teddy bear clinic — an annual event at Grand Strand Regional aimed at allaying childrens' fears of hospitals. Pre-schoolers bring their "injured" teddy bears into the emergency room where doctors and nurses apply bandages, splints, stitches and the odd button.

Georgetown Memorial Hospital

606 Black River Rd. *527-7000*
Georgetown (from Myrtle Beach) 626-9040

This is a private, nonprofit acute-care medical facility that is currently licensed for 142 beds. More than 50 physicians representing 20 areas of specialty practice are members of the active medical staff. The hospital also owns and operates two associated facilities: Waccamaw Neck Medical Center in Murrells Inlet and Andrews Medical Center in the Town of Andrews. Medical services include ambulatory surgery, birthing suites, cardiac diagnostic, catheterization and rehabilitation, cholesterol screenings, full emergency and lab services, magnetic resonance imaging, pathology, radiology, renal dialysis and respiratory therapy. For patient convenience, the hospital also houses a pharmacy, offers cholesterol screening, dietary consultation and discharge planning. Established since 1950, Georgetown Memorial has consistently expanded services to keep up with the

needs of its community and has recently added pre-op bays and a fifth surgical suite.

Loris Community Hospital

3655 Mitchell St.
Loris *756-4011*

Some visitors at the northern end of the Grand Strand might find it quickest to visit Loris, a nonprofit community hospital. Loris has a capacity of 105 patients, all in private rooms. The hospital also runs a separate 88-bed nursing home known as the Loris Community Hospital Extended Care Facility.

Loris Hospital offers 24-hour emergency service, cardiac rehabilitation services, same-day surgery, respite care for the elderly, a modern intensive care unit, magnetic resonance imaging, CT scanner, outpatient services, an obstetrics unit with childbirth classes and nutritional counseling. Current expansion includes the construction of a 25,000-square-foot Wellness Center that will house cardiac rehabilitation, physical therapy, hydrotherapy, exercise programs and meeting facilities. Surgical suites, the in-house pharmacy and radiology are also being revamped and enlarged. Anticipated for the spring of 1995 is the opening of a mental health wing that will service individuals and families who previously had to travel outside the county for psychiatric care. With the recent opening of a full complement of medical offices in North Myrtle Beach and the LCH Family Health Center clinic, Loris Hospital is fast becoming one of the most full-service medical facilities in the area.

McLeod Regional Medical Center

555 E. Cheves St.
Florence *667-2000*

About 75 miles from Myrtle Beach is McLeod Regional Hospital — a regional referral center for 12 counties in southeastern South Carolina. McLeod was established in 1906 as a small infirmary; today, it's a large high-tech medical center, with 331 beds and a variety of services. Many Horry countians depend on McLeod's neonatal intensive care unit to tend premature babies and full-term babies born with special problems.

The hospital's breast imaging center is designed to detect breast cancer early. McLeod has the state's first permanent magnetic resonance imaging (MRI) system — a high-tech machine that uses a magnetic field to see into the body in a much clearer way than other scanning machines allow.

McLeod also provides comprehensive inpatient, outpatient and diagnostic facilities including an extensive 24-hour laboratory, computerized tomography, angiography, computer-enhanced nuclear medicine, ultrasound, mammography, EEG, EKG, echocardiography, a vascular laboratory, osteoporosis screening, a sleep center and 24-hour emergency care. The Florence hospital is the state-designated regional trauma center.

The facility has recently added a five-story freestanding Women's Pavilion connected to McLeod. The entire hospital is devoted to meeting women's special health care needs. The pavilion houses a mammography unit, outpatient surgery rooms, and a special section for labor and delivery or Caesarean sections.

Hospital officials are also interested in tending to the special needs of children, so they created the Pediatric After-Hours Care Center, where children 16 and younger can receive treatment for about 40 ailments. The After-Hours Center takes over when the doctors' offices close, handling minor cuts and scrapes, earaches, tummy aches,

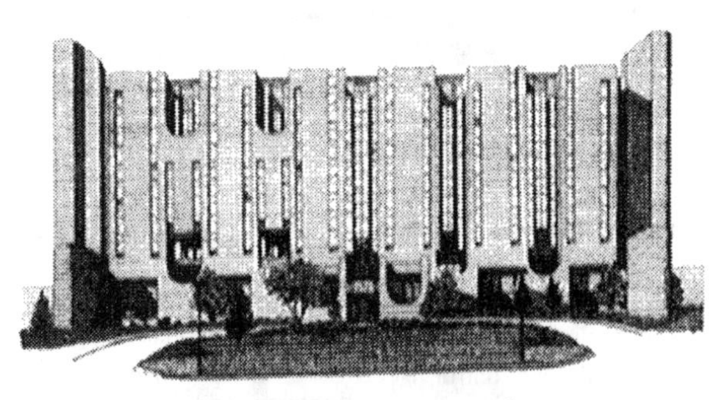

even coughs and fevers. Nine pediatricians work in rotation from 6:30 PM to 10:30 PM. It's also less expensive than an emergency room visit.

A wide range of support departments buttress the hospital's services. These include rehabilitative services, pain management, cardiac rehabilitation, respiratory services, counseling and discharge planning, Hospice, infection control, pastoral services, patient representatives, volunteer services, computer services and marketing.

Mental Health/Addictions

The Waccamaw Center for Mental Health

Horry County
164 Waccamaw Medical Park Dr.
Conway *347-4888*
Georgetown
2710 Highmarket St.
Georgetown *546-6107*

Waccamaw Center is a public, nonprofit agency that handles any sort of mental health issue on an outpatient basis. Fees are established by a sliding-scale method. You pay only what you can afford, based on income and expenses, and most insurances are accepted. Staff is on call 24-hours a day, seven days a week to respond to emergencies and crises. All clinics offer adult services, child and adolescent therapy, alcohol and drug abuse counseling, programs for the chronically mentally ill and emergency stabilization. Special community programs are continuously being developed by The Waccamaw Center to institute prevention of growing mental health problems. A BabyNet program counsels pregnant mothers and follows the child's development from birth to 3 years of age. The school-based program operates out of Myrtle Beach Primary and Elementary schools, offering on-site help to children and their families. The Center will also refer clients to an appropriate inpatient facility if needed.

Coastal Carolina Hospital

U.S. 501 *448-1481*
W. Conway *(800) 922-0742*

Coastal Carolina is a specialty hospital providing both inpatient and outpatient psychiatric and chemical dependency services. Outpatient assessments and therapy cover almost any problem from marriage and family conflicts to drug and alcohol treatment. Coastal is best known for its inpatient services which include acute psychiatric treatment for adults and children, plus detoxification and a residential treatment center for adolescents. Their helpline is available 24-hours a day, seven days a week (see the above-listed 800 number). Coastal accepts commercial insurance, Champus and Medicare. Visa and MasterCard are accepted.

Health Related Associations

Alzheimer's Support Group

151 Quail Run
Conway *347-1496*

This group provides a listening ear, encouragement, coping techniques, moral support and practical information. Respite services are also available, including adult day-care programs, home health aids and short-stay nursing home programs.

American Cancer Society

514 Alder St.
Myrtle Beach *448-2562*

The Cancer Society holds quarterly support group meetings and provides a loan closet of wheelchairs and walkers. Gift items and counseling for breast cancer patients are also provided, as well as a transportation program for anyone afflicted with a cancer.

Arthritis Foundation

1314 Spring St. N.W.
Atlanta, Ga. (800) 283-7800

The Arthritis Foundation provides the above-listed toll-free number to answer folk's questions about various types of arthritis and, when appropriate, refers callers to community organizations. The foundation is also prepared to help clients and their families with financial support.

Department of Health and Environmental Control

303 Hazzard St.
Georgetown 546-5593
101 Elm St.
Conway 448-9121

DHEC performs physical exams, blood tests, immunizations, family planning and tuberculosis screening. The agency can provide health care to the homebound, depending upon the particular circumstances.

Diabetic Outreach

300 Singleton Ridge Rd.
Conway 626-9461

A registered nurse and dietitian are on hand for this group's monthly meetings, held the first Thursday of every month at 1:30 PM in the auditorium of Conway Hospital.

Inside Media

For the first time in about 10 years, the Grand Strand's world of media seems to have finally stabilized into neat market share packages of audiences and airwaves.

Especially in radio programming, stations have spent the better part of a decade jockeying for specific formats that might appease the stable population during the winter off-season and grab the ears of thousands of diverse visitors coming into the area during the spring, summer and fall.

To a Grand Strand local, it has never been an unusual experience to tune into a favorite morning FM station only to discover that your beloved DJ was replaced and the rock 'n' roll tunes had been cast aside in favor of a country music format. And we were never the least bit surprised a year later if the same station began playing Top 40 hits and our old buddy was back in the DJ's seat!

Because a resort area is playing host on any given day to people from any given town, city or country, the local media always seemed to be caught in a Catch 22 of trying to be all things to all people and reaching no one in particular. But, at this point in time, it seems as if local radio has relaxed desperate strategies for bigger advertising dollars and ratings and has finally settled into a state of consistent programming.

With that in mind, we feel pretty confident that the electronic media listed here will remain constant for at least the next year.

Newspapers

The Sun News

P.O. Box 406
Myrtle Beach 29578 *626-8555*

This is the only daily newspaper along the Grand Strand, offering comprehensive local and international news, stock market reports, weather forecasts and a full classified advertising section. On Fridays, the paper includes the "kicks!" section, which provides an impressive look at upcoming entertainment and reviews. The Sunday edition is chock-full of extras including a separate real estate section, TV guide, coupons and *Parade* magazine.

The Myrtle Beach Herald

P.O. Box 7116
Dunes Station
Myrtle Beach 29577 *626-3131*

Found mainly in area book and grocery stores, this broadsheet paper comes out every Thursday morning. Editorial coverage investigates the Grand Strand from Little River to Murrells Inlet.

The Times

P.O. Box 725
North Myrtle Beach *249-3525*

Published on Wednesdays, *The Times* attempts to zero in on Grand Strand-related issues such as the local option sales tax and further development of the local transportation infrastructure. You can find it in bookstores and brochure racks at local restaurants and businesses.

Coastal Observer

P.O. Box 1170
Pawleys Island 29585 — *237-8438*

This weekly newspaper hits the streets on Thursdays and covers the region known as the Waccamaw Neck: Georgetown, Pawleys Island, Murrells Inlet, Litchfield Beach and Garden City Beach. A number of native Georgetonians seem to think that the *Observer* presents good in-depth coverage of their area.

The Georgetown Times

P.O. Drawer G
Georgetown 29442 — *546-4148*

A well-established local newspaper, *The Times* is published on Tuesdays, Thursdays and Saturdays to reflect Georgetown and its surrounding communities. You'll find copies in news racks throughout the county.

Radio Stations

Adult Contemporary

WWMX-FM 97.7

This station promises to give you the hot Top 40 hits. The morning DJ, Billy Smith, has been a local for years and has a reputation for bending the rules. His show usually features conversations with local-yokels you have to hear to believe.

WNMB-FM 105.9, WGSN-AM 900

Mainstream adult contemporary music is the mainstay of these sister stations, airing the best hits from the 1970s, '80s and '90s. These stations appeal to the 30-something set that prefers soft rock music.

WDAI-FM 98.5

Kiss FM 98.5 blends non-rap music with solid urban oldies and features the Tom Joyner morning show.

Country Music

WGTR-FM 107.9

Even though "Gator" is the newest radio station to the area, it swept all others in The Overall Adult category (Monday through Sunday) when 1994 Arbitron ratings were made public.

WJXY-FM 93.9/AM 1050

This station offers a country format on its FM frequency and gospel music on AM.

WYAK-FM 103.1/ 94.9

"Yak" used to be the only game in town when it came to country music. Tab Allen is the morning DJ and has been a favorite local personality for years.

Easy Listening

WJYR-FM 92.1

Called "Joy 92", this format is a delight to those who want to be lulled by their radio selections. You'll hear lots of instrumental versions of popular songs as well as Big Band numbers.

Oldies

WSYN-FM 106.5

If you love music from the 1950s and '60s, turn your dial no further than "Sunny" 106. This station specializes in the best of that era plus selections from later years.

Rock

WYAV-FM 104.1

Going out on a limb last year, "Wave" took a controversial chance by bringing *The Howard Stern Show* to town. Infamous "shock-jock" Stern can be heard live from New York City every morning on this station and is followed by classic rock music for the rest of the programming day.

WKZQ-FM 101.7/AM 1520

Hear the most up-to-date rock music on the oldest consistent-format station in the area. AM jock "Banana" Jack Murphy is known for his local cable TV show as well as his on-air antics.

Talk Radio

WRNN-FM 94.5

Locally owned and operated, this is the first and only talk radio station to hit the Grand Strand. G. Gordon Liddy can be heard from 10 AM to noon, followed by Rush Limbaugh from noon to 3 PM. Allan Colmes comes on from 3 to 4 PM and Dr. Dean Edelle talks from 4 to 5 PM. The rest of the day is filled with local talk programming.

Television Stations

ABC Affiliates

WPDE-TV 15
WWAY-TV 3
WCBD-TV 2

CBS Affiliates

WBTW-TV 13
WCSC-TV 5

Photo: Jody Hazzard, The sun News

The Sun News *is the daily newspaper for the Grand Strand.*

NBC Affiliates

WECT-TV 6
WIS-TV 10
WCIV-TV 4

FOX Affiliates

WTAT-TV 24
WSFX-TV 26

United Paramount Affiliate

WWMB-TV 21

Independent

WGSE-TV 43

Educational

WITV-TV 7
WHMC-TV 23
WJPM-TV 33
WUNJ-TV 39

Scroll Channels

COX Cable and Jones Intercable

Scroll channels offer a constant listing of local information and public service announcements accompanied by easy listening music. They are a favorite in many hotel rooms since they supply Grand Strand visitors with updated information.

Inside Volunteer Opportunities

Want to get the pulse on a seemingly erratic resort area in a hurry? Become a volunteer! We highly recommend this pastime as one of the best ways to become entrenched in the community. Whether you're a newcomer to the Grand Strand or have chosen this sandy coast as your retirement home, joining a volunteer corps can open an insightful window to local politics, culture and people.

For those who are coming into town to tackle a new job assignment or career, a number of area businesses encourage volunteer activity by paying club membership dues for their employees. Civic, which means "of citizenship," organizations can often plug you right into a networking circuit of business contacts. Even *Fortune 500* magazine recently listed volunteer experience as a highlight many American corporations now look for on resumes.

On a purely social level, civic involvement in a specific club will serve you up a slice of local life. Each organization presents its own microcosm or cross section of Grand Strand citizenry, where you're bound to meet an interesting friend or two and, perhaps, the man or woman of your dreams. For singles, we can assure you that meeting native people through volunteer activity will beat a Werewolf lifestyle of moonlit barstalking.

Volunteer opportunities abound up and down the Grand Strand strip and its pockets of sub-communities. To get a fairly comprehensive listing of volunteer outlets, we suggest dropping into the main office of the Myrtle Beach Area Chamber of Commerce on Oak Street to pick up the free-to-the-public guide, *Civic & Service Organizations of the Myrtle Beach Area*. You can also get updated volunteer information from *The Sun News* on Sundays. Civic and support group meetings can be found in the "Coastal Living" section of the newspaper.

Included here are some volunteer organizations to start with that we know would gratefully welcome your help.

American Red Cross

236-1350

If you prefer hands-on, in the trenches sort of work, volunteering with the Red Cross could be just the ticket. The helping organization needs people to teach CPR courses, to assist with Bloodmobiles, to work in hurricane shelters and to train for emergency disaster relief.

City of Myrtle Beach

626-7645

If you want to get right into the thick of things, consider volunteering for the city. Work taking surveys, coaching or performing a number of office duties. Volunteer positions are available in the departments of planning, construction, police, finance, engineering, public services and parks and recreation.

The Myrtle Beach Jaycees sponsor the Sun Fun Little Olympics every year.

Civitan Club

Contact James McIlrath *Home 626-6878*
Work 448-2019

These "builders of good citizens" primarily focus on projects that deal with youth. Civitans are the official local sponsors of Special Olympics for disabled children. The club currently has 30 to 35 members and meets at 1 PM on the second and fourth Tuesdays of each month.

Grand Strand Humane Association

448-5891, 448-9151, 449-2778

This is definitely the right place for animal lovers to donate their time and energy. People are needed to assist in the care of animals in the North Myrtle Beach and Myrtle Beach shelters and to help with fund-raising and community interest programs.

Grand Strand Regional Medical Center Auxiliary

Contact Gay Cooke, CDVS *497-2184*

Volunteers are utilized in every department and on every floor of this major hospital. If interested, you must book an appointment for more information or to make application for volunteer work. Individuals are matched to particular positions at the hospital according to the skills they bring with them. Orientation and training are provided.

Hi Newcomers

Contact Lorraine Pennywitt *Home 650-3087*
Work 272-3166

As the name suggests, this 300-member-strong organization is for those who have taken up permanent residency in the Grand Strand area within the last year. From September through May, members meet for coffee, informative luncheons and to organize charity functions. Members are allowed to stay in for three years and then are invited to join Newcomers Alumnae of the Grand Strand (NAGS).

Horry County Arts Council

248-7200

Arts enthusiasts are invited to volunteer with this council at any time. In operation year round, it needs plenty of help with bulk mailings and phone-a-thons to recruit sponsors and members.

Horry-Georgetown County Guardian Ad Litem Program

248-7374

Volunteers in this program are specially trained to become advocates for abused and neglected children, representing the child's best interests through the Family Court system. This is interesting, viable work and a wonderful opportunity to learn the legal system firsthand.

Kiwanis International

Contact Phil Frank *651-7956*

A club for men and women older than the age of 18, Kiwanis clubs internationally are mandated to serve their communities. They run four or five major fund-raisers each year, and all monies raised must be donated or spent in the home town. The group does a fine job of helping support many area services such as Helping Hand and Meals On Wheels.

Optimist Clubs

Contact Jeff Ciuba *651-0372*

Call for referrals to any Optimist Club operating along the Grand Strand. Optimists meet morning, noon and night in a variety of places, so there should be a chapter that suits your schedule. Calling themselves the "Friends of Youth," Optimists are the official area ponsors of the "Just Say No" program to educate and discourage the use of drugs and alcohol by school-aged children; they also sponsor sports teams through the YMCA.

Pilot Club

Contact Linda Harrington *448-1642*

Open to men and women of all ages, the Pilot Club meets the third Tuesday of each month to coordinate ongoing community projects. The organization's main thrust is to service citizens with disabilities and the elderly. High schoolers may serve through the organization's Anchor Club.

Surfside Beach Fire Department

238-2314

Well, here's your chance to live out that childhood dream of riding along in a screeching fire-engine, wearing a shiny red hat and big boots, with your arm slung around a dalmatian. Volunteer firefighters are always needed, and the department requires no previous experience. They will train you.

The Myrtle Beach Jaycees

448-7305

The Jaycees are definitely a "doers" club, relying far more on the participation of members than fees to run the organization. At present count, the group has a membership of about 100 men and women between the ages of 21 and 40 and runs upward of 50 projects and programs every year, covering a wide range of activities from charity fund-raising to public speaking competitions. This is a good club to join for socializing and to foster people-management skills. Anyone is welcome to attend any of their meetings, which are held on the second and fourth Mondays of every month at 7 PM.

Volunteer Rescue Squads

Myrtle Beach *626-7352*
Murrells Inlet *651-2902*
North Myrtle Beach *272-3144*

Yes, the Grand Strand has a complete emergency ambulance service run solely by volunteers. Not one paid employee works at any of the area rescue squads. They operate from 7 PM to 7 AM, seven days a week responding to emergency 911 calls dispatched from police departments. Volunteers serve as drivers, crews and trained medical assistants. You must be 18 or older to volunteer.

Inside
Places of Worship

Horry and Georgetown counties are situated smack in the heart of the God-fearing Bible Belt. Consequently, the denominational makeup of the area has traditionally been largely Protestant and more than a little fundamentalist in nature. However, as the spiritual temperature of the nation is changing, so are things changing in Horry County. The Bible Belt has loosened its strap a notch or two, and the religious scene now features plenty of players in addition to Presbyterians, Methodists and Baptists.

Newcomer or visitor, you're guaranteed to find a church (and a friendly congregation!) that speaks to your spiritual needs. Here's an abbreviated list of choices: charismatic, interdenominational, nondenominational, Catholic, Protestant, Jewish, Christian Scientist, Church of Jesus Christ of Latter Day Saints, Free Will Baptist, Primitive Baptist, Southern Baptist, Greek Orthodox, United Presbyterian U.S.A., Reformed Presbyterian, Presbyterian Church in America, Jehovah's Witness, Pentecostal Holiness, Episcopalian, Lutheran, United Methodist, Southern Methodist, Assembly of God, Apostolic, Full Gospel, Church of God, Assembly of God, Unity, Seven Day Adventists or African Methodist Episcopal. You'll even find an Indian mysticism retreat, The Meher Spiritual Center, located on the oceanfront just to the north of Myrtle Beach.

If you're staying in one of the Grand Strand campgrounds, you can probably count on an opportunity to worship without leaving the premises. Lakewood Campground and Ocean Lakes Campground have their own full-time chaplains who hold Sunday worship services and plan weekday activities for the campers. Kirk Lawton, chaplain at Ocean Lakes, which bills itself as the world's largest campground, said it isn't unusual for 1,200 people to show up on summer Sunday mornings.

At least five other campgrounds are provided chaplains during the summer months by Myrtle Beach Campground Ministries: Apache, Myrtle Beach Travel Park, Myrtle Beach KOA, Springmaid Beach and the Myrtle Beach State Park. Chaplains, usually seminary students, serve from Memorial Day to Labor Day. This ministry is funded by First Baptist Church of Myrtle Beach, Ocean View Baptist Church, Trinity Episcopal Church, First Presbyterian of Myrtle Beach, St. Phillips Lutheran and First United Methodist of Myrtle Beach.

The **Campground Ministries** program, under the direction of Bert Wright, 626-3171, also coordinates as many as 60 youth groups per summer. They see the Grand Strand and its enormous campgrounds as a field ripe for harvest. The kids who participate come from as far away as Ohio. In addition to helping with

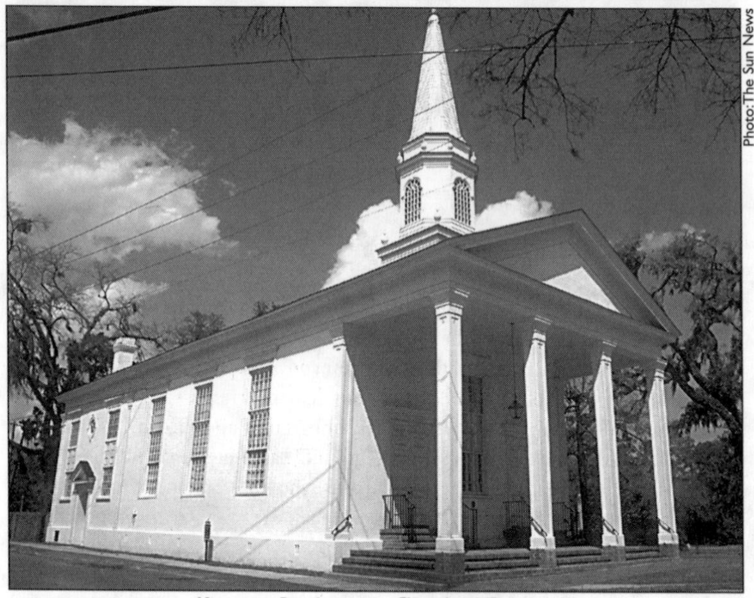
Photo: The Sun News

Kingston Presbyterian Church in Conway.

the evening services, they hold day camps during the week from 9:30 to 11:30 AM. Activities include craft classes, games, Bible stories, singing, drama and puppet shows. Groups taking part in this ministry must be approved by Mr. Wright and must send a leader to a training session in the spring. Wright and his wife also coordinate **Grand Strand Ministry**, which recruits college students to minister to lifeguards.

Area churches, dynamic and growing, are often at the center of the residents' social lives. Not only are many of the area's private schools church-sponsored, many of its best day-care programs are too. Frequently, churches organize activities for youth of all ages, for singles and for senior citizens. Some offer concert series and plays.

All of the Horry and Georgetown municipalities have large downtown sanctuaries. Because the Grand Strand was still a frontier less than a century ago, many, if not most, of its churches sport large, modern facilities. But, there's history to be found too. In Georgetown, particularly, many of the beautiful churches boast rich histories. And, in Conway, the Kingston Presbyterian Church, listed on the National Register of Historic Places, is literally steeped in history.

One of the busiest days in the religious life of the Grand Strand is Easter Sunday. Extremely popular sunrise services are held up and down area beaches. Some draw thousands of sleepy-eyed participants! Three of the most popular are the Grand Strand Ministerial Association's at the Myrtle Beach Pavilion, Ocean Lakes Campground's on the beach in front of the campground and the North Strand's service on the horseshoe at the end of Main Street in Ocean Drive. The sunrise services are held at different times each year depending on the time the sun rises. Check the newspaper if you want to go. They are usually well advertised, but if you can't find the ads, check the time for sunrise and head to the beach.

There are simply too many churches to mention them all; so please check your phone book to find listings and worship times. The Myrtle Beach Area Chamber of Commerce also prints a free listing of area churches and synagogues.

Here's a smattering of additional information about several of the area's churches.

Prince George Winyah Episcopal Church

Highmarket St.
Georgetown *546-4358*

If history is important to you and yours, don't miss Prince George Winyah.

The Parish of Prince George, formed in 1721, was named for the man who eventually became George II of England. The first sanctuary was situated in a bend on Black River, roughly 12 miles north of the current Georgetown location. Due to the area's growth, the parish divided in 1734. Since the original church fell within the boundaries of the newly established Prince Frederick's Parish, commissioners were appointed to build a new sanctuary for the Parish of Prince George. The first rector, sent by the English Society for the Propagation of the Gospel in Foreign Parts, held an initial service in Prince George on August 16, 1747.

The church building was ravaged by enemy troops in both the Revolutionary War and the War Between the States. In 1809, following the Revolution, the existing gallery and chancel were added. The steeple that overlooks the shady streets of Georgetown was added in 1824.

The box pews still used today were a customary feature in colonial churches. As heating systems were nonexistent, pew owners usually brought charcoal burners to their own boxes in winter. The design of the box pews helped to retain some of the heat lost to the beautiful building's high ceilings.

The stained-glass window that graces the back of the altar is English stained glass and was originally in St. Mary's Chapel at Hagley Plantation on the Waccamaw River. St. Mary's was a lovely little sanctuary built by Plowden C.J. Weston for his slaves. (Colonial churches did not have stained glass-windows.) The windows on either side of the church were installed early in this century. There are still four of the original clear windows. Prince George is one of South Carolina's few original colonial church buildings still in use.

The Plantation Tour, an annual fundraiser sponsored by Prince George Winyah, has become one of the area's most popular events. For two days each spring, visitors can tour area plantation grounds, as well as the interiors of a few select homes. The tour begins at Prince George Winyah and includes a bag lunch. For dates and other details, contact the Georgetown Chamber of Commerce at 546-8436.

All Saints Episcopal Church

River Rd. at Chapel Creek
Pawleys Island *237-4223*

All Saints was established by an act of the Colonial Assembly of South Carolina on May 23, 1767, primarily because it was very difficult for worshippers to get from the Waccamaw Neck area all the way to Georgetown for services at Prince George Winyah. The first chapel was built on land donated by George Pawley

The Day Religion Came to the Strand . . .

Local historian C.B. Berry says one of North Myrtle Beach's first churches was formed when George Whitefield, a fiery disciple of John and Charles Wesley, hit the area on a New Year's Day in 1740. He stayed in a home near the community of Nixon's Crossroads, about 5 miles from the North Carolina line.

Accounts of his visit indicate that Whitefield was horrified when he witnessed Horryites getting ready to celebrate the New Year with country dances. He preached passionately to the people and thought he had convinced them to abandon this sinful behavior. Later, when Whitefield went to bed in his upstairs room, he heard merry music and what sounded like much dancing coming from below. Berry speculates that this was the beginning of the Cedar Creek Methodist Church. That church was torn down in 1930, but a cemetery remains on the site. The present day Little River United Methodist Church on U.S. 17 apparently has replaced it.

II. In 1992, the church celebrated its 225th anniversary.

After the War Between the States, All Saints came close to perishing due to a lack of funds. The church's only income came from the rental of a house built in 1854 for the rector's summer home. By 1876, the Rev. William Habersham Barnwell was hired at a salary of $700 a year, and All Saints sped toward recovery. It is an understatement to say that All Saints is a lovely church. Overhung with enormous oaks, the historic setting is peaceful and genuinely captivating. The cemetery offers a fascinating history lesson in itself. Today, All Saints flourishes. Two services are held on Sunday mornings. The church also operates a preschool program that is held in high regard by local moms and dads.

Pawleys Island Baptist Church

U.S. 17 S.
Pawleys Island *237-4449*

With approximately 260 members, Pawleys Island Baptist is considered a bit "nontraditional" for a Baptist church — there are no weekly altar calls. Recognizing that most busy families value time together at home, there is no Sunday evening worship service. The church has a strong music program. The extraordinarily talented piano player performs at the Carolina Opry. Music Director John Czerwinski is well known along the Grand Strand for his superb vocal ability. Hearts and Hands, a ministry organized and supported by the church, reaches out to the surrounding community by meeting the special needs of the elderly and disadvantaged. The church has lots of children, an active youth program and seniors group and an exceptionally friendly atmosphere. It is accessible to the handicapped.

Garden City Chapel and Retreat

50 N. Dogwood
Garden City *651-2223*

The Garden City Chapel only looks

small and cozy; inside there are comfortable seats for about 1,100 people. Services run from May 1 through Labor Day. It is not your typical church in that it has no members and is interdenominational. The retreat is open year round to youth groups seeking solitude, coastal beauty and wholesome fun. Annually, as many as 12,000 youngsters from more than 20 states spend time at the retreat. There are enough rooms to accommodate 600 kids, divided into 11 groups, at any one time. Each dorm has a kitchen, chapel and dining room. Youngsters plan their own programs but join other guests for Sunday morning worship services and Tuesday evening socials. There is also a Junior Olympic-size swimming pool, basketball and volleyball courts and a canteen. College students are employed each summer to work in the canteen and lead Bible studies. Every year, the retreat's board of directors reserves time for disadvantaged youngsters who could not otherwise afford a beach vacation.

Rev. David Welch also organizes a popular senior citizen ministry that involves cross country pleasure trips on chartered buses.

Photo: Cecelia Knoyn, The Sun News

A worker puts the finishing touches on a window at St. Paul's Waccamaw United Methodist Church in Litchfield Beach.

Living Faith Church

4513 U.S. 17 Bypass S.
Myrtle Beach *293-1000*

Based on its exterior appearance, Living Faith Church is one of the Grand Strand's most unusual sanctuaries; it's painted bright purple and decorated with geometric designs. Inside, things are also a bit different from mainstream, but extremely popular. This spirit-filled, charismatic church features its own stage and has a live band every Sunday.

Although it is a fairly new church, it already has 450 members and adds about 10 new members each month. The church has a Sunday morning celebration, Thursday evening Bible teaching and intercessory prayer. Other activities include home Bible studies, men's fellowship and activities for youngsters 8 to 18. A Lightkeepers group holds get-togethers for people older than 50. Soulwinning teams visit with potential congregants one Saturday each month and invite them to church.

Mt. Olive A.M.E. Church

1108 Carver St.
Myrtle Beach *448-5541*

Mt. Olive Church has about 300 members and holds Sunday School at 9:30 AM and worship at 11 AM each Sunday. The church has a day-care program with about 15 children and has an active youth department. One unusual offering by this church is a tutorial program. Any high school student who needs help in his or her studies can go to the church and find encouragement and instruction. Mt. Olive also has an active senior citizens program.

Grand Strand Christian Church

1226 Burcale Rd.
Myrtle Beach *236-1121*
1298 S.C. 9 W.
North Myrtle Beach *361-0678*

Grand Strand Christian Church in Myrtle Beach is part of a worldwide brotherhood of local congregations known as Christian Churches or Churches of Christ. In a nutshell, they seek to exalt Christ and His Word above all human creeds. Additionally, they believe New Testament Christianity is neither sectarian nor denominational. With 600 members and two worship services on Sunday morning, at 8:30 AM and 11 AM, this is indisputably a fast-growing church. About themselves, they like to say, "Not too wild. Not too mild. Just right." If you're on the North Strand, try the North Myrtle Beach "branch." Both locations hold Bible study classes on Thursday nights. Call for more information.

First United Methodist Church

901 N. Kings Hwy.
Myrtle Beach *448-7164*

First United Methodist Church has about 1,850 members and may be Myrtle Beach's oldest continuously meeting church — at the same location anyway. The church has a day-care program and preschool for 3-year-olds and 4-year-olds.

First Presbyterian Church

1300 N. Kings Hwy.
Myrtle Beach *448-4496*

First Presbyterian Church is growing at a phenomenal pace. In the past few years, $2.5 million went to the construction of a new sanctuary and fellowship hall, complete with basketball court and stage. The church has services each Sunday and works to make sure the building stays busy the rest of the week. The church also sponsors a day-care center for about 100 children. The program is so well thought of, its waiting list hovers at about 50.

A youth director takes great pains to keep the community's kids busy playing volleyball and basketball. Two full-time singles directors organize activities for singles younger than 40. Music Director Brown Bradley was renowned in professional circles before making his home in Myrtle Beach, so the music program is considered top-of-the-line. There are even two bell choirs! A group called the FPC players puts on plays and hosts four or five annual concerts.

Trinity Episcopal Church

3000 N. Kings Hwy.
Myrtle Beach *448-8426*

Trinity Episcopal is yet another fast-growing church. It has about 300 families. The church is particularly proud of a puppet ministry, called God's Gang, which meets on Sunday evenings at 6 PM.

In addition to communion and unction services, the church holds a mass of prayer and praise with guitarists providing the music. The church has a youth rector and offers an active young people's program.

Ocean Drive Presbyterian Church

410 Sixth Ave. S.
North Myrtle Beach *249-2312*

Ocean Drive Presbyterian Church was organized in the 1940s. Growth was minimal until the late 1980s when things started to take off. The church now has

Meher Center Flourishes

Meher Baba (1894-1969) was a great spiritual master born in Poona, India, to Persian parents. He is considered by many people throughout the world to be the Avatar, one who awakens humanity to the love of God. The universal work of Meher Baba was not to prescribe a new creed, rather to renew the truth of love for God and fellow human beings that is at the core of all the great world religions. "I have come," he said, "not to teach but to awaken."

Founded in the 1940s at Meher Baba's request, Meher Center is a retreat for "rest, meditation, and the renewal of the spiritual life" — a place for all who are genuinely interested in learning more about Meher Baba's universal message of love and truth. Each year, thousands of day visitors and overnight guests come to experience the center. The peace and quietude they find have made Meher Center "a place of pilgrimage." Retreat guests are given many opportunities for silence, mediatation and prayer. Miles of trails are maintained for meditation and nature walks by individuals and groups. A library and reading room provide writings from all the world's great faiths and a quiet environment for reading and study. Spiritual renewal also comes from interaction with others through discussion, singing, talks and other activities.

Today, more than 40 years after it was founded, the center, located at 10200 N. Kings Highway, remains an island of stillness surrounded by a sea of activity. As commercial development expands nearby, every acre of the center's land becomes more crucial, providing a buffer that protects the sanctity and silence of its atmosphere. Since the spiritual purposes of the center are also served by preserving and protecting the natural wonders of God's creation, the center has been designated a South Carolina Wildlife Sanctuary. Meher Center provides protection for more than 100 species of birds, and river otters, black bear, bobcats and mink are among the 44 species of mammals that have been sighted. More than 200 plant species have been collected and documented as well.

The spiritual renewal found at Meher Center does not end at its gate. For years, many members of Meher Center, inspired by Meher Baba's life of love and service, have served others in South Carolina and in communities throughout the United States. For Meher Baba, love of God is inseparably linked to selfless service. To love God, he said, one must "love others, make others happy, serve others even at discomfort to yourself."

For more information, please call Barbara Plews at 272-8793.

700 members and receives about 100 new members each year. There are two services each Sunday. A large portion of the church's members are older, but church officials are quick to point out that the church is getting younger all the time. Many families with young children have joined in the past few years, and the church has responded by offering an active program for high school students and single adults.

Photo: Bill Scroggins, The Sun News

The Sanctuary of All Saints Episcopal Church in Pawleys Island.

The Travelers Chapel

U.S. 501
Conway *No phone listing*

Travelers who need a few minutes of rest, meditation or prayer are encouraged to make a stop at the tiny Travelers Chapel, about 3 miles east of Conway. The charming little building is 16 feet by 10 feet and can comfortably accommodate a small group of about 12. The idea for this well-used and much-loved chapel came from Dr. Gaylord Kelley, a Conway chiropractor, who fell in love with a similar chapel in Washington State. Dr. Kelley drummed up support for the building and made it a community project. Local community members contributed the site, materials, pews, carpeting, lighting, paint, heating and air-conditioning, labor and landscaping. It was built by the Rev. Emory Young, his son, Bruce, and other volunteers. A guest register in the chapel shows that it has been used by people from all across the country. Very small weddings have even been performed in the charming little chapel.

Kingston Presbyterian Church

800 Third Ave.
Conway *248-4200*

Kingston Presbyterian Church is on the National Register of Historic Places and is designated as an American Presbyterian and Reformed Historical Site. No one knows exactly when Presbyterians started meeting in Conway, but local historians believe it was before 1754. The church was assigned its first preacher in 1756, the Rev. William Donaldson.

One of the first churches on the site overlooking Kingston Lake was destroyed in a storm, probably a hurricane, in 1798 and wasn't rebuilt until the 1830s. In fact, one local historian, Catherine Lewis, says Conway went about 40 years without any churches at all. Conwayites didn't neglect their worship during those years. They simply met in private homes and at a campground outside the town. In 1858, the present building was erected. Since then, it has been extensively renovated.

The Kingston Presbyterian Churchyard is undoubtedly one of the most serene and captivating spots in the Grand Strand area. The lake, the huge oaks, dogwoods, camellias and azaleas add to the sense of history and beauty. A community burial ground that dates to the 1700s makes for a fascinating afternoon excursion.

First United Methodist Church

1001 Fifth Ave.
Conway *248-4251*

First United Methodist Church, organized in 1828, is listed on the National Register of Historic Buildings and on the Register of United Methodist Historic Sites. The original church, now home to the Hut Bible Class, was built in 1844 and was replaced by a Gothic building in 1898. The mission-style church, now a fellowship hall, was built in 1910. The present Georgian-style sanctuary was built in 1961. Of special interest is the cemetery with graves dating back to the 1830s.

Inside
Real Estate

Considered one of the top vacation destinations along the East Coast, Myrtle Beach and the Grand Strand attract an estimated 10 million visitors annually. Many of those visitors pack up and depart with notions of one day making the South Carolina coastline home. Little wonder. Life on the Grand Strand is living at its absolute sweetest.

Since the '70s, population growth has been phenomenal. *American Demographics* magazine placed Horry County fifth among the top 20 fastest growing retirement communities. And *Southern Living* listed Myrtle Beach and Pawleys Island among the "Top 10 Family Beaches." Obviously, a lot of people already know what you're about to learn: Our Strand is much more than a great place to visit; it's a great place to live. Countless residential options, glorious beaches, an ever-expanding cultural foundation, restaurants, history, shopping, medical facilities, educational opportunities . . . there are many reasons — smart reasons — you'll never want to leave once you've settled in.

The Myrtle Beach area appeals to active retirees, singles and brand new families. Value packed residential opportunities abound: friendly communities nestled around stunning golf courses; country clubs with stately clubhouses, sprawling residences and plentiful amenities; smaller neighborhoods with charming patio homes, bridge clubs, pool parties and well-tended borders; crisply designed condominium villages that are blissfully low maintenance and convenient; retirement or family communities, or a combination of both. From the private and unpretentious to the stately and memorable. Bustling. Reserved. On course. Off course. Panoramic views or quiet seclusion. Affordable. Extravagant. Whatever you're looking for . . . whatever you need, you can find it here.

Every study shows that Myrtle Beach and the surrounding area are growing at a phenomenal pace. Music theaters, a new trend in entertainment, abound, as do golf courses — there are currently more than 85 championship courses; by the year 2000, that number is expected to exceed 100. New shopping facilities and restaurants are taking shape and climbing skyward every day. Grand Strand developers considered 1994 their busiest year since the building boom of the '80s. More than $1 billion worth of construction is either under way or about to be started. Given this unprecedented growth, we cannot see how the value of real estate investments in this area can do anything but climb . . . and climb some more.

Enthusiastic as we are about the area's potential, we feel obligated to point out that while tourism is increasing, entertainment and attractions are growing, the population is on the rise and the wide, blue attractive Atlantic is going nowhere,

the number of available properties increases every year, too. So, take care to analyze your real estate purchases carefully — whether for investment or permanent occupancy. Particularly on the south end of the Strand, you should consider the long term potential of the property. Is high tide already lapping at the back deck? Is insurance a manageable expense? Is an oceanfront view worth it, or should you consider a purchase off the ocean . . . on a lake, the Waccamaw River or a golf course? Do zoning ordinances protect the long-term integrity of your investment? And, don't forget to inquire about homeowner association fees. They are not included in your mortgage and can be assessed monthly or annually. And they can increase rather considerably — and unexpectedly.

Myrtle Beach boasts many communities that are reputable and well-established. Historically, these areas tended to be concentrated on the North Strand. That is changing, albeit slowly. Enduring communities like The Dunes, Pine Lakes and anything on Ocean Boulevard from 30th Avenue North to 80th Avenue North, will certainly prove a strong purchase. Here, zoning laws are already in place to protect the value of your purchase. As a result, such properties come with a hefty price tag. But there are plenty of newer developments well worth your consideration all over the Strand. Remember, these days "a place at the beach" doesn't necessarily mean "on the beach."

From south to north, here are a few of our favorite communities, followed by a sampling of the (many dozens of) real estate agencies with strong reputations.

DeBordieu

U.S. 17, 1801 Luvan Way
Georgetown 546-4176

DeBordieu is a private oceanfront residential community of exceptional quality, encompassing 2,700 acres of age-old oaks and pines, tidal marshes and creeks with access to the Atlantic Ocean. This may be the most prestigious address on the length of the Grand Strand. Justifiably so, they bill themselves as purveyors of "splendid isolation."

This community offers a variety of homesites and villas with ocean, forest, marsh and fairway views, and all are served by central water and sewer systems and underground utilities. All streets are — or soon will be — paved.

DeBordieu Club's golf course has been nationally acclaimed as one of Pete Dye's best. The Club's colonial-style clubhouse is spectacular. The Beach Club, with its lovely pool overlooking the ocean, offers superb dining. The Tennis Center has eight composition courts and an excellent pro shop.

Access to DeBordieu is controlled by a security entrance that is staffed 24 hours a day. Roving patrols are on duty during selected hours.

Living here is a pricey proposition, but if money is not an object and you don't mind the half-hour drive to Myrtle Beach, there's no prettier place or better investment. Homesites range upward from $100,000.

Heritage Plantation

U.S. 17
P.O. Box 2010 237-9824
Pawleys Island 29585 (800) 448-2010

Blessed with a unique combination of 300-year-old oaks, giant magnolias, scenic rice fields and Waccamaw River vistas, Heritage Plantation is one of South Carolina's most beautiful properties. First-time visitors often fall in love with its special magnetism; some won't even consider a purchase anywhere else.

Amenities are excellent. There's a clubhouse with a 75-foot heated pool and Jacuzzi, lighted tennis courts, a fitness center, card room and a social area for entertaining. Property owners enjoy abundant golfing opportunities, including special privileges on six of the Grand Strand's top rated courses: Oyster Bay, Marsh Harbour, all three Legends courses and Heritage Club itself, where members get reserved tee times. The beautiful beaches of Pawleys Island are only 3 miles away.

The Heritage offers an outstanding selection of real estate. Homesites range from $40,000 to $170,000. Homes start around $160,000.

Pawleys Plantation

U.S. 17
P.O. Box 2070 237-8497
Pawleys Island 29585 (800) 367-9959

Pawleys Plantation is a world-class golf and country club built on 582 acres of natural wetlands, salt marshes, lakes and rolling green fairways. Bordered on the south by a 645-acre nature preserve, this private community offers homesites and golf villas for purchase, and accommodations and golf packages for those who want to vacation in the country club atmosphere.

The Pawleys Plantation golf course is an 18-hole championship layout designed by Jack Nicklaus. Among the most unforgettable features are a tremendous double green, a dramatic split fairway and breathtaking lake and marsh views. An antebellum-style clubhouse ranks with the finest club facilities in the Southeast.

In addition to golf, the lifestyle at Pawleys Plantation includes a clubhouse swimming pool and private tennis courts.

Neighborhoods of villas throughout the plantation offer comfortable year-round living or a perfect getaway for the second home buyer. Lots feature a variety of views. Homesites start at about $20,000, and villas start at $100,000.

Litchfield By The Sea

U.S. 17
P.O. Box 97 237-4000
Pawleys Island 29585 (800) 476-2861

For over 37 years, The Litchfield Company has been developing one of the finest collections of private seaside communities on the East Coast. Litchfield By The Sea has become synonymous with beautiful beaches and marshlands, lush

Lowcountry golf courses and the gracious hospitality of the Waccamaw Neck.

Amenities includes pools, spas, tennis, volleyball, horseshoes, fishing, picnic areas and three of the finest golf clubs in the Lowcountry.

Throughout this spacious resort, you can choose from homes, single-family homesites, and a variety of quality townhomes or villas overlooking miles of clean, white beaches, marshland, lakes or golf course fairways.

Willbrook Plantation

U.S. 17 — *237-4000*
Litchfield Beach — *(800) 476-2861*
P.O. Box 97
Pawleys Island 29585

The natural profile of Willbrook Plantation has changed little since it operated as three colonial rice plantations. Deer and fowl remain abundant, as do towering cypress trees, Carolina pines and age-old oaks.

Considered one of the finest achievements in Lowcountry courses, the Willbrook Plantation Golf Club is just one part of a setting that accentuates the exclusivity of the homes and homesites. Residents can also take advantage of the community's classic amenities, including beach access privileges. A proposed marina nearby and the planned Residents' Club round out future attractions.

Half-acre lots, priced from $49,900, are available for sale throughout the Plantation. Single family homes are available in a community called Allston Point.

Centex Builders, one of the nation's largest and most sought-after contractors, recently announced plans for a new community within Willbrook. Called "The Tradition," this community will be built around a new 18-hole championship golf course. Several different single-family floor plans will be offered starting at $189,000. (Homesites are included.) In addition to swimming, tennis and the extensive clubhouse, Tradition residents can also take advantage of the amenities enjoyed in Litchfield By The Sea. Private beach access, a beach club, tennis and bike trails set the stage for a lifestyle that's tough to beat. Prices begin at $99,000.

Wachesaw Plantation

U.S. 17 — *651-0115*
Murrells Inlet 29576 — *(800) 451-0115*

Wachesaw Plantation is one of our favorite residential communities. Conve-

A Word About Homebuilders

Without a doubt, there's nothing quite so wonderful as moving into a brand new home. Crisply painted walls, unsullied carpets and pristine baseboard coupled with the pride of ownership . . . it's clearly an unparalleled experience. Unfortunately, the excitement can be compromised early in the process if you're intimidated by the idea of building from scratch. Choosing a reputable, friendly and fully licensed home builder can help to relieve your anxieties.

If you're considering building, you should know about the local Horry-Georgetown Home Builders Association (HGHBA). This dynamic group, comprised of builders and associated firms like architects, suppliers and marketing professionals, represents the interests of the building industry and the general public in Horry and Georgetown counties. The HGHBA has grown to more than 350 members since its inception in 1969. Its goals include, but are not limited to, establishing and maintaining high standards of professional conduct among members, providing forums for sharing information on business concerns and enhancing professional development, and providing community services. If you have questions about an area builder, call HGHBA at 347-7311.

One exceptionally friendly local contractor you might want to consider is Forbes Homes. Boasting a family tradition of more than 115 years in the residential construction industry, Paul Forbes and his associates can help you decide on a home design that will complement your lifestyle without breaking your budget. Forbes has the in-house expertise and understanding to build affordable residences that showcase old fashioned quality and first-rate craftsmanship. Utilizing the latest in computer-aided design (CAD) technology, Forbes Homes makes the sometimes difficult process of designing a home easier and far more enjoyable. Sitting comfortably in front of a large color monitor, you can watch while Forbes' professionals bring your dreams, ideas and requirements to life. Give them a call today at 237-3654.

nient to everything yet worlds away in atmosphere, we think this is the kind of place where everyone would choose to own property — if they could. This community was carved from a historically rich land, once a flourishing rice plantation. Archaeological surveys have been orchestrated by the developers so as to protect this legacy.

There's a beautiful clubhouse, eight tennis courts, a swimming pool and a Tom Fazio-designed private golf course.

Even when placed beside tough competition, Wachesaw stands on its own as a truly premier community. There's a variety of real estate options from lots and townhomes to mammoth-sized residences. Choose a home on the course or on the Waccamaw River. Prices start from $50,000. Wachesaw Plantation East, a new development phase, is a private community offering a health club and a semi-private golf course.

Indigo Creek

U.S. 17 Bypass S.
9457 Pinckney Ln. — *650-9475*
Murrells Inlet — *(800) 654-9202*

The moment you drive into Indigo Creek, you'll know you're in a truly special place. This parcel of land, thick with

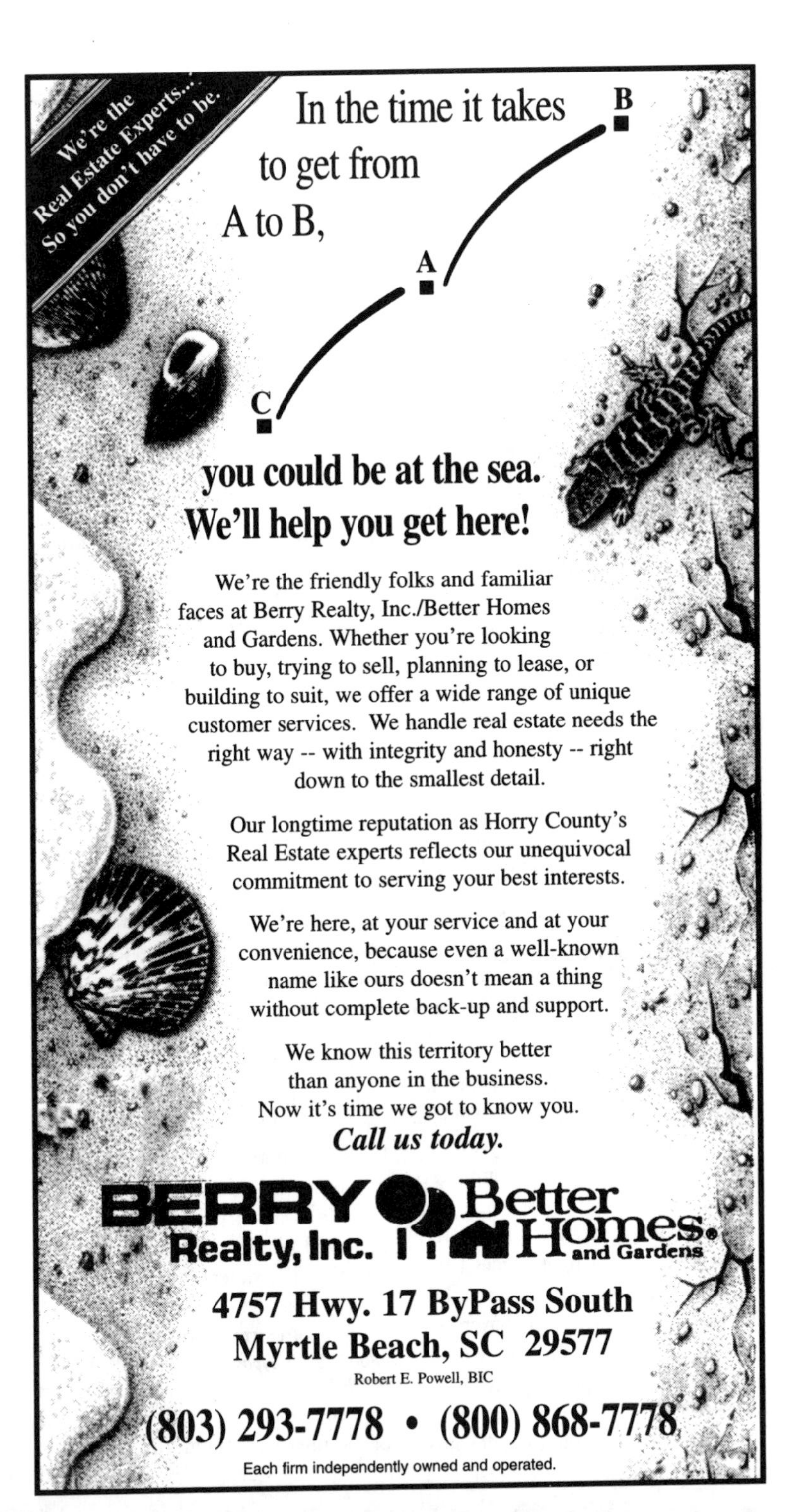
We're the
Real Estate Experts...
So you don't have to be.
In the time it takes
to get from
A to B,
B
A
C
you could be at the sea.
We'll help you get here!
We're the friendly folks and familiar
faces at Berry Realty, Inc./Better Homes
and Gardens. Whether you're looking
to buy, trying to sell, planning to lease, or
building to suit, we offer a wide range of unique
customer services. We handle real estate needs the
right way -- with integrity and honesty -- right
down to the smallest detail.
Our longtime reputation as Horry County's
Real Estate experts reflects our unequivocal
commitment to serving your best interests.
We're here, at your service and at your
convenience, because even a well-known
name like ours doesn't mean a thing
without complete back-up and support.
We know this territory better
than anyone in the business.
Now it's time we got to know you.
Call us today.
BERRY
Realty, Inc.
Better
Homes®
and Gardens
4757 Hwy. 17 ByPass South
Myrtle Beach, SC 29577
Robert E. Powell, BIC
(803) 293-7778 • (800) 868-7778
Each firm independently owned and operated.

forest and sprinkled with lakes, is rich in natural beauty. The central location, a breeze from Myrtle Beach on the U.S. 17 Bypass, is less than five minutes from restaurants, entertainment, shopping, medical facilities and beaches. Indigo Creek boasts the features of a community committed to preserving long-term value: privacy, attractive landscaping, well-lit streets with curbs and gutters, underground utilities and an architectural review board. Even when the local real estate market was sluggish, Indigo Creek was setting records.

An 18-hole championship, Willard Byrd-layout offers an indisputably challenging game of golf. There's a private pool complex, too.

Astonishing product diversity offers something for every lifestyle. There are no fewer than seven award-winning floor plans to choose from. Boasting "Best Single Family Design," "Best Interior" and "Best Bath" awards, these designs are truly a cut above the norm. Plus, there are a couple of patio home communities to consider. Lots are priced from $30,000, and homes begin at about $100,000.

Prestwick Country Club

S.C. 544 — *293-6000*
Surfside Beach — *(800) 521-8522*
P.O. Box 2800
Myrtle Beach 29578

If location is everything, Prestwick may be the perfect place to call home. Since opening more than five years ago, this beautiful country club community has become one of the most sought after addresses on the Strand. (The Gatlin Brothers recently bought homes here!) Prestwick is perfect for retirees seeking an active lifestyle, investment buyers pursuing second homes, relocating families, and vacation-home purchasers.

Situated around a private, $6 million Pete and P.B. Dye-designed golf course, there's also one of the finest tennis complexes (thirteen clay courts and a stadium court) around. There's a health club facility with a sauna, whirlpool, exercise areas, and indoor and outdoor pools. Security is provided 24 hours a day.

Prestwick features condominiums and homes, with direct fairway or lake views, ranging from $100,000 to $400,000. Custom-built residences are also available. Homesites run from approximately $40,000 to $96,000. Patio homes are priced from $130,000 to more than $180,000.

Tidewater Golf Club & Plantation

4901 Little River Neck Rd. — *249-1403*
N. Myrtle Beach — *(800) 843-3234*

Like more than a few residential communities in this area, Tidewater is probably best known for its highly rated golf course. But what home buyers are discovering is that this premier golf community offers some of the area's finest choices in lifestyle, architecture and homesite values. Densely wooded homesites start around $41,000, and spacious villas sport prices that begin under $100,000. Without visiting Tidewater, you cannot appreciate the value-packed opportunity those prices represent. On-course, off-course, custom homes or cottages, everything this exclusive neighborhood offers is extraordinarily beautiful and of the highest quality. The sales center is open Monday through Saturday from 9 AM until 5 PM. On Sunday, drop in between 10 AM and 5 PM. Take U.S. 17 N. to the Cherry Grove Exit and turn right on Little River Neck Road. Ignore the drive; Tidewater is worth it.

Plantation Point

3800 U.S. 17 Bypass
Myrtle Beach — *Inquire through local Realtors*

Plantation Point is well known as one of the finer communities in the Myrtle

Beach area. Its location on the Bypass in Myrtle Beach is as close to perfect as you could hope for: It sits right in the heart of everything. Yet, it was developed in such a way that it retains a valuable sense of privacy and separation from the hustle and bustle. The Myrtlewood Golf Club wraps around the development. Some lots and homes are located on the Intracoastal Waterway.

There are many different residential options to choose from at Plantation Point, and what you choose determines what amenities you may access. There are lots, estate homes, single-family homes and townhome communities in a wide range of prices.

THE PARK

48th Ave. N. *277-7704*
Myrtle Beach *(800) 277-7704*

The Park has been tremendously successful. It's hard to believe this quiet residential community is smack-dab in the heart of Myrtle Beach. There are no amenities to speak of, but who cares when you live in a beautiful home so close to everything?

The Park at 48th offers the latest designs in single-family courtyard homes. All homes are brick. You can choose from two-, three- and four-bedroom plans. Courtyards are ample, and every home features a two-car garage. Prices start in the upper $130s.

KINGSTON PLANTATION

9770 Kings Rd. *449-6400*
Myrtle Beach *(800) 382-3332*

Kingston is in a class by itself. Its 145 heavily-forested acres of parklike settings and freshwater lakes border a half-mile of secluded beach. Kingston prides itself on its location and unspoiled setting. Expect to see wildlife including black swans, egrets, mallard ducks and sea turtles.

The amenities are unmatched anywhere in the area. A $4.5 million-health club crowns the package. The health club alone features an indoor pool, three squash and racquetball courts, an aerobics studio, weight-training and cardiovascular equipment, sauna, whirlpool and locker room facilities. There's even a professional masseuse on staff. Outdoors, you'll find a junior Olympic pool and exceptional tennis facilities. In addition, Kingston's different communities typically feature unique amenities.

From luxury oceanfront residences to clusters of lakeside villas and townhomes, Kingston has a home to suit every taste. Prices vary dramatically — from roughly $115,000 and up and up.

DUNES COUNTRY CLUB

9000 N. Ocean Blvd.
Myrtle Beach *Inquire through local Realtors*

If appearances are important to you, this is the place to choose; it's the most prestigious address on the Strand. The homes, sold through various Realtors, are all beautiful — though many are older than you might expect. Appropriately, the upscale Dunes Golf Club anchors this community. Many homes feature golf vistas; a precious few feature ocean views.

Buying a home here doesn't qualify you to enjoy the amenities; memberships are additional and the prices are steep.

If you're wondering about prices, you probably shouldn't consider a home in the Dunes.

Realtors

As you drive along the Strand, it will probably seem that there's a real estate office on every corner. Despite the plethora of choices, however, you should give much time and consideration to choosing your agent. More often than with many other occupations, people enter the real estate field from widely disparate backgrounds. Consequently, the first salesperson you stumble across may or may not be a good fit for you. Scan first, then narrow down. Interview different people and choose someone with whom you're truly comfortable. After all, this is probably one of the biggest investments you'll ever make, and you deserve someone you can speak with honestly, confide in frequently and respect. If you're coming from another area, speak with a real estate agent you know and trust back home. Often, they have contacts in the industry that will help you zero in on the perfect person.

When looking for the perfect property, *The Sun News* should be a primary resource. It is estimated that at least one third of realty transactions begin with a newspaper ad. Realtors use it religiously — though not always to advertise their best buys. (Can't tip off the competition!) They usually advertise a broad and respectable selection of their listings, hoping to attract prospective buyers for the hidden bargains too.

Listed below are some area Realtors who can help with the purchase of a new residence or an investment property. Please consider that the area has dozens of professional Realtors — many of which will not be detailed here. This list is in no way meant to reflect upon the qualifications of the real estate professionals not included. If you'd like information about other companies in the area, call the Grand Strand Board of Realtors at 272-6113, the Greater Horry County Association of Realtors at 626-3638 or the Georgetown Board of Realtors at 237-4000.

North Strand

Callier Realty

3810 S.C. 9 E. at Baytree *249-8220*
(800) 882-8674

Callier Realty has been in business for eight years and has established itself as one of the top rental companies in the area. Three agents also handle real estate sales — primarily residential and condominiums. The personalized service is excellent.

Century 21 Coastal Carolina Properties, Inc.

1906 U.S. 17 S. *272-9947*
(800) 328-9008

Coastal Carolina Properties was founded in August of 1973 as a general brokerage and development agency. In

1978, a decision was made to concentrate on general brokerage, and Coastal Carolina Properties joined the renowned Century 21 system. They have grown to employ approximately 20 agents and staff a property management division. In 1994, the company earned Century 21's prestigious Quality Service Award and was one of the Top 21 producing companies in the Carolinas. Their slogan is "Dedicated to Serving You," and they have a reputation for doing exactly that.

Century 21 Thomas Realty, Inc.

625 Sea Mountain Hwy. *249-2100*
(800) 249-2100

This Century 21 agency recently earned the 1994 Centurion award, signaling membership in the top percentage of the nearly 6,500 Century 21 offices worldwide. This award is given to those offices that reap in excess of $1 million in gross closed commission during the calendar year. Century 21 Thomas Realty is currently home to 15 sales associates, serving the community in residential and commercial sales, rentals and property services.

ERA Callihan Teal Skelley & Associates

1240 U.S. 17 S. *449-8900*
(800) 833-6330

This three-partner firm has been in business for approximately five years and has around 45 agents — several of which have won national awards for volume. In 1994, this agency recorded more transactions than any ERA agency in the nation. Serving North Carolina, as well as the Myrtle Beach area, ERA Callihan Teal Skelley & Associates handles everything from general real estate to planned residential communities. Well-reputed in all areas of the industry, they are probably best known for their experience with planned residential developments. Their sister company is Pinehurst Builders which provides a "one-stop-shop" advantage to real estate shoppers seeking custom work. A strong company.

RE/MAX Southern Shores

100 U.S. 17 S. *249-5555*
(800) 729-0064

With offices throughout North America, RE/MAX Realtors are recognized as full-time professionals. RE/MAX serves residential, commercial and investment needs and has just completed six successive years of record sales — earning them the No. 1 Market Share in residential sales for the Little River and North Grand Strand areas. Currently they have 14 agents and are well respected in the community.

Myrtle Beach

Berry Realty Inc. Better Homes & Gardens

4757 U.S. 17 Bypass S. *293-7778*
(800) 868-7778

Berry Realty has served the beach since 1976 and has been affiliated with Better Homes & Gardens since 1981. This is the only Better Homes & Gardens franchise on the Strand. Berry Realty's territory covers from the North Carolina state line to Winyah Bay in Georgetown to the rural town of Aynor. Berry specializes in residential properties — primary, secondary and investment. They also have a property management division that orchestrates annual rentals. Currently, Berry has 12 agents but expects to grow to 20 in 1995. Berry is particularly proud of their in-house training program.

The Prudential Burroughs & Chapin Realty, Inc.

7421 N. Kings Hwy. 449-9444
(800) 277-7704

Anyone who knows anything about the history of Myrtle Beach will recognize the Burroughs and Chapin names. The parent company has been around for more than a century. With 24,000 acres, they're one of the largest landowners in the county. This firm was recently recognized as Prudential's "Top Southeast Agency." Burroughs & Chapin Realty had 38 agents at the time this book was written, but the that number likely has climbed.

Chicora Real Estate

10225 U.S. 17 N. 272-8700

Chicora is a well-respected local firm. In addition to the location listed here, they have three other offices throughout the Strand, as well as sales centers at Myrtle Pointe, Southcreek, South Wood, SweetWater, Covenant Towers, Ashton Glenn and Eastport. They bill themselves "#1 in sales and listings" and have approximately 26 agents. In addition to residential and resort offerings, Chicora represents many commercial and industrial properties.

Century 21 Boling & Associates

7722 N. Kings Hwy. 449-7449
(800) 634-2500

This Century 21 office opened for business in 1986. In five years, Penny I. Boling, broker-in-charge, took the company — at the time, one of the least productive in the region — and made it the No. 1 Century 21 office in the South Carolina region for the fourth year in a row. Boling & Associates controls approximately 200 listings at any given time, including condos, townhomes, residential, commercial, multifamily and land in various price ranges.

This agency thrives on a team concept. The majority of the sales associates have been with the company for more than five years. A property management division coordinates annual rentals. In the words of Ms. Boling, "We're the best we can be to our customers and clients."

Century 21 Broadhurst & Associates, Inc.

3405 N. Kings Hwy. 448-7169
(800) 845-0837

Century 21 Broadhurst & Associates is a full-service real estate company with 27 professionally trained property specialists. In business since 1974, this firm is one of the largest Century 21 offices in the Carolinas. Serving clients in all phases of real estate, they offer one-stop shopping for residential, vacation, commercial and investment properties.

Fitzgerald Realty, Inc.

4615 U.S. 17 Bypass S. 293-7053
(800) 593-7053

Established in 1985, Fitzgerald Realty now has approximately 20 full and part-time agents. This is a full-service real estate firm specializing in residential properties in the Grand Strand area. They are members of numerous professional associations including, among others, the Greater Horry County Association of Realtors, Myrtle Beach Chamber of Commerce and the Surfside Beach Merchants Association. Their affiliation with these organizations enables them to serve their customers knowledgeably and professionally. They have one additional office at 900 Mt. Gilead Drive in Murrells Inlet. They pride themselves on a "no surprises"

Many people relocate to the Grand Strand to enjoy the great fishing the region offers.

sales process — from home selection through the final closing.

Leonard, Call & Associates, Inc.

3501 N. Kings Hwy. 626-7676
(800) 280-7676

For more than 22 years, Leonard, Call & Associates, one of the Southeast's leading real estate firms, has been developing and marketing the Carolinas' most outstanding communities. They have established an extraordinary reputation for a commitment to integrity, performance and professionalism. LCA offers an impressive range of real estate services that include brokerage, consulting, development, marketing, market research and property management. A leader in residential, resort and commercial real estate.

Merrill Lynch

600 27th Ave. N. 946-2000, (800) 937-0848

Merrill Lynch is considered a topnotch firm on Wall Street and an industry leader among peers. Employees are trained to take great pride in principles and client commitment. This office has been in the Myrtle Beach area since 1988 and is the working home to 13 brokers.

South Strand

The Barony Company

Three Center Marsh Ln. 237-4202
Pawleys Island (800) 868-8412

The name Barony is derived from an early 17th century term used by King George to grant land holdings to the colonies in South Carolina. This is a full-service real estate company serving the Waccamaw Neck and historic Georgetown in residential, resort and commercial areas. Their inventory includes the highest quality properties.

Coldwell Banker The Roberts Agency

14792 Ocean Hwy.
Pawleys Island 237-1686

This agency, established in 1989, has a second location at 701-A Front Street in Georgetown. Their annual sales volume exceeds $38 million, and they have approximately 22 full-time agents — many of which are multimillion dollar producers. Their own training facility accommodates 50 students and specializes in continuing education for professionals and new agents. Very active in community organizations, The Roberts Agency is committed to professional excellence and enjoys a strong reputation throughout the region.

Garden City Realty, Inc.

608 Atlantic Ave. 651-0900
Garden City Beach (800) 395-5930

Since 1973 Garden City Realty has been a focal point for South Strand real estate transactions and has earned a reputation for scrupulously ethical and fair dealing. As a full service agency, Garden City Realty can serve all of your real estate needs — buying, selling or renting. The experienced, well-trained staff has access to more than 4500 listings of Myrtle Beach area homes, condos and land parcels. They offer nearly 400 rental properties on the South Strand.

The Litchfield Company

U.S. 17 S. 237-4000
Litchfield Beach (800) 476-2861

For more than 37 years, The Litchfield Company has developed one of the finest collections of private seaside communities on the East Coast. Its name alone brings to mind the beautiful beaches and marshlands, lush Lowcountry golf courses and traditional Southern hospitality. The company has land holdings that include more than 20 percent of the remaining oceanfront land available for development in South Carolina.

The Litchfield Company has developed a unique collection of communities including Litchfield By The Sea, River Club, Willbrook Plantation, Clubhouse Creek and Inlet Point South. It is the largest real estate development firm in Georgetown County.

Pawleys Island Realty Company

N. Causeway 237-4257
Pawleys Island (800) 937-7352

Pawleys Island Realty was created in 1962 by R. Linwood Altman, who was elected to the S.C. House of Representatives in 1978. In 1987, Alan Altman was added as a partner. Through prudent planning, hard work and a commitment to honest, excellent service, Pawleys Island Realty has remained a constant in the area's ever-changing real estate industry. Professional associates can answer your questions about any property in Georgetown County, including all the developments.

Photo: Jody Hazzard, The Sun News

Chapin Park in downtown Myrtle Beach is a popular place for children to play.

Rose Realty

1711 U.S. 17 S. — 650-9274
Surfside Beach — (800) 845-6706

Rose Real Estate came into existence as a vehicle for resolving management problems within the very popular resort and residential community of Oceanside Village. Comprised of modular and manufactured homes, this amenity-packed community recently introduced The Keys on Ocean Boulevard, a new section. Like the rest of Oceanside, this newest phase has met with tremendous success. In addition to sales and rentals within Oceanside Village, Rose Real Estate has its own general brokerage division.

The president of Rose Real Estate, Fran Sugar, is a former director of the Greater Horry County Board of Realtors and has been active in Grand Strand real estate since 1982. You can rest assured that Ms. Sugar and her associates will utilize their experience and go "above and beyond" to ensure your satisfaction.

Photo: Bill Scroggins, The Sun News

Conway residents have gone to great lengths to protect the beautiful oak trees throughout the city.

Inside Services and Utilities

We hope this chapter will steer you in the right direction to services you may need as a visitor or a new resident of the Grand Strand area. If you are searching for medical care, volunteer opportunities, senior citizen centers or any other specific resources, please refer to those particular chapters for information.

Emergency Assistance

As you could well imagine, emergency assistance personnel in a resort area are some of the most overworked people you'll ever know. With hundreds of thousands of people coming to the Grand Strand every balmy weekend, their work load literally increases by a hundred times or more! We urge visitors and residents alike to use sound judgment before contacting any of these folks, since they spend a lot of precious, potentially live-saving time responding to "panic calls" as well as bona fide emergencies.

Note: For any *emergency* situation, call 911 first.

Fire Departments

MYRTLE BEACH

1101 Oak St.
Myrtle Beach 448-3111

NORTH MYRTLE BEACH

1015 2nd Ave. S.
North Myrtle Beach 249-2233

SURFSIDE BEACH

115 U.S. 17 N.
Surfside Beach 238-2811

Police Departments

MYRTLE BEACH

1101 Oak St.
Myrtle Beach 448-3111

NORTH MYRTLE BEACH

1015 2nd Ave. S.
North Myrtle Beach 280-5511

SURFSIDE BEACH

115 U.S. 17 N.
Surfside Beach 238-2621

Rescue Squads

Myrtle Beach 626-7352
Murrells Inlet 651-2900
Surfside Beach 238-1216

Crisis Intervention

CITIZENS AGAINST SPOUSE ABUSE (CASA)

P.O. Box 912
Myrtle Beach 29578 626-7595

This temporary emergency shelter and its telephone crisis lines are open 24-hours a day. The shelter also offers counseling, legal advocacy and children programs.

GM Parts Mr. Goodwrench

CAR PROBLEMS?

We service all
Makes & Models

Factory Trained & Certified Technicians

•

No Appointment
Necessary

•

ON VACATION?

Drop your car off at Atlantic...
We'll deliver you to your
desired destination*.
Golf Course • Beach • Hotel

Wherever!

*within 10 mile radius of dealership

FREE
Oil Change
&
27 Point Inspection
Limit 1 per vehicle. Must present ad.

SMART PLAN
Several different types of financing to suit *your* needs from the dealership with heart!

Bud Ward's

ATLANTIC
Geo CHEVROLET Geo

Located across from Bay Tree Golf Course
on Hwy. 9 in North Myrtle Beach

399-4400

The moonrise over the beach can be just as impressive as the sunrise.

Grand Strand Community Against Rape

P.O. Box 613
Myrtle Beach 29578 *448-7273*

Twenty-four hours a day, seven days a week, this organization responds to rape victims. A crisis hotline is available, and trained volunteers serve as victim-advocates throughout any legal proceedings.

National Child Watch

24-hour service *(800) 222-1464*

A division of the National Child Safety Council, this hotline takes any information concerning missing children, anywhere in the United States.

Poison Control Center

(800) 922-1117

Even hospital emergency room per-

sonnel and doctors call this hotline to get fast, efficient information about any commercial product or poisonous substance. Poison Control Center's database boasts information on 90 percent of all products made and/or sold in the nation plus facts on all plants and drugs. If you suspect a toxic reaction to some substance or exposure to a poison, these operators can give you advice and treatment options fast.

Disaster Services

American Red Cross

4808 U.S. 501
Myrtle Beach *236-1350*

The Red Cross is always there to give emergency assistance to disaster victims of floods, fire, hurricanes, etc. They also provide emergency communications between military personnel and their families, collect blood and offer citizens health and safety instruction and certification.

Public Utilities

Water, Sewer and Sanitation

City of Myrtle Beach Water Department

626-7645

The City of Myrtle Beach Water Department handles all water, sewer and trash pickup from the old Myrtle Beach Air Force Base, north to Briarcliffe Mall. If you need these services for any other area, simply contact the local water and sewer department. To give you an idea of costs, hookup by the City of Myrtle Beach will require a $30 deposit from a homeowner and a $60 deposit from a renter. There is a basic $20.06 charge per month for the use of up to 4,000 gallons of water. Base-line cost will vary if the size of a water meter is larger than the norm, such as a business or duplex. In the City of North Myrtle Beach, a $90 deposit is required for a single family home and you will be charged $25 per month for up to 3,000 gallons of water.

Gas and Electric Service

Santee Cooper Electric Cooperative

1703 Oak St.
Myrtle Beach *448-2411*

For most of the Grand Strand area, Santee Cooper will fulfill your electric needs. For service, the cooperative requires a $100 deposit. However, if you can produce a "letter of credit" from your previous electric company stating that you were a customer in good standing for at least one year, and can provide two pieces of identification, Santee Cooper will waive the deposit.

Horry Electric Cooperative

1708 Oak St.
Conway *248-2211*

Horry Electric services 95 percent of the Socastee area and 100 percent of Longs and the area along S.C. 9. The co-op offers customers energy management programs such as Good Cents — for new and improved homes — and the H_2O Advantage. With H_2O Advantage, a homeowner installs an 80-gallon hot water heater with a control timer that monitors the unit to heat water only during low energy usage times of the day. Participating customers get a $300 rebate on the water heater and a $3 credit on their monthly bills.

South Carolina Electric & Gas Corporation

U.S. 501
Myrtle Beach *236-6413*

If you want or need it, this is the area's only natural gas outlet.

Telephone Service

GTE South

Kings Festival Plaza
Myrtle Beach *(800) 532-2311*

Except for a few outlying areas, GTE is your telephone service provider along the Grand Strand. Basic charges for a touch-tone phone are around $20 plus tax. Hookup fees include a $105 deposit and a $44 connection charge that will be added to your first billing. GTE will wire for additional phone jacks, and initial service as well, for $69.

Horry Telephone Cooperative

3480 U.S. 701 N.
Conway *293-2151*

If you need telephone services in the Socastee or Wampee areas of the county, or live along S.C. highways 707 or 544, Horry Telephone will be your phone company. Basic service is provided for $14.10 a month. New residents will be required to pay a $50 deposit — refunded after two years of timely payment or when service is disconnected — a $10 membership fee and a $64 service initiation fee. If your home is not wired for telephone service, it will cost $15 for wiring and $10 to $12 for each phone jack.

Cable Television

Your local cable hookup gives television viewers an array of entertainment choices such as HBO, Cinemax and the Disney Channel. Rates vary by area and company.

Cox Cable

1901 Oak St.
Myrtle Beach *626-2922*

Cox serves Myrtle Beach, Conway (west of the Intracoastal Waterway, including the Forestbrook area), Cypress Creek, Tarpon Bay, Burcale Road, Little River, North Myrtle Beach and Atlantic Beach.

Jones Intercable

U.S. 17
Murrells Inlet *651-6699*

Contact Jones Intercable if you require service in the areas of Surfside Beach, Garden City Beach, Murrells Inlet, Pawleys Island, Pawleys Plantation, Hagley, Socastee or Litchfield Beach.

Horry Telephone Cooperative

Conway *365-2151*

Horry Telephone provides cable television service to Loris, Longs, Wampee, Bucksport and Socastee, west of the Intracoastal Waterway.

Atlantic Telephone

North Carolina *(910) 754-4211*

This is your cable provider if you want service in Holden Beach, Ocean Isle mainland, Longwood, Ash, Shallotte, Seaside, Bolivia, Sunset Beach, Winnabow and most of Brunswick County.

Cablevision Industries

Georgetown *546-2476*

Service is provided for the Georgetown County area, except in the Town of Andrews.

Genesis Cable

Pawleys Island *527-2447*

Genesis exclusively serves the DeBordieu area.

Cablevision

Garden City *650-7450*

Hook up with Cablevision if service is sought in Briarcliffe, the Forest, the Arcadian section, the Shore

Drive section and county areas surrounding Surfside Beach.

SOUTHERN CABLE

Longs *399-9222*

This is the cable company to call if you need service in The Preserve, Colonial Charters, Little River Inn or The Spa at Little River.

Driver's License/License Plates/Motorist Information

In the Grand Strand area, all drivers must pay in full an annual property tax on their motor vehicle before procuring license plates. The tax is levied according to the value of your automobile, which should decline each successive year you own the same motor vehicle.

SOUTH CAROLINA HIGHWAY DEPARTMENT

4103 U.S. 701
North Conway *365-0500*
North Strand Plaza
North Myrtle Beach *272-3870*

SOUTH CAROLINA HIGHWAY & PUBLIC TRANSPORTATION OFFICE

21st Ave. N.
Myrtle Beach *626-9183*

AAA CAROLINA MOTOR CLUB

845 Briarwod Dr. *272-1141*
North Myrtle Beach *(800) 477-4222*

HIGHWAY PATROL OFFICE

4195 U.S. 701
Conway *365-5001*

HIGHWAYS & PUBLIC TRANSPORTATION DRAWBRIDGES

399-3539

Voter Registration

To become a registered voter or to acquire information about your voting district, contact:

HORRY COUNTY BOARD OF REGISTRATION

1316 First Ave.
Conway *626-1382*

Animal Services

ANIMAL CONTROL

1866 S.C. 90
Conway *347-3898*

GRAND STRAND HUMANE SOCIETY

10th Ave. Ext.
Myrtle Beach *448-9151*

Pet Boarding and Care

This is a touchy subject to those of us who love and treat our pets like members of our family. If you need to board your beloved cat or dog, *be very careful where you leave them*!! We strongly suggest that you personally view the kennel you are considering using. From personal experience and accounts, there is nothing worse than picking up your pet from a boarding facility to find them dirty, sick and exhausted. If a kennel owner doesn't want to show you the pet accommodations and exercise area, be suspicious. If your pet literally leaps into your arms after a stay or runs for the door, there's usually good reason. Take the time to look around and ask plenty of questions, for your pet's sake as well as your own peace of mind.

If you'd like an alternative to kennel boarding, we recommend you call Care 'n Company at 650-7387. While you're away, trained sitters come to your home twice a day to take care of your pets. Usually for the same price as kennel boarding, sitters will also take in your mail and newspapers.

Employment Services

Employment Security Commission

1100 Legion St.
Myrtle Beach *448-1677*

The commission offers such services as job listings, unemployment compensation and assistance in making job choices.

Waccamaw Regional Planning Commission

1063 Howard Pkwy.
Myrtle Beach *238-0590*
1230 Highmarket St.
Georgetown *546-8502*

The Waccamaw Regional Planning Commission in both Horry and Georgeton counties administers the Job Training Partnership Act program, which enables elderly individuals to gain employment through job retraining.

Legal Assistance

Better Business Bureau

1601 N. Oak St.
Myrtle Beach *626-6881*

The bureau monitors advertising, promotes self-regulation with businesses and handles customer complaints.

Horry County Probate Court

1201 Third Ave.
Conway *248-1294*

Court officials provide probate wills, issue marriage licenses, perform marriage ceremonies and conduct hearings concerning mental health and drug cases.

Georgetown County Probate Court

Courthouse
Georgetown *527-6325*

The probate court provides probate wills, issues marriage licenses, performs marriage ceremonies and conducts hearings concerning mental health and drug cases.

Neighborhood Legal Assistance, Inc.

607 Main St.
Conway *448-2976*
201 King St.
Georgetown *546-2491*

This agency provides legal aid for low-income individuals and, in special instances, persons 60 years of age and older.

South Carolina Lawyer Referral Service

950 Taylor St.
Columbia *799-7100*

Sponsored by the South Carolina Bar Association, referrals are made to attorneys throughout the state. Once referred, there is a $25 limit on consultation fees for the first half-hour and a $40 limit for the first hour.

Government Offices

If you need to get in touch with a particular sector of government or public works, the following contact numbers for each city or town should gain you access to such departments as planning, zoning, taxes, etc.

City of Myrtle Beach *626-7645*
City of North Myrtle Beach *280-5555*
Town of Surfside Beach *238-2590*
Horry County Offices *248-1365*
City of Georgetown *546-2000*

Libraries

Chapin Memorial Library

400 14th Ave. N.
Myrtle Beach *448-3338*

Chapin is a full-service library that offers large print and recorder books. Special yearly programs include book discussion groups, afternoon films, genealogy programs, business topic breakfasts and income tax preparation assistance.

Horry County Memorial Library

799 Second Ave. N.
North Myrtle Beach *249-4164*

Free library services are available Monday and Wednesday from 9 AM to 6 PM; Tuesday and Thursday from 9 AM to 8 PM; Friday 9 AM to 5 PM; and Saturday 9 AM to 1 PM.

1032 10th Ave. N.
Surfside Beach *238-0122*

This Surfside Beach branch offers free library services to Horry countians from 9 AM to 6 PM, Monday through Friday.

Georgetown County Library

45 Cleveland St.
Georgetown *546-2521*

Georgetown's main library also offers free library services and programs. The branch is open Monday through Thursday from 9 AM to 8 PM; on Fridays from 9 AM to 5 PM; and from 2 PM to 5 PM on Sundays.

Waccamaw Neck Library

15 Library Ln.
Pawleys Island *237-4646*

This branch offers free library services to citizens of Georgetown County, Pawleys Island and Litchfield Beach. For all others, there is a $1 charge to check out books. The library is open from 9:30 AM to 6 PM, Monday through Thursday and 9:30 AM to 5 PM on Friday and Saturday. Waccamaw Neck Library is closed on Sundays.

Social Services

Associated Charities

10th Ave. N.
Myrtle Beach *448-6321*

On Tuesdays, Associated Charities gives away clothing and furniture to needy citizens. They also open the Thrift Store for low-cost goods every Thursday. The charity also provides assistance with home fuel and heating bills where appropriate.

Churches Assisting People (C.A.P.)

911 Lakewood Dr.
Conway *248-2484*

Of the same mission as Helping Hand (see subsequent listing), C.A.P. offers a food pantry, limited rental assistance and help in purchasing prescription drugs and paying utility bills. Supported by 14 Conway churches, C.A.P. operates from St. Paul's Episcopal Church.

Community Volunteer Services, Inc.

P.O. Box 2150
Conway 29526 *248-7240*
800 Canal St.
Myrtle Beach *448-9277*

Serving the medically and financially needy, Community Volunteer Services offers a wide array of programs including health services, a child development center and assistance with purchasing eyeglasses.

Family Support Services of Horry County

P.O. Box 2057
Conway 29526 *248-5392*

Programs include Welcome Baby for new mothers, prenatal checkups and support for mothers of young children and non-teen mothers.

Helping Hand, Inc.

P.O. Box 2886
Myrtle Beach 29578 *448-8451*
900 Pearlie St.
North Myrtle Beach *272-8327*
812 Poplar Dr.
Surfside Beach *238-4594*

Helping Hand provides acute crisis intervention over a 48-hour period, distributes food and secondhand goods, provides financial aid for utility bills and rent and gives toys and food baskets at Christmas.

Horry County Department of Social Services

P.O. Drawer 1465
Conway 29526 *365-5565*

This agency offers a food stamps program, Medicaid eligibility, homemaker services, family management and counseling, foster care, protective services, emergency medical and food assistance and aid to families with dependent children.

Salvation Army

1415 Second Ave.
Conway 29526 *248-5417*

Homeless persons and families can access emergency food, clothing, household items, prescriptions, rent, utilities and lodging. Assistance with food and toys is also available at Christmas.

Services for the Disabled

Disabled American Veterans (DAV)

2987 Church St.
Myrtle Beach *448-6483*

The DAV assists vets with wheelchairs, walkers and crutches and provides transportation to the VA Hospital in Charleston. A food bank is also available.

Grocery Delivery for the Disabled

21st Ave. N.
Myrtle Beach *497-8294*

Three Kroger grocery stores cooperate with Coastal Cab to deliver foodstuffs and prescriptions to elderly people who are homebound or without transportation. The delivery fee is $3.

South Carolina Handicapped Services Information System

University of South Carolina
Columbia *(800) 922-1107*

With one phone call, you can access more than 200 providers of such services as support groups, residential care, case management, home health care, infant stimulation, medical treatment, education services, protection/advocacy, specialized equipment and summer camps.

Automotive Services and Car Dealerships

There are plenty of places on the Grand Strand to buy a fine ride or to get your vehicle in tip-top shape. We recommend the following establishments:

Bud Ward's Atlantic Chevrolet-Geo

3740 S.C. 9 E.
Little River *399-4400*

This shop offers new and used vehicles and services all makes and models.

Bob Bible Honda/Isuzu

1100 Third Ave. S.
Myrtle Beach *626-3741*

Bob Bible has been in business for 25 years and offers new and used vehicles, plus a full-service parts and service department.

Fowler Motors

2351 U.S. 501
Conway *(800) 951-2463*

This 53-year-old establishment sells BMW, Mercedes-Benz, Cadillac, Oldsmobile, Jeep and Eagle, offers new and used vehicles and has full-service parts and service departments.

Index of Advertisers

Index

C

D

ORDER FORM
Fast and Simple!

Mail to:
Insiders Guides®, Inc.
P.O. Drawer 2057
Manteo, NC 27954

Or:
for VISA or
Mastercard orders call
1-800-765-BOOK

Name
Address
City/State/Zip

Qty.	Title/Price	Shipping	Amount
	Insiders' Guide to Richmond/$14.95	$3.00	
	Insiders' Guide to Williamsburg/$14.95	$3.00	
	Insiders' Guide to Virginia's Blue Ridge/$12.95	$3.00	
	Insiders' Guide to Virginia's Chesapeake Bay/$14.95	$3.00	
	Insiders' Guide to Washington, DC/$14.95	$3.00	
	Insiders' Guide to North Carolina's Outer Banks/$14.95	$3.00	
	Insiders' Guide to Wilmington, NC/$14.95	$3.00	
	Insiders' Guide to North Carolina's Crystal Coast/$12.95	$3.00	
	Insiders' Guide to Charleston, SC/$12.95	$3.00	
	Insiders' Guide to Myrtle Beach/$14.95	$3.00	
	Insiders' Guide to Mississippi/$12.95	$3.00	
	Insiders' Guide to Boca Raton & the Palm Beaches/$14.95 (8/95)	$3.00	
	Insiders' Guide to Sarasota/Bradenton/$12.95	$3.00	
	Insiders' Guide to Northwest Florida/$12.95	$3.00	
	Insiders' Guide to Lexington, KY/$12.95	$3.00	
	Insiders' Guide to Louisville/$14.95	$3.00	
	Insiders' Guide to the Twin Cities/$12.95	$3.00	
	Insiders' Guide to Boulder/$12.95	$3.00	
	Insiders' Guide to Denver/$12.95	$3.00	
	Insiders' Guide to The Civil War (Eastern Theater)/$14.95	$3.00	
	Insiders' Guide to North Carolina's Mountains/$14.95	$3.00	
	Insiders' Guide to Atlanta/$14.95 (4/95)	$3.00	
	Insiders' Guide to Branson/$14.95 (12/95)	$3.00	
	Insiders' Guide to Cincinnati/$14.95 (9/95)	$3.00	
	Insiders' Guide to Tampa/St. Petersburg/$14.95 (9/95)	$3.00	

Payment in full (check or money order) must accompany this order form.
Please allow 2 weeks for delivery.

N.C. residents add 6% sales tax

Total

Who you are and what you think is important to us.

Fill out the coupon and we'll give you an Insiders' Guide® for half price ($6.48 off)

Which book(s) did you buy? ______________________

Where do you live? ______________________

In what city did you buy your book? ______________________

Where did you buy your book? ❑ catalog ❑ bookstore ❑ newspaper ad

❑ retail shop ❑ other ______________________

How often do you travel? ❑ yearly ❑ bi-annually ❑ quarterly

❑ more than quarterly

Did you buy your book because you were ❑ moving ❑ vacationing

❑ wanted to know more about your home town ❑ other ____________

____

Will the book be used by ❑ family ❑ couple ❑ individual ❑ group

What is you annual household income? ❑ under $25,000 ❑ $25,000 to $35,000

❑ $35,000 to $50,000 ❑ $50,000 to $75,000 ❑ over $75,000

How old are you? ❑ under 25 ❑ 25-35 ❑ 36-50 ❑ 51-65 ❑ over 65

Did you use the book before you left for your destination? ❑ yes ❑ no

Did you use the book while at your destination? ❑ yes ❑ no

On average per month, how many times do you refer to your book? ❑ 1-3 ❑ 4-7

❑ 8-11 ❑ 12-15 ❑ 16 and up

On average, how many other people use your book? ❑ no others ❑ 1 ❑ 2

❑ 3 ❑ 4 or more

Is there anything you would like to tell us about Insiders' Guides? ____________

____

____

Name ______________ Address ______________

City ______________ State _____ Zip ______

We'll send you a voucher for $6.48 off any Insiders' Guide© and a list of available titles as soon as we get this card from you. Thanks for being an Insider!

BUSINESS REPLY MAIL

FIRST CLASS PERMIT NO. 20 MANTEO, NC

POSTAGE WILL BE PAID BY ADDRESSEE

The Insiders' Guides®, Inc.
PO Box 2057
Manteo, NC 27954